BODENSTOWN REVISITED

To my wife Penny

Bodenstown revisited

The grave of Theobald Wolfe Tone, its monuments and its pilgrimages

C. J. WOODS

FOUR COURTS PRESS

Typeset in 10.5pt on 12.5pt Ehrhardt MT Pro by
Carrigboy Typesetting Services for
FOUR COURTS PRESS LTD
7 Malpas Street, Dublin 8, Ireland
www.fourcourtspress.ie
and in North America for
FOUR COURTS PRESS
c/o IPG, 814 N Franklin St, Chicago, IL 60622.

A catalogue record for this title is available
from the British Library.

ISBN 978-1-84682-738-9

Printed in England
by TJ International, Padstow, Cornwall.

Contents

Illustrations

appear between pages 150 and 151

Abbreviations

B.M.H., W.S.	Bureau of Military History, Witness statement (N.L.I. and on-line)
Bowyer Bell, *Secret army* (1979)	J. Bowyer Bell, *The secret army: the I.R.A., 1916–1979* (new ed., Dublin, 1979)
Comerford, *Fenians in context*	R. V. Comerford, *The Fenians in context: Irish politics and society, 1848–82* (revd ed., Dublin, 1998)
Coogan, *I.R.A.*	Tim Pat Coogan, *The I.R.A.* (revd ed., London, 2000)
Devoy's post-bag	*Devoy's post-bag*, ed. William O'Brien and Desmond Ryan, ii (Dublin, 1948)
Dickason papers	Tone MSS held by the late Mrs Katherine Dickason of Short Hills, New Jersey
D.I.B.	*Dictionary of Irish biography*, i–ix, ed. James McGuire and James Quinn, x–xi, ed. James Quinn (Cambridge, 2009, 2018)
English, *Armed struggle*	Richard English, *Armed struggle: the history of the I.R.A.* (London, 2003)
Foster, *Vivid faces*	R. F. Foster, *Vivid faces: the revolutionary generation in Ireland, 1890–1923* (London, 2014)
Freeman's Jn.	*Freeman's Journal*
Hanley, *I.R.A.*	Brian Hanley, *The I.R.A., 1926–1936* (Dublin, 2002)
Hanley & Millar, *Lost revolution*	Brian Hanley and Scott Millar, *The lost revolution: the story of the Official I.R.A. and the Workers' Party* (Dublin, 2009)
Ir. Indep.	*Irish Independent*
Ir. Press	*Irish Press*
Ir. Times	*Irish Times*
Kildare Arch. Soc. Jn.	*County Kildare Archaeological Society Journal*
Le Roux, *Clarke*	L. N. Le Roux, *Tom Clarke and the Irish freedom movement* (Dublin, 1936)
MacAtasney, *Clarke*	Gerard MacAtasney, *Tom Clarke: life, liberty, revolution* (Dublin, 2013)
MacAtasney, *MacDiarmada*	Gerard MacAtasney, *Seán MacDiarmada: the mind of the revolution* (Manorhamilton, Co. Leitrim, 2004)
MacEoin, *I.R.A.*	Uinseann MacEoin, *The I.R.A. in the twilight years, 1923–1948* ([Dublin]: Argenta, 1997)
McGee, *I.R.B.*	Owen McGee, *The I.R.B.: the Irish Republican Brotherhood from the Land League to Sinn Féin* (Dublin, 2005)

Nat. Arch., Dublin	National Archives of Ireland, Dublin
Nat. Arch., Kew	National Archives, Kew, Surrey
N.L.I.	National Library of Ireland
N.M.I.	National Museum of Ireland
Ó Beacháin, *Destiny of the soldiers*	Donnacha Ó Beacháin, *Destiny of the soldiers: Fianna Fáil, Irish republicanism and the I.R.A., 1926–1973* (Dublin, 2010), pp 105–06
Ó Broin, *Revolutionary underground*	Leon Ó Broin, *Revolutionary underground: the story of the Irish Republican Brotherhood, 1858–1924* (Dublin, 1976)
Life of Tone	*Life of Theobald Wolfe Tone ... edited by his son William* (2 vols, Washington, 1826)
T.C.D.	Trinity College, Dublin
Tone, *Writings*	*The writings of Theobald Wolfe Tone, 1763–98*, ed. T. W. Moody, R. B. McDowell and C. J. Woods (3 vols, Oxford, 1998–2007)
Travers, 'Tone of national commemorations'	Kathleen Travers, 'The Tone of national commemorations: the annual Wolfe Tone commemorations at Bodenstown' (M.A., University College, Dublin, 2002)
Walker, *Ir. parlty election results, 1918–92*	Brian Walker, *Parliamentary election results in Ireland, 1918–92* (Dublin, 1992)

Preface

B ODENSTOWN HAS BEEN much visited but little studied. A short paper by me read at the Irish studies conference held at Halle-an-der-Saale in September 1988 and published as 'Tone's grave at Bodenstown: memorials and commemorations' in a volume edited by the late Dorothea Siegmund-Schultze, *Irland: Gesellschaft und Kultur VI* (Halle, 1989), has attracted some interest and, its publication being obscure, produced some requests for copies. It was originally provoked, or inspired, by Professor Tom Dunne's assertion, in his very stimulating *Theobald Wolfe Tone, colonial outsider* (1982), that 'Tone did not become a central figure for later nineteenth-century nationalists, not even for the Fenians', and his suggestion that he was ignored until 1913 when Patrick Pearse in his famous speech at Tone's grave proclaimed him 'the greatest of Irish nationalists' and his grave 'the holiest ground in Ireland'. Any merit in a paper only marginally about Theobald Wolfe Tone written thirty years ago must surely by now have diminished considerably. In 1989, too, appeared the definitive biography of Tone by Professor Marianne Elliott, *Wolfe Tone, prophet of Irish independence*; recently it has gone into a revised edition. In 1998, the bicentenary of Tone's death, appeared both a popular new edition by Professor Thomas Bartlett of William Tone's *Life of Theobald Wolfe Tone* (originally published in 1826) and the first of the three volumes of a definitive edition by T. W. Moody, R. B. McDowell (both now deceased) and myself of the collected writings of Tone, the final volume of which was published in 2007. *Bodenstown revisited*, however, readers should be warned, is about the dead Tone, his grave, its monuments or memorials and, most of all, the phenomenon of the annual pilgrimages that began in the 1870s and did much to create an historical memory of Tone (true or false) and to strengthen Irish nationalist sentiment. The paper read in the ci-devant German Democratic Republic was limited in its purpose, which I stated as being 'to investigate popular awareness of Tone after his death and throughout the nineteenth century from the evidence of his mortal remains'. Bodenstown was the focus of this awareness. Since then the concept of 'place' in history and in popular memory, expounded collectively by different authors in several volumes under the direction of Pierre Nora in *Les lieux de mémoire* (1984–92), has caught the attention of Irish historians. What follows is more ambitious, an attempt to reconsider, revise and expand that paper and to revisit 'Tone's grave at Bodenstown'. In these revisits I am attempting to give a grand narrative. The result may be considered rather encyclopedic. Tone's burial at Bodenstown in 1798 is established almost to a certainty; the different memorials erected successively on his grave (the first mention was in 1829) are considered, and the pilgrimages to the grave which began in the 1870s and have recurred annually are described. My terminal date, 1983, was determined originally by the date of publication of Professor Dunne's book; it was reinforced by the thirty-year rule imposed by T. W. Moody and R. Dudley Edwards as first editors of *Irish Historical Studies* to distinguish between history and mere contemporary studies. The rule is one for which I am thankful. Only occasionally have I breached it.

For various kindnesses acknowledgements are due to Mario Corrigan, Seamus Cullen, David Dickson, Paul Ferguson, Anthony J. Gaughan, Brian Griffin, Brian Hanley, Peter Harbison, Mick Healy, Jacqueline Hill, Lar Joye, Liam Kelly, Matthew Kelly, Michael Laffan, Jim Lane, Linde Lunney, Gerard MacAtasney, Brian McCabe, James McCafferty, Owen McGee, Edward McParland, Patrick Maume, David Murphy, Éamon Murphy, Aileen Murray, Brendan O'Cathaoir, Eva O'Cathaoir, Éamonn Ó hÓgáin, Seán O'Mahony, Turlough O'Riordan, Gary Owens, Matthew Parkes, Jacinta Prunty, James Quinn, Marta Ramón García, Regina Richardson, Matthew Stout, Jim Tancred, Mark Thompson, Mary Weld and Audrey Whitty. For reading through, and commenting on, earlier drafts, I am grateful to R. V. Comerford, Marianne Elliott, Brian Walker, Thomas Bartlett, Kevin Whelan and especially, for commenting rigorously on a later draft and contributing to the index, to Sylvie Kleinman. Most of all, I thank my wife Penny for her advice, help and patience during the five-year gestation of *Bodenstown revisited*, and for laboriously reading the final draft.

May I express my gratitude also to Tim Pat Coogan for permission to quote a passage from his book, *The I.R.A.* (revd ed., London: HarperCollins, 2000); and to Aileen Murray, Celbridge Post Office, for permission to quote from the diaries of the 4th Baron Cloncurry (1840–1928) in her possession. I must acknowledge also the director of the National Library of Ireland for permission to reproduce various illustrations and the text of a letter in the Thomas Davis papers (N.L.I., MS 1791, ff 24–7).

All responsibility for the content of *Bodenstown revisited* remains however entirely my own.

C. J. WOODS
4 July 2018

Introduction

IN BODENSTOWN CHURCHYARD lie the remains of Theobald Wolfe Tone, the Irish revolutionary who in 1798, under sentence of death, took his own life to avoid being hanged for treason. This study is of Tone's grave, of the monuments erected upon it, and of the organised pilgrimages to the grave which began 75 years after his death. It is *not* a study of Tone while he was living — the narrative begins with Tone lying dead. It treats of place and of changing times. The Tone who appears is not the Tone of the 1790s, he is the Wolfe Tone of popular memory, as seen through the prism of Bodenstown.

Bodenstown is situated in County Kildare about 27 kilometres, as the crow flies, W.S.W. of Dublin, the Irish metropolis, and lies on the right bank of the River Liffey about 3 kilometres upstream of Clane, a sizeable village, and 5 kilometres north of Naas, the county town.[1] Its geographical co-ordinates are 53° 24' 86 N. and 06° 66' 00 W. Bodenstown is both a civil parish and a townland (one of nine) within that parish. The route there from Dublin recommended by Tone to his friend Richard Sharkey in 1787 was via the turnpike to Naas and then the road to Clane.[2] It would have been shorter, if less reliable, to turn off before Naas at Kill and take a back road direct to Bodenstown. It could also be reached conveniently along the western road to Lucan and then via Celbridge and Straffan. Any of these routes could have been taken by 'pilgrims' many years later. By 1798 the southern part of the parish was traversed by the Grand Canal, which took a straight line from its 'basin' or 'harbour' in the Liberties of Dublin through open country to quays at Sallins, a new village the canal had brought into existence straddling the boundary of Bodenstown and the adjacent parish of Kerdiffstown. By 1846 a railway was completed parallel to the canal as far as Sallins. A station close to the canal 'harbour' was opened in August, the railway quickly displaced the Grand Canal for passenger traffic. Sallins was now less than an hour's journey from Dublin. By any of these routes the distance is little more than 35 kilometres.

The population of Bodenstown parish in the 1790s (as now) was thin and scattered, there being no nuclear settlement. The most conspicuous building in the townland of Bodenstown at the end of the eighteenth century must have been, as it has remained, the church on the south side of (and almost abutting) a minor road,

---

1 For much of what follows in this introduction I draw on my 'Theobald Wolfe Tone and County Kildare' in William Nolan and Thomas McGrath (eds), *Kildare: history and society* (Dublin, 2006), pp 387–98. An expanded version is in progress. 2 *The writings of Theobald Wolfe Tone, 1763–98*, ed. T. W. Moody, R. B. McDowell and C. J. Woods (3 vols, Oxford, 1998–2007), i, 6.

a country lane, a 'boreen', running east from the Clane–Naas road. When Theobald Wolfe Tone was born in 1763 it had already been a ruin for a hundred years or more. The churchyard remained a burial ground for local people. Directly opposite in Tone's day, on the north side of the boreen, was the farmhouse occupied by his father Peter. The view through any north window would have been across open fields to the townland of Blackhall, the residence of the Wolfes, the gentry family of the district after whose son Theobald, we can presume, the revolutionary was named. By the 1840s the Tone farmhouse was, as stated later by a visitor, John Gray, 'much dilapidated, though still habitable'.[3] In the 1980s only a few foundation stones could be seen. The exact location of the small 'cottage' that Tone made his home in 1792 or 1793, playfully named Château Boue ('Castle Mud'), after establishing himself in his legal career, has not been ascertained. One of Tone's biographers, Frank MacDermot, stated that according to 'local tradition' it was amongst farm buildings at Blackhall; a local historian, Seamus Cullen, thinks it may have been on the west side of the road to Naas in the townland of Cassumsize (renamed Castlesize).[4] The Ordnance Survey map of 1839 shows, a short distance further along the minor road where it crosses another, a blacksmith's forge, probably the forge where Gray and his companion Thomas Davis luckily found a guide when they visited Bodenstown in 1843. Unlike the scattering of buildings near Bodenstown churchyard, Clane (a separate parish) was a nuclear settlement, as was, by the 1790s, Sallins too. In the history of Tone's grave, its monuments and pilgrimages, Sallins is the more important. Its urban infrastructure, brought about after the Grand Canal reached the place in 1777, various canal facilities including an hotel completed in 1784 and eventually (evident in the Ordnance Survey map published in 1839) streets laid out on a grid pattern and lined with buildings, made Sallins the gateway to Bodenstown.[5]

The earliest known date of a Tone connexion with Bodenstown is 1755 when Tone's grandfather William Tone leased land from a certain Andrew Nash.[6] William Tone was a farmer, evidently a working farmer as he died from a fall from a cornstack, on 24 April 1766. His name, his age at death and the date of his death were to be seen clearly on a gravestone that marked the Tone family plot in Bodenstown churchyard until it was damaged by an explosion in 1969. Whether William Tone and his son Peter were born and brought up in Bodenstown is not known. What is certain is that Peter prospered as a coach-builder in Dublin until he gave up his trade in the mid-1770s and took over the farm that, as William's eldest son, he had inherited. He must soon have become a man of some standing in County Kildare, as in 1779 he was named in connexion with a proposal to raise a

---

3 For the visit of John Gray to Bodenstown with Thomas Davis in 1843, see below, chap. 1. 4 Frank MacDermot, *Theobald Wolfe Tone: a biographical study* (London, 1939), p. 130; Frank MacDermot and John Doyle, 'Wolfe Tone's house' in *Kildare Arch. Soc. Jn.*, xiv, no. 4 (1969), p. 376; info. Seamus Cullen. Tone called it a 'cottage'. 5 Ruth Delany, *The Grand Canal of Ireland* (Newton Abbot, 1973), pp 23, 130–1. 6 Registry of Deeds. Dublin, 488/296/310911. The document is in fact a memorial of a deed dated 1794 and referring to 'William Tone, Blackhall,

troop of mounted Volunteers to be approved by duke of Leinster.[7] Though Theobald, aged thirteen or so when Peter took over the farm, remained in Dublin to complete his education, it is a fair guess that he regularly visited his parents at Bodenstown during vacations and probably stayed with them and so became familiar with the place. In July 1785, before completing his studies at Trinity College, he got married. Tone and his wife, Martha or (as he preferred) Matilda, aged only 16 or 17, soon moved in with his family at Bodenstown. A daughter, Maria, was born there some time in 1786. When Tone went to London to study for the bar, his wife remained with her parents-in-law. Tone was called to the Irish bar in the early summer of 1789 and commenced practice as a barrister on the Leinster circuit. In the same year Peter Tone was ousted, by proceedings in chancery, from the Tone family farm by his unmarried brother Jonathan, who apparently had worked it in the years between their father's death and when Peter took over. The struggling barrister and his small family lived in lodgings in Dublin for the next few years whilst managing to keep on good terms with Jonathan Tone despite his natural sympathy with his father in the inevitable acrimony between the two brothers. When, in September 1792, Jonathan was on his death bed the nephew visited him at Bodenstown and commented afterwards in his diary, 'sorry for him after all'; two days later he was seeking medical assistance for his bachelor-uncle. Jonathan was living not in the farmhouse opposite the old church but in the townland of Cassumsize (which is closer to Sallins).[8] By 1793, probably in 1792, Tone had possession of 'Château Boue', the nearby cottage that he made a home for his growing family and a rural retreat for himself. It was to remain his home until May 1795, when, about to emigrate to America and soon move on to France, he sold it to a local man, Matthew Donnellan. He was to return to Ireland three-and-a-half years later and to die in prison aged 35. He was buried, like his grandfather, father, uncle Jonathan, sister Fanny, brother Mathew and infant son Richard, in the churchyard adjacent to the farmhouse where once he had lived with his young wife and infant daughter.

What raised Bodenstown out of its obscurity and made it an Irish place of pilgrimage was the discovery of Tone's grave in 1843 by the young nationalist writer Thomas Davis, who quickly wrote and published a touchingly romantic poem, 'Tone's grave' with the first line beginning 'In Bodenstown churchyard', and then arranged for an inscribed stone to mark the spot. Tone's reputation when he set foot in Ireland again in 1798 was as a political reformer, Catholic emancipationist, United Irishman and political exile. He had disembarked in French military uniform from a French naval vessel, one of a fleet attempting to effect a landing and invasion. He was a marked man and was promptly arrested. The drama of his return to Dublin in irons and the *cause célèbre* of his trial for treasonable service with

Co. Kildare, gent., since deceased'.   7 George Wolfe, 'Naas Volunteers, 1779' in *Kildare Arch. Soc. Jn.*, xi, no. 4 (1933), p. 465.   8 Tone, *Writings*, i, 274, 280. In *Life of Theobald Wolfe Tone … edited by his son William* (2 vols, Washington, 1826), the words 'after all' are suppressed, suggesting later memories were fonder. For Jonathan Tone, see Tone, *Writings*, ii, 261, 281–2, iii, 471.

revolutionary France quickly followed by the tragedy of his suicide in prison enhanced his reputation amongst Irish democrats. The publication in 1826 of his engaging, frank and revealing autobiography and diaries, an *apologia* for his embrace of the Catholic cause and the French revolution, and the sympathetic notice it was given in a speech to the Catholic Association in Dublin by a brilliantly eloquent orator, Richard Sheil, enhanced Tone's reputation further in democratic circles and among the Catholic chattering classes. Sheil was briefly prosecuted, which brought his speech more attention. To speak or write sympathetically of Tone remained incautious in Ireland until the publication of 'Tone's grave' removed restraints. By the 1860s the names 'Wolfe Tone' and 'Bodenstown' were evoking passions among Irish nationalists.

Bodenstown became a place of annual political pilgrimage in the 1870s. A new stone was laid on Tone's grave and a protective railing erected. The pilgrimages, as regularly reported in the Dublin press as the Dublin Horse Show, made the place famous for nationalist commemoration of Tone and for advocacy, and eventually commemoration, of Irish national independence. It was an emotional place, some said a holy place, one that during the years before and after independence, evoked popular memory of the past and promising ill-defined freedom in the future. Yet its fame, unlike Tone's, has never been studied. What follows is 'Bodenstown-centric'. An attempt will be made here which will at least be a contribution to a history of its famous grave, its monuments and its pilgrimages. Some of the pieces of information it brings to light may even be useful additions to the general narrative of Irish history during the nineteenth and twentieth centuries. Similarly they may be drawn on for biographical treatment of some of the illustrious men and women who made their way, previously unnoticed by historians, along the pilgrims' route from Sallins to Bodenstown churchyard.

Tone's burial at Bodenstown in 1798 and virtual oblivion

T ONE'S DEATH OCCURRED on 19 November 1798, 'very early in the morning', in the Provost prison at the Dublin barracks (on the north bank of the Liffey).[1] With little delay the Irish chief secretary, Viscount Castlereagh, gave permission for his body to be given to his 'friends', but 'on the express condition that no assemblage of people shall be permitted and that it be interred in the most private manner'.[2] Tone's body was collected by two relatives, William and Peter Dunbavin (both apparently cousins of his), and laid out at No. 65 High Street, where William had his business as a tallow chandler.[3] The house, a four-storey building, belonged to William's mother Mary, a sister of Peter Tone; it stood on the edge of the Liberties district lying to the west of the city's core until demolished in 1944.[4] Tone's widow, Matilda, later explained to her daughter-in-law, Catherine Tone, that his body was taken to his aunt's house because his parents were living in lodgings. She added that Tone's hair was cut and divided, some being sent to her in Paris (her home from 1797 until her remarriage in 1816), and that a plaster cast was taken of his face — taken, R. R. Madden believed, by James Petrie (who took a cast of Robert Emmet in 1803). Her source of information was a conversation with an unnamed person who had spent the night with the body.[5] Madden tapped other family sources for the chapters on Tone in his *United Irishmen*, written in the early and mid-1840s and revised for a new edition ten years later. He states that the body was laid out in a room on the second floor, remained for two nights and 'a great number of persons came and sat in the room'. Madden's informants were a son, two daughters and a nephew of William Dunbavin. They had a purely family feeling for

---

1 *Saunders' News Letter*, 21 Nov. 1798. The location is put beyond doubt by four letters written by Tone in his prison nine days before his death (Tone, *Writings*, iii, 401–4).   2 Castlereagh to General Craig, 19 Nov. 1798 (T.C.D., Courtsmartial proceedings, MS 872, f. 153r).   3 The main source for the days between Tone's death and burial is R. R. Madden, *The United Irishmen*, 1st ed., 3rd ser. (Dublin, 1846), i, 121–2, 158–9. It is replicated with changes in a new edition or series (4 vols, Dublin, 1857–60), ii, 143, 160–61. William Dunbavin is identified by Madden as an uncle; Peter is named only by Joseph Hammond (see below, n. 8).   4 The house is illustrated in Henry Shaw's *Dublin pictorial guide & directory of 1850* (facs. ed., Belfast, 1988). Dunbavin's name is shown engraved over the front as a previous occupant. It was reported in 1944 that the house where Tone was waked, 46 High Street (previously 65), 'is being demolished by the Corporation as a dangerous building' ('An Irishman's diary' in *Irish Times*, 19 June 1944).   5 Matilda Tone to Catherine Tone (née Sampson), 22 Dec. 1829 (Dickason papers).

Tone and did not seek to promote him as an heroic figure.[6] Another source, a maverick, populist journalist, Walter Cox, who claimed also to have been present at the vigil, recalled that Tone's 'former companions and political associates of rank and distinction in the city kept away'.[7] Another source is Joseph W. Hammond (1882?–1965), whose grandfather Joseph Hammond (1785?–1873) was as a child present at the wake and later became acquainted with Peter Dunbavin; Joseph's mother, Elizabeth (née Fisher?), a friend of Matilda Tone, had taken him along. Matilda had on 14 August 1784 (when aged 15) been present at St Mark's church, Dublin, at the marriage of Elizabeth to John Hammond as a friend of the bride.[8] From this it may be deduced that among the 'great number' at the wake were mostly family, friends and respectful members of the public. Madden states that 'at length an order came from government that the interment should immediately take place, and as privately as possible … The funeral, in conformity with the orders of the authorities, was attended by only two persons.' He names them as William Dunbavin and James Ebbs, a brazier of Bride Street.

Theobald Wolfe Tone was buried in the Tone family grave in Bodenstown in County Kildare. About the date, 21 November 1798, a Wednesday, there is no doubt.[9] About the place some doubt was expressed by the late Frank MacDermot in his life of Tone,[10] and later by Tom Dunne in his study of Tone's ideas.[11] It is desirable therefore to give some proof here. The only *contemporary* evidence found relating to Tone's place of burial is a report in the *European Magazine* for December 1798 that 'he was buried in the same vault with his brother'.[12] This does not, unfortunately, indicate the location of the 'vault'; easy to identify, however, is the brother, Mathew Tone, hanged on 29 September for his part in the French invasion of General Jean-Joseph Humbert. There is the evidence of contemporaries recorded later. Madden's key informant was Nicholas Dunbavin, a son of William Dunbavin and so a grandson of Peter and Jonathan Tone's sister Mary.[13] Madden states that William Dunbavin was a native of Bodenstown; probably he had an interest in property there inherited by his mother Mary from Jonathan; certainly he was connected with Naas — four of his children who died in infancy were buried there between 1802 and 1814.[14] If Nicholas was living in 1798 he was perhaps a small child

---

6 For Madden, see above, n. 3.   7 The words are those of Madden, who wrote from a memory of seeing Cox's account 'in one of the publications of that wayward being … which I cannot call to mind'. Attempts to trace this have not been successful.   8 This Hammond family lore is contained in a letter from Joseph W. Hammond in *Dublin Evening Mail*, 8 July 1944, and a letter from him to Dr Charles Dickson, 10 Nov. 1946 (photocopies in Moody papers to be donated to T.C.D. and numbered MS 10048).   9 *Saunders' News Letter*, 22 Nov. 1798.   10 Frank MacDermot, *Theobald Wolfe Tone and his times* (2nd ed., Tralee, 1968), pp 3, 273. The original edition, *Theobald Wolfe Tone: a biographical study*, was published in London in 1939.   11 Tom Dunne, *Theobald Wolfe Tone, colonial outsider* (Cork, 1982), p. 13.   12 *European Magazine and London Review*, xxxiv (July–Dec. 1798), p. 427.   13 'Genealogy of Theobald Wolfe Tone' in *The writings of Theobald Wolfe Tone, 1763–98*, ed. T. W. Moody, R. B. McDowell and C. J. Woods, iii (Oxford, 2007), pp 488–9.   14 The youngest known was born in 1794 or 1795 and so William Dunbavin must have been born no later than the early 1770s; he died perhaps in 1830, certainly

and so it is open to question how much he recalled from then, even if he can be supposed to have been present at the wake. It can at least be supposed that Nicholas Dunbavin learnt from his father, or from his uncle Peter, where the burial took place as well as other details of Tone's fate; it can be conjectured that he visited Tone's grave, perhaps with his father. Nicholas Dunbavin later informed Madden of the events of November 1798, and in 1842 accompanied him on a visit to the grave at Bodenstown which Madden unquestioningly portrays as the grave of T. W. Tone.[15]

Circumstantial evidence is abundant: the Tones were from the parish of Bodenstown; Dunbavin had some sort of connexion; Theobald Wolfe Tone lived there as a young man on the family farm and later, before going to America in the summer of 1795, as the occupier of a cottage; a Tone family plot existed in the churchyard, the remains of William Tone and 'also 3 of his children' lying there, as recorded on a gravestone; it would have seemed to Peter Tone to be the most obvious place to bury his eldest son. It would moreover have been highly acceptable to the authorities in Dublin Castle, for it would have ensured privacy from the Dublin crowd. William Dunbavin, finding himself guardian of the body, would conveniently have been able to make the necessary arrangements including its transport to Bodenstown churchyard from his house in Dublin. And might another reason have been that the body could be conveyed by water, both the Dunbavin house in High Street and the churchyard at Bodenstown being within two kilometres of the Grand Canal? A passage boat was scheduled to leave the Grand Canal basin each morning at 8 o'clock and to reach Sallins at 12.30 p.m.[16] The convenience of such a journey is evident in the account of an English traveller who went that way two years later.[17] It would have been barely light at 7 o'clock when the body left High Street, the time and place of departure reported in *Saunders*. Bodenstown churchyard is little more than half an hour on foot from the Sallins quays (exactly 1.8 kilometres), the significance of which will become evident.

A piece of evidence not previously cited is an obituary of an insurgent United Irishman, Luke Doyle, whose home was at Sallins. It makes it clear that Tone's burial was indeed at Bodenstown. The obituarist (whose source was presumably Doyle himself) states that 'when the news came that General Tone's remains were being brought down to be buried at Bodenstown, about a dozen haggard, hard-hunted outlaws' — Doyle among them — 'assembled around the coffin ... as it was borne up the boreen, by his father's house, to its last resting-place beside the old abbey'.[18] (He meant the ruined parish church.) Another piece of retrospective evidence not

by 1837 (*Dublin Morning Register*, 1 July 1837; gravestone inscriptions in grounds of St David's Church, Naas, transcribed by Brian McCabe, Kill). **15** Madden, *United Irishmen*, 2nd ed. (4 vols, Dublin, 1857–60), ii, 143, 160–61. On the Dunbavins this edition (really a new series) is more useful than the 3rd series of the 1st edition (published 1846 but probably written about 1842), as it correctly gives Nicholas as the son (not brother) of William, contains additional information received from Thomas Dunbavin (son of Nicholas) in 1847, and mentions Madden's visit to Bodenstown in 1842. **16** *Watson's Gentleman's and Citizen's Almanack*, 1798, p. 117. **17** C. J. Woods (ed.), 'An account of a journey through County Kildare and Queen's County in 1800' in *Kildare Arch. Soc. Jn.*, xxi (2016–17), pp 257–69 at pp 259–61, 268. **18** *Nation* (Dublin), 29 May 1852.

previously cited is that of Michael Cavanagh who, when visiting Bodenstown in 1861, was told by a local man of an old insurgent named Toal, no longer living, who had confirmed that the churchyard was truly Tone's burial place.[19] A concluding if not conclusive piece of circumstantial evidence is that Tone's widow, Matilda, unquestioningly believed he was buried at Bodenstown. Writing to her daughter-in-law in 1829 she recalled the exact place: 'I knew the spot right well, it is only separated by the road from the farm his father occupied', which was 'where I went soon after I was married ... The ruin of the church was very picturesque, overgrown with ivy.'[20] Matilda Tone — more correctly then Matilda Wilson, as she had married a Thomas Wilson in 1816[21] — was living in Georgetown, in the District of Columbia, the capital territory of the United States. She would presumably have learnt that Bodenstown was her first husband's burial place from correspondents in Dublin, for example from her sister Catherine Heavyside and from her mother-in-law Margaret Tone.[22]

If only two persons from Dublin and a dozen or so local insurgents attended the burial of Theobald Wolfe Tone at Bodenstown in 1798, 'huge crowds of ordinary people' were attracted there in August 1805 for the funeral of his father Peter, in his last years a quiet, retiring man who took no part in politics.[23] His death had occurred, suddenly, at Monk Place, Phibsborough, a northern suburb of Dublin.[24] It requires little imagination to conclude from this that the 'ordinary people' were paying their respects to Peter Tone not as a local farmer but as a proxy for his famous son buried there with little ceremony seven years before. (Significantly too the funeral in Paris of Tone's adolescent daughter Maria in March 1803 'drew together all the Irish refugees'.[25]) But Bodenstown churchyard was not yet an arena for political demonstrations. During the next thirty-eight years the grave of Theobald Wolfe Tone was tended by local residents, as will be seen. Tone was not forgotten, but public mention of his name was very imprudent until after publication of the *Life of Theobald Wolfe Tone*, copies of which reached Ireland from America at the end of 1826.[26] Only one, brief account of a visit to the grave during those years has been discovered. It first appeared, under the heading 'Theobald Wolfe Tone', in the *Dublin Morning Register*, 10 October 1829, and was credited to

19 For Cavanagh's account, not published until 1898, see below, chap. 2.   20 Matilda Tone to Catherine Tone, 22 Dec. 1829 (Dickason papers).   21 For this marriage, see Jane Rendall and C. J. Woods, 'Thomas Wilson (1758–1824) of Dullatur, the Scottish second husband of Matilda Tone: the unravelling of a mystery' in *Journal of Irish and Scottish Studies*, vi, pt I (2013), pp 25–49.   22 Catherine Heavyside to Matilda Tone, 30 Nov. 1798 (Tone, *Writings*, iii, 436); Matilda Tone to Margaret Tone, 11 May 1810 (T.C.D., MS 873/35); Matilda Tone to Catherine Heavyside, 10 Oct. 1812 (Royal Irish Academy, Burrowes papers, MS 23/K/53).   23 Elliott, *Partners*, p. 34, where however the place of Peter Tone's funeral is given as Naas. Madden, from whom the indication of Peter Tone's character is taken, states more plausibly, on the evidence of a Mrs Walsh, a 'confidential friend' of William Dunbavin, that he was buried at Bodenstown (*United Irishmen*, 2nd ed., ii (1857), pp 142, 160).   24 *Saunders' News Letter*, 27 Aug. 1805.   25 J. G. Alger, *Napoleon's British visitors and captives, 1801–1815* (London, 1904), p. 154.   26 Discussed by me in 'The writings of Theobald Wolfe Tone: provenance, publication and reception' (unpublished).

'a correspondent' who had written in. 'I believe it is generally supposed', the account began, 'that the ashes of Theobald Wolfe Tone repose in some gaol or barrack-yard in Dublin'. Apparently, Tone's burial at Bodenstown was not widely known. The account continues: 'a few days since, I visited an old abbey, a relic of Catholic times, near Sallins, in the burial ground of which I discovered the grave of this celebrated man. A simple stone, with the name of Theobald Wolfe Tone, rudely inscribed, marks the spot.'[27] No other clue to the identity of the visitor was given. Somehow the report came to be reprinted (on 19 December) in a New York newspaper, the *Truth Teller*, and so to the attention of Matilda Tone, who wrote indignantly to her daughter-in-law: 'I never heard the supposition that his ashes reposed in some geol [sic] or barrack yard, or I should have contradicted it'.[28] No other evidence of the existence of a stone bearing the name of the revolutionary as early as 1829 has been found. Perhaps the visitor misread the inscription on the stone over the grave of Tone's grandfather, described below. Perhaps the report was hardly noticed in Ireland; it has been found in only five other Irish newspapers. Even though the *Dublin Morning Register* does not identify Bodenstown by name, it at least gives good evidence that Tone is buried there and stands out as the first newspaper to identify his place of burial.

At a time not ascertained, but no earlier than 1766, a stone bearing the name of Tone's grandfather William Tone was placed just outside the south wall of the ruined Bodenstown church. Matilda Tone, in a letter to her daughter-in-law, recalled reading its inscription 'hundreds of times' before she and her family left Bodenstown (in 1795).[29] It can still be deciphered, albeit badly damaged. It could once be clearly read:

> This Burial Place Belongs
> Wm Tone & His family. Here
> lieth the Body of the above
> who Departed this Life ye 24
> of April 1766 aged 60 years
> also 3 of his Children

A century later, sometime between 1873 and 1895, a graphic representation of the stone was made by a local clergyman, William Sherlock.[30] His contribution will be discussed later. Only the name of William Tone appears. Matilda Tone, in the same letter to her daughter-in-law, claimed to have read the name of William's wife Mary, but she must have been mistaken; she recalled, with some accuracy, the words 'here

---

27 It was reprinted in *Pilot*, 12 Oct. 1829, *Saunders' Newsletter*, 14 Oct. 1829, *Tipperary Free Press*, 17 Oct. 1829, and *Limerick Evening Post*, 27 Oct. 1829. There was never an abbey at Bodenstown; the building visited was an old parish church.   28 Matilda Tone to Catherine Tone, 22 Dec. 1829 (Dickason papers).   29 Ibid.   30 William Sherlock, 'Bodenstown churchyard, a place of Irish pilgrimag' in *Kildare Arch. Soc. Jn.*, vi (1909–11), p. 227; repr. in *Journal of the Association for Preservation of Memorials to the Dead, Ireland*, viii , no. 4 (1911), pp 350–52, where a transcription

lie also three of their children'. The word 'lieth' (the archaic form of 'lies') in the third line suggests that the last line was added later; Matilda Tone's recollection dates it to no later than 1795. The three children have not been identified. In the same letter, Matilda named as buried at Bodenstown William's son Jonathan, who died in 1792, and Peter's daughter Fanny, who died at about the same time.[31] The stone was the only clue to the exact whereabouts of the remains of Theobald Wolfe Tone until long after his death. The location of his grave at Bodenstown must have become more widely known on being mentioned in the entry on the parish in Samuel Lewis's *Topographical dictionary of Ireland* (1837): 'the celebrated Theobald Wolfe Tone was a native of this parish and lies in the same grave with his father in the churchyard'.[32] Lewis, a London publisher, stated that he solicited and obtained his information from 'resident gentlemen'. Four such men were named in the entry on Bodenstown, three of whom appeared in the list of subscribers; the fourth was the occupier of Blackhall, one 'P. Wolfe', presumably Peter Wolfe who was high sheriff of Kildare in 1805 and died in 1848.[33] It is unlikely however that the grave would have been regularly visited from afar until the 1840s. The very name of Bodenstown was missing from Tone's literary remains — his autobiography, journals, correspondence and political writings — published in the *Life* in 1826. Tone referred to his home as Clane (the nearest village in his day) or as Blackhall (the nearest 'big house').[34]

The most momentous visit to Bodenstown was that made by John Gray and Thomas Davis some time towards the end of 1843. Gray was owner of the *Freeman's Journal*, the Dublin daily newspaper most read by Catholics. Davis was the most respected of the Young Irelanders, young men, most of them Catholics (Davis was an exception), with romantic, nationalistic ideas who had their counterparts in other European countries in the 1840s.[35] At that time, Young Ireland was little more than a youthful element, at most a militant tendency, in Daniel O'Connell's movement for repeal of the union of Ireland and Great Britain. Davis was the principal contributor to the *Nation*, a weekly newspaper owned and edited by another Young Irelander, Charles Gavan Duffy, which had a readership (or audience, for it was regularly read aloud) and an influence wider than any other newspaper in Ireland. That Davis did visit Bodenstown, and in 1843, probably early or mid November (close to the forty-fifth anniversary of Tone's death), is implicit in the words of the poem 'Tone's grave', composed by him (using the pseudonym 'The Celt') and published in the *Nation* for 25 November 1843. It begins:

by Lord Walter FitzGerald is given. **31** Matilda Tone to Catherine Tone, 22 Dec. 1829 (Dickason papers). For the death of Jonathan Tone, see Tone, *Writings*, i, 274, 280, iii, 471, 480; for Fanny, see also *Life of Tone*, ii, 561. **32** Samuel Lewis, *A topographical dictionary of Ireland* (2 vols, London, 1837), i, 214. **33** Ibid., preface and list of subscribers. For Peter Wolfe, see *Anglo-Celt*, 26 May 1848. **34** *Life of Theobald Wolfe Tone … edited by his son William* (2 vols, Washington, 1826). Tone refers in his journal for 8 September 1792 to going to his home in 'County Kildare' and sleeping 'at Clain', and in his autobiography (written in 1796) to living as a young man 'near Clain' and 'at Blackhall' (ibid., i, 22, 28, 181). **35** Davis and Young Ireland have received much attention from historians, most recently and perceptively by James Quinn in his

> In Bodenstown churchyard there is a green grave
> And wildly along it the winter winds rave.

The narrator recounts how:

> Once I lay on that sod — it lies over Wolfe Tone
> And thought how he perished in prison alone.

If the poem derived from Davis's experience, and not from his imagination, it could be considered as a source of information on popular awareness of Tone. His muse, he relates, ended abruptly.

> I was woke from my dream by the voices and tread
> Of a band, who came into the home of the dead;
> They carried no corpse, and they carried no stone,
> And they stopp'd when they came to the grave of Wolfe Tone.
>
> There were students and peasants, the wise and the brave
> And an old man who knew him from cradle to grave.
> ...
> ...
> But the old man, who saw I was mourning there, said
> 'We come, sir, to weep where young Wolfe Tone is laid,
> And we're going to raise him a monument, too —
> A plain one, yet fit for the single and true'.

Of course, Davis had licence to make free with his imagination and to resort to wishful thinking. Students, peasants and old men were close to every romantic's heart. It would have been quite possible, just the same, for him to have met an old man who had known Tone, for when Tone left Bodenstown 48 years before he had been living there, off and on, for nearly half of his 32 years. It is likely that memories of the Tone family survived there in 1843. An odd, curious thing about the poem, in which there is numbering for ten verses, is that verses 8 and 9 are left blank. Did Davis suppress what he had written?

Confirmation and reinforcement of Davis's poetic narrative comes from a letter Gray wrote thirty years later to the editor of the *Freeman's Journal*, the newspaper he had acquired in 1841 and owned until his death in 1875. Gray recounts how he and Davis 'made an excursion to Bodenstown' having 'resolved if possible to discover the grave'. They took a boat on the Grand Canal to Sallins (as Tone had done one day in 1792)[36] and easily found their way to Bodenstown, but could not find the grave. Then they had an idea.

Young Ireland and the writing of Irish history (Dublin, 2015).　**36** Diary for 12 Sept. 1792 (Tone, *Writings*, i, 274).

The blacksmith at the cross-roads was thought of as a 'likely' man to know the gossip of the district, its traditions and memories. A few minutes brought us to the forge. The son of Vulcan was plying his trade with unwonted industry, but as we darkened his door the anvil ceased to ring and he bid the strangers a kindly welcome ... The Tones were delicately talked of as people who once lived there when a new thought seemed to flash across the brain of the man of thews and sinews, who, with a frankness I never can forget, became at once the questioner from being the questioned. 'Gentlemen', said he, with flashing eye, 'you must be relatives of the counsellor's, or at least his friends?'. We briefly told him our mission — that we sought Wolfe Tone's grave and failed to find it in the churchyard hard by. 'No wonder, as you are strangers; but if you come to a burial you could easily know it, for old and young pay it reverence, and while every other grave in the place is walked over, no one walks on that grave. And even the children are taught by the gray-haired men not to harm it, as my father taught me to respect the counsellor's grave.' The good man at once left his smithy and, accompanied by a neighbour who was in the forge when we called, the four of us repaired to Bodenstown to see the grave of Tone. A slight elevation of the ground near the church wall indicated the resting place of Tone; but there was no inscription, no slab, no head stone. Our newly-made acquaintance pointed out the soft freshness of the sod that covered the grave and spoke with fervid enthusiasm of the care with which the little mound, hardly four inches above the surrounding level, was tended. Davis and I each took a rooted daisy and shamrock from the green turf, having first asked and obtained permission from the good blacksmith, who seemed to be the self-constituted guardian of the counsellor's grave.[37]

The 'son of Vulcan' was William Reddy, a resident of Bodenstown or Clane; his sons make a brief appearance later in this story.[38] Gray sent his daisy and shamrock to Tone's widow, who lived near Washington in America.[39]

The truest significance of Davis's 'Tone's grave' was the impact it had on the popular imagination in Ireland and the awareness it created of the Irish revolutionary and of his grave deep in the Kildare countryside. The poem was reprinted in the enlarged series of *The spirit of the nation*, a miscellany of verse first published in the *Nation* newspaper, which Davis brought out at the beginning of 1845.[40] It was reprinted too in the posthumous collection of Davis's verse brought out by his friend Thomas Wallis in 1846 (another edition in 1869), as well as in two versions of Madden's *United Irishmen* (1846 and 1858). *The spirit of the nation* was

---

37 *Freeman's Jn.*, 16 Sept. 1873. 'Counsellor' was the title given to Tone as a barrister-at-law. This usage was obsolescent.   38 *Nation*, 28 Mar. 1874. For more on the Reddys, see chap. 3.   39 Matilda Tone to Catherine Tone, 18 May 1844 (Dickason papers).   40 *The spirit of the nation* (2nd ser., Dublin, 1845), pp 129–30. The preface is dated 1 January 1845 and the copy presented by Davis to Thomas Moore held now by the Royal Irish Academy is inscribed March 1845.

more important, as this book was continually reprinted; by 1877 it had gone through 50 Dublin impressions and a new edition appeared in 1934. And the inclusion of 'Tone's grave' in broadsheets of Young Irelanders' verse regularly reprinted and distributed ensured the widest possible public.[41] Thus it became well established as a piece in the repertoire of Young Ireland and its spiritual successors.

41 G. D. Zimmerman, *Irish political street ballads and rebel songs, 1780–1900* (Geneva, 1966), pp 80, 81.

Thomas Davis's memorial slab, 1843–72

TWENTY-THREE DAYS AFTER 'Tone's grave' first appeared in print, Tone's widow Matilda, who throughout her long widowhood cherished deeply the memory of her patriot-husband and who had been the moving force in the publication of his literary remains, wrote from America to John Gray appealing to him to undertake for her the 'duty of marking the spot where he lies'.[1] Gray had begun a correspondence with her early in 1843 when he was more interested in Tone's friend Thomas Russell than in Tone himself.[2] Her letter, a *cri de cœur*, dated 18 December 1843 at First Street, Georgetown, District of Columbia (her home for some years preceding her death), and addressed to Gray at the *Freeman's Journal* office in Dublin, is worth reproducing in full:

> Although personally unacquainted, I may presume to say that we are not strangers to each other, and the admiration I feel for your character encourages me to delegate to you an office dear and sacred to my heart. It is now above forty-five years since Theobald Wolfe Tone, the husband of my youth and of my love, the father of my children, laid down his life a self-devoted martyr for his country — for that country to which after untiring exertions in her service, to use his own words, when in the hands of a Ruthless Power, he says, 'I have sacraficed [*sic*] all my views in life, I have courted poverty, I have left a beloved wife unprotected and children whom I adored fatherless, — it is no great effort to-day to add the sacrafice of life'. And yet that generous heart moulders in an obscure grave *and no stone tells where he lies*, his family are destroyed, his race extinct, save one fair girl, the only child of our eldest son. For a long time I entertained the hope that at some period I might be enabled to return to my native country and fulfill the last sad duty of marking the spot where he lies, commemorating his virtues and making my last long home there. Even this, time and fate and 75 years with their infirmities forbid. Will you, Sir, undertake this holy office for me? Will you do it speedily enough that I may have the last consolation of hearing that it is done? I remain with true esteem and respect,
>
> your most obedient
> Matilda Wolfe Tone[3]

1 Matilda Tone to John Gray, 18 Dec. 1843 (N.L.I., Davis papers, MS 1791, ff 24–7). 2 John Gray to John A. Russell, 14 Apr. 1843 (T.C.D., Madden papers, MS 873/699, ff 1–3); Matilda Tone to Catherine Tone, 16 Apr., 2 May 1843 (Dickason papers). 3 Matilda Tone to John Gray,

This letter demonstrates how passionately, how persuasively, Matilda Tone promoted the laying of a stone on Tone's grave and so how unwittingly she was a progenitor of what was to become the annual cult of Tone at his grave. It does not mention the daisy and shamrock that Gray thirty years later recalled plucking for her in Bodenstown churchyard; they are mentioned in a letter she wrote to her daughter-in-law in May 1844.[4] We can speculate that the correspondence started by Gray many months before was the reason for Matilda Tone directing her request to Gray in particular. There is a hint of this in the opening sentence of her letter. It is highly unlikely however that, when she wrote the letter, she knew of Davis's poem — not only does she make no mention it, but the *Nation* of 25 November 1843 would hardly have reached her across the Atlantic and inland to Georgetown by 18 December, twenty-three days later, even though packet-ships were sometimes making the passage from Liverpool to New York by steam in less time.[5]

Gray passed on to Davis the letter received from Matilda Tone.[6] Already, Gray recalled many years later, he and Davis, inspired by their experience at Bodenstown, had resolved 'to put a stone over the grave, entrusting the work to a local artist recommended by the blacksmith'.[7] There is some confirmation of this in Davis's poem, 'Tone's grave'. A few Young Irelanders — 'a few friends', Charles Gavan Duffy, himself a Young Irelander, calls them — subscribed money.[8] No doubt Duffy was one. Gray remembered as subscribers two more, John Pigot and John Blake Dillon, and also R. R. Madden (who from November 1843 until August 1846 was in Lisbon as correspondent of the *Morning Post*).[9] The result was that 'a plain black marble slab, very massive', was chosen.[10] A 'slab' is a recumbent stone as distinct from a standing stone. Words of Davis's composition were to be inscribed as follows:

Theobald Wolfe Tone
Born 20th June 1763
Died 19th November 1798
For
Ireland[11]

18 Dec. 1843 (N.L.I., Davis papers, MS 1791, ff 24–7). She was born on 17 June 1769 and so 74 when she wrote. Here 'office' has the archaic meaning of 'duty'.   4 Matilda Tone to Catherine Tone, 18 May 1844 (Dickason papers).   5 The westward passage took on average 33 days; but one steamship, *Roscius*, had in Dec. 1839 made it in 19 days, and another, faster, the *Great Western*, had been averaging 16 days (Boyman Boyman, *Steam navigation, its rise and progress* (London, 1840), pp 146–7). The eastward passage was faster than the westward. But a letter dated 19 Oct. 1842 that Matilda Tone sent from Georgetown to the New York *Truth Teller* was not reprinted in the Dublin *Freeman's Journal* until 14 Dec., i.e. 54 days later. It was quickly reprinted in the *Nation* of 17 Dec., which reported on another page that the *Roscius*, carrying news from America, had left New York on 25 Nov. and made the passage across the Atlantic in 19 days.   6 It is among the Davis papers. It had been seen by Davis by 17 April 1844 (Charles Gavan Duffy, *Thomas Davis: the memoirs of an Irish patriot, 1840–1846* (London, 1890), p. 200).   7 *Freeman's Jn.*, 17 Sept. 1873.   8 Duffy, *Davis*, pp 199–200.   9 *Freeman's Jn.*, 17 Sept. 1873.   10 Davis to Pigot, 17 Apr. 1844 (Duffy, *Davis*, p. 200).   11 Ibid.

Gray and Davis revisited the grave at Bodenstown on 17 April 1844 to prepare for the laying of the 'slab' the following Sunday (the 21st).[12] Davis when writing his poem had envisaged letting 'winter and winds rave' around Tone's grave 'till Ireland, a nation, can build him a tomb';[13] but, as he explained to Pigot (on 23 May) when telling him all about the monument, 'the reason of its being put down now is that Mrs Tone wrote to say she wished it ... She says she had wished and had hoped to have done this last office and to have laid her bones beside his, but the infirmities of seventy-six years prevent her.'[14] Gray had replied to Matilda Tone's letter of 18 December. In writing to her daughter-in-law on 18 May she referred to having received 'a letter from Doctor Gray in answer to mine'. It contained a daisy and shamrock (plucked from Tone's grave on the November visit?) and Gray's news that 'most probably before the close of next day the gates of a prison will close upon him'. In the same letter was 'a sketch of the tomb' and the news that 'a procession' had gone from Dublin 'to place it'.[15] The date of Gray's letter is not stated. It must have been after 12 February, the date on which he and others were convicted of conspiracy. As it would normally have taken at least five weeks to reach its destination, Gray could hardly have despatched it much later than the second week in April. It is just about possible that he entrusted it to a traveller taking a direct passage from Ireland and blessed with a rare easterly wind, in which case the 'procession' she refers to may have been a misunderstanding of the preparatory visit Gray and Davis made on 17 April in anticipation of laying their stone on the 21st. If not, they, perhaps with others, must have made an investigative visit earlier.

The Young Irelanders' memorial slab was not laid on the intended day. On 23 May 1844, Davis told Pigot: 'the tomb is *not* set up. It was taken to Bodenstown and all the parties were to have gone down to have lent a hand in placing it over the sod where he lies; but some of the "conspirators'" counsel objected to its being done just then; so it was postponed and will, I think, not be done till the end of June. Do not speak of *any* of these facts.'[16] The 'conspirators' were Daniel O'Connell and eight other Repealers who had on 12 February been found guilty in the high court in Dublin of conspiracy and were now awaiting sentence. One of the eight was Gray himself, another was Duffy.[17] In postponing the Bodenstown ceremony Davis and other Young Irelanders were recognising the likelihood that any public display of admiration for Tone would be interpreted as tantamount to sedition and be detrimental to the interests of the Repealers, whose cases had still to be decided. On 30 May, O'Connell, Gray, Duffy and the others were imprisoned, an appeal was lodged, and not until 6 September were they released.[18] During that summer Matilda Tone, aware of the delicacy, even danger, of the situation, wrote that the 'simple, unpretending' stone with an 'appropriate epitaph' prepared by Gray, Davis

12 Ibid.   13 'Tone's grave' (*Nation*, 25 Nov. 1843).   14 Duffy, *Davis*, p. 200.   15 Matilda Tone to Catherine Tone, 18 May 1844 (Dickason papers). No such sketch has been found.   16 Davis to Pigot, 23 May 1844 ('Letters of Thomas Davis to J. E. Pigot' in *Irish Monthly*, xvi (1888), pp 268–9). The date is given here, but not in Duffy, *Davis*.   17 *Freeman's Jn.*, 13 Feb. 1844. 18 *Freeman's Jn.*, 31 May, 7 Sept. 1844.

and others had not been laid, as 'the present crisis in Irish affairs ... forces them to stop'. She then introduced another factor, her own role, a reminder of the ownership of the grave: 'they have laid it aside till they can get from me authority for its erection. As from me, it would be perfectly legal, but their doing it unauthorized would be liable to malicious construction.'[19] Davis, writing to Pigot on 28 May, acknowledged receipt of 'the £1' (presumably a contribution) and added 'I dare say you'll be with us when the stone is laid'; but twelve days later he wrote only of the imprisonment and made no allusion to the stone; similarly in later letters to Pigot there is none.[20] The laying of the monument on Tone's grave seems to have been done quietly some time after the release of the prisoners, most likely in the autumn of 1844. It is nowhere mentioned in Duffy's *Nation* or in Gray's *Freeman*. Duffy, who says so much about the early stages of the project in his life of Davis, is strangely silent about the outcome. Indeed no report even of the existence of the stone has been found in these papers during the 1840s and 1850s. Tantalisingly, the exact date of Davis's stone being laid is not known; nor is any graphic representation. Wonderfully, a fragment, if not the whole, survives and is now in the National Museum of Ireland. What survives seems to be in size about one-third of what must have been the original stone. Its authenticity as the stone described by Davis in his letter to John Pigot of 17 April 1844 is established by what remains of the first three lines of the inscription: 'Tone' (at the end of the first line), '763' (at the end of the second line, in 'old style' numerals), and 'ber 1798' (at the end of the third line, numerals in 'old style').[21]

One man present did give an account of the ceremony. He gave it to Michael Cavanagh, who as a young man supported the Young Irelanders and took part in the abortive Irish rebellion of 1848.[22] His account is to be found in a memoir by Cavanagh, 'A pilgrimage to Bodenstown', written perhaps long after the events it recounts and published in 1898 in a nationalist magazine, *Shan Van Vocht*. Cavanagh records for posterity a conversation he had on a journey from Sallins to Bodenstown in 1861 with an unnamed local Sallins man, a jarvey, who recalled being present when 'the tombstone was first put over' Tone's grave. 'I heard an old man be the name o' Toel' — no doubt correctly O'Toole or Toal — 'who lived near us thin', the jarvey informed Cavanagh, 'tell the strange gintlemen all about the family o' the Tones that had a farm thereabouts whin he was a young man. He told 'em about 'Ninety-eight too, for he had a hand in it himself when Prosperous was burned and the "Yeos" massacred. An' he showed 'em where Wolfe Tone was buried, though he wasn't at the berrin', an' good reason why, he was on the *shaughran* himself at the time along with a good many more United Min.'[23] Those 'strange gintlemen' were

19 Matilda Tone to —, summer 1844 (Dickason papers). Only a fragment of this letter has been seen. It was probably addressed to a relation, possibly her daughter-in-law. 20 Davis to Pigot, 28 May, 9 June 1844 ('Letters of Thomas Davis to J. E. Pigot' in *Irish Monthly*, xvi (1888), pp 269–70); the later letters, Sept. 1844 to Aug. 1845, are in ibid., pp 366–48. 21 For this discovery in Sept. 2016 and for supplying a photograph I am grateful to Dr Audrey Whitty, N.M.I. 22 Cavanagh (1822–1900) is the subject of an article in the *D.I.B.* by Maureen Murphy and James Quinn. 23 Michael Cavanagh,

no doubt Young Irelanders; an insurgent then 'on the *shaughran*' would now be said to be 'on the run'. The 'yeos' were yeomanry, locally recruited forces deployed during the 1798 rebellion.[24]

Madden states in the volume of his *United Irishmen* in which he first treats of Tone at great length — published in July 1846, when Davis's stone had probably been in position for most of two years — that there was at Bodenstown 'no monument to his memory, in stone or marble'.[25] It is possible that Madden was out of touch, as he had left Ireland for Portugal in November 1843 — three or four months before Gray could have received Matilda Tone's letter — and did not return until August 1846.[26] It is more likely that he learnt of the stone but was unable to amend his text before publication. In a revised version of his treatment of Tone (published in 1858) Madden does refer to a stone on Tone's grave with his name inscribed, explaining that 'a monumental slab was placed there' as a result of 'the successful efforts of Davis' and that the time of its placement was 'a little later' than Davis's visit. Madden states that the inscription read:

Sacred
to the memory of
Theobald Wolfe Tone
who died for Ireland
on the 19th of November 1798.[27]

These words are significantly different from the words stated by Davis in his letter to Pigot. Except for the existence of a fragment of Davis's stone in the National Museum, this would raise the questions whether the slab that Davis and Gray had ready for laying in May 1844 really was laid 'a little later' than Davis's visit, and whether indeed it was not laid at all but instead a new slab or stone was prepared and laid. It would certainly have been unwise to place a memorial on Tone's grave during Gray's trial or before his release from prison in September 1844. If Madden's statement that there was no stone to Tone's memory was correct when it was published in 1846, the 'monumental slab' he describes in the volume of his *United Irishmen* published in 1858 could have been laid between those years. Davis died on 16 September 1845. The possibility that he was not himself present at the laying of the slab could be inferred from a statement by John Mitchel (another Young Irelander) concerning Tone and Bodenstown: that it was 'where Thomas

'A pilgrimage to Bodenstown' in *Shan Van Vocht* (Belfast), 4 July 1898. A shorter version is in Alice Milligan, *Life of Theobald Wolfe Tone* (Belfast, 1898), pp 113–16.   **24** In 1798 a large rebel force set fire to buildings at Prosperous, west of Clane, occupied by a government force of Welsh fencibles (Ancient Britons) and Cork City militia; men of the Clane yeomanry were nearby but escaped the massacre (Mario Corrigan, 'Prosperous' in Seamus Cullen and Hermann Geissel (eds), *Fugitive warfare: 1798 in north Kildare* (Clane, 1998), pp 145–62).   **25** Madden, *United Irishmen*, 1st ed., 3rd ser. (1846), i. 159; *Freeman's Jn.*, 11 July 1846.   **26** C. J. Woods, 'R. R. Madden, historian of the United Irishmen' in Thomas Bartlett et al. (eds), *1798: a bicentenary perspective* (Dublin, 2003), p. 498.   **27** Madden, *United Irishmen*, 2nd ed., ii (1858), p. 143.

Davis *caused* a monumental slab to be erected in his memory'.[28] (The italics are mine.) The subtly more nationalistic tenor of the inscription stated in Madden's account — 'Sacred to the memory' and 'died for Ireland' — in comparison with simply Tone's name, 'born' and 'died' followed by the dates and, at the foot, 'For Ireland' might have signified some heated discussion among the 'friends'. Banal as the words 'died for Ireland' are in the twenty-first century, they verged on the seditious in 1844. But it has to be recognised, not for the first time, that Madden's accuracy is in doubt.

'Tone's grave' appeared not under Thomas Davis's name or initials but under a nom-de-plume. Until the mid-1840s it was still considered imprudent to make a hero of Tone in Ireland. Publication of 'Tone's grave' even in the gently minatory *Nation* was acceptable because it was a pseudonymous piece of romantic verse. And yet it was the most positive identification of his grave in print to come nearly half a century after Tone's death. More than anything else it broke the taboo on depicting him as a hero. That the laying of the stone intended for his grave had to be postponed and that its very existence was never mentioned in the press until much later are reminders that commemoration was not yet prudent. What is truly significant about Davis's stone or slab is that it is an early example — the earliest? — of a monument to a hero of 'Catholic Ireland'.[29] Joep Leerssen makes the point that in Ireland 'there are almost no pre-1850 monuments or *lieux de mémoire* embodying a "national" Irish, anti-Ascendancy historical consciousness'.[30] He cites as the first of many the O'Connell monument in Sackville Street (later O'Connell Street), the main broad thoroughfare in Dublin, the foundation stone of which was laid in 1864. This monument to O'Connell, completed in 1882, was conspicuous, but it never became, like the monument over Tone's grave at Bodenstown even earlier, a destination for pilgrims.

Matilda Tone died aged nearly 80 on 18 March 1849. It has not been ascertained how much she learned of the results of her letter to Gray of 18 December 1843. Her own remains were placed in a grave at the Presbyterian burying-ground at Georgetown in the District of Columbia. It is described by the Washington reporter of the *Boston Pilot* who visited it in 1869. Matilda's dates of birth and death were inscribed on the gravestone with the eulogy that she was 'revered and loved as the heroic wife of Theobald Wolfe Tone'.[31] Later, in 1891, her remains, those of her son William (who died in 1828) and those of her second husband, Thomas Wilson (who died in 1824), were reburied, in Green Wood Cemetery, Brooklyn, New York. This was done at the request of her great-granddaughter, Katherine Anne or Kate

---

28 John Mitchel, *The history of Ireland from the treaty of Limerick to the present* (2nd ed., Dublin, 1869), ii, 75. **29** This expression is made explicit in the title of W. G. O'Brien's doctoral thesis: 'Imagining Catholic Ireland: the nationalist press and the creation of national identity, 1843–1870' (Ph.D., Univ. of Limerick, 2007). **30** Joep Leerssen, 'Monument and trauma: varieties of remembrance' in Ian McBride (ed.), *History and memory in modern Ireland* (Cambridge, 2001), pp 204–22, at p. 210. **31** *Nation* (Dublin), 7 Aug. 1869. Curiously, the sexton who held the key was a man named Kickham, a first-cousin of the Tipperary poet and Fenian Charles Kickham.

Maxwell, by a Brooklyn undertaker, James Benson, a native of Athy, County Kildare, who on a visit to Ireland in 1893 called at the office of the *Leinster Leader* at Naas and supplied some information. The graves at Georgetown had been cared for by the Irish American Union of Washington until the Presbyterian burying-ground was sold (probably for development); another such society, the Irish Society of New York, provided a new monument. The reburial took place on 31 October, the eve of All Saints' day, in accordance with the rites of the Protestant Episcopal Church. The original gravestones were re-erected.[32] Matilda Tone's mantle as custodian of Tone 'lore' (as well as of Tone's papers) had fallen first on her only grandchild, Grace (alluded to in her letter to Gray). Grace, who married an Irishman, Lascelles Edward Maxwell, briefly appears, in the early summer of 1899, in the story of her illustrious grandfather's grave, as the donor, with her daughter, the aforementioned Kate, of £20 to the Wolfe Tone and '98 Memorial Association, then organising a visit to Bodenstown.[33] It was a renewal of contact between Tone's descendants and his native island.

THE GRAVE LITTLE VISITED

The coming of the Famine in the autumn of 1845, at its height in 1847, caused the graveyard to be used more often by local people and perhaps to be visited less by strangers. Michael Cavanagh's informant recalled that 'poor Mr Toal', the last of the United Irishmen 'in these parts', died 'in the "year of the starvation", like many a stronger man. The ould churchyard was visited often that year.'[34] Developments in Irish politics after Davis's death in September 1845 were that Young Irelanders became increasingly militant under the influence of John Mitchel, who assumed responsibility for the *Nation* and used it to write strident political articles; Duffy, Mitchel and other Young Irelanders left the Repeal Association in July 1846, refusing to accept O'Connell's requirement that members repudiate violence to achieve political aims; and in January 1847 Duffy and others formed the Irish Confederation, which gave rise to numerous local Confederate clubs, generally more democratic than the early Young Irelanders, and distinctively plebeian. Clubs formed at Waterford and Cork were given the name 'Wolfe Tone Club'.[35] There was also a Wolfe Tone club at Kill, County Kildare, which in July 1848 had 50 members and intended 'holding a district meeting near Wolfe Tone's grave at Bodenstown' (six kilometres away) on Sunday the 16th and inviting 'Repealers' of Kildare and Dublin to attend.[36] But Mitchel, appalled by the Famine, distanced himself from the Confederate leadership, founded his own weekly, the *United Irishman*, which applauded the outbreak of revolution in France in February 1848 and espoused

32 *Leinster Leader*, 1 July 1893. See also Alice L. Milligan, *Life of Theobald Wolfe Tone* (Belfast, 1898), pp 118–21.   **33** *Freeman's Jn.*, 16 June 1899. Kate Maxwell's covering letter, dated New York, 17 May 1899, is printed in this issue.   **34** Cavanagh, 'A pilgrimage to Bodenstown' (see above, n. 23).   **35** *Nation*, 15 Jan., 26 Feb., 1 Apr., 17 June, 1, 22 July 1848.   **36** *Nation*, 8 July 1848.

republicanism and egalitarianism. Eighteen forty-eight became the year of revolution in Ireland as elsewhere. Mitchel was arrested in May and, on conviction of treason-felony, transported; Confederates rose hopelessly in rebellion in July and were scattered. Another rising, in 1849, similarly met with failure.[37] Some of the survivors of these rebellions were to be the progenitors of Fenianism some ten years later.

More has to be said of Fenians and Fenianism, words used frequently, and sometimes undiscriminatingly, by contemporaries and by historians. In 1858, on St Patrick's day, in Dublin, James Stephens, a veteran of the Irish rebellion of 1848 who had returned from exile in Paris, formed a secret, oath-bound society of Irish revolutionaries; he gave it no name, but it soon became known as the Irish Revolutionary Brotherhood or Irish Republican Brotherhood or, more commonly, the I.R.B. Six months later, Stephens visited New York and encouraged Irish nationalists there, led by John O'Mahony and Michael Doheny, fellow veterans and fellow exiles with Stephens in Paris, to form a similar but society. O'Mahony, a Gaelic scholar inspired by the ancient warriors of Irish antiquity, the Fianna, gave it the name Fenian Brotherhood. The name 'Fenian' came to be applied to members of the I.R.B. no less than to members of the Fenian Brotherhood.[38] The ideology of the Fenians (which in essence never changed) was summarised by T. W. Moody. 'The founders of fenianism', he wrote, had a single aim — Irish independence from Great Britain — and they insisted that 'all other questions were a secondary consideration'; they sought to achieve their aim

> by secret organisation, by the high morale of their followers and by choosing the moment to strike when circumstances, especially the international situation, would be adverse to Great Britain … A crucial fact about this largely working-class movement was that its thinking was simply nationalist. It had no specific social programme for the democratic Irish republic of its dreams … It had no specific doctrine of nationalism, but accepted the national creed of Wolfe Tone and the United Irishmen, of Thomas Davis and Young Ireland.[39]

The conspiratorial nature of the Fenian movement, the lowly social position of its adherents and the connexion between Ireland and the United States of America — no friend of Great Britain until the twentieth century — brought Fenians to the constant attention of the British authorities. Yet in the early spring of 1867 the I.R.B. attempted an insurrection in Ireland, an event that became a point of reference for friends and enemies alike.

---

37 For Irish nationalism during these years, see Marta Ramón, *Provisional dictator: James Stephens and the Fenian movement* (Dublin, 2005), chap. 1; James Quinn, 'The I.R.B. and Young Ireland: varieties of tension' in Fearghal McGarry and James McConnell (eds), *The black hand of republicanism: Fenianism in modern Ireland* (Dublin, 2009), pp 3–17 esp. pp 3–4.   38 R. V. Comerford, 'Conspiring brotherhoods and contending elites, 1857–63' in *A new history of Ireland*, v (Oxford, 1989), pp 414–50 at pp 418–19; Ramón, *Provisional dictator*, pp 83–97, 161; idem, 'Stephens, James' in *D.I.B.*   39 T. W. Moody, *Davitt and Irish revolution, 1846–82* (Oxford, 1981), pp 40–41.

The narrative of Tone's career as the Irishman who had gone to revolutionary France and twice returned to Ireland with a French army in an attempt to expel the English, only to forfeit his life in prison, would have been well known in Ireland in political and literary circles by the time Davis first visited his grave in 1843. It had been established and had spread suddenly and rapidly in consequence of the arrival of copies of the apologetical and engaging *Life of Tone* in 1826 and of Sheil's virtual exoneration of Tone to the Catholic Association a month or two later.[40] Awareness of the existence and location of Tone's burial place at Bodenstown would have spread to nationalists and separatists all over Ireland in consequence of the publication of Davis's 'Tone's grave'. A more exact knowledge of Tone's career would have become available even to ordinary people with the republication in the spring of 1846 of his autobiography and, in the following December, of long extracts from his Continental diaries, by a Dublin publisher, James McCormick, who offered them for sale at the astonishingly low price of fourpence each.[41] Significantly they were written when Tone was imbued with republican ideas as a serving French officer. By the mid-1840s Tone was common knowledge. But how widely known Davis's memorial slab would have been, and how often the grave would have been visited, in the years immediately following, is impossible to determine, no *contemporary* evidence having been found. There is at least retrospective and deductive evidence that during the thirty years to 1873 the memorial did in fact receive attention from visitors.

VISITS IN THE 1860s

By the 1860s, it is clear from *retrospective* evidence, visits to Tone's grave, by individuals or by small private groups, were customary. One such piece of evidence meriting credence is Michael Cavanagh's account (already mentioned).[42] Cavanagh's visit was on 9 November 1861, the day before the funeral in Dublin of Terence Bellew McManus (who had taken part in the abortive rebellion in Ireland in 1848); Cavanagh was one of a party of nine (or ten?), two of them women, who went to Bodenstown expressly to see Tone's grave; he and others in the party had accompanied McManus's body from America.[43] (Bodenstown had earlier been

40 The impact of the publication of the *Life of Tone* and the significance of Sheil's speech to the Catholic Association are discussed in C. J. Woods, 'The writings of Theobald Wolfe Tone: provenance, publication and reception' (unpublished).   41 They were mentioned or advertised in the *Nation*, 22 Apr. 1846 and 11 Dec. 1846 respectively. They are discussed further in Woods, 'Writings of Tone'.   42 Cavanagh, 'A pilgrimage to Bodenstown'.   43 Their visit to Bodenstown was reported in *Freeman's Jn.*, 13 Nov. 1861. Seven men are named, also a 'Miss McManus' (presumably McManus's sister Isabella) and a 'Mrs Doheny' (presumably Ellen O'Dwyer, wife of Michael Doheny, one of the seven); they travelled by the 12 o'clock train to Sallins; one of the seven is named as 'Jeremiah Cavanagh', probably a confusion of Michael Cavanagh and Jeremiah Kavanagh, both of whom accompanied the body from New York. The forename of McManus's sister has been kindly supplied by Marta Ramón. For the whole affair, see Louis R. Bisceglia, 'The Fenian funeral of Terence Bellew McManus'in *Éire-Ireland*, xiv (1979), no. 3, pp 45–64.

proposed as a burial place for McManus, no doubt for political reasons; he was buried at Glasnevin, a Dublin cemetery mentioned below.)[44] Like countless visitors in years to come, the party went by train to Sallins, where a station had been opened in 1846. It was on the Great Southern and Western Railway's line from Dublin to the south; passengers starting from Dublin would board a train at the Kingsbridge terminus, within sight of Dublin barracks where Tone died. On the way from Sallins railway station to Bodenstown, the party stopped briefly at a public house kept by a John Magrath; on the party's way back, for 'a most agreeable hour', Magrath, his sister and others present were, on learning the party's purpose, 'most demonstrative in their welcome' and were effusive on the subject of the grave. Cavanagh recounts — on the basis, it can only be inferred, of what his party learnt in the public house at Sallins — that, after the scattering of Young Irelanders in 1849, 'Bodenstown was but rarely visited by strangers. Consequently, the "Martyr's grave" received little attention and that only when some local admirer, attending a funeral in the lonely little churchyard, went to draw hope and inspiration from the sacred spot.'

Cavanagh describes Tone's monument as 'a heavy limestone slab about six inches in thickness. The slab stood quite close to the centre of the south wall of the ruin. It was elevated about a foot from the ground, and rested on six stone supporters.' This description of the 'slab' is the most detailed to have been found. Cavanagh's measurement of its thickness accords almost exactly with that entered in the acquisitions register of the Art and Industrial Division of the National Museum in 1941. There is however an apparent discrepancy. Davis told Pigot, in his letter of 17 April 1844, published in 1890 (in Duffy's *Thomas Davis*), that it was to be 'a plain black *marble* slab, very massive' (my italics). Matthew Parkes of the National Museum, having examined the fragment, gives his opinion, 'based on colour, texture, fracturing, weathering and general appearance', that it is 'Irish Carboniferous limestone … Marble is a stonemason's term. Any limestone that can take a good polish, usually a dark, fine-grained micrite as this probably is, is generally termed a marble in the stone trade.'[45] The wording of the inscription stated in Cavanagh's account published in *Shan Van Vocht* in 1898 corresponds precisely to the wording stated by Davis in his letter to Pigot. As has been discussed above, it differs from that stated by Madden in the volume of his *United Irishmen* published in 1858. Cavanagh cannot however be considered to have put the matter beyond doubt. It is possible that he did not write down the inscription on his visit in 1861 and that he could not later recall it, but took it from Duffy's *Davis*, or that, failing this, the editor of *Shan Van Vocht*, Alice Milligan, did so. Cavanagh found Tone's grave somewhat neglected. He added that, 'with the advent of Fenianism, a reaction in national sentiment set in' and 'the lone grave in Bodenstown became again the resort of enthusiastic pilgrims'.[46] Cavanagh, who also took part in the Irish rebellion of 1848, was in North America a friend of, and secretary to, John O'Mahony,

44 R. V. Comerford, *The Fenians in context: Irish politics and society, 1848–82* (revd ed., Dublin, 1998), pp 76, 254. Comerford's source is *Irishman*, 20 July, 3 Aug. 1861.   **45** Matthew Parkes to Audrey Whitty, 20 Nov. 2017. To both I am grateful.   **46** *Shan Van Vocht*, July 1898.

founder there in 1859 of the Fenian Brotherhood; one of Cavanagh's companions at Bodenstown was Michael Doheny, also a rebel in 1848 and an associate of O'Mahony in 1859.[47] Cavanagh's recollection of the slab as limestone is consistent with Davis's promise of marble, and he amply confirms the statements of Davis, Madden, Mitchel and Gray that the memorial to Tone was indeed a slab, 'an inscribed though humble flagstone', Gray also called it.[48]

Another piece of information on visits during the 1860s is ultimately from a Fenian source. It is that some time before 28 March 1864 several people, one of them John Devoy, acquired soil taken from Tone's grave, for each sent samples to the Fenian-organised 'Great Irish National Fair' which opened in Chicago on that date.[49] Devoy, born in 1842 in County Kildare, at Kill, a village six kilometres from Naas and the same distance from Bodenstown, was in 1862 or 1863 a local organiser for the I.R.B. in the Naas area. It is likely that Bodenstown was part of his territory. Devoy was arrested in February 1866, pleaded guilty to a charge of seducing soldiers from their allegiance, and spent five years in prison in England before emigrating to America, where he soon joined Clan na Gael, a society formed in 1867 with the object of reconciling the two factions into which the Fenian Brotherhood had split two years before. For many years he was the strongest link between the Fenians there and the I.R.B. in Ireland. To the organisers of the pilgrimage to Bodenstown in 1903 he sent a cablegram expressing support.[50] His death in New Jersey in September 1928 was marked by an obituary in the London *Times*, the writer of which described him as 'the most bitter and persistent, as well as the most dangerous, enemy of this country which Ireland has produced since Wolfe Tone'.[51] Devoy was buried in Ireland, at Glasnevin, on 17 June 1929, because of which the annual pilgrimage to Bodenstown of the Irish government and defence forces had to be postponed to allow for his funeral.[52]

The three Sullivan brothers Timothy, Alexander and Denis, in the first edition of their *Speeches from the dock*, could write of Tone in 1867: 'his mortal remains repose in Bodenstown churchyard, County Kildare, whither parties of patriotic young men from the metropolis and the surrounding districts often proceed to lay a green wreath on his grave'.[53] An instance of such a visit being expected in September 1869 appears in a report that reached Dublin Castle: nationalists planned

47 Doheny is in the *D.I.B.*, in an article contributed by Desmond McCabe and James Quinn. 48 Gray to the editor, n.d. (*Freeman's Jn.*, 17 Sept. 1873). 49 Brian Griffin, '"Scallions, pikes and bog oak ornaments": the Irish Republican Brotherhood and the Chicago Fenian Fair, 1864' in *Studia Hibernica*, xxix (1997), pp 85, 90. Another exhibit was 'a window shutter handle from Wolfe Tone's residence in Grafton Street', donated by Stephen Lambert of Wilbrook, a 94-year-old veteran of the battles of New Ross and Foulkesmills (loc. cit., p. 91). 50 *Freeman's Jn.*, 22 June 1903. For Devoy, see Patrick Maume's article in *D.I.B.* For Clan na Gael, see Comerford, *Fenians*, pp 205–6. 51 *The Times*, 1 Oct. 1928. It is possible that the writer was John Woulfe Flanagan, an Irishman who was the paper's chief leader writer for many years (C. J. Woods, 'Flanagan, John Woulfe (1852–1929)' in *D.I.B.*). 52 *Ir. Indep.*, 17 June 1929. 53 T. D., A. M. and D. B. Sullivan, *'Guilty or not-guilty?': speeches from the dock* (Dublin, 1867), p. 23. It was advertised as 'now ready' in *Nation*, 1 Feb. 1868.

an excursion to Bodenstown, perhaps to stage a 'mock funeral'; in the end the expected groups from Dublin, to be accompanied by the Skinners' Band, did not appear; only local people went to Tone's grave and there they had a picnic.[54] Evidence of visits, albeit fleeting, evidence that is deductive and unspecific, can also be found in a mention of the grave by a knowledgeable follower of the Kildare Hounds that in February 1871 passed 'through the large grass fields of Bodenstown'; the tombstone, he commented, 'is growing small by degrees from the many pieces knocked out of it by visitors'.[55] Evidence of the dilapidated state of the stone and so implicitly of many earlier visits is more explicit in a report of an organised visit two years later in the *Freeman's Journal* (still owned by Gray); Tone's grave had, it stated, 'many and many a time been the object of loving interest to those whom chance or opportunity may have brought to its vicinity, and seldom has it been seen without some trifling object of respect — a flower, green wreath, or garland — being observed upon it'; the original stone had, 'from the fact that portions of it were being constantly removed as *souvenirs* of the spot, become utterly unworthy of the object for which it had been erected'.[56] On the same occasion, the reporter of the *Irish Times* referred to pieces of the stone being 'repeatedly chipped off and carried away by visitors' and of the stone being 'accidentally broken some short time ago by a young man in his endeavour to get a piece to bring to America with him'.[57]

The last statement, together with the existence of a large fragment of the stone in the National Museum in Dublin, supports accounts given many years later by two men who would have grown up learning of the fate of Davis's stone. It is implicit in both accounts that the incident of the stone being broken occurred in the late 1860s or early 1870s, certainly before September 1873. The first of the two was Joseph William O'Beirne, who took part in pilgrimages to Tone's grave in the early 1890s (recounted below); O'Beirne would at least have picked up much folklore about the stone. According to O'Beirne, the Dublin 'half' was removed to the premises in Great Britain Street (later renamed Parnell Street) of James Dillon, a bill-poster (known popularly as the 'dead wall decorator'), where it remained until the late 1880s, when it was moved to 17 Moore Lane; it came into the keeping of 'a prominent Dublin Nationalist', whose descendants still held it in the late 1930s.[58] The second to give an account was John J. Whelan, perhaps a son or grandson of the Whelan brothers — or were they cousins? — John R. and Edward R., who were prominent at pilgrimages in the 1890s. If his account be reliable, the stone was broken in two at 'one of the annual pilgrimages' in consequence of 'a row started between two faction parties'; a 'wealthy American', perhaps of Kildare ancestry, on visiting the grave 'decided to remove one half to his home in Philadelphia'; Dillon the bill-poster drove to Bodenstown in his pony-trap and removed the other 'half' to his premises in Dublin; a local chimney-sweep named Rooney removed it one

54 Nat. Arch., Dublin, Fenian papers, 4763/R. I am grateful to Brian Griffin and Gary Owens for this information.   55 *Leinster Express*, 4 Mar. 1871.   56 *Freeman's Jn.*, 15 Sept. 1873.   57 *Ir. Times*, 15 Sept. 1873.   58 J. W. O'Beirne, 'How Tone's grave was found' in *Ir. Press*, 24 July 1937.

night to his home in Moore Lane, confiding to his neighbour at No. 17, John McDonnell, a basket maker and poor-law guardian, John J. Whelan's grandfather and no doubt the 'prominent Dublin Nationalist', who in turn removed and hid it in his own premises; years later McDonnell moved it to 78 Pill Lane (renamed Chancery Street), where he had it on exhibition in a glass case, attracting many visitors, among them, more than once, John Howard Parnell (eldest brother of Charles Stewart Parnell); he moved it again, on retirement in 1906, to 49 Bolton Street, where on his death in November 1916 it passed to Whelan's sister Catherine; it was on exhibition in 1936 by Éamonn Whyte of the Capel Book Shop; a year or more later Catherine presented it to O'Beirne, who, accompanied by John Doran (another veteran pilgrim and an associate of John R. Whelan in the Young Ireland League) and John J. Whelan himself, presented it to the National Museum.[59] What is verifiable beyond question is that the 'half' of the stone which the National Museum holds was donated formally by O'Beirne in 1941 on behalf of the Wolfe Tone Commemoration Committee.[60] It is really only about one-third of what must have been the original stone. Its authenticity has been discussed above.

59 John J. Whelan to the editor, n.d. in *Dublin Evening Mail*, 22 June 1944.   60 Info. Dr Audrey Whitty, N.M.I., 30 Sept. 2016.

3

The Wolfe Tone Band's memorial slab and
organised pilgrimages, 1873–90

IN THE SUMMER OF 1872, a reader of the *Nation* signing himself 'Dun
Padruic' wrote to the editor with a proposal about Bodenstown that was to prove
prophetic. It was subsequently published under the heading 'A good suggestion':

> Many citizens of Dublin make excursions on summer Sundays to places
> within easy access of the city by rail for mere pleasure. Could not these
> excursions be systematised and utilised, made to keep the national spirit in a
> state of healthy vitality, and to promote that rational education on the general
> diffusion of which the speedy or remote realisation of our hopes of national
> independence rests? Suppose a series of excursions to places of historic
> interest within reach of Dublin were organised, could they not be made
> conducive to the end we all have in view? Let the first be to visit the grave
> where the grass grows greenest in the pleasant fields of Kildare. Twenty-eight
> years have passed since Thomas Davis — then the unknown 'Celt' of the
> Poet's Corner of the *Nation*, now regarded at home and in every spot on the
> surface of the globe to which our people have been dispersed as the very
> personification of the cloudy and lightning genius of the Gael — wrote his
> heart-stirring stanzas over the 'Green grave' in 'Bodenstown Churchyard'
> where the noble heart of young Wolfe Tone has become Irish earth; and still
> that grave is green, for no stone marks the spot where the martyr for Ireland
> lies. An excursion thither, either to hold a pic-nic near the sacred spot or (each
> excursionist to bring his or her commissariat in his or her pocket), to hear a
> lecture or address by some well-qualified person on the life of our young hero,
> might enable us to combine patriotism and pleasure. No doubt some of the
> popular and patriotic bands of Dublin would give their services for the
> occasion.

Though this proposal was before long to be carried out, the correspondent's further
proposals, significantly (it will be argued), were not.

> Another excursion of the succeeding Sunday might be made to the Beech of
> Fassaroe, near Bray, the famous trysting tree of Michael Dwyer and his gallant
> guerillas of '98. The next Sunday an excursion might be made to Glendalough

or some other scene of triumph of Pheagh MacHugh O'Byrne over the foreign robbers ...

The correspondent went on to suggest 'Clontarf, to visit the field where the victorious Brian overthrew the fierce Vikings and all their power', and 'Howth, the historic associations of which ... would form ample theme for the orator of the day', and further 'the Hill of Donore and Schomberg's Obelisk, the scene of the battle at the Boyne's ill-fated river ..., Tara of the Kings and of the Croppies' graves' and 'the Druid's Altar beyond the Fifteen Acres in the Park'.[1] Why Bodenstown proved to be the outstanding success will become evident.

The custom of, and model for, organised excursions to Bodenstown were the creations of the forty members of the Dublin Wolfe Tone Band who visited Tone's grave in 1873. Their stated purpose was to replace the badly-damaged and broken memorial slab. Accounts of the well-attended ceremony at Tone's grave on Sunday, 14 September, appeared in the *Freeman's Journal* and also in the *Irish Times*, the *Leinster Express* and the *Belfast News Letter*. As the *Freeman*'s correspondent reported,

> By the half past nine o'clock train from King's Bridge the members of the band we have mentioned proceeded to Sallins, accompanied by a large concourse of well-dressed people of both sexes, and thence walked to Bodenstown, carrying flags and bannerets, and everyone displaying a ribbon or rosette of the national colour. Crowds flocked in from Sallins, Newbridge, Naas and the neighbouring districts, and towards evening there were at least between two and three thousand people present. The old slab was removed, and the new one, which was admirably cut by Mr Thomas H. Dennany, of Glasnevin, placed in its stead.[2]

After the placing of the new slab, a flowery speech was made by a Mr Keegan of the Dublin Wolfe Tone Band — probably the Richard Keegan mentioned on a later occasion. The full text was printed in the *Irishman* the following Saturday.[3] It was a precedent for annual orations at Tone's grave. Another was the orderly behaviour of the crowd. As the *Freeman* reported, 'though an extra force of thirty constabulary was drafted to Sallins for the occasion, ... their interference was in no way required'.

The new tombstone was described by W. F. Wakeman, an archaeological illustrator who visited the graveyard in 1886, as a 'prostrate flag' and as 'lying over the grave'.[4] In these respects it resembled the stone that it was replacing. It was inscribed, as reported in the *Freeman's Journal*:

1 *Nation*, 3 Aug. 1872. Was 'Dun Padruic' perhaps Charles Kickham?   2 *Freeman's Jn.*, 15 Sept. 1873.   3 *Irishman* (Dublin), 20 Sept. 1873, 28 Mar. 1874.   4 W. F. Wakeman, 'The grave of Theobald Wolfe Tone' in *Graves and monuments of illustrious Irishmen* (Dublin, 1887), pp 22–4. This book consists of articles reprinted from the *Evening Telegraph* (Dublin), Oct.–Dec. 1886. It was advertised, with mention of Tone, in *Freeman's Jn.*, 20 Mar. 1888.

THEOBALD WOLFE TONE
Born 20th June 1763
Died 19th November 1798 for Ireland
The original Slab having been accidentally broken,
the members of the Wolfe Tone Band in
respect for their noble patron,
erected this slab,
14 September 1873
GOD SAVE IRELAND

There are small differences in the version given in the *Irish Times*. The third and fourth lines are said to be separated by 'a harp surrounded by shamrocks'; the sixth line is said to read 'respect to the memory of their noble patron'. More significantly the new memorial is described as 'a plain black stone similar to the original'.[5] A Dublin photographer, Adolphe Le Sage of Lower Sackville Street, 'succeeded in getting some admirable views'.[6] No photographs have been found. There is, however, a sketch of the slab, shown lying at the foot of the standing stone marking William Tone's grave with the two in a railed area; it was made by William Sherlock, evidently before 1895 as a new stone replaced it that year. Sadly, by then the upper part showed signs of damage, the first three lines of the inscription were missing, there was no trace of any harp surrounded by shamrocks, and on the ground in space between the two stones there were three fragments, on one of which the word 'Tone' (in capitals) could be distinguished.[7]

How were funds for the new stone raised? It is likely money was collected mainly in Dublin by the Wolfe Tone Band. In one report of the slab-laying ceremony it is stated that the bandsmen took the initiative and 'that in an inconceivably short time the requisite funds were at hand'.[8] This rapidity suggests the existence of bountiful friends. It also suggests that there were nationalists eager to restore Tone's grave to its earlier condition. An apocryphal account of an initiative being taken in County Kildare merits attention. If a claim made in a speech, in a politically-fraught situation, twenty years later can be relied upon, a pupil at Clongowes Wood College, John Redmond (born in 1856 and at the school from 1868 until 1874),[9] paid visits to Tone's grave — about six kilometres distant from the school — and, becoming aware that repair was needed, 'started a collection among his comrades in the college for the purpose'. The claim was made in a speech at Bodenstown in 1893 by J. L. Carew.[10] Now Carew (born in 1853) had also been at Clongowes (1867–8); he was elected member of parliament for North Kildare in 1885, remained loyal to Charles Stewart Parnell after the split in the Irish home-rule party in 1890, and lost his seat

5 *Freeman's Jn.*, 15 Sept. 1873; *Ir. Times*, 15 Sept. 1873.   6 *Freeman's Jn.*, 15 Sept. 1873. The photographer's name has been corrected.   7 William Sherlock, 'Bodenstown grave-yard: a place of Irish pilgrimage' in *Kildare Arch. Soc. Jn.*, vi (1909–11), p. 227, illus. Sherlock, like Wakeman, has 'in respect to the memory ...'.   8 *Ir. Times*, 15 Sept. 1873.   9 Timothy Corcoran, *The Clongowes record, 1814 to 1932* (Dublin, 1932), p. 212.   10 *Leinster Leader*, 1 July 1893; *Kildare*

in 1892. When Carew spoke at Bodenstown, Redmond was leader of the Parnellite faction of the home-rulers. Carew's claim was rejected by anti-Parnellite rivals.[11] Certainly, Redmond had credibility as an admirer of the United Irishmen, being the author of a vindicatory pamphlet, *The truth about '98* (Dublin, 1886). He was to speak and write vigorously in 1898, the centenary of the United Irish rebellion, in praise of the rebels.[12] Carew's statement can at least be treated as evidence of the existence of a public fund for a new stone in the early 1870s. Donations of schoolboys would hardly have sufficed.

Mysteriously, in Mainham Cemetery, between Clane and Rathcoffey, there is now to be seen a Celtic cross inscribed in Gaelic lettering: 'this cross is carved from the original tomb of Wolfe Tone'. It surmounts an upright gravestone inscribed 'to the memory of Peter Mackey who died 23rd March 1872 aged 28 years erected by his brother Thomas Mackey, R.I.P.'. The Mackeys have not been identified. No explanation is forthcoming.[13]

A PROTECTIVE RAILING ERECTED

On 22 March 1874 — barely six months after the descent on Bodenstown churchyard by the Wolfe Tone Band — a crowd assembled there again. Only four weeks after the laying of the slab there was a rumour in Naas of 'some evil-disposed person' having broken it; the rumour quickly spread and in the evening a large number of people from Clane and Naas, and from as far away as Celbridge and Newbridge, appeared in the graveyard to find that 'a small "chip" had been broken from off the under part of the slab'; a subscription was quickly got up for 'an ornamental railing' to be placed around the monument 'to prevent parties removing chips from the stone' as mementoes.[14] In 1874, as in 1873, the Wolfe Tone Band arrived at Sallins and proceeded to Bodenstown joined by a large, growing crowd of local people. A reporter from the *Nation* explained and described the scene:

> To save the new stone from meeting the fate of the old, the men of Kildare
> have recently enclosed it with an iron railing, which arches over at the top, at
> a height of about eight feet, and effectually protects it from all chance or
> injury. The railing is of a tasteful pattern and displays a range of spear-heads
> and shamrocks on the crown of the arch. There is a door to the enclosure, for
> which two keys are kept, one by the Wolfe Tone Band, Dublin, and the other

---

Observer, 1 July 1893.   11 I am indebted to Gary Owens for information on Carew's claim. For his career, see the obituary in the *Leinster Leader* (which he owned), 5 Sept. 1903, and William Murphy, 'Carew, James Laurence (1853–1903)' in *D.I.B.* He is listed in Corcoran, *Clongowes record*, p. 171.   12 Timothy J. O'Keefe, '"Who fears to speak of '98?": the rhetoric and rituals of the United Irishmen centennial, 1898' in *Éire-Ireland*, xxvii, no. 3 (fall 1992), pp 67–91 at pp 68, 78, 80–1.   13 I am grateful to Professor R. V. Comerford for drawing my attention to this cross and for his opinions on it. I am grateful too to my wife Penny for her opinions.   14 *Leinster Express* (Maryborough), 18 Oct. 1873.

by the Kildaremen who have taken part in this patriotic work ... A large number of persons, including the Wolfe Tone Band and the Volunteer Band, left Dublin for Sallins on Sunday morning by the 9.30 train. The fine brass band of the Coopers proceeded in a drag drawn by four horses and displaying their trade banner to the place of meeting.

There were local Kildare bands too: brass bands from Clane and Kilcock, bands from Newbridge and Naas, and 'a band from the town of Kildare accompanied by a large number of stalwart men'. About three thousand were present, 'all were well dressed, orderly and intelligent', and among them 'a considerable number' of women. T. D. Sullivan (one of the three brothers who had produced *Speeches from the dock*) spoke about Tone's career. Then the bands 'marched around the tomb playing national airs ... Before quitting Bodenstown each of them halted and performed some music in front of the house of Messrs Reddy, whose father, in the year 1844, pointed out the grave of Tone to Thomas Davis, Sir John Gray and others who had gone from Dublin to discover it.'[15] Gray's letter (quoted above) describing his visit and how a local blacksmith had pointed out the grave had been published the previous September.[16]

The imprecision about 'the men of Kildare', about 'the Kildaremen who have taken part in this patriotic work', poses the question of what co-operation existed between Tone's admirers in Dublin and his admirers in Kildare. Money for the erection of the railing was, as stated, raised locally out of alarm that damage was being done. Convincingly, Carew had a reliable source, a Clane man, Peter Clory or Clowry.[17] This Clory (or Clowry?) seems to have been the chief donor and also the organiser. In September 1874, six months after the erection of the railing, Clory was given a pen-and-ink drawing of the dilapidated Bodenstown church made from the north side by J.O.C. Robinson of Blackrock; nine months later still, the same artist drew for Clory the church from the south side 'with the grave of W. Tone', as the legend explained, 'beautifully rebuilt by Mr Peter Clory of Clane, Co. Kildare'.[18] Clory's role no doubt made him popular as well as respectable. He may have been the Peter Clowry (*sic*) of Clane who was present at the commemorations at Bodenstown in 1891, 1892, 1893 and 1896; he was later president of the Clane '98 Centenary Association;[19] this Peter Clowry was a local builder.[20]

Robinson depicts clearly the exterior of the south wall of the church. Most striking is the railing enclosing Tone's grave. Barely discernible is a heart-shaped plaque with the word 'erected' and the initials 'P.C.'. Wakeman deciphered the inscription as 'the men of the Co. Kildare have erected this railing to protect the

15 *Nation*, 28 Mar. 1874. The year of the first visit of Davis and Gray was however 1843. The Reddys' house was on the east side of the Naas–Clane road, just north of the turn into the boreen (info. Seamus Cullen, Ger MacCarthy and Jim Tancred).   **16** *Freeman's Jn.*, 26 Sept. 1873.   **17** *Leinster Leader*, 8 July 1893.   **18** N.L.I., Department of Prints and Drawings.   **19** *Freeman's Jn.*, 23 June 1891, 20 June 1892; *Leinster Leader*, 1 July 1893, 27 June 1896, 25 June 1898.   **20** *Kildare Observer*, 20 Aug. 1887, 20 July 1889, 5 Mar. 1892, 14, 21 Oct. 1893, 21 Mar. 1896.

grave of Wolfe Tone'. The grave when he visited Bodenstown churchyard in 1886 was not altogether secure, for the lock on the railing was disintegrating, in consequence, Wakeman believed, of being 'broken by violence'.[21] Removal of portions of the memorial as souvenirs had continued. There is evidence that the practice continued into the 1890s in William Sherlock's account, most tellingly in the accompanying sketch showing the Wolfe Tone Band's recumbent slab positioned, as it was, at the foot of William Tone's standing stone. The upper part shows signs of damage, the first three lines of the inscription are missing; on the ground in space between the two stones are three fragments, on one of which the word 'Tone' (in capitals) can be discerned. Sherlock, referring to the slab placed in 1873 and then to the slab placed in 1844, comments:

> it will be noticed that the edges have been chipped off by enthusiastic pilgrims who have carried the pieces with them as sacred relics. Not content with this, they have even (as the transcription on the slab which rests above the grave informs us) broken up and carried away the original stone placed over Wolfe Tone. The second slab, which replaced this, is in process of being similarly destroyed … At present the railing placed to protect it by the men of Kildare is of little service, as the lock has been forced and the gate lies open.[22]

In fact the inscription stated that the damage was accidental. But Sherlock (whose interest was antiquarian) would have had local knowledge of overenthusiastic admirers of Tone chipping away pieces of stone as souvenirs. He was not merely a local Protestant clergyman and historian, he was the rector of Bodenstown and a denizen of the adjacent parish of Sherlockstown, where Sherlocks were established in 1299.[23] He would therefore have kept Bodenstown churchyard under close observation. In our own age it is appalling that pilgrims should routinely damage what they have come to see; yet in the nineteenth century even respected archaeologists on occasion made a point of chipping away at historic monuments for samples. When, for instance, Sir George Petrie was visiting prehistoric sites in Connacht in or around 1820 he took a hammer and chisel and removed grouting at Hag's Castle in Lough Mask.[24]

PILGRIMAGES BECOME ANNUAL

Organised summer visits to Bodenstown in the later 1870s brought gatherings 'of both city and country people'.[25] Such visits took on the character of a religious pilgrimage — a word soon to recur in contemporary reports. After the erection of

21 Wakeman, 'The grave of Theobald Wolfe Tone', pp 22–4. 22 Sherlock, 'Bodenstown churchyard' (1909–11), pp 227–8. 23 J. F. M. Ffrench, 'Notes on the family of Sherlock chiefly gathered from the state papers and other official documents' in *Kildare Arch. Soc. Jn.*, ii, pt II (1897?), pp 33–47, at pp 34, 45–6. 24 William Stokes, *The life and labours in art and archaeology of George Petrie* (London, 1868), p. 215. 25 *Freeman's Jn.*, 18 Aug. 1879.

the protective railing in 1874 the *Nation* commented: 'the grave of Wolfe Tone is now a conspicuous object in the graveyard … and it will doubtless be the scene of many a pious pilgrimage of the sons of Ireland in ages yet to come'.[26] The word 'pilgrim' was employed too. In 1899 the excursionists were referred to as 'the pilgrims to the grave of our hero-martyr'.[27]

The 'pilgrimage' of 26 September 1875 was organised by the Amnesty Association. This was a body campaigning for the release of 'political prisoners', men who had engaged in Fenian activities of various kinds, most particularly the rebellion that occurred in the early spring of 1867. The planned gathering was previously advertised, but heavy, prolonged rain into which only a hundred or so pilgrims ventured to take the train from Dublin to Sallins spoilt the day. Bandsmen from Kill arrived after walking in 'pelting rain'; a member of parliament for County Kildare invited to speak, Charles Henry Meldon, did not venture far. Despite the weather, speeches were eventually delivered by the association's secretary, Robert J. Dunne, and by the deputy editor of the *Irishman*, James O'Connor.[28] O'Connor himself had been arrested in September 1865, convicted of treason-felony and eventually released from prison with forty-eight others in February 1869 as a result, partly at least, of the campaign. His membership of the I.R.B. began in the early 1860s; he became closely associated in 1863 with James Stephens, who had founded the secret organisation in 1858; O'Connor was in the early 1870s treasurer of its governing body, the Supreme Council.[29] The *Irishman* was in the 1870s the Dublin weekly newspaper that appealed most to Fenians.[30] It was O'Connor who presided the following year, on 13 August, at another pilgrimage to Bodenstown organised by the Amnesty Association; this time the weather was insufferably hot, 'hundreds' took an early train to Sallins, at least seven bands played and Dunne again made a speech; when it came to the vote of thanks a second chair was taken by James Egan of Wolverhampton.[31] One report, surely with exaggeration, put the attendance at five thousand or more.[32] Egan (b. 1847), an Irishman, seems to have been working for the I.R.B. as an arms agent in Birmingham; he was arrested in April 1884 and subsequently served nine years' imprisonment; later, from 1898 until his death in 1909, he was Dublin municipal sword-bearer, a sinecure, during which period his name appears in reports of Bodenstown pilgrimages.[33]

What proved to be a very successful pilgrimage in 1877 was at first proposed as an excursion to take place on the last Sunday in July for members and friends of the 'Court Wolfe Tone No. 1' of the Irish National Order of Foresters.[34] The Irish National Foresters were a benefit society some branches ('courts') of which had

---

26 *Nation*, 28 Mar. 1874.   **27** *Freeman's Jn.*, 18 July 1899.   **28** *Nation*, 25 Sept. 1875; *Irishman*, 25 Sept., 2 Oct. 1875; *Ir. Times*, 27 Sept. 1875.   **29** Comerford, *Fenians in context*, pp 47–8, 98, 164–5; Owen McGee and Georgina Clinton, 'O'Connor, James (1836–1910)' in *D.I.B.* **30** Comerford, *Fenians in context*, pp 146, 171, 181, 182, 210.   **31** *Freeman's Jn.*, 14, 17 Aug. 1876; *Irishman*, 19 Aug. 1876.   **32** *Leinster Express*, 19 Aug. 1876.   **33** E.g. *Leinster Leader*, 30 June 1900, 27 June 1903. For his career, see Desmond McCabe and Owen McGee, 'Egan, James Francis' in *D.I.B.*   **34** *Freeman's Jn.*, 12 July 1877.

since 1874 separated from the Ancient Order of Foresters (which was British-based), chiefly because of Irish members' support for the Amnesty Association.[35] Other clubs became involved; the date was put back to 12 August, which proved to be a fine day; three trains were needed to convey enthusiastic 'demonstrationists' with their bands and banners to Sallins at an early hour; 'large bodies of the country people and well-to-do farmers on their outside cars from neighbouring and outlying districts swelled the ranks'; the procession set off for Bodenstown at 11.30 a.m. headed by the Martyrs' Band and interspersed by four other bands; in the churchyard Handel's 'Dead march in Saul' was played by all five; political speeches were made from a platform in a field nearby; a certain James Carey of Dublin took the chair; a speech was made again by Dunne of the Amnesty Association and again Egan of Wolverhampton took a second chair to call for a vote of thanks.[36] The Martyrs' Band was named after the three members of the I.R.B. hanged at Salford, near Manchester, in 1867 in consequence of the rescue, organised by Ricard O'Sullivan Burke, of two Fenians from a prison van. The three were remembered, and commemorated ever after, as the 'Manchester martyrs'. There can be little doubt that James Carey was the man of this name who in the 1870s was an active member of the Dublin directory of the I.R.B.; this James Carey left the I.R.B. about 1878 and was one of the group known as the Invincibles who in 1882 murdered the Irish chief secretary and under-secretary in the Phoenix Park, in Dublin, which eventually brought about his own murder in July 1883.[37] The significance of the pilgrimage of 1877 was that it displayed so many of the features that were to characterise Bodenstown in the 1890s and most of the twentieth century.

One of these features merits further treatment here. The 'field nearby' was almost certainly the field mentioned in later reports of pilgrimages. A more exact location was not indicated until 1923, when one reporter referred to 'a large field near the little graveyard' occupied by 'troops drawn up in review form facing the graveyard', and, more exactly still, in 1933, when another referred to pilgrims having, after the graveside ceremony, 'proceeded to the field at the other side of the laneway' to hear the oration.[38] Unmistakably this was on the north side of the boreen, directly opposite the entrance to the churchyard, and was where Peter Tone's house once stood. Matilda Tone refers to it in 1829 as 'the glebe field'.[39] In her day it would have been rented from the Protestant church; it has not been fully ascertained where ownership lay after church disestablishment in 1871. It must at some time have passed to one of the Reddy family, a descendant of William Reddy who led Davis and Gray to Tone's grave in 1843. William Reddy, described as 'a farmer and blacksmith' of Clane, died in June 1869; his will was disputed by a niece in Kildare County Court in 1882.[40] As stated above, sons of his were living at Bodenstown in 1874. They were presumably the Thomas and William Reddy who were present

35 *Freeman's Jn.*, 17 Aug., 28 Sept. 1877. The history of the Irish National Foresters has yet to be written.   36 *Irishman*, 4 July, 18 Aug. 1877.   37 James Quinn, 'Carey, James' in *D.I.B.* 38 *Evening Herald* (Dublin), 25 June 1923; *Leinster Leader*, 1 July 1933.   39 Matilda Tone to Catherine Tone, 22 Dec. 1829 (Dickason papers).   40 *Kildare Observer*, 17 June, 22 July 1882, 16

among the pilgrims in June 1892. Whether Thomas or another Reddy acquired ownership, or whether William Reddy the elder ever rented the field from the church, is not known. What is known, from local sources, is that Reddys were living at Bodenstown in the farmhouse near the corner of the boreen with the Sallins-Clane road before or until February 1922 and that Mrs Eliza Reddy gave the glebe field some time before her death in 1935 to a niece, Mrs Ciss Daly (wife of a Sallins shopkeeper, Thomas Daly). In the early 1960s it became the property of a family named Lyons, who sold it in the 1990s.[41] Whatever its ownership, the glebe field was an obvious place for very large gatherings of pilgrims. It was used on such occasions from 1911 until 1915, again in 1918 and from 1923 until 1937. In none of the many reports examined is there any indication of awareness that it was once the location of Peter Tone's farmhouse.

Despite the resounding success in 1877, only one, very slight piece of evidence has been found of a pilgrimage in 1878, merely a fleeting, incidental mention in a private diary. Lord Cloncurry (a resident of Lyons, County Kildare) records in his diary for 17 March, a Sunday, meeting near Oughterard a Mr Ritchie who told him that 'all his men had gone off with the bands to W. Tone's grave and he had to look after his ewes and lambs that day by himself'.[42] This at least confirms the importance of music in creating local interest. In August of the following year, 1879, the *Freeman's Journal*, reporting what it called 'the annual commemorative visit, or pilgrimage, to Wolfe Tone's grave', stated that 'the attendance was very small' and 'confined to the members of the Wolfe Tone Band' and 'a few local sympathisers' awaiting them at Sallins railway station; it added that 'a few years ago the event used to attract a large gathering'.[43]

The commemoration at Bodenstown in the summer of 1880, on 22 August, showed new interest. It was reported in some detail as 'the annual pilgrimage of the Martyrs' Band to the grave of Theobald Wolfe Tone'. As before, people arrived from nearby villages (Sallins, Naas, Clane and Celbridge are named) and by train from Dublin. They heard the Martyrs' Band and afterwards a speech by John Daly of Limerick.[44] This band had played in 1877. Daly (1845–1916), active in the I.R.B. in his native city in the 1860s, was the body's chief travelling organiser in the 1870s (facts not stated publicly); he was in 1880 living in Brighton in the south of England still engaged in I.R.B. activity and was to be sentenced in 1884 to penal servitude for life, from which he was freed in 1896.[45] Daly's speech, reported at length only in the *Leinster Express*, was characteristically Fenian in its dismissal of the Land League, all agrarian agitation, constitutionalism and parliamentarianism. Were Tone alive, Daly insisted, 'they might call him a coward if he would not be a Land Leaguer — they might charge him with a want of courage sufficient to burn a haystack'.[46]

Feb. 1884.   41 For this information I am grateful to Mrs Mary Weld, Clane.   42 Diaries of 4th Baron Cloncurry (1840–1928) in the possession of Aileen Murray, Celbridge Post Office. I am grateful to Jim Tancred for drawing these to my attention.   43 *Freeman's Jn.*, 18 Aug. 1879. 44 *Freeman's Jn.*, 23 Aug. 1880.   45 Desmond McCabe and Owen McGee, 'Daly, John' in *D.I.B.* 46 *Leinster Express*, 28 Aug. 1880.

A similar commemoration, reported as being 'the annual visit to Bodenstown churchyard', occurred on 14 August 1881, the Martyrs' Band arriving from Dublin and local people joining the procession from Sallins.[47] In charge of the band in both years was a 'Mr Bracken'. Evidently, from a police report, this was Thomas Bracken, the band's president and an I.R.B. man.[48]

The interest shown in 1873 and 1874 by members of the Wolfe Tone Band and of local people in north Kildare may have been largely civic and social: replacing and securing the damaged stone was a combination of bandsmen's bonding and enjoyment of a summer outing; for locals it was an opportunity to show local pride and to hear local and Dublin bands. The appearance in 1875, 1876 and 1877 of politically motivated orators known, publicly or not, to be Fenians was the beginning of what was to be an essential element of the pilgrimages — a political rally with oratory by a man of pronounced nationalistic opinions. The recreational element remained, however, and was indispensable. The pilgrimages were from the beginning social occasions. The excursion of the Wolfe Tone Band in the early autumn of 1873 was a day's outing into the countryside for the bandsmen's friends and relations as well as for themselves. Local bandsmen, from Naas and Newbridge, joined in. Not only the music but the colour made the occasion jolly and enjoyable. As the *Leinster Express* recorded, 'a procession was formed at Sallins station and set out with flags, banners, sashes and rosettes'; later 'large crowds came from Naas, Clane, Newbridge, Kilcullen and the surrounding neighbourhood. Most of the people had either green sashes, or rosettes, or green leaves in the hatbands, and many of the female portion of the crowd had green veils'; a photographer captured the view of 'the members of the band standing in a group to the right and the left of the monument'.[49] The participation of bands was an essential and lasting feature. The Wolfe Tone Band had been in existence since 1870 or earlier; its president, Keegan, had joined other band enthusiasts in forming in that year the Dublin Bands' United Alliance.[50] By 1887 there existed as many as 30 bands in that city.[51] In 1875 local bands, from Celbridge, Kill and Naas, attempted to play despite the very wet autumn weather; in 1876, on a 'sweltering day' in August, there was a large turnout of Dublin and local musicians; named in one report were the City of Dublin Band, Inchicore Fife and Drum Band, Leixlip Band, Ardclough Brass Band, Clane Fife and Drum Band, Celbridge Brass Band and (from the same village) Celbridge Fife and Drum Band.[52] Various bands were to entertain the crowds over the next hundred years and no doubt made the events more attractive to some than the political speeches that similarly became regular features.

47 *Freeman's Jn.*, 15 Aug. 1881. **48** Owen McGee, '"God save Ireland": Manchester-martyr demonstrations in Dublin' in *Éire-Ireland*, xxxvi, nos 3–4 (fall–winter 2001), pp 39–66 at pp 45, 60. Bracken ('Tom Bracken, a noted Fenian') is mentioned by Andrew Kettle as having shown an interest in agrarian reform in the 1870s (*Material for victory: the memoirs of Andrew J. Kettle*, ed. L. J. Kettle (Dublin, 1958), p. 13). **49** *Leinster Express*, 20 Sept. 1873. **50** *Nation*, 3 Sept. 1870. **51** Timothy Dawson, 'The city music and city bands' in *Dublin Historical Record*, xxv (1971–2), pp 102–16; see also McGee, 'God save Ireland', pp 67–8. **52** *Ir. Times*, 27 Sept. 1875; *Irishman*,

Why did the annual pilgrimages to Bodenstown begin in the 1870s and not before or after? Eric Hobsbawm showed that in Great Britain, France, Germany and other parts of Europe during the 1870s and subsequent two decades traditions of various kinds were created and proved persistent. He defined this 'invented tradition' as 'a set of practices ... of a ritual or symbolic nature' designed 'to inculcate certain values and norms' in a way that implies 'continuity with the past'. He cited and discussed, among his examples, the erection of monuments, formalisation of sports and joining mutual bodies. These traditions served to create popular national awareness and solidarity.[53] Bodenstown may fit into Hobsbawm's thesis if account is taken of the chronological position of the first pilgrimage (1873) occurring between the laying of the first stone of the O'Connell monument (1864) and the formation of the Gaelic Athletic Association (1884); and more exactly of the Irish branches of the Ancient Order of Foresters separating themselves on nationalistic grounds from the British branches to form the Irish National Foresters (*c.*1874–7), which eventually became by far the most popular Irish benefit society, and of the formation of the Society for the Preservation of the Irish Language (1876), which quickly secured the teaching of Irish in state-supported schools.[54] It may not be out of place to point out that in November 1873, only weeks after the replacing of the damaged stone and a few months before the erection of the protective railing, there took place in Dublin a conference that brought into existence the Home Rule League, a political association composed of Irishmen, both inside and outside parliament, committed to promoting some form of Irish self-government and other specifically Irish interests.[55] It was to have a continued existence until 1918, with changes of name and shifts of policy, as an Irish nationalist party resembling nationalist parties elsewhere in Europe. Perhaps more relevant to the creation of the Bodenstown tradition, certainly to its timing, was the coming into effect of two legislative measures that had a liberating effect. The first of these was the Irish Church Act of 1869, effective on 1 January 1871, as a result of which the ruined Bodenstown church and its churchyard would have been removed from the control of the Protestant minister of the parish. A minister might previously have objected to people unrelated to the Tone family replacing the gravestone that had been authorised by Tone's widow, or to the churchyard being used for political demonstrations. The second measure was the repeal in June 1872 of the party processions acts. These had been passed in 1850 and 1860 in attempts to control political parades that in Ulster and, to a lesser degree, elsewhere in Ireland were causing disturbances.[56] It was barely one month later that 'Dun Padruic' wrote his

19 Aug. 1876.   **53** Eric Hobsbawm, 'Mass-producing traditions: Europe, 1870–1914' in Eric Hobsbawm and Terence Ranger (eds), *The invention of tradition* (Cambridge, 1992), pp 1–14, 263–307.   **54** The histories of the last two remain to be written.   **55** David Thornley, *Isaac Butt and home rule* (London, 1964), chap. 4.   **56** For these acts of parliament, see T. W. Moody and C. J. Woods, 'Ireland under the union, 1801–1921' in *A new history of Ireland, viii: a chronology of Irish*

letter to the *Nation* proposing that Irish people should 'keep the national spirit in a state of healthy vitality' by going on 'excursions' for 'picnicks' at destinations that were what historians now call 'places of historic memory'. Bodenstown was the place he most recommended. He did not suggest a procession there, though he might have known that the location and the logistics of enthusiasts reaching it from the metropolis would necessitate a walk from the railway station. The repeal of the party processions acts made processing to Bodenstown with flags and banners lawful. It may have been that 'Dun Padruic' saw a new opportunity to promote the type of Irish patriotism he preferred and that members of the Wolfe Tone Band, politically like-minded, seized that opportunity to process in the following year with music playing as well as flags flying.

A STRANGE HIATUS, 1882–90

No evidence has been found of any comparable pilgrimage from Dublin to Tone's grave during the eight years from 1882 to 1890. None was reported in the newspapers examined; none is mentioned in the other sources examined. In 1893 a local Naas newspaper, the *Leinster Leader*, referring vaguely to the period before the revival that occurred in 1891, stated that 'for some years' Tone's anniversary 'was allowed to pass almost unheeded'.[57] It did not elaborate.

One possible explanation is preoccupation with the 'land war', the agrarian agitation that began in Connacht in 1879 and was throughout the 1880s the consuming popular political concern. Arguably it was (except briefly in 1886) a distraction from concern for Ireland's constitutional position, from Tone and from events of ninety years before, a distraction too from 1848, from Fenianism and 1867. The weekly *Irishman*, a paper read in the 1870s and into the 1880s by men of Fenian sympathies, did not report the 1880 pilgrimage, though it found ample space for the Land League, and it took its report of the 1881 pilgrimage from the *Freeman's Journal*, publishing it abridged, without mentioning Daly; its columns were again filled with news of the agrarian agitation.[58] It is significant that while Daly at Bodenstown praised Tone for his determination in resorting to force and to French assistance, he denounced the Land League as a distraction from the aim of Irish independence. Tone could not be cited as a friend of farmers. In his writings he shows little interest in landlord-tenant relations and no empathy with tenant farmers; his only mention is his endorsement of the view of 'a parcel of squires' in 1791 that 'a farm at a smart rent [is] always better cultivated than one at a low rate', recalled and repeated when he was in America in 1795.[59] Daly's view was not one that would have won favour if expressed by Parnell or Michael Davitt. No evidence has been found of either ever visiting Bodenstown.[60]

history (Oxford, 1982), pp 342, 344, 345; R. V. Comerford, 'Gladstone's first enterprise, 1864–70' in Ibid., *v: Ireland under the union, I: 1801–70* (Oxford, 1989), pp 443–4. **57** *Leinster Leader*, 1 July 1893. **58** *Irishman*, 28 Aug. 1880, 20 Aug. 1881. **59** Tone, *Writings*, i, 146, ii, 30. **60** Davitt,

Such an explanation is unconvincing. The interest in Tone's grave in the 1870s, in the 1890s and in later decades came from Dublin, from men of a certain social class, the 'class above the masses',[61] the class that produced the bandsmen who went enthusiastically to Bodenstown in 1873. This class was that of the petty bourgeoisie and the artisans; it was urban, it was dependent economically on knowledge and skills, not on occupancy of land. It was the class to which Fenianism appealed. Fenianism did flourish in Dublin in the 1880s. The annual November marches to Glasnevin cemetery to commemorate the Manchester Martyrs flourished throughout the decade, as in the previous decade.[62] It may have been that the politically motivated murders of the Irish chief secretary and his under-secretary in the Phoenix Park on 6 May 1882 and the apprehensiveness that ensued spoilt any idea of a pilgrimage in the summer of that year. This interruption of the custom begun in 1873 could have been a factor in there not being a pilgrimage in 1883 or subsequent years. Yet during the same period some Dublin men who were in the I.R.B. or at least of Fenian sympathies were drawn into the Young Ireland Society, an association more cultural than political when it began in 1881. Matthew Kelly, in his study of Dublin Fenianism in the 1880s, has described it as the 'crucible' of 'cultural nationalism'. It became as much political as cultural after being taken over in 1883 by Fenians led by Fred Allan, a member of the I.R.B.'s supreme council.[63] A 'national monuments committee' was formed; it gave all its attentions to Fenian graves in Glasnevin cemetery and not until 1889 were they turned to the grave at Bodenstown of Theobald Wolfe Tone, as will be discussed in the next chapter. There were police reports of groups of 'suspects' — suspected Fenians, no doubt men of Fenian sympathies — making 'excursions into the country during the summer' and of 'picnic parties and other large excursions'; Bodenstown, however, was not mentioned. Dr Kelly concludes by defining Dublin Fenianism in the 1880s as a 'socio-cultural space where people met'.[64] It was a tight space.

Despite the absence of evidence, it would be hard to believe that the Young Ireland Society did not, through its national monuments committee, show an interest in Tone's grave. It would be harder when it is considered that the Young Ireland Society came under the influence of an alluringly romantic old Fenian, John O'Leary, after his return to Ireland from long exile in 1885 and that the society was absorbed in the early 1890s by the Young Ireland League.[65] This was the body that (as will be shown) organised the Bodenstown pilgrimages in 1892 and annually until the Wolfe Tone Memorial Committee was formed in 1897. Similarly, it might have been expected that Bodenstown would have been the destination of summer

however, requested (and received) Tone's memoirs when in prison in 1881 (Moody, *Davitt*, p. 477). **61** The words of a senior military man, Lord Strathnairn, in 1869, cited in K. Theo Hoppen, *Elections, politics and society in Ireland, 1832–1885* (Oxford, 1984), p. 359.   **62** McGee, 'God save Ireland', passim.   **63** For Frederick Allan (1861–1937), see the article by C. J. Woods and Owen McGee in *D.I.B.*   **64** Matthew Kelly, 'Dublin Fenianism in the 1880s: "the Irish culture of the future"?' in *Historical Journal*, xliii (2000), pp 729–50, esp. pp 731–2, 735, 741–2, 749.   **65** Kelly, 'Dublin Fenianism in the 1880s', p. 735.

excursions and a secluded spot for picnics. Yet the Young Ireland Society's commemoration of the 'Wolfe Tone anniversary' held in June 1886, apparently on the initiative of Allan, was held in the society's hall in Dublin and not at Bodenstown; it was little more than a concert of nationalistic music and song with a lecture on Tone during an interval.[66] A reason for there being in the 1880s no regular pilgrimages on the model established in the 1870s may have been that there was no continuity of organisation during the earlier decade. The Dublin Wolfe Tone Band took the initiatives in 1873 and 1874; the Amnesty Association did so in 1875 and 1876; a branch of the Irish National Foresters took the initiative in 1877 and other bodies joined in; there was apparently no organised pilgrimage from Dublin in 1878; the Wolfe Tone Band went, with few followers, in 1879; the Martyrs' Band, through the initiative of Thomas Bracken, organised pilgrimages in 1880 and 1881. There was no permanent committee, there was no pilgrimage in 1882. If any thought of organising pilgrimages came to members of the Young Ireland Society, action was prevented by want of initiatives or, as was the case after 1905, want of finance.

An account of one outing to Bodenstown, not a pilgrimage on the earlier model but evidently one of a series of customary outings, shows that Tone's grave did still receive group visits. It was stated in this account that every three years until 1885 'the students of the senior division' of the Catholic national seminary at Maynooth would go on a cross-country ramble to Bodenstown, which lies some 13 kilometres south of the college. An inference is that these triennial rambles began in the late 1870s or even earlier. Another ramble, though not due, occurred on 18 April 1887. It is recounted in some detail by one of the ramblers, Laurence Kieran or O'Kieran. Seventy-six of the eligible two hundred or more students set off headed by the dean.[67] It is evident from Kieran's account that the ramble had a recreational purpose and that much of the satisfaction was in the fun and adventure it afforded. Though his description of Tone's grave is in the romantic tradition of Thomas Davis, Kieran's behaviour, and that of his fellow students, demonstrates a mentality far removed from the staunch secularism permeating Tone's own extensive writings; they were moved to pray at the grave but, receiving no cue from the dean and realising that Tone had been a Protestant, shied away.[68] Demonstration of party political feeling, however, was acceptable. The leader of the college choir sang 'God save Ireland'; then 'the son of an old veteran, now in the Irish party, who in his young days was sentenced to be hung, drawn and quartered' — a son of J. F. X. O'Brien, once a member of the I.R.B., now of Parnell's Irish home-rule party, whose

66 Young Ireland Society minute book, Jan. 1885–Oct. 1886 (N.L.I., MS 19158); *Freeman's Jn.*, 24 June 1886.   67 'A walk to Wolfe Tone's grave' in Agnes O'Farrelly (ed.), *Leabhar an Athar Eoghan: the O'Growney memorial volume* (Dublin and London, [1904?]), pp 102–3, 227–30. It was first published in the *United Irishman*, 26 Oct. 1901, where it is misattributed to Eugene O'Growney, amongst whose papers the MS was discovered.   68 The two deans in Apr. 1887 were James Donnellan and Daniel O'Loan (John Healy, *Maynooth College* (Dublin, 1895), pp 510–12, 704). Nothing has been ascertained of their doctrinal tendencies.

sentence, for leading a force in the Fenian insurrection in 1867, was commuted — gave a rendering of 'The memory of the dead'; finally, from the entire gathering, came 'the anthem proper to the scene'. This was Davis's 'Tone's grave', better known by its evocative first line, 'In Bodenstown churchyard there is a green grave'.

A fleeting glimpse of Bodenstown by young men from another college in the vicinity two or three years later is immortalised in fiction. James Joyce, with poetic licence but no doubt from the experience of being driven jauntily, with other pupils, from Clongowes Wood College to the railway station at Sallins, writes that 'they drove merrily along the country roads. The drivers pointed with their whips to Bodenstown. The fellows cheered.' This appears in his *Portrait of the artist as a young man*, in which Joyce personifies himself in Stephen Dedalus.[69] Joyce was a pupil at Clongowes from the autumn of 1888 until Christmas 1891. Although he was not yet ten when he left the school for good, he was precocious and he does capture the mood of senior boys, who must have known, as the drivers did, that Tone lay buried in Bodenstown churchyard. Their mood was perhaps little different from that of the seminarians.

The men of the Dublin Wolfe Tone Band did not fully realise the significance of their initiatives in 1873 and 1874. They unknowingly invented a tradition 'of a ritual or symbolic nature' designed 'to inculcate certain values and norms' which has been identified by Hobsbawm as beginning elsewhere in Europe in the 1870s and 1880s. 'Dun Padruic', who remains anonymous, was prescient.

---

69 James Joyce, *A portrait of the artist as a young man* (first published in New York by Huebsch, 1916).

4

Pilgrimages revived, the Kildare Gaels' stone and the Wolfe Tone Memorial Committee, 1891–1910

A REVIVAL OF organised visits to Bodenstown came in the 1890s. The first of these took place on 21 June 1891. They were to continue regularly every June to the present day, with only one complete break (1906–10) and with several of their earlier features unchanged. Already, in 1879, the word 'pilgrimage' had been used to describe the phenomenon — 'the annual commemorative visit, or pilgrimage, to Wolfe Tone's grave'.[1] The pilgrims continued to be mainly men (and even women too) of 'advanced' nationalist opinions travelling by train from Dublin to Sallins, proceeding on foot to Bodenstown churchyard and being joined by others, mostly from other parts of Kildare travelling by other routes and by other means. Unlike the earlier visits, the pilgrimages after 1891 were always on the Sunday closest to, or a Sunday close to, the anniversary of Tone's birth. This, he stated in his autobiography and in his diary, was 20 June 1763.[2] Of the annual mass pilgrimages reported in Dublin daily newspapers between 1891 and 1980, only three were held on days other than a Sunday in June.[3] Another innovation was travelling by road, on horse-drawn brakes or (from the early 1890s) bicycles. As the fame of Tone's grave and of its pilgrimages spread, pilgrims travelled from afar.

What brought about the revival of the pilgrimages in 1891? The answer may lie in the familiar story of the rise and fall of Charles Stewart Parnell. The very effective home-rule party, largely created and successfully led by Parnell, dominated Irish Catholic politics throughout the 1880s. While Irishmen of 'advanced' nationalist tendencies were wary of 'constitutional' politics and the I.R.B. was quite dismissive, some of them at least shared the high regard for Parnell almost universal among Irish Catholics. After the 'conversion' to Irish home rule in 1886 of W. E. Gladstone, the leader of the English Liberal party, an alliance was formed between the two parties (the 'union of hearts'). Parnell's sudden 'fall' in December 1890 was caused by adverse publicity in a divorce case in which he was co-respondent. After details of Parnell's role became known, Gladstone, deferring to English Nonconformist

---

1 *Freeman's Jn.*, 18 Aug. 1879. 2 Tone, *Writings*, ii, 261, iii, 308. There is however a discrepancy in the baptismal register (ibid., i, 1). 3 The exceptions were in 1905 (Sunday, 9 July), 1911 (Saturday, 8 July), 1921 (Sunday, 3 July) and 1929 (Monday, 17 June, official pilgrimage). No reports have been found of any mass pilgrimages in the years 1906 to 1910. That planned for 19

opinion on which his party depended, stated that the alliance could not continue were Parnell to remain leader. This intervention precipitated a bitter split in the home-rule party, the anti-Parnellites quickly emerging as the majority in the country, the Parnellites retaining dominance in popular politics in Dublin. Throughout 1891, Parnellites and Fenians were together in loudly castigating Gladstone for what they perceived as his treachery and the anti-Parnellites for their acceptance of English dictation.[4] Parnell himself praised Tone in a speech in Belfast in May of that year, a few months before his death.[5] To strong nationalists Parnell now personified, like Tone, rejection of any prospect of English support for Irish independence and the firm conviction that Irishmen should look to their own resources. The revival of the pilgrimages occurred six months after Parnell's 'fall'; by then his struggle to regain his position was most intense and his most earnest supporters were Dublin's 'advanced' nationalists. Four months later it was those same nationalists who, with remarkable co-ordination and efficiency, organised Parnell's funeral and formed the very large crowd that walked in mourning to his open grave at Glasnevin;[6] in years to come it was Dublin nationalists who, on a smaller scale, walked annually to Tone's grave at Bodenstown.

THE NATIONAL CLUB AND THE YOUNG IRELAND LEAGUE

It was the National Club Literary Society, in conjunction with the Leinster Literary Society, which organised the pilgrimage in 1891. Other 'national bodies' were invited, and also 'the various trade and labour organisations, Gaelic clubs, Irish National Foresters and the city bands'.[7] The National Club, the creation of John O'Leary with money largely from the I.R.B., opened in June 1887 at 41 Rutland Square, Dublin.[8] So-called 'literary' societies discussed political matters more than literature. The Leinster Literary Society (formed in 1888 as the Leinster Debating Society) had as its president in 1891 a man whose name was to become famous: Arthur Griffith.[9] Six of the small number of men present at the National Club to make arrangements are significant for the recurrence of their names in reports of pilgrimages in the 1890s: Griffith, Henry Dixon, Patrick Lavelle, George Lynch, John Murphy and John R. Whelan. Each year from 1892 to 1896 the organising body was the Young Ireland League, formed in September 1891. The organisers in 1897 were the '98 Centenary Committee, the body formed in that year to organise a grand festival of commemoration of the 1798 rebellion. Part of this

June 1921 was banned.   **4** See esp. M. J. Kelly, *The Fenian ideal and Irish nationalism, 1882–1916* (Woodbridge, Suffolk, 2006), pp 9–12. Parnell's relations with 'advanced nationalists' is discussed also in C. J. Woods, 'Parnell and the Catholic church' in D. G. Boyce and Alan O'Dea (eds), *Parnell in perspective* (London, 1991), pp 9–37.   **5** *Northern Whig*, 12 May 1891, cited in Paul Bew, *C. S. Parnell* (Dublin, 1980), p. 129.   **6** Emmet Larkin, *The Roman Catholic church in Ireland and the fall of Parnell* (Liverpool, 1979), pp 285–6.   **7** *Freeman's Jn.*, 30 May, 19 June 1891.   **8** Owen McGee, *The I.R.B.: the Irish Republican Brotherhood from the Land League to Sinn Féin* (Dublin, 2005), pp 162–3, 234.   **9** Leinster Debating Society minute book, 1888–92 (N.L.I., MS 19935).

commemoration was the pilgrimage to Bodenstown on 19 June 1898. The committee continued in existence as the Wolfe Tone and '98 Memorial Association and took on responsibility for the pilgrimages of 1899 and successive years. Early variants of its name were Wolfe Tone and '98 Memorial Association and Wolfe Tone and United Irishmen Memorial Committee. In reports of the pilgrimages the name was the Wolfe Tone Memorial Committee in 1902 and 1903; it was the Wolfe Tone and United Irishmen Memorial Committee in 1904 and 1905. The shorter form became usual. Apparently this committee with the changing name was made permanent in June 1898 under the presidency of O'Leary; later it rented accommodation at 41 Rutland Square from the Irish National Foresters, who purchased the building after the National Club closed down in June 1899.[10] No doubt the social and political complexion of the organising body remained the same whatever the name. No. 41 Rutland Square, which had been the home of Francis Macdonogh, Q.C., who died there in 1882,[11] remained a centre for nationalist activity into the 1930s, still in the ownership of the Irish National Foresters. During the Irish War of Independence it was frequented largely by individuals connected with, even if not sworn into, the I.R.B.,[12] the sort of nationalists sponsoring the Bodenstown pilgrimages since the 1890s; about ten years later it provided accommodation for the National Graves Association,[13] the voluntary body that eventually took charge of Tone's grave. Attempts by the city corporation to change the name to Parnell Square began in 1911.[14] The new name was quickly adopted by nationalists and was definitive by 1920.

The first of the revived pilgrimages, on 21 June 1891, was reported at considerable length in the *Freeman's Journal* and in the *Leinster Leader*. The latter (owned by J. L. Carew from 1885 until his death in 1903) was the more strongly nationalistic of the two. The report in the *Nation* extended to a mere six lines, a sign that its nationalistic fervour in the middle years of the century had abated. As in the 1870s, people attended from surrounding villages, one of them Peter Clory or Clowry, instigator of the railing in 1874; a local band, the Naas Labour Union Fife and Drum Band, provided the music. Members of the National Club Literary Society were prominent. One, Henry Dixon, gave an oration summarising reasons for commemorating Tone: it was 'not merely because he had removed the disabilities which existed against Catholics' or that he 'had started the first democratic movement which was established in Ireland', it was 'because the memory of Wolfe Tone placed before them the only true interpretation of the principle of national independence'. A guest was Carew, who besides owning one of the two local newspapers, was the member of parliament for North Kildare, in which constituency Bodenstown was situated. Carew had taken the side of Parnell in the split that had occurred just six months before. He probably captured the mood of

---

10 McGee, *I.R.B.*, p. 270.   11 *Freeman's Jn.*, 19 Apr. 1882.   12 Leon Ó Broin, *Revolutionary underground: the story of the Irish Republican Brotherhood, 1858–1924* (Dublin, 1976), p. 189. 13 *Ir. Indep.*, 17 Mar. 1930, 5 June, 3 Oct. 1935, 27 Apr. 1938.   14 *Freeman's Jn.*, 28 Sept. 1911.

his Parnellite audience, wavering ambiguously between the traditions of 'moral force' and 'physical force', in saying that while 'Wolfe Tone had been compelled to take only the method open to him to obtain his objects, namely open warfare', they now 'happily lived in other times, when other and if more peaceful, also more effectual, methods were available'.[15]

The pilgrimage that took place on 19 June 1892, organised by the Young Ireland League, seems to have been less successful notwithstanding a glowing report in the *Freeman's Journal* of 'a large number' taking part, some travelling in brakes from the National Club premises in Rutland Square, 'many others' by train or on bicycles. Among the pilgrims named were Fred Allan, other members of the organising body and local men from Naas, Clane, Bodenstown and Straffan. As well as Peter Clowry, two local names stand out: Thomas Reddy of Bodenstown and William Reddy of Naas, apparently sons of the William Reddy who had identified Tone's grave for Davis and Gray in 1843. Not reported were the names of the chairman and any other speaker. Music was provided (as in 1874) by the Naas Fife and Drum Band.[16] But an official report dismissed the pilgrimage of 1892 as a 'complete failure'.[17] One likely explanation of any failure is the mid-1892 general election campaign in which the Parnellites and Fenian sympathsers were preoccupied in fighting bitterly their anti-Parnellite foes. The new Parnellite *Irish Daily Independent*, full of election campaign news, ignored Bodenstown. Another factor may have been the differences (discussed below) which had developed between the Young Ireland League and the Kildare Gaelic Association over necessary restoration of the site of Tone's grave. One of Allan's companions was J. W. O'Beirne. He is mentioned above but merits further mention here. O'Beirne was in 1892 a fellow I.R.B. man of Allan's as well as a colleague on the *Irish Independent* (and by 1916 a journalist on the *Freeman*); he had a few months before been one of the group accompanying Parnell's body from Holyhead to Dublin; he was to be a founder member of the Wolfe Tone Memorial Committee, and he was to donate the remnant of the original Tone gravestone to the National Museum in 1941.[18]

In 1893 the *Leinster Leader* gleefully reported the pilgrimage on 25 June as having been 'one of the largest and most magnificent demonstrations which ever took place within the confines of the Co. Kildare'. Two special trains, 'closely packed with the men — and women too', arrived at Sallins from Dublin; a procession formed and marched to Bodenstown 'with bands playing and banners waving', a scene which, 'apart from its picturesqueness, was significant of the undying spirit of patriotism and independence which animates the Irish breast'. Carew, who had lost his seat in the 1892 elections, presided this time and gave a long speech in praise of Tone. At

---

15 *Freeman's Jn.*, 23 June 1891; *Leinster Leader*, 27 June 1891.   16 *Freeman's Jn.*, 20 June 1892; *Leinster Leader*, 25 June 1892.   17 Nat. Arch., Kew, CO 904/16. For this reference I am most indebted to Dr Matthew Kelly and also for documents in the same series cited below.   18 Joseph William O'Beirne (1870?–1942) was by 1916 a journalist on the *Freeman*; he also wrote a short guide to Glasnevin cemetery (*Freeman's Jn.*, 31 Mar. 1908; *Ir. Indep.*, 4 Aug. 1937, 13 Oct. 1931, 26 July 1938, 9 July 1942; Nat. Arch., Dublin, Census of Ireland, 1911).

least six groups of pilgrims were from branches of the Parnellite Irish National League.[19] The *Kildare Observer* perceived that though the gathering 'was supposed to consist of persons belonging to both sections of the nationalists, ... there was a most decided flavour of Parnellism'.[20] This assessment is confirmed in the month's constabulary report from County Kildare stating that the crowd was largely of Parnellites and 'independents'.[21] No parliamentarian appeared again until after 1919.

The pilgrimage of 1894 was the largest so far. The procession of pilgrims to Tone's grave began at Naas; participants came from further afield; one train started at Kilkenny and called at Carlow, Athy, Kildare town and Newbridge along the main line of the Great Southern and Western Railway to deposit pilgrims at Sallins; other trains came from the Dublin direction; some Dubliners travelled by car or cycled; it was a large, merry crowd, contingents marching behind their local bands, the men in ranks four deep. Parnellites and anti-Parnellites alike were present. A discourse on Tone's career was given by George Lynch of the Young Ireland League.[22] A police report put the number of participants at two thousand and characterised some of the Dubliners as belonging to 'lower classes'.[23]

THE GAELIC ATHLETIC ASSOCIATION

It was damage to the stone over Tone's grave which brought about, in 1873 and 1874, the first large excursions organised from Dublin. A new stone was laid in place of the original and a railing erected to protect it from further depredation. Yet fifteen years later — because of neglect — the new gravestone needed repair. In September 1889 there appeared in the *Kildare Observer* a report of a plan to meet the need. The County Kildare Committee of the Gaelic Athletic Association (G.A.A.) was planning a tournament the proceeds of which were to be forwarded to the Young Ireland Society's monuments committee for the repair of the Wolfe Tone monument in Bodenstown churchyard. A 'valuable set of crosses' was to be purchased as a prize for the successful team.[24] A report in the *Leinster Leader* was less precise and made no mention of the Young Ireland Society or its monuments committee.[25] The committee, dignified as the National Monuments Committee, was formed in or after 1883 under the auspices of the Young Ireland Society, a predecessor of the Young Ireland League. Among its active members in the early 1890s were Lavelle, Henry Dixon, John MacBride and J. W. O'Beirne.[26] All of these were regular participants in the revived Bodenstown pilgrimages. It remains unknown what liaison there was between Kildare Gaels and the National Monuments Committee *before* September 1889. Little more was done about the tournament until August 1890; the Kildare

19 *Leinster Leader*, 1 July 1893. 20 *Kildare Observer*, 1 July 1893. 21 Nat. Arch., Kew, CO 904/61. 22 *Freeman's Jn.*, 25 June 1894; *Ir. Daily Indep.*, 25 June 1894; *Leinster Leader*, 30 June 1894. 23 Nat. Arch., Kew, CO 904/55. 24 *Kildare Observer*, 14 Sept. 1889. 25 *Leinster Leader*, 7 Sept. 1889. 26 McGee, *I.R.B.*, p. 235.

committee then decided that the 'grand football tournament' to benefit the 'restoration' of the 'monument' should begin on 7 September; each participating club was to pay an entrance fee of 7s. 6d. to the county secretary. Only fourteen clubs entered and enthusiasm was moderate; nonetheless the semi-finals were played on 14 December, and the final, between Kilcullen and Sallins, was to be played on the 27th.[27] From then on events conspired to thwart and delay the intentions of the Gaels. Frost caused a postponement until the following Sunday, when the Sallins team walked off the pitch before the end, protesting at the referee's insistence on allowing a goal to Kilcullen despite the ball having been, they said, 'thrown' illegally; the repeat match allowed by the county committee also had to be postponed and when it was finally being played, on 25 January, a fight broke out between rival players resulting in the suspension of both clubs from the county championship matches, the withdrawal of the aggrieved Kilcullen club from the G.A.A. and irate letters to local newspapers.[28]

The final rounds of the Wolfe Tone tournament were played against a background of general acrimony caused by the splitting of Parnell's home-rule party. A consequence was that the Kildare G.A.A. began going through a troubled period; the split divided Gaelic clubs in the county and was not finally healed there until 1895.[29] About three months after the ill-tempered final the chairman and secretary of the county committee resigned, as did two or three other members of what was quite a small body. On 7 June a new chairman was elected and the treasurer was directed 'to communicate with the secretary of the National Monuments Committee with reference to the disposal of the proceeds of the Wolfe Tone Tournament'; in the issue of the *Leinster Leader* reporting this was a notice from Patrick Lavelle of the National Club Literary Society of the planned 'visit' to Tone's grave on the 21st.[30] The new chairman was John T. Heffernan, in the 1870s a strong supporter of the Amnesty Association, in the 1880s a militant Land Leaguer, still a Parnellite, and now prominent as an auctioneer at Kildare town and a Naas poor law guardian.[31] Neither the G.A.A. county committee nor the National Monuments Committee was mentioned in reports of the 21st, but the members of the winning Sallins team were present proudly showing their crosses, and the county commttttee did cancel all football and hurling matches for the occasion.[32]

The fortunes of the G.A.A. in County Kildare did not improve. A convention held at Heffernan's premises at Kildare on 6 March 1892 in an attempt to mend them, the association having 'almost become extinct in the county', drew representatives from only five clubs. The fund raised from the Wolfe Tone Tournament, referred to as being 'in aid of the objects of the National Monuments Committee', was reported to stand at £22 16s. 6d. The treasurer, William Kennedy,

27 *Leinster Leader*, 19 Apr., 16, 23 Aug., 6, 20 Sept., 8 Nov., 20 Dec. 1890.   **28** *Leinster Leader*, 3, 10, 24 Jan., 7, 21, 28 Mar. 1891; *Kildare Observer*, 7 Feb. 1891.   **29** Eoghan Corry, *Kildare G.A.A.: a centenary history* (Newbridge, 1984), pp 31, 42, 44, 49.   **30** *Leinster Leader*, 13 June 1891. **31** For Heffernan (1850?–1907), see Thomas Nelson, 'The political career of John T. Heffernan' in *Kildare Arch. Soc. Jn.*, xix, no. 6 (2006–7), pp 619–31.   **32** *Leinster Leader*, 20 June 1891.

reported that the National Monuments Committee had failed to guarantee that the whole amount would, if handed over, be spent on Tone's grave, and, no less disquietingly, had indicated an indefinite delay in starting work; the chairman, Heffernan, thought it injudicious to hand over the funds, 'as they might be used for other objects in different parts of the country'; there was agreement to his proposal that a sub-committee be appointed by a new county committee 'to visit the Bodenstown churchyard and recommend the most suitable way of laying out the money'. At another convention two months later, supported by eight clubs and with a new treasurer present, Heffernan stated that, no reply having been received from the National Monuments Committee, the former treasurer, Kennedy, was justified in retaining the tournament money 'until the county committee was properly constituted'.[33]

The writer of editorial matter in the *Leinster Leader* in the issue reporting the 1892 pilgrimage gave a rather different view of the connexion between the National Monuments Committee and the Gaelic Athletic Association:

> Some years ago the National Monuments Committee inaugurated a series of Gaelic football and hurling tournaments for the purpose of raising funds for the erection and repair of the monuments of those brave patriots who in troubled times gave their lives for Ireland. A considerable sum was realised and in County Kildare a very successful tournament was held. But strange to say, the proceeds of the tournament in the county Kildare remain in the hands of the Gaelic County Committee. Why has the money not been spent in honour of Wolfe Tone at Bodenstown? The condition of the grave is a standing reproach. The old monument lies broken and disfigured, and the grounds are ill kept. In justice to the Kildare Gaelic Committee the circumstances in which they have been placed should be stated.

The explanation he gave was that

> after the tournament they intimated to the Monuments Committee their desire that the proceeds should be spent exclusively on the grave of Wolfe Tone. No satisfactory reply was received, the money was retained, the Gaelic Association became disorganised, and nothing further was heard of the matter till the committee met a few months ago in Kildare for the purpose of reviving the association. The committee were willing to hand over the money to the Monuments Committee upon a promise being given that it would be spent in accordance with the desire already expressed.

A 'representative' of the *Leinster Leader* had raised the matter at Bodenstown with one of the Young Ireland League. Now, it seemed, there was a prospect of progress; Allan, who had had some part in forming the committee, was promising to

33 *Leinster Leader*, 12 Mar., 7 May 1892. See also *Kildare Observer*, 12 Mar. 1892.

communicate with Heffernan, who presided, and thereby rouse the committee from its 'state of apathy'.[34]

This did not however settle the matter. In March of the following year Kennedy still held the proceeds, reluctant to hand them over to the County Kildare Committee until he received assurances from them that they would be used for no other purpose than 'repairing the grave of Wolfe Tone' and that they intended proceeding with the work.[35] Two months later this assurance was given by the formation of a working committee of seven, three members from Naas, two from Clane, the secretary, a J. C. McGrane, from Sallins; an appeal was made, in Dublin as well as locally, for more money, and a letter sent to the Young Ireland League.[36] Thus in 1893 the Kildare Gaels seized from the Young Ireland League ownership of the project.

The damage was made worse at the pilgrimage on 25 June 1893, as widely reported. The *Freeman's Journal* gave some detail while defending the Young Ireland League:

> The condition of the grave is hardly creditable. The work of vandalism has gone on to such an extent as to be a serious reproach. The slab which some twenty years ago was placed over the grave has been broken almost to pieces, despite the precaution taken of surrounding and covering it with an iron railing. Yesterday no sooner had the crowds reached the place than quite a horde of persons set to work to break away portions of the stone work — even what ought to be the sacred precincts enclosed beneath the railings were invaded, and the revolting noise of hammering chips off the slab was heard almost up to the time of the commencement of the formal meeting which was held. The ruined walls of the old church were scaled and the ivy dragged down mercilessly and flung to the people beneath. It is right to say that for this in no way can the Young Ireland League be said to be responsible. On the contrary, many gentlemen present protested against such a desecration, and many actors in the scene desisted from sheer shame. A blade of grass or an ivy leaf would surely suffice as a memento of the scene.

The culprits were, the *Freeman* surmised, 'enthusiastic and thoughtless individuals'.[37] In an editorial the *Kildare Observer*, as usual censorious of excessive nationalist fervour, deplored that some of the crowd should have got inside the railings and one person have broken a portion of the sundered slab 'into small pieces for the purpose of taking them away as mementoes', and no less that that the ivy pulled from high off the church walls should have been 'thrown to the crowds beneath, who fought with each other for possession'. 'Such', it retorted, 'is the boundless enthusiasm of Nationalists!'.[38] More sympathetic and understanding,

34 *Leinster Leader*, 25 June 1892.   35 *Leinster Leader*, 4, 11 Mar. 1893.   36 *Leinster Leader*, 20, 27 May 1893; *Evening Herald*, 2, 19 June 1893.   37 *Freeman's Jn.*, 26 June 1893.   38 *Kildare Observer*, 1 July 1893.

United Ireland, the Parnellite weekly, attributed 'very good intentions' to the 'few persons' who had taken away portions of the gravestone 'to possess themselves of a memento of the place and of the great patriot buried there'.[39]

A year later, the *Leinster Leader* lamented that only 'portions of a broken slab' mark 'Tone's last earthly habitation. The missing parts of the stone have been taken away by souvenir seekers who visited the grave from time to time.'[40] But already the local working committee had made good progress. On 30 May 1894 the Naas Board of Guardians (in whom the churchyard was vested under provisions of the Irish Church Disestablishment Act of 1869) gave permission for the committee's 'memorial slab' to be placed on Tone's grave.[41] By March of the following year it was ready. It was cut from Tullamore limestone by Thomas Farrell and Son, a firm of monumental stonemasons in existence at Glasnevin since 1834; two months later the working committee was congratulated by its parent body, the G.A.A. county committee, for completing its work whilst Farrell's stonemasons too were praised.[42] How much this had eventually cost has not been ascertained. A guess can be made from the expenditure of £50 on the erection in 1896 of a stone on the grave at Ballycreen, County Down, of Betsy Gray, her brother and her lover, whose lives were lost in the rebellion of 1798. It was comparable to the G.A.A.'s stone except that it was much less elaborate and that the expenditure included a simple wrought-iron railing.[43] The railing erected around Tone's grave in 1874 was retained.

At the June pilgrimage in 1895 the new tombstone was the centre-piece. But neither Heffernan nor any of the G.A.A. county committee was present, and only three G.A.A. clubs are named: Clane, Newbridge and Kilcock.[44]

William Sherlock was later able to observe cheerfully: 'a new headstone has been erected; the railing has been repaired and painted; and the grave is now well cared for by the County Kildare Gaelic Association'.[45] The inscription read:

THEOBALD WOLFE TONE
BORN 20th JUNE 1763
DIED 19th NOVR 1798
FOR IRELAND
THIS STONE
HAS BEEN ERECTED BY MEMBERS OF THE
KILDARE GAELIC ASSOCIATION
IN MEMORY OF
THEOBALD WOLFE TONE

---

39 *United Ireland*, 1 July 1893.   40 *Leinster Leader*, 30 June 1894.   41 *Leinster Express*, 2 June 1894.   42 *Irish News* (Belfast), 23 Mar. 1895; *Leinster Leader*, 25 May 1895.   43 *Belfast News Letter*, 22 Aug. 1896; *Irish News*, 13 May 1898; W. G. Lyttle, *Betsy Gray, or hearts of Down* (Newcastle, 1968), pp 60–1.   44 Reported in *Kildare Observer* and *Leinster Leader*, 29 June 1895. 45 William Sherlock, 'Bodenstown churchyard: a place of Irish pilgrimage' in *Kildare Arch. Soc. Jn.*, vi (1909–11), p. 228, n. 1. The footnote seems to have been written long after the text.

TO REPLACE A FORMER MONUMENT ERECTED BY
THE WOLFE TONE BAND
WHICH AS WELL AS THE ORIGINAL STONE
HAS FALLEN INTO DECAY

Above the inscription is a harp motif, below are motifs of shamrocks, two Round Towers, a recumbent wolf hound and a ruined church.[46] These were all motifs of Irish cultural nationalism. Despite this creditworthy endeavour of 'the Kildare Gaels', the Gaelic Athletic Association — usually known by just its initials — hardly ever after 1895 received mention in reports of Bodenstown pilgrimages. A rare instance was in 1902 when the Wolfe Tone Memorial Committee 'secured a field in the immediate vicinity of Bodenstown graveyard' for hurling and football matches to begin at 4 p.m. — after the procession, wreath-laying and speech-making would be over.[47] Probably the pilgrimages were too controversial in G.A.A. circles. Whereas the social basis of militant nationalism was (as will be argued) urban and a combination of the skilled working and clerical classes, that of the G.A.A. was rural and perhaps socially wider. The Kildare Gaels' concern in 1890 was not for Tone's grave to become a neater and tidier destination for annual pilgrimages (of which there had been none since 1881), it was for a decent memorial to a local patriot. The G.A.A. did not engage again until 1970, when its national treasurer donated £500 towards the 'restoration' of the Kildare Gaels' memorial.[48]

The memorial stone did not suffer the same dilapidation as the earlier ones. It was reported in 1897 that

> Tone's grave is well cared for by a local committee of Nationalists. It is enclosed by strong railings, which are neatly painted in black each year. This railing was deemed absolutely necessary to prevent the various admirers of Tone, especially visitors from America, from taking off pieces of the wall or of the tombstone which was originally erected over the grave as souvenirs of their visit.[49]

It did not need major refurbishment until the 1940s, when Thomas Farrell and Sons, still in existence, were again employed. A reason for its endurance may have been that the custom of chipping away fragments as souvenirs gave way to one of taking away small pieces of ivy from the wall of the old church. Reporting on the commemoration of June 1899 a police sergeant stated that of 8,000 pilgrims (probably an overestimate) most 'took away small pieces of ivy leaves from the wall over Wolfe Tone's grave'.[50] It seems likely that once pilgrimages were again a regular and organised event, as they were from 1891 after the hiatus of nine years, the organising committee made and enforced a rule that the gravestone be left intact.

---

46 The inscription and detail are taken from a later photograph. The stone was damaged in 1969. For its fate, see below, chap. 9. **47** *Freeman's Jn.*, 21 June 1902. **48** *Ir. Press*, 15 Sept. 1970. **49** *Ir. Daily Indep.*, 21 June 1897. **50** Rep. by Patrick Daly, 28 June 1899 (Nat. Arch., Dublin, C.S.O., Crime Branch Special).

Why did the project take six years? Davis and associates had taken a few months, the Dublin Wolfe Tone Band probably little longer. There are several likely explanations. One is that the Kildare Gaelic Athletic Association was weak: the Wolfe Tone tournament was delayed and ended acrimoniously; the county committee could barely raise quorums and was quarrelsome; there were very few affiliated clubs in the county; and there was distraction and division because of the split between Parnellites and anti-Parnellites. Another explanation is the mistrust between the G.A.A. in Kildare and the National Monuments Committee in Dublin. The work of renovating the Wolfe Tone's Band's memorial was to be undertaken by this committee, but there was unexplained apathy on its part. The reason for this apathy was probably that it was already committed to another project: a large monument to 'the members of the Irish Republican Brotherhood' for erection at Glasnevin. It was eventually completed in November 1895 at the considerable expense of £500.[51] Although this grandiose project was not reported in the newspapers, there was probably awareness of it among well-informed men in County Kildare and hence the unwillingness of the county committee to pass on to the National Monuments Committee the proceeds of the tournament, intended as they were for a monument in Bodenstown churchyard. This unhappy relationship may explain the rather odd lack of co-operation between the G.A.A. and the Young Ireland League, one concerned for the repair of Tone's grave, the other for the grave as a destination for pilgrimages. As the National Monuments Committee was a subsidiary of the Young Ireland League, some of the organisers of the annual pilgrimages had prior commitments to the Glasnevin monument. Only Heffernan, a chairman at Bodenstown in 1892 and 1894, and the chairman of the G.A.A. county committee from 1891 to 1894, involved himself prominently in both.

THE 1798 CENTENARY AND WOLFE TONE MEMORIAL COMMITTEE

The Kildare Gaels' stone was in place for all to see on the pilgrimage of 23 June 1895. A higher than usual proportion of participants were Kildare people no doubt proud of a local achievement. An official account recorded as many as 4,000 pilgrims reaching Bodenstown. Edward R. Whelan of the Young Ireland League gave the address. Some months earlier at least one active member of the league had expressed criticism of the G.A.A.'s achievement; Whelan commented on it only a briefly, qualifying his praise by urging the G.A.A. to do more to build up 'a belief in the principles of Tone'.[52] According to the same official source, Whelan spoke of a need to wean politics from clerical control.[53] But in an account of the event in a Dublin

---

51 McGee, *I.R.B.*, p. 228. It was not erected until 1933.   52 *Ir. Daily Indep.*, 20 Mar. 1895; *Evening Herald*, 25 June 1895. The orator is named as 'E. R. Whelan' of the Young Ireland League. Present too was a brother or cousin, John R. Whelan, also of the Young Ireland League (Owen McGee, *Arthur Griffith* (Dublin, 2016), pp 17, 18).   53 Nat. Arch., Kew, HO 164/65/32. This is also the source of the figures for attendance, which seem rather high. For this reference I am

evening paper, the *Evening Herald*, this anti-clerical remark is not mentioned despite Whelan's speech (largely about Tone's career) being reported at great length. As well as the expected Kildare Gaelic clubs, there were present at least four Dublin branches of the Irish National League. The importance of the part of 'the Kildare men' was acknowledged by Allan in thanking the chairman, a Naas man, Robert Dorrian.[54]

A new phenomenon occurred at Tone's grave on 21 June 1896. This was 'decoration of graves'. Various nationalistic bodies, such as the Irish National Foresters (dressed in their colourful insignia), joined the pilgrimage, representatives of which in turn laid elaborate wreaths on Tone's grave. Similar ceremonies occurred on graves of 'patriots' elsewhere during the same week.[55]

By the summer of 1897 preparations had begun for the commemoration of the centenary of the United Irish rebellion and French invasion. It was the 'Ninety-eight Commemoration Committee, jointly with the Young Ireland League, which organised and advertised the pilgrimage to Bodenstown that took place on the Sunday that happened to fall, most appropriately, on Tone's birthday.[56] The usual oration was given by Charles Doran of Queenstown, County Cork, as reported in the *Freeman*.[57] That he was a senior member of the I.R.B. was not publicly stated.[58]

The culmination of these early demonstrations at Bodenstown came in 1898. It was the centenary of the United Irish rebellion, and of the French invasion that cost Tone his life, and so a year of universal commemoration by Irish nationalists.[59] There was another warrant too. Timothy O'Keefe argues that the recent success of Queen Victoria's diamond jubilee celebrations in 1897 by their political opponents gave nationalists an 'opportunity to demonstrate Ireland's true loyalty — loyalty to its own heroes and the continuing struggle against British rule'.[60] The nationalists' celebrations, held all over Ireland, particularly in places associated with the events of 1798, were to have long-term consequences for Bodenstown. The Centennial Committee formed to organise these celebrations, though ostensibly representative of all shades of nationalist opinion, was dominated by the I.R.B. It set up a new Wolfe Tone and United Irishmen Memorial Committee that excluded prominent politicians. This committee replaced the Young Ireland League in organising future annual pilgrimages to Bodenstown. The *Leinster Leader*, in its account of the pilgrimage on 19 June 1898, reported that 'at least five thousand' arrived at Sallins from Dublin by special trains and that at 3 o'clock 'the road leading to Bodenstown was one dense mass of people, the members of the numerous city centenary clubs marching up and down in the closest of order, headed by their bands'.[61] Large

grateful to Dr Matthew Kelly. **54** *Evening Herald*, 25 June 1895. **55** *Ir. Daily Indep.*, 22 June 1896; *Freeman's Jn.*, 22 June 1896. **56** *Freeman's Jn.*, 7, 14 June 1897; *Leinster Leader*, 19 June 1897. **57** *Freeman's Jn.*, 21 June 1897. **58** McGee, *I.R.B.*, p. 244; C. J. Woods, 'Charles Guilfoyle Doran (1835–1909)' in *D.I.B.* **59** For these commemorations, see Timothy J. O'Keefe, 'The 1898 efforts to celebrate the United Irishmen' in *Éire-Ireland*, xxiii, no. 2 (summer 1988), pp 51–73 and, for astringent treatment, R. F. Foster, 'Remembering 1798' in his *The Irish story* (London, 2001), pp 211–34. **60** O'Keefe, 'Efforts to celebrate the United Irishmen', p. 53. **61** *Leinster Leader*, 25 June 1898.

numbers had flocked in from the surrounding counties; by 2 o'clock the first processionists were arriving at the churchyard; their bands and banners, the 'heavenly' weather and 'the abundant and verdant foliage', the green branches of the trees waving in a gentle breeze and looking 'as if they were part of the great pageant'.[62] The orator, identified only as W. J. Ryan and as a member of the central executive of the '98 Commemoration Committee, declared that 'Tone's anniversary ideal was that the people of Ireland had in themselves all the constituent elements of a nation'. Among his listeners were three old Fenians 'of special eminence', John O'Leary, Charles Underwood O'Connell and James Stephens.[63] William James Ryan (1865?–1926), a native of either County Wexford or King's County (records conflict), was often mentioned in later years, but his forenames were never spelt out, and he remains almost unknown to historians despite his association with nationalist luminaries of his day; as a member of the '98 Commemoration Committee, he would have been close to its treasurer, Fred Allan, during the 1890s the energetic and influential business manager of the *Irish Daily Independent*. Ryan too may have been employed by this newspaper, certainly he was involved in its transformation into the *Irish Independent* in 1905 and was employed by it editorially for many years after; he seems to have become a public speaker when in Liverpool in the 1880s.[64]

The Bodenstown demonstration was, according to a monthly police report, largely a Fenian affair, as many as 5,200 of the ten thousand present being identifiable as advanced nationalists.[65] The climax of this year of commemoration by Irish nationalists was the placing of a bust of Tone on his grave by O'Leary, with his long beard the grand old man of Fenianism.[66] Could this have been the bust displayed on a pedestal at a celebratory St Patrick's day dinner in 1862 in the Round Room of the Rotunda in Dublin attended by two hundred and more members of the crypto-Fenian National Brotherhood of St Patrick?[67]

HIGHS AND LOWS, 1899–1905

After all the enthusiasm and razzmatazz of 1898, the pilgrimage of the following year came not as an anticlimax but as a renewed opportunity for demonstration. The *Freeman's Journal*, probably relying on information obtained from the organisers, estimated the turn-out at Bodenstown on 25 June 1899 to be 'at least 8,000'.[68] In a confidential report ('The Wolfe Tone pilgrimage to Bodenstown') a sergeant of the Royal Irish Constabulary based at Naas put the figure at close to 4,000, but still

62 *Freeman's Jn.*, 20 June 1898.   **63** *Leinster Leader*, 25 June 1898; *Shan Van Vocht*, 4 July 1898. **64** *Ir. Indep.*, 23 Mar. 1907, 18 Dec. 1911, 15, 17 Nov. 1917, 4 Sept. 1926; Patrick Pearse to W. J. Ryan, 1, 2 Feb., 4 Dec. 1905, pr. in *The letters of P.H. Pearse*, ed. Séamus Ó Buachalla (Gerrards Cross, 1980), pp 91–4, 99–100; McGee, *I.R.B.*, p. 249; Census of Ire., 1901, 1911. See also below, n. 143.   **65** Nat. Arch., Kew, CO 904/68. For this reference I am indebted to Dr Matthew Kelly. **66** Marcus Bourke, *John O'Leary: a study of Irish separatism* (Tralee, 1967), p. 218.   **67** For this celebration, see *Freeman's Jn.*, 18 Mar. 1862.   **68** *Freeman's Jn.*, 18 July 1899.

reckoned that, except for the previous year, a special case, 'this was the largest pilgrimage to Bodenstown for a number of years'.[69] In the monthly report of the inspector general for June 1899 it was stated that the demonstration at Bodenstown 'was purely Fenian in its inception and was mostly composed of a large contingent of Dublin extremists. Violent revolutionary speeches were made.'[70] The 'panegyric' was delivered by Maurice Moynihan of Tralee. Moynihan was a member of the I.R.B., the so-called 'head centre' in County Kerry[71] — a political connexion not stated publicly. As the *Leinster Leader* put it,

> the keynote of Mr Moynihan's address was antagonism to England and to a certain extent he carried his audience with him; his references to an Irish Republic were enthusiastically cheered by a section of the Dublin men, but when he touched upon secret societies as a means for accomplishing a revolution he trod upon dangerous ground and following the advice of counsellors wiser than he [*sic*], he got away from it.

Moynihan's avowed republicanism did not inhibit a young interrupter from shouting out: 'Fred Allan drank the health of the Queen at Malahide on the 3rd of June'. This toast was a sore point within the I.R.B., as the secretary of its Supreme Council, Fred Allan, a powerful figure on the organising of the '98 Centenary Committee, had conflicting loyalties, being also treasurer of the Irish Journalists' Association, some members of which would have been monarchists. There was 'confusion' and at one point a supporter of Allan 'finally lost his temper and rushed in the direction of the interrupter brandishing a stick'. Towards the end of his long discourse on Tone, during which he endorsed Tone's belief that 'a united Ireland was necessary to break the connection' with England, Moynihan made it known that 'he did not wish to decry any existing organisation in connection with land or labour, but they only promoted class interest, they did not voice the nationalist sentiment, they did not assert the unalienable right of Irishmen to independence'.[72] This epitomised Fenian doctrine. The heckler was identified elsewhere as James Connolly, the labour leader shot as an insurgent in 1916 and who in 1899 was the owner-editor of a socialist newspaper, the *Worker's Republic*.[73] Moynihan (1864–1918), of Tralee, County Kerry, was to become the father of Maurice Gerard Moynihan (1902–99), from 1937 until 1961 secretary to the Department of the Taoiseach, the cabinet office of independent Ireland.[74]

69 Rep. by Sgt John Breslin, 29 June 1899 (Nat. Arch., Dublin, C.S.O., Crime Branch Special, 19565/S). **70** Nat. Arch., Dublin, C.S.O., Crime Branch Special. **71** For Maurice Moynihan (1868–1918), see *Kerryman*, 19 Jan. 1918; J. A. Gaughan, *A political odyssey: Thomas O'Donnell* (Dublin, 1983), pp 23–4. **72** *Leinster Leader*, 1 July 1899. **73** Fred Allan to editor, 27 June 1899, and reply (*Worker's Republic*, 1 July 1899); Report by Supt B. Lanktree, Dublin Metropolitan Police, G division, 10 July 1899, which states that an associate of Connolly received 'a black eye' (Nat. Arch., Dublin, Crime Branch Special 19572/S). I am grateful to Gary Owens for photocopies of these. **74** For Maurice Gerard Moynihan (1902–99), see Deirdre McMahon's article in *D.I.B.*

At this Bodenstown pilgrimage in 1899 copies of the *United Irishman*, strongly recommended to the crowd by Moynihan, were distributed by Arthur Griffith.[75] This weekly newspaper had been started three months previously by Griffith and William Rooney. Griffith had been present at the meetings at the National Club Literary Society in 1891 at which the first of the revived pilgrimages was planned and from then on he regularly took part in pilgrimages until 1896.[76] He left Ireland for South Africa in January 1897 and did not return until the autumn of 1898, therefore missing the centenary commemorations. There can be little doubt that he was on later pilgrimages, certainly he was in 1903 and 1905.[77] As he was an energetic cyclist who enjoyed leading cycling tours into the Dublin hinterland, he quite likely visited Bodenstown on other occasions too.[78] Griffith was to be credited with the formation in 1907 of a political party, Sinn Féin, and was to play a role in the second revival of the Bodenstown pilgrimages in 1911; he died in 1922 as president of the provisional parliament of the nascent Irish Free State.[79]

Excitement at the war between Britons and Boers in South Africa was at a height in 1900 when another pilgrimage took place (on 24 June). Heavy rain forced the orator, William O'Leary Curtis, to keep his remarks brief. What he had prepared, a lengthy narrative of Tone's life and career, was later printed in five columns of small type in Griffith's *United Irishman*.[80] The rain did not prevent William Rooney delivering a short speech in Irish.[81] Rooney, who was on at least five pilgrimages, had been, with Griffith, an active member of the Leinster Literary Society and was an early member of the Gaelic League, founded in 1893; he was to die on 6 May 1901 aged twenty-seven.[82] But there was still excitement and merriment among the crowd, which was large, 'three long special trains' having left Dublin for Sallins with, it was stated, 'quite 3,000 persons' on board.[83] The reports of the two Naas newspapers, the anti-Boer *Kildare Observer* and the pro-Boer *Leinster Leader*, were affected by their political sympathies. The *Observer* reported that 'the visitors either lingered around Sallins enjoying themselves as best they could, or proceeded in straggling bodies to Bodenstown'; after the laying of wreaths 'a few young men with Boer flags sang Nationalist songs and indulged in the usual extravagant epithets against England, the Queen and the Empire … Cheers were given now and then for Kruger and the Boers, France and America, whilst the object of the pilgrimage was completely ignored. The same young men burned a Union Jack amidst cheers and groans'. The proceedings over, the visitors proceeded to Sallins, where

75 D.M.P. report dated 10 July 1899 (Nat. Arch., Dublin, Crime Branch Special, 19572/S, Box 15). For this reference, I am grateful to Dr Matthew Kelly.　76 *Freeman's Jn.*, 30 May, 19, 23 June 1891, 26 June 1893; *Ir. Daily Indep.*, 25 June 1894, 22 June 1896.　77 *Kildare Observer*, 27 June 1903; *Freeman's Jn.*, 10 July 1905.　78 This information about Griffith as a cyclist comes from Brian Griffin with the suggestion that he may well have included Bodenstown in his itineraries. 79 Griffith (1871–1922) has received much attention from historians, most thoroughly in Owen McGee, *Arthur Griffith* (Dublin, 2015). The best summary is Michael Laffan, 'Griffith, Arthur Joseph' in *D.I.B.*　80 *United Irishman*, 30 June 1900.　81 *Leinster Leader*, 30 June 1900. 82 *Freeman's Jn.*, 26 June 1893; *Ir. Daily Indep.*, 25 June 1894; *Leinster Leader*, 29 June 1895, 27 June 1896, 26 June 1897; William Murphy, 'Rooney, William'; in *D.I.B.*　83 *Freeman's Jn.*, 26

the excursionists from Dublin made fun for themselves. A good deal of drinking, shouting, cheering and jostling prevailed, and coming towards 7 o'clock matters took a serious turn by two parties falling into the canal, but they were promptly rescued. A large part of the crowd had come into Naas, and as they left Naas Station for Dublin by the 8.25 p.m. train, they, needless to say, created no little amount of noise and confusion.[84]

The *Leinster Leader* reported more favourably. The various contingents 'marched from Sallins headed by their bands and banners to the churchyard at Bodenstown'. Quite picturesque were 'the Irish National Foresters garbed in their full regalia of green tunic edged with gold, buff trousers, top boots, cocked hat and plume' accompanied by 'a band of lady Foresters, sporting green and gold sashes'. Many of the men, the report continued,

> carried halberts or pikes while the green flags and bannerettes were borne aloft and fluttered side by side with the national colours of the South African Republics. Approaching Bodenstown the majority of the processionists uncovered and sang 'Who fears to speak of '98' and other national airs ... A diversion was caused by the carriers of the Boer standards, who clambered up the walls of the dismantled old ivy-grown church and from this pinnacle called lustily for three cheers for the 'Transvaal Republic'.

A Union Jack flag was then 'torn into shreds and the remnants burned'. If the *Leader* and not the *Observer* is to be believed, 'in the evening the processionists proceeded to their destinations peaceably'.[85] These reports illustrate how contemporary political issues and passions came to subsume commemoration of Theobald Wolfe Tone and how excursions to Bodenstown provided entertainment and even merriment as well as personal bonding and political expression.

After 1900 popular enthusiasm for mass pilgrimages to Bodenstown was unabated. The ability of the Wolfe Tone and United Irishmen Memorial Committee to organise them was however not commensurate with this enthusiasm. On the appointed day in 1901 pilgrims arrived notwithstanding constant rain; a group of Irish National Foresters 'dressed in their picturesque regalia' and five bands were unperturbed.[86] A police report put the attendance as high as 2,500.[87] It was the occasion when Maud Gonne, a woman of the upper class already famous as an agitator, took a party of children to Bodenstown as a reward for regular participation in Irish history and Gaelic language classes.[88] It was also the occasion when, by coincidence or otherwise and if their plans went well, five Dublin cycling clubs descended on Bodenstown as the destination of their Sunday outings.[89]

June 1900.   **84** *Kildare Observer*, 30 June 1900.   **85** *Leinster Leader*, 30 June 1900.   **86** *Ir. Daily Indep.*, 24 June 1901.   **87** Nat. Arch., Dublin, Crime Branch Special, 1901, Box 19, 24841. For this reference I am indebted to Dr Matthew Kelly.   **88** *Freeman's Jn.*, 22 June 1901; *Ir. Daily Indep.*, 24 June 1901; Ann Matthews, *Renegades: Irish Republican women, 1900–1922* (Cork, 2010), pp 28–30, 56–8.   **89** *Evening Herald*, 22 June 1901.

In 1902 attendance was large, about 1,400 pilgrims and two bands arriving by train from Athlone in County Westmeath.[90] Athlone, much further inland, was three times the distance of Dublin; the railway made a day trip to Bodenstown feasible. The train was a 'special' arranged by Thomas Cook & Son on the initative of the Celtic Literary Society at Tullamore to give 'the Nationalists of the Midlands' their first opportunity to join 'the Nationalists of Dublin and Kildare'; the return fare from Athlone was 2*s*. 6*d*. (less from intermediate stations); departure from Athlone was at 10.30 a.m., arrival at Sallins at about 1 p.m.[91]

In 1903 the pilgrimage was the largest so far. At least four trains arrived from Dublin; long 'specials' carrying pilgrims (mostly young men) came from towns as far away as Cork and Limerick served by the Great Southern and Western Railway; bands and banners came too; the Charleville fife and drum band from County Cork headed the procession formed at Sallins, which took an hour to reach Bodenstown churchyard.[92] Pilgrims had not previously travelled in large numbers from Munster and, except for 1914 and 1915, were not to do so again until 1931. The invited orator was an important visitor from the United States, John T. Keating, a native of Cork. He was no mere 'returned American'. On his arrival in Dublin on the evening before the pilgrimage he was welcomed by a large crowd with bands and banners which accompanied him in procession to the City Hall for a civic reception, stopping en route at places associated with popular heroes of 1798. The *Freeman* reported significantly that the procession was followed by 'a large force of police'.[93] Keating was introduced in Ireland as a former president of the large fraternal organisation of Irish Catholics in the United States, the Ancient Order of Hibernians; in Ireland privately and in America publicly he was known to be chairman of the main Fenian organisation there, Clan na Gael, whose secretary was John Devoy.[94] Keating was chairman of Clan na Gael's executive from 1900 until, it appears, his death in 1915.[95] A cablegram of good wishes from Devoy in New York was acknowledged and Keating in his speech expressed his gladness 'to be near the townland where was born his old friend and colleague John Devoy'.[96] Keating's presence and the Fenian connexion was a likely reason for so many travelling from afar. A greater degree than usual of organisation would have been necessary. It is likely that an important role in this was played by John Daly, who three years after his appearance at Bodenstown in 1880 spent some months in America negotiating with Clan na Gael and becoming acquainted with Devoy; he subsequently served a twelve-year prison sentence in England for unlawful possession of explosives; after release he revisited America and Devoy at the beginning of 1898 and later that year started an increasingly profitable

---

90 *Ir. Daily Indep.*, 21 June 1902.   **91** *Leinster Express*, 7, 14 June 1902.   **92** *Ir. Daily Indep.*, 22 June 1903; *Leinster Leader*, 27 June 1903.   **93** *Ir. Daily Indep.*, 22 June 1903; *Freeman's Jn.*, 22 June 1903.   **94** His public reception in New York on his return is reported in *New York Times*, 31 July 1903.   **95** *Chicago Eagle*, 3 July 1915; Sean Cronin, *The McGarrity papers* (Tralee, 1972), p. 30.   **96** *Freeman's Jn.*, 22 June 1903; *Ir. Daily Indep.*, 22 June 1903; McGee, *I.R.B.*, pp 297, 303–4.

bakery business in his native Limerick.[97] An inference that can be drawn from all this is that in 1903 the Wolfe Tone Memorial Committee was playing a role in a special effort being made by the I.R.B. jointly with its Fenian counterpart in America to revitalise 'advanced' nationalism in Ireland.

For reasons not explained publicly, but will be suggested below, the Wolfe Tone Memorial Committee in the following year, 1904, announced that, 'having consulted the national associations of Dublin', it had decided 'that it would not be advisable this year' to bring 'thousands of persons from Dublin and elsewhere' for the purpose of 'keeping up the time-honoured custom of visiting Tone's grave and placing wreaths'; instead, about a score or more of committee members and other activists ('nationalists') travelled by road from Dublin for wreath-laying and speech-making; they were joined at the grave by 'a few score of country people'. Many years later, Seán McGarry, reflecting on the success of the first official pilgrimage held after the establishment of the Irish Free State, recalled seeing in the graveyard in 1904 'only three people'.[98]

At the demonstration held in 1905 (on 9 July, not on a Sunday near 20 June as usual) the main attraction was surely the chairman, John MacBride, an Irish nationalist hero for having commanded an Irish brigade fighting on the side of the Boers in the recent South African war.[99] 'Major' MacBride (as he was known to Irish nationalists) had recently returned to Ireland after more than five years' absence and was able to arouse his audience by hinting at armed rebellion in Ireland:

> Here by the grave of Tone he asked them to solemnly renew their vow of allegiance and to promise that as long as God gave them health and strength they would never cease working until they had ousted foreign rule from Ireland. They had often been accused of foolishly arguing on the country the necessity of appeals to arms. This was not true. They had lamented, and still lamented, the waste of Irish money upon the Parliamentary movement, the cost of elections and so on. Their contention was this, that if this countless wealth which was thrown away from O'Connell's time to our own were employed in maintaining what was left of our industries and placing arms in the hands of the young Irish, then when an occasion like the Boer War arose they in Ireland would be in a position to add a new republic to the republics of the west.

The formal oration, by Patrick Devlin, a member of the Wolfe Tone Memorial Committee, was barely reported. The reports in the *Freeman's Journal* and the

---

97 For Daly's acquaintance with Devoy in 1883 and 1898, see *Devoy's post-bag*, ed. William O'Brien and Desmond Ryan, ii (Dublin, 1948), pp 183–5, 339. For Daly's closeness to Devoy and his ability to finance I.R.B. activities after taking up business in Limerick I am indebted to discussions with Gerard MacAtasney, who has examined Daly's papers held at the University of Limerick. **98** *Freeman's Jn.*, 27 June 1904, 26 June 1923. **99** For MacBride, see Donal P. McCracken, 'MacBride, John (1865–1916)' in *D.I.B.*

Leinster Leader suggest many hundreds of pilgrims arrived from Dublin or elsewhere, some on excursion trains (one from Athlone), and formed a lively enough audience; both however acknowledge that the number was lower than in previous years.[100] The *Irish Independent* — 'Daily' had been dropped from its title — stated that in comparison it was 'not well attended. Only one band was present, though it was nothing unusual to see ten, and even a dozen, bands in former years.'[101] The Kildare county inspector of the Royal Irish Constabulary, while recording in his monthly report to Dublin Castle a participation of 'about 600 persons', dismissed the event's importance 'save as an indication of the failure of treasonable or revolutionary demonstrations in Ireland at the present day'.[102] MacBride's audience seems to have been made up largely of the usual supporters, which may account for this lack of concern. A factor not accounted for is public interest in the divorce case brought by his wife Maud Gonne, another stage of which was to begin in Paris later in July. The sympathies of advanced nationalists were with MacBride.[103] Was the committee's invitation to MacBride intended to give him moral support as well as to encourage the usual faithful?

ANOTHER HIATUS, 1906–10

No report has been found of any mass pilgrimage to Bodenstown during the next five years, although meetings of the Wolfe Tone Memorial Committee were regularly reported. There was at least the 'excursion' on 17 July 1910 of members of the Old Guard Union (a sort of mutual or benefit society for old Fenians); they enjoyably travelled out from Dublin in five brakes.[104] This body had been represented at the organised pilgrimages discussed above from 1896 to 1904 and was to form a fifty-strong contingent at the 'great pilgrimage' in 1914. There was a private visit on 3 October 1909 by an old (but disenchanted) Fenian, Edward Condon, sentenced to death, but reprieved, for his part in the rescue of two Fenians from police custody for which the 'Manchester martyrs' were hanged; Condon, travelling from America, broke his journey at Sallins en route to Dublin from Kilkenny after receiving the freedom of the city.[105] Another visit was by a writer, a native of Loughrea, County Galway, who moved to Naas in 1906 to be editor of the *Leinster Leader*. This was Seumas O'Kelly, who, like Davis before him, was inspired to write, probably in the following year, a poem, 'In Bodenstown', evoking a visit he had obviously made to Tone's grave:

100 *Freeman's Jn.*, 10 July 1905; *Leinster Leader* 15 July 1905. **101** *Ir. Indep.*, 10 July 1905. **102** Nat. Arch., Kew, CO/904/117 (July 1905). **103** Caoimhe Nic Dháibhéid, '"This is a case in which Irish national considerations must be taken into account": the breakdown of the Gonne-MacBride marriage, 1904–08' in *Irish Historical Studies*, xxxvii, no. 146 (Nov. 2010), pp 241–64. **104** *Freeman's Jn.*, 20 June, 11 July, 8 Aug. 1910; McGee, 'God save Ireland', p. 68; Kelly, *Fenian ideal*, p. 99. **105** *Ir. Indep.*, 4 Oct. 1909.

> Wave, grasses tall, and whisper wind
> A low, soft cadence o'er the tomb
> Where one great dead among his kind
> Lies gathered to the common womb
> And if for Freedom still he prays
> Sing him a restful lullaby.

Twelve more lines and then two more verses follow.[106] O'Kelly (1880?–1918) was an associate of Griffith and contributor to his *United Irishman*; after his health deteriorated in or around 1911, his brother Michael took over his editorship.[107] And there were surely many private visits by nationalists of which no record has been found.

What was the reason for this hiatus? What was the reason for the pilgrimage of 1904 being restricted to members of the Wolfe Tone Memorial Committee? Why was the pilgrimage of 1905 addressed by John MacBride less than a resounding success? The statement made by the committee in June 1904 that any pilgrimage on the scale of those of earlier years was not 'advisable' concealed a crisis on the committee. Its inability to organise a public pilgrimage in that year was a delayed consequence of the extravaganza of 1898. By excluding public men of standing from the committee, the national organisers had forgone sources of funds otherwise available to them; moreover, local nationalists preferred to raise and spend money for commemorating local heroes. By mid-1899 there was a deficit of over £200. The secretary, John P. Dunne, was inept and had to resign.[108] The committee's finances might have recovered but for a falling away of practical support. There is a hint in the *Leinster Leader*'s report of Keating's visit in 1903 that Keating would rescue the situation; it is explicit in a letter from P. T. Daly (a member of the committee) to Devoy in April 1905: 'For God's sake, try and do something about the Wolfe Tone Memorial. It is destroying us. Keating's promises when he was here — public promises — are being thrown in our teeth every day.'[109] For the weakness of the committee's finances there is strong evidence in a financial report it made public shortly before the pilgrimage of 1905. At one time its credit balance had been down to 19*s*. 11*d*.; recently it had been up to £380 1*s*. 6*d*. with 'steady work' in progress by what was a renewed committee.[110] Aggravating the situation was a 'long-disputed trusteeship question' not settled until the close of 1907.[111] It is at least plausible that the committee was hoping that the presence at Bodenstown of MacBride would attract a large number of pilgrims and thereby revivify the custom. MacBride was still, despite recurring and embarrassing newspaper reports of his divorce case, an

---

106 *Gaelic American*, 12 July 1924. I am grateful to Seamus Cullen for sight of this poem. It may have been first published much earlier.   **107** Patrick Maume, 'O'Kelly, Seumas' in *D.I.B.*; James Durney, 'The brothers O'Kelly, writers, poets, editors and nationalists' (<www.jamesdurney.com/ the-brothers-okelly>, accessed 7 Jan. 2016).   **108** O'Keefe, 'Efforts to celebrate the United Irishmen', pp 71–2.   **109** *Leinster Leader*, 27 June 1903; *Devoy's post bag*, ii, 354.   **110** *Ir. Indep.*, 22 June 1905.   **111** *Freeman's Jn.*, 31 Mar. 1908.

heroic figure to many Irish Catholics outside as well as inside the smallish circles of
the I.R.B. In the eyes of Fenians he had the rare and creditable distinction of having
led Irishmen in battle against an English army. But the police report on the 1905
pilgrimage referred to 'a complete lack of enthusiasm' and 'a veritable gloom'
surrounding the whole proceedings.[112] Leon Ó Broin perceived the I.R.B. leadership
as being 'dormant' that summer because of lack of funds and as having a rank-and-
file that was 'apathetic' and unwilling to collect money because of the leadership's
earlier 'squandering of the funds'.[113] Whatever the truth of the matter of the 'turn-
out' at Bodenstown in 1905, there is little doubt that the finances of the organisers,
the Wolfe Tone Memorial Committee, were in a sorry state. The fundamental reason
was that Irish revolutionaries were poor, a reality pointed out by Owen McGee.[114]

A few days after the 1905 pilgrimage the *Kildare Observer* referred angrily to 'the
annual desecration of the little burial ground at Bodenstown ... by the hundreds of
trippers who throng the road from Sallins to Bodenstown yearly. Ballad-mongers,
with their wretched rhymes, stand on the graves of the dead and bellow forth their
wares. Sellers of oranges and other edibles erect their stands on tombs and loudly
claim the custom of the excursionists.'[115] This paper had reported unruly behaviour
by departing pilgrims in 1900. In 1903 it criticised behaviour it considered
inappropriate for a graveyard such as ballad-singing and hawking oranges and
lemonade; it commented that 'the whole scene would remind one of a festival after
a fair, or an excursion party gone mad'.[116] Evidently, to the minds of some local
people the pilgrimages had been unruly for a number of years because of the
presence of Dubliners who regarded them as opportunities for recreation. There is
a hint of this unruliness and of the need to contain it in a report of a tentative
proposal made in 1911 to resume pilgrimages — 'the difficulty of preventing
the presence of thimble-riggers and their fraternity who ... desecrated the
commemoration a few years ago'.[117] Evidently the Wolfe Tone Memorial Committee
had been unable to keep good order. The pilgrimages may therefore have alienated
its local supporters and have become something of an embarrassment.

There may also have been another, more obvious reason for the discontinuance
of pilgrimages after 1905. If the reports, in the *Freeman's Journal*, of regular
meetings of the Wolfe Tone Memorial Committee are to be given face value, most
of its attention was given to its other business, ostensibly its main business — raising
money for the erection of a fitting memorial to Theobald Wolfe Tone in Dublin.[118]
Lucien Bonaparte had predicted, in a speech before the Conseil des Cinq Cens on
9 Brumaire VIII (31 October 1799), that one day 'the independent people of Ireland'
would erect a monument to Tone on the site of the scaffold where he was to have
been hanged. The committee's intended site was, however, not in front of Green
Street Court House (prepared for Tone's execution in 1798) but at the north-west

---

112 Nat. Arch., Kew, CO/904/117 (July 1905).   113 Ó Broin, *Revolutionary underground*, p. 129.
114 McGee, *I.R.B.*, p. 282.   115 *Kildare Observer*, 15 July 1905.   116 *Kildare Observer*, 30 June
1900, 27 June 1903.   117 *Irish Freedom* (Dublin), Apr. 1911.   118 *Life*, ii, 553–4.

corner of St Stephen's Green where, in 1898, O'Leary had laid a foundation stone. The site was lost to nationalist memory a few years later when, in 1907, a memorial was erected instead to the men of the Royal Dublin Fusiliers who lost their lives in the Boer War of 1899–1901 — 'ignobly', protested Patrick Devlin (the formal orator at Tone's grave in 1905), 'warring against freedom'.[119] Leon Ó Broin saw the 'setback in erecting the Wolfe Tone memorial' as one of the things 'impeding the collection of money'.[120] But as late as June 1913, if we are to take at face value a private statement by a very active member of the committee, the memorial project was still regarded as its primary objective and the publicity generated by a pilgrimage to Bodenstown as a means to that end.[121] This was probably pretence, as will be argued. After Bodenstown pilgrimages were resumed in 1911, and periodically until 1922, the Wolfe Tone Memorial Committee was named in press reports as the body under whose auspices the pilgrimage was held. It survived 'in one fashion or another' until 1964, when it was reconstituted by legal deed and, after acquiring the remaining funds of the I.R.B. (which became defunct in 1924), was able to contribute £11,635 towards the cost of a memorial to Tone in Dublin, the balance of which was met by the Irish government.[122] The original committee could not have foreseen that nearly 70 years would pass before its efforts would have the desired outcome. On 18 June 1967, a bronze and stone statue representing Theobald Wolfe Tone, situated in the *north-east* corner of St Stephen's Green, the work of Edward Delaney, was unveiled by the president of Ireland, Éamon de Valera. At the unveiling ceremony were thirteen of Tone's descendants, among them his great-great-granddaughter Katherine Dickason (née Maxwell) who, three-and-a-half years before, had presented to Trinity College a batch of Tone's papers.[123] The story of these papers is being told elsewhere.[124] But the long, tortuous history of the Wolfe Tone Memorial Committee and its travails will be left for others to tell fully.[125]

The Wolfe Tone Memorial Committee had another, secret purpose that may go to explain its inactivity in organising pilgrimages after 1905. It was really a 'front' for the I.R.B. As early as 1899 a Naas police sergeant expressed his opinion 'that the Wolfe Tone and '98 Memorial Association is an I.R.B. association pure and simple'.[126] When Thomas Barry, who was initiated into the I.R.B. in London 1895, moved to Dublin ten years later he found that 'the Wolfe Tone Memorial Committee was the public body under cover of which the I.R.B. operated'. He recalled that 'the circles had Wolfe Tone clubs under various names ... The public proceedings of

---

119 *Freeman's Jn.*, 8 Oct. 1906.   **120** Ó Broin, *Revolutionary underground*, p. 129.   **121** Thomas Clarke to John Daly, 18 June 1913, printed in Gerard MacAtasney, *Tom Clarke: life, liberty, revolution* (Dublin, 2013), p. 264.   **122** Ó Broin, *Revolutionary underground*, pp 221–2.   **123** *Ir. Times*, 27 Apr. 1964, 18, 20 Nov. 1967.   **124** Woods, 'Writings of Theobald Wolfe Tone' (unpublished).   **125** It is mentioned significantly in Gary Owens, 'Nationalist monuments in Ireland, *c.*1870–1914: symbolism and ritual' in Raymond Gillespie and Brian P. Kennedy (eds), *Ireland: art into history* (Dublin, 1994), pp 103–17. Its archives were presented to the N.L.I. and added to the Tom Clarke and Kathleen Clarke papers and are now MSS 49,355/1.   **126** Rep. by Sgt John Breslin, 29 June 1899 (Nat. Arch., Dublin, C.S.O., Crime Branch Special, 19565/S).

these clubs were reported.'[127] (A 'circle' was the smallest unit of the I.R.B. organisation.) Barry's recollection of this in 1947 confirms what Louis Le Roux learnt in the 1930s — that the Wolfe Tone clubs, while ostensibly branches of the Wolfe Tone Memorial Committee, functioned as branches of the I.R.B.[128] Apparently these 'Wolfe Tone clubs' dated from 1898 and owed much to Allan's early support; in 1901 their secretary was P. T. Daly; in 1906, when John O'Hanlon, an I.R.B. veteran from the 1880s had charge, three in every four of the thousand-strong I.R.B. membership in Dublin belonged to one of these clubs.[129] In October 1910 the joint-secretaries of the Wolfe Tone Memorial Committee claimed thirteen affiliated clubs of the kind.[130] Not long before that date appeared a new regulatory body, the Wolfe Tone Club *(sic)*. In its formal constitution, datable to 1909 or 1910, the Wolfe Tone Memorial Committee is stated to be the sponsoring body, provision is made for the regulation of satellite clubs and their primary purpose is defined as being 'to propagate the principles and to disseminate the teachings of Theobald Wolfe Tone and the other true Irishmen who in 1798, 1803, 1848 and 1867 strove for the complete independence of Ireland'. A requirement was that each club should raise money for the erection of the proposed monument in Dublin.[131] But there was no mention of Bodenstown.

It is explained, in an article entitled 'The Wolfe Tone clubs', in *Irish Freedom*, December 1910, that the clubs 'first began to grow gradually out of the branch Wolfe Tone Memorial associations'; in the same article is a report of the formal inauguration on 12 November 1910 of the Dublin Central Wolfe Tone Club. This was the body that two months before had made final arrangements for the publication of *Irish Freedom*.[132] It was undoubtedly the same as the body provided for in the aforementioned constitution. The clubs were largely confined to Dublin, the home ground of the I.R.B. Again there is no mention of Bodenstown. Two young political activists in the period retained memories of the clubs. Donal O'Hannigan recalled that in 1910 and 1911 the Wolfe Tone clubs were organised in different parts of Dublin 'at the instance of the executive of the I.R.B.'.[133] Desmond Ryan, recalling events in 1913, stated plainly that 'meetings of the Wolfe Tone clubs … were a cover for the I.R.B.'.[134] Another I.R.B. man, Patrick Kearney, recalled attending a meeting of his circle at 41, Rutland Square 'under the guise of the Wolfe Tone Memorial Committee'.[135] A telling piece of circumstantial evidence

---

127 Thomas Barry, 22 Feb. 1947 (Bureau of Military History, W.S. 1, p. 1). 128 L.N. Le Roux, *Tom Clarke and the Irish freedom movement* (Dublin, 1936), pp 89–90. For Le Roux, see below, chap. 5. 129 McGee, *I.R.B.*, pp 270, 299, 349, 351–2; Joseph O'Connor, 13 Oct. 1948 (B.M.H., W.S. 157, p. 2). 130 Wolfe Tone and United Irishmen Memorial Committee, Secretaries' annual report, 29 October 1910 (printed); copies in N.L.I., McGarrity papers, MSS 17,500 and 17,641. 131 'Constitution of the Wolfe Tone Club', n.d. (N.L.I., Clarke papers, MS 49,355/1/26). No doubt it was the 'new scheme for organising Wolfe Tone Clubs' mentioned as having been 'approved by the Committee' in the Wolfe Tone Memorial Committee's report for 1909–10; most likely the constitution was drafted about 12 months later, as is evident in the next paragraph. 132 Le Roux, *Clarke*, pp 89–90. 133 Donal O'Hannigan, 2 Dec. 1948 (B.M.H., W.S. 161, p. 2). 134 Desmond Ryan, 5 Sept. 1952 (B.M.H., W.S. 725, p. 2). 135 Patrick

of the true nature of the Wolfe Tone Memorial Committee is the promptness and diligence with which an older, well-connected and very energetic I.R.B. man, Thomas Clarke, joined it in 1908 after his return from America, and the forcefulness with which in 1912 he got himself elected president and his no less energetic young I.R.B. protégé Seán MacDermott elected treasurer jointly with James Stritch.[136] Stritch had been a founder member in 1898 and treasurer since 1905. Clarke's role in the resumption and continuance of the Bodenstown pilgrimages will be discussed in the next chapter. It would be hard to avoid the conclusion that the purpose of the Wolfe Tone Memorial Committee was not entirely, or even mainly, the erection of a monument or the organising of pilgrimages. There was something very appropriate about supplementing its funds with frozen I.R.B. funds in 1964 to realise its stated purpose of erecting a memorial to Tone in St Stephen's Green.

THE ORATIONS

The precedent of orations delivered at Tone's grave, if little more than a recital of the events in his career, was set by Richard Keegan in 1873. By the mid-1890s crowds as large as 4,000 assembled to hear political speeches by orators who could be accounted 'Fenians', ones for whom Tone's republicanism, his advocacy of the twin causes of the freeing of Catholics from legal disabilities and the separation of Ireland from Great Britain, demonstrated by deed as well as by word, were congenial. In 1894, George Lynch of the Young Ireland League 'read an eloquent and interesting paper on Wolfe Tone' — reported as some length in the *Freeman's Journal* and, in a special supplement, in the *Leinster Leader*, which devoted four columns to reproducing Lynch's speech.[137] Tone's career was to be recounted many times. Often the speeches were illustrated by dicta taken from Tone's autobiography or journals. In 1895, another member, Edward R. Whelan, abstracted 'Tone's views and objects, as stated by himself' as being 'to break the connection with England, and to assert the independence of his native country; to unite the whole people of Ireland; to abolish the memory of past dissensions, and to substitute the common name of Irishmen for the denominations of Protestant, Catholic and Dissenter'.[138] Such dicta were to be reiterated. Whilst Tone and Ireland in the 1790s, and Tone's words in his literary remains, remained recurring themes, some orators were unafraid to court controversy by treating of present-day topics, most forcefully John MacBride in 1905 and by successive orators later in the new century.

Kearney, 18 June 1953 (B.M.H., W.S. 868, p. 2).   **136** Gerard MacAtasney, *Seán MacDiarmada: the mind of the revolution* (Manorhamilton, Co. Leitrim, 2004), pp 58, 190; Clarke to Patrick McCartan, 11 Apr. 1912 (N.L.I., McCartan papers, MS 17666/1).   **137** *Freeman's Jn.*, 25 June 1894; *Leinster Leader*, 30 June 1894; McGee, *I.R.B.*, p. 244, n. 53.   **138** *Evening Herald*, 25 June 1895.

THE PILGRIMS

What sort of people were the Bodenstown pilgrims in the early days? What sort of people were the leading lights? From what evidence there is of the social position of the more prominent participants, they were almost exclusively from the lower levels of the middle class and upper levels of the working class. As shown above in chapter 3, the earliest known organised outing or pilgrimage was that of the Dublin Wolfe Tone Band in 1873. This was probably a group of working men sufficiently prosperous to be able to afford musical instruments and an outing into the countryside. For the speedy erection in 1874 of the protective railing in the graveyard the involvement of prosperous local artisans like Clory would have been essential. James O'Connor, who held the audience in 1875 and 1876, was a journalist. The people who revived the pilgrimages in the 1890s, members of the Young Ireland League, were men of the middle or lower middle classes. Patrick Lavelle who made a speech in 1891 was a university graduate and by 1901 a solicitor;[139] Henry Dixon who followed him was a solicitor's clerk;[140] Edward R. Whelan (1895) was a solicitor's clerk too;[141] John Murphy, 'of Clontarf' (1896) was editor of the *Weekly Independent*;[142] Charles Doran (1897) was a builder or civil engineer; W. J. Ryan (1898) was connected with the *Irish Daily Independent*;[143] Maurice Moynihan (1899) was a butter-buyer in Kerry for Messrs Shanahan's of Cork;[144] William O'Leary Curtis (1900), a minor Dublin literary figure, was later a sub-editor on the staff of the *Irish Independent*;[145] P. N. Fitzgerald (1901) was a commercial traveller;[146] P. T. Daly (1902) was a compositor on the *Irish Daily Independent* and later prominent in trades-union and labour circles.[147] But John T. Keating (1903), described in the *Kildare Observer* as 'one of the pillars of the "advanced" Nationalist movement in America', was more precisely chairman of the Clan na Gael, on a lecture tour in Ireland and so probably successful in a profession.[148] John MacBride (not an 'orator' but the chairman in 1905), born into a shop-keeping family at Westport, County Mayo, worked for a wholesale chemist before emigrating to the Transvaal in 1896; back in Ireland, having separated from his well-to-do English-born wife, in 1905 he was probably unemployed.[149]

Their audiences, the mass of pilgrims, would have been made up largely of men of a somewhat lower rank than themselves. Evidences of their social status are frequent mentions of political clubs, musical bands, bicycles and the Irish National

---

139 McGee, *I.R.B.*, pp 163, 235; *The collected letters of W. B. Yeats*, i (Oxford, 1986), p. 273. fn.; Kelly, *Fenian ideal*, p. 182; Census of Ire., 1901.   140 McGee, *I.R.B.*, p. 146. For Henry Dixon (1859?–1928), see *Ir. Indep.*, 5, 6 Dec. 1928.   141 Census of Ire., 1901.   142 Ibid., p. 244. 143 For Ryan, see above, n. 64, and below, chap. 5.   144 For this Maurice Moynihan, see above, n. 71.   145 O'Leary Curtis (d. 1923) was imprisoned in 1918 for making a seditious speech (*Ir. Indep.*, 13 July 1918, 28 Feb. 1923).   146 For Fitzgerald, see Owen McGee, 'Patrick Neville Fitzgerald (1851–1907)' in *D.I.B.*   147 For Daly, see Desmond McCabe and Owen McGee, 'Patrick Thomas Daly (1870–1943)' in *D.I.B.*   148 *Kildare Observer*, 27 June 1903; McGee, *I.R.B.*, pp 303–4.   149 MacBride is described in a notebook concerning his divorce as being 'without profession' (N.L.I., Allan papers, MS 29817).

Foresters. The social positions of such men warrants Sean O'Casey's comment, made in 1938 and referring to 1913 (when he was secretary of the Wolfe Tone Memorial Committee) that the I.R.B. 'appealed only to clerks and artizans'.[150]

As for the politics of Bodenstown orators, T. D. Sullivan, who presided at the completion of the railing in 1874, could come over as a strong nationalist without however overt Fenian tendencies; he was a regular contributor to the *Nation*, owned by one of his brothers, and in 1876 assumed ownership himself. Speechifying at Bodenstown in 1875 and presiding in 1876 was James O'Connor, who was a member of the I.R.B. and was employed on the *Irishman*, a paper much read by Fenians. Five years later, in 1880, the guest speaker was John Daly of Limerick, another I.R.B. man, one who was to be a vital financial backer thirty years later and whose name will recur. The Young Ireland League, mentioned above for the social classes of its membership, was a Dublin political club formed on 17 September 1891 at a convention chaired by John O'Leary. It absorbed the Young Ireland Society and also apparently the National Club Literary Society. Naturally its tone, if not entirely its tendency, was Fenian. Lavelle and Dixon (both of whom spoke in 1891) were at the time members of the National Club Literary Society and were 'almost certainly' in the I.R.B.; Joseph Doyle (1893), George Lynch (1894) and Edward R. Whelan (1895) were members of the Young Ireland League, Whelan was a socialist; John Murphy (1896) was reputedly a member of the I.R.B.[151] From 1897 this was the body that, directed by Fred Allan, secretary of its Supreme Council and secretary too of the '98 Centenary Committee, organised the pilgrimages. Naturally the Bodenstown orators thenceforward were usually I.R.B. men: Charles Doran (1897); probably W.J. Ryan (1898), certainly Maurice Moynihan (1899); perhaps William O'Leary Curtis (1900); certainly P.N. Fitzgerald (1901) and P.T. Daly (1902). It was the 'Fenian chief' himself, John O'Leary, who presided in 1898, the centennial year. John T. Keating, the guest orator in 1903, belonged to Clan na Gael, the I.R.B.'s fraternal society in the United States. John MacBride (who presided in 1905) had been in the I.R.B. and in a short-lived splinter group, the Irish National Association; his anti-British credentials were that he had commanded an Irish unit fighting on the side of the Boers in the South African War. Another member of the association who went to South Africa was John R. Whelan, one of the group present at the National Club who in 1891 revived the pilgrimages and afterwards a regular at Bodenstown in the Young Ireland League contingent; a university graduate, he left Ireland in January 1897, some time after Griffith (a maternal cousin), was in Mafeking during the siege, and for his pains was held under arrest there as a Boer sympathiser; his commitment to Irish independence could not have diminished, as he went with John Murphy to Bodenstown in 1912.[152] A special case, very different

---

150 *The letters of Sean O'Casey, 1910–41*, ed. David Krause (London, 1975), pp 29, 697. Cf. 'that old craft and petit bourgeois Fenianism' pervasive in Dublin (David Dickson, *Dublin* (London, 2014), p. 486).   **151** McGee, *I.R.B.*, esp. pp 207, 209, 234, 244.   **152** *Freeman's Jn.*, 26 Feb., 24 June 1912; Donal P. McCracken. *MacBride's brigade: Irish commandos in the Anglo-Boer war* (London, 1999), pp 17, 19, 34; McGee, *Griffith*, p. 70.

from MacBride, was J. L. Carew, who presided in 1891 and again in 1893. Carew, a barrister by profession, owner of a local nationalist newspaper and the local member of parliament loyal to Parnell after the 'split' in December 1890, was engaged in 1891 in the Parnellite campaign against the anti-Parnellites which sought and drew much of its support from nationalists of Fenian tendencies; in 1893, defeated in the recent general election, he aspired to revive the Parnellite cause.

Almost invariably, Bodenstown organisers and pilgrims were Catholics, practising Catholics. A rare exception was Fred Allan, a Methodist. One reason for the absence of Protestants was that reverence for Tone was founded on two perceptions, one that he had played the leading role in a campaign in the 1790s for the removal of Catholic disabilities, the other that he had pressed for the separation of Ireland from Great Britain and its establishment as an independent state, activities that ultimately brought about his downfall and death in dramatic circumstances, a tragedy that turned him into a hero. Both objectives, Catholic liberties and Irish self-government, were in the nineteenth century and well into the twentieth perceived by Protestants as conducive to Catholic empowerment and so to Protestant decline. There was another, imperative reason for Protestants taking no part in Bodenstown pilgrimages. It was that they took place on a Sunday, the day observed by Protestants as a day of prayer and rest to the exclusion of political activities. Sabbatarianism was conventional amongst Irish Protestants until the final quarter of the twentieth century.

BODENSTOWN A SOCIAL AND CULTURAL PHENOMENON

The journey to Bodenstown with like-minded travellers was part of the enjoyment of the pilgrimages. The mysterious Dun Padruic in 1872 recommended popular visits to Tone's grave on social as well as political grounds. The railway train was not merely the speediest means of travel from Dublin into the Kildare countryside, it was convenient. The members of the Wolfe Tone Band went in 1873 and 1874 by the regular 9.30 a.m. train from Dublin. The Kingsbridge terminus was 2.25 kilometres upstream of O'Connell Bridge and so within walking distance of the artisanal districts of the Liberties and Oxmantown.[153] Dun Padruic's advice to hire 'excursion trains' was followed in 1877 when organisers made a special arrangement with the railway company.[154] It was a regular practice from 1893 until 1902. The special return fare advertised in 1893 was one shilling, which the committee believed would enable 'most nationalists' to 'avail themselves of the opportunity'; the fare was to be on a 'Cook's train'[155] — a 'special' arranged by Thomas Cook & Son, already well known as travel agents in Ireland as well as in Britain. One shilling was manageable for a skilled or semi-skilled working man. This can be imagined, for example, from an advertisement in the *Freeman's Journal* of 6 January 1891 of a

153 *Freeman's Jn.*, 15 Sept. 1873; *Nation*, 28 Mar. 1874.   154 *Irishman*, 18 Aug. 1877. 155 *Freeman's Jn.*, 17 June 1893; *United Ireland*, 24 June 1893.

vacancy for an experienced provisions and grocery assistant (who 'must know his trade thoroughly') at a wage of £30 per year, which works out at 11s. 6d. per week (and probably included accommodation). The railway was convenient too for pilgrims setting off from places along the line: Inchicore (an industrial suburb of Dublin), Clondalkin, Lucan and Celbridge; it was particularly convenient for bandsmen and their instruments. The 'special train' was to remain a necessary requirement for transporting pilgrims and paraphernalia en masse until the 1970s.

As early as 1892, bicycles were being used for travel from Dublin and no doubt from nearer places. Several instances are given above. For a man able to save up for some time or obtain credit, purchase of a bicycle was manageable too. In the *Kildare Observer*, 25 March 1905, M. & J. Dawson, of Maynooth, advertised cycles ('new machines, fully guaranteed') from £5 10s. ('cash and easy payments'). By then the 'free wheel' and pneumatic tyres were becoming the norm. One can imagine that some of the bicycles that went to Bodenstown had been purchased second-hand at lower prices.[156] This mode of transport was technically in its infancy in the 1870s and unavailable for travel to Bodenstown; technical improvements in the 1890s made the 'safety bicycle' ideal. This revolution was as significant as the railway revolution that made easy the journey from Dublin to Sallins. Cycling there was increasingly popular among the physically fit, suddenly so in 1918 when fares rose sharply.

In some instances the journey from Dublin was made by horse-drawn vehicle, as in 1874 when the Dublin coopers' band travelled 'in a drag drawn by four horses', and in 1904 when, weary of organising a mass pilgrimage, the Wolfe Tone Memorial Committee went quietly by road, a course adopted by members of the Old Guard Union in 1910. A particular means of transport was the 'brake', typically a four-wheeled carriage with low sides but no roof drawn by two horses, its passengers seated facing each other on two longitudinal benches. So pleasant and companionable means as this (in good weather) was availed of in 1891 and 1892 by the organising party, departing in the morning from the National Club in Rutland Square.[157] Though reports give no details, it can be imagined that the locals who travelled from Clane, Sallins and beyond did so on foot or on horse-back, or on pony-traps, ass-carts or other domestic horse-drawn vehicles. They thereby incurred no additional expenditure, which must partly account for the local popularity of the pilgrimages. The first mention of motor-cars as conveyances to Bodenstown was not until 1917; motor-buses and 'charabancs' (open buses for pleasure trips) were first mentioned in 1920.

A great attraction of the pilgrimages was the playing of music in the open air by local and visiting and bands. The custom was an essential feature from the very beginning of the phenomenon. The tunes and songs were always 'popular', some were also political. Indeed any peculiarly Irish melody appealed to Irish nationalists. What is most striking is the abundance of bands in the countryside. From Dublin

---

156 For the advent of bicycles in Ireland, see Miriam Daly, 'The return to the roads' in Kevin B. Nowlan (ed.), *Travel and transport in Ireland* (Dublin, 1973), pp 134–49; Brian Griffin, *Cycling in Victorian Ireland* (Dublin, 2006).   157 *Freeman's Jn.*, 23 June 1891, 16, 20 June 1892.

too bandsmen with their instruments travelled to Bodenstown, several in 1894; two arrived from Tullamore in adjacent King's County in 1902 and one in 1903 from Charleville, County Cork; the railway was essential for transport of instruments over long distances. On one occasion, in 1899, as many as a dozen different bands performed. Perforce all bands were marching bands with colourful costume and insignia, as the walk or march from Sallins was also an essential feature of pilgrimages.

The Bodenstown phenomenon in the 1890s and the first few years of the new century can be perceived, like the Celtic twilight and the Gaelic revival, as a cultural phenomenon. All three arose in the aftermath of the split in the short-lived but monolithic and briefly-powerful nationalist movement built up in the 1880s by Parnell, the tragedy of whose rise, downfall and death became, like the tragedy of Tone's, a potent impulse. The coincidence of the occurrence of the first Bodenstown pilgrimage in the new series six months into Parnell's struggle to regain his position and the Fenian tendencies of his most earnest supporters have been noted above, as has the vital role of Dublin Fenians in organising his massive funeral four months later. The evidence is that it was Dublin nationalists, more than a few of them in the I.R.B., who organised the June pilgrimages to Tone's grave. Processions to graveyards and the concomitant ritual are, arguably, cultural and social phenomena, moreover, in the case of a revered political figure, politics, culture and social activity are blended.

Bodenstown pilgrimages were also recreational. The prospect of an outing into the countryside in early summer was attractive to Dubliners of the lower middle and artisanal classes. What was enticing to country people was the prospect of hearing popular tunes played by visiting as well as local bands. The outings were made even more congenial by the renewing and making of friendships with like-minded people. A particular delight for younger people would have been meeting members of the opposite sex in a relaxed mood. Perhaps it was in consideration of this recreational aspect, as well as to mark the anniversary of Tone's birth, that from 1891 the pilgrimages were held on the Sunday closest to 20 June, the day conveniently with the greatest amount of daylight (if not the 21st). To mark the anniversary of his death (19 November) would have been impractical owing to paucity of daylight. Another aspect of Bodenstown as a social phenomenon was the political bonding effected by the walk from Sallins station to Bodenstown churchyard, a distance of barely one Irish mile, not too long for men unaccustomed to walking, long enough for comradeship to form.[158] There were pleasant spots along the route and around and inside the graveyard for gatherings or picnics. Access to the graveyard is along a side-road, largely free of vehicular traffic even at the present day, with hardly any building but the ruined church in the vicinity. Such was the popularity of visits to

158 For more on the Bodenstown pilgrimages as a social phenomenon, see C. J. Woods, 'Pilgrimages to Tone's grave at Bodenstown, 1873–1922: time, place, popularity' in *History Ireland*, xxiii, no. 3 (May–June 2015), pp 36–9.

Bodenstown that 'Wolfe Tone's grave' was recognised officially as a man-made feature of County Kildare by being marked as such on the Ordnance Survey 25-inch map of 1897–1913, for which Bodenstown was surveyed in June 1908.[159] On this evidence, it is likely that by the eve of the First World War the grave was finger-posted, both at the Bodenstown turn on the Clane–Sallins road and at the entrance to the churchyard.[160] By then also it was, one Sunday each June, a less idyllic spot than when discovered by Thomas Davis.

159 County Kildare Burial Grounds Survey, carried out apparently in 2009, copyright Kildare County Council Heritage Office, 2011.   **160** To my personal recollection, in the mid-1960s there were signposts in these places.

5

Thomas Clarke, the Easter rising and its aftermath, 1911–21

T HE PILGRIMAGES WERE REVIVED again in 1911. Initiatives were taken by Thomas Clarke, immortalised for his part in the insurrection that broke out in Dublin in April 1916.[1] Clarke, born in 1857, was the principal in the organisation of the five pilgrimages that preceded it. A member of the I.R.B. since 1878, he had served 15 years' harsh imprisonment in England (for unlawful possession of explosives), settled briefly in Dublin on his release, and in 1900 moved to New York. In America he became assistant to John Devoy of Clan na Gael. While in New York, Clarke started a custom of an annual pilgrimage, around 20 June, to the grave of Matilda Tone at Greenwood cemetery in Brooklyn.[2] His connexion with Devoy was to be of consequence in Ireland. Devoy encouraged and facilitated Clarke's return to Ireland in November 1907 and provided through Clan na Gael regular subventions to the I.R.B., normally £300 per annum, later £600.[3] Six months after his return Clarke was auditing the accounts of the Wolfe Tone Memorial Committee as 'requested by several subscribers and sympathisers' in America.[4] He was co-opted on to the Supreme Council of the I.R.B. as treasurer in April 1910 and the following September was entrusted with the editorial direction of *Irish Freedom*, nominally the publication of the Dublin Central Wolfe Tone Club but really the main medium of I.R.B. opinion. In much of what he did he was also aided financially, and helped in other ways too, by John Daly of Limerick, who had interested him in the I.R.B. in 1878 and whose niece, Kathleen Daly, Clarke had married in 1901.[5] 'Tom' Clarke was a small, wiry man whose occupation as a small shopkeeper in Dublin belied his great organising ability and his single-mindedness in his pursuit of Irish

---

1 On Clarke, see Gerard MacAtasney, *Tom Clarke: life, liberty, revolution* (Dublin, 2013), also James Quinn, 'Clarke, Thomas James' in *D.I.B.* (2009), and, still, L. N. Le Roux, *Tom Clarke and the Irish freedom movement* (Dublin, 1936). Le Roux (d. 1944), a Breton nationalist, was present at the Republican pilgrimage in 1931; he later lodged with Clarke's widow Kathleen when researching for his book and got information from her, her sister Madge and other paticipants in the 'Irish revolution' incl. Patrick McCartan and P.S. O'Hegarty (*Ir. Press*, 28 Dec. 1931, 17 Dec. 1934, 8 Aug. 1944; *Ir. Times*, 18 Feb. 1933, 15 Aug. 1944; N.L.I., Le Roux papers, MS 44,684 / 1– 5). 2 Le Roux, *Clarke*, p. 72; Info. John Carroll, *c*.1935 (N.L.I., Le Roux papers, MS 44.684/3). 3 Ó Broin, *Revolutionary underground*, p. 134. 4 *Sinn Féin*, 20 June 1908; *Ir. Indep.*, 13 June, 11 Aug., 16 Nov. 1908; Clarke to James Reidy, 3 Jan. 1909, pr. in MacAtasney, *Clarke*, p. 235. 5 For Kathleen Clarke (1878–1972), who was to become lord mayor of Dublin, see the article on her in

independence. Clarke presided or spoke at Bodenstown each year from 1911 till 1915.[6]

The first of these pilgrimages took place on Saturday, 8 July 1911. No pilgrimage on the model created in the 1870s had taken place since 1905. The circumstances of the revival suggest that it owed as much to a plan for a royal visit to Ireland and a dispute in the I.R.B. as it did to Clarke's undoubted charisma, determination and diligence. George V had succeeded in May 1910. When early in February 1911 the date of his coronation was known, Clarke informed Devoy, 'we have secured the Mansion House for 22 June (Coronation Day) to hold a nationalist demonstration by way of celebrating Wolfe Tone's birthday'.[7] A few weeks later it was known publicly that the 'central executive' of the Wolfe Tone Clubs was contemplating 'the revival of the pilgrimage to Bodenstown on the last Sunday of June'.[8] This would be on the 25th, but it did not take place on that day. Once the royal visit was announced, advanced nationalists' antipathy to British royalty became more pronounced. On the initiative of the Sinn Féin party, a committee was formed on 24 March, under the chairmanship of the party's leading light, Arthur Griffith, to oppose any form of welcome to the king. Called the United National Societies Committee, it had representatives of Wolfe Tone Clubs — ostensibly branches of the Wolfe Tone Memorial Committee but really covers for 'circles' of the I.R.B. — and was supported by men and women of various nationalist opinions, among them Major MacBride, Constance Markievicz (a bellicose gentlewoman, estranged wife of a Polish count and leader of the National Boy Scouts) and Patrick McCartan (an assertive young member of the I.R.B.).[9] The Dublin Central Wolfe Tone Club is not named in newspaper reports; it seems to have been barely distinguishable from the Wolfe Tone Memorial Committee. Mrs Sidney Czira (née Giffard), who in 1911 was an active member of Inghinidhe na hÉireann, a nationalist women's club connected to this committee, recounted over forty years later how some wanted an overt protest to be made against the royal visit — to take place from 7 to 12 July. Partly from her own recollection, partly from information received recently from McCartan, she stated how he and another young member of the I.R.B., Seán MacDermott, had called for such a protest contrary to the requirement of the I.R.B.'s supreme council, influenced as it was by its secretary, Fred Allan, that no public statement be made concerning it.[10] The reason for the supreme council's position remains unclear. Perhaps Allan's republicanism was compromised on this royal occasion by his being, like other men of republican principles (MacBride and Stritch, for example), an employee of Dublin city corporation. (Certainly Allan, later, in his official capacity as secretary to the lord mayor accompanied him as he paid his respects to the royal visitor.)[11] Another consideration is the likely mood of the public. It was a period

the *D.I.B.* by Frances Clarke (no relation).   **6** *Freeman's Jn.*, 10 July 1911, 24 June 1912, 23 June 1913, 22 June 1914, 21 June 1915.   **7** Clarke to Devoy, 10 Feb. 1911, pr. in *Devoy's post-bag*, ii, 395–6.   **8** *Irish Freedom*, Apr. 1911.   **9** *Freeman's Jn.*, 25 Mar., 1, 15 Apr. 1911 et passim; *Irish Freedom*, Apr. 1911.   **10** Mrs Sidney Czira, 29 Dec. 1953 (B.M.H., W.S. 909, pp 4–6). She makes no mention of it in her published recollections, *The years flew by* (Dublin, 1974).   **11** MacAtasney,

when Irish Catholics had high hopes of the concession of home rule by a Liberal government dependent since February 1910 on the Irish nationalist members for its majority in parliament. Clarke supported McCartan in opposition to Allan.[12] No doubt to defuse the situation, a decision was taken to hold a demonstration at Bodenstown on the day that the royal party would process along Dublin streets.

There is evidence of this dispute and its remedy in a report reaching the Dublin Metropolitan Police. Dated 3 July, it stated that 'more extreme members' of the Wolfe Tone Memorial Committee were to be given 'an opportunity of being out of Dublin' in order to 'prevent them witnessing their majesties' entry'.[13] There is some substantiation in McCartan's memoirs published fifty years after the event.[14] Further substantiation is in a series of articles, 'Memories', by Countess Markiewicz, published in 1923. She recalled that a committee was formed 'from all the national societies' and met 'to consider how best we might make profit for Ireland' from the planned royal visit. The majority, led by Griffith, 'seemed to be in great dread of a riot ... The others considered that the best way to make the royal visit unpopular with the people was if we could get the police to attack us, and we were willing to take the risk'. Disagreement was resolved 'in co-operation with the I.R.B.' when a 'huge excursion to Bodenstown' was arranged for the day 'the British royalties were advertised to make their triumphal entry into Dublin'.[15] It was to be, advised the I.R.B.'s paper, *Irish Freedom*, 'no mere merry-making excursion but a gathering of Nationalist men and women'; a train would leave Dublin at 9.30 and arrive back at 6.30 at a fare of 1s. 6d.[16]

Two thousand people, according to the *Sunday Independent*, assembled at Bodenstown on 8 July. An alternative figure is 'about 200', all 'followers of the extreme Nationalist parties in Dublin with about 100 local people' — this in a report for the Dublin Metropolitan Police.[17] Unlike the earlier pilgrimages, it was held in July and on a Saturday — a bank holiday for the royal visit. As the paper explained, 'the usual time for holding the pilgrimage was departed from this year, and in the public notice announcing the pilgrimage Irishmen and Nationalists were invited to ignore the royal visit and to join in paying a tribute to the memory of Wolfe Tone'. It was described as 'the pilgrimage of the members of the Wolfe Tone city clubs'.[18] At 11.30 a.m. pilgrims gathered at Kingsbridge railway station, the majority displaying a white badge with black lettering spelling out the words 'Thou art not conquered yet, dear land', others placards bearing the quotation from John Mitchel, 'England, damn your concessions, we want our country'. According to the *Freeman's Journal*, thirty-two extra carriages had to be deployed. (Thus would suggest the police estimate of attendance was too low.) Having alighted at Sallins, pilgrims formed into a procession and set off for Bodenstown singing marching songs

MacDiarmada, p. 57.   **12** Mrs Sidney Czira, 29 Dec. 1953 (as above).   **13** Nat. Arch., Kew, CO 904/13, f. 204.   **14** 'Extracts from the papers of the late Dr Patrick McCartan', ed. F. X. Martin, in *Clogher Record*, v (1963), pp 42–4.   **15** Constance Markiewicz, 'Memoirs' in *Éire: the Irish Nation*, 16 June, 14 July 1923.   **16** *Irish Freedom*, July 1911.   **17** Nat. Arch., Kew, CO 904/13, f. 186.   **18** *Sunday Independent*, 9 July 1911.

(among them 'A nation once again' and 'O'Donnell Abu'); they were met at the graveyard by National Boy Scouts who had marched there the previous evening (to camp overnight), and by cyclists who had pedalled from Dublin; all present reformed and filed slowly, two abreast, past Tone's grave; prayers were recited in Irish. On a less solemn note after the speeches were over, an *aeraíocht* (a cultural festival with music, song and dance) was held in the field opposite the churchyard presided over by Cathal Brugha; a dozen songs and recitations are named in reports, one of them 'Tone is coming back', another Davis's 'Tone's grave'. After arriving back in Kingsbridge 'the entire gathering of fully 2,000 people' sang again the nation song.[19] Before that, however, came the main business.

Clarke, described discreetly in the *Freeman* as 'an old Fenian', proposed John MacBride as chairman.[20] MacBride had been best-man at Clarke's wedding and was a close friend of Allan and his wife Clara. Both Clarke and MacBride were to lead insurrectionists in 1916 and to suffer death in consequence. The guest orator in 1911 was James Mark Sullivan, who made a long rambling speech. Sullivan (1873–1935), a relation of T. D. Sullivan and brought up in America, was a lawyer and a man of some importance in Irish-American circles, particularly in Clan na Gael; his business in Ireland was probably to help Clarke establish *Irish Freedom*, the first issue of which appeared in November 1910; his host in Ireland, where he stayed for many months, was John Daly in Limerick.[21] Another speaker, not mentioned in newspaper reports in 1911 but recalled by a former National Boy Scout, was James Stritch, a Dublin city corporation employee since 1882 and a low-profile I.R.B. man.[22] Stritch, whose Fenian credentials (if an account of his career published at the time of his death in 1933 is to be credited) stretched back to collaboration with the 'Manchester martyrs' when he was 17, was one of the group headed by Fred Allan which welcomed the old Fenian O'Donovan Rossa on his arrival in Dublin from America in 1894; Stritch was at Bodenstown in June 1896 as a member of the Irish National Foresters; he was present at the public meeting at the Rotunda in 1898 which started the Wolfe Tone and United Irishmen Memorial Fund (to which he subscribed £1); and he was treasurer of the Wolfe Tone Memorial Committee in 1905 and for long after; he attempted, without success, around this time, to persuade John McDonnell, the custodian of the 'half' of Davis's stone, to return it to Bodenstown churchyard.[23] Also identified as present in 1911 were four other members of the I.R.B.: Allan, MacDermott, Bulmer Hobson and John O'Hanlon.[24] MacDermott,

19 *Freeman's Jn.*, 10 July 1911; *Leinster Leader*, 15 July 1911. The report in the latter is identical except that it includes the quotation from John Mitchel.   **20** *Freeman's Jn.*, 10 July 1911. **21** Ibid.; Maryanne Felter and Daniel Schultz, 'James Mark Sullivan and the Film Company of Ireland' in *New Hibernia Review*, viii, no. 2 (summer 2004), pp 24–40; MacAtasney, *Clarke*, p. 72. **22** Robert Holland, 18 July 1949 (B.M.H., W.S. 280, pp 1–2).   **23** *Freeman's Jn.*, 26 June 1894, 22 June 1896, 21, 30 June 1898, 18 May 1899; *Ir. Daily Indep.*, 22 June 1896, 27 June 1904; *Ir. Indep.*, 22 June, 12 July 1905; *Ir. Press*, 25 Feb. 1933; Census of Ire., 1901, 1911. See also David Fitzpatrick, *Harry Boland's Irish revolution* (Cork, 2003), passim; David Flood, 'Dublin Corporation employees' in John Gibney (ed.), *Dublin City Council and the 1916 rising* (Dublin, 1916), p. 291.   **24** Nat. Arch., Kew, CO 904/13, ff 186, 210.

mentioned above as a close associate of Clarke, was to share the fate of Clarke and MacBride in 1916. Hobson, born the son of a grocer in 1883 and educated at the Friends' School, Lisburn, was trained as a printer and was many years later to edit and publish some of Tone's letters and an abridged version of his autobiography; he joined the I.R.B. in 1904 and by 1911 was one of the leadership; he spoke after Sullivan.[25] O'Hanlon, a Dublin compositor and an I.R.B. man, was from 1901 a stalwart of the pilgrimages and of the Wolfe Tone Memorial Committee; in 1911 he was president of the Wolfe Tone clubs. He was to follow Allan out of the I.R.B. in March 1912 and to die in November 1918.[26]

The National Boy Scouts were to be a regular presence at Bodenstown pilgrimages. A nationalist youth movement, more militaristic than the Baden Powell Scouts and known also as 'Fianna Éireann' ('Irish Warriors'), they had been started formally in August 1909 by Bulmer Hobson and Countess Markievicz.[27] Louis Le Roux states that Fianna Éireann were formed 'at the instigation of the I.R.B. supreme council' at Hobson's suggestion. Whilst this is plausible, the evidence now available indicates that Hobson did not consult the I.R.B. formally and that the I.R.B. played no role in the formation of the Fianna, who were and remained independent until 1913.[28] The 'countess', wife of a Polish count, was born Constance Gore-Booth into a life of privilege. Since about 1908 she had also involved herself in other nationalistic bodies, Sinn Féin and Inghinidhe na hÉireann. She had been present at a function of the Wolfe Tone Memorial Committee in 1910, a dance in aid of funds, on that occasion awarding 'the prize for the neatest and prettiest frock of Irish material'.[29] Though she was to be an *habituée* at Bodenstown, she was not present there with the Fianna in 1911, instead absenting herself, indignant at being deprived by Allan of an opportunity to demonstrate in Dublin.[30] Only a few days before the event she had been involved there in a fracas.[31] In 1912 a Fianna circle of the I.R.B. was formed by Hobson (by then its Dublin 'centre'); just before Fianna Éireann's annual conference in July 1913 a small group of Fianna officers who were I.R.B. members gained control of the Fianna Éireann organisation; one in this group, probably, was Liam Mellows, who throughout that year served as Fianna's travelling organiser, turning that youth body into a regular source of recruits for the I.R.B. Countess Markievicz remained its figurehead until her death in 1927.[32] Many

25 On Bulmer Hobson (1883–1969), see Patrick Maume's long article in *D.I.B.* and Marnie Hay, *Bulmer Hobson and the nationalist movement in twentieth-century Ireland* (Manchester, 2009). **26** Nat. Arch., Kew, CO 904/13, ff 186, 210. For John or Jack O'Hanlon, see esp. *Ir. Daily Indep.*, 22 June 1903, *Ir. Indep.*, 17 Oct. 1905, 16 Nov. 1908, 18 Nov. 1918; *Freeman's Jn.*, 31 Mar. 1908, 8 Nov. 1909; McGee, *I.R.B.*, esp. pp 255, 349–53. **27** For the Fianna Éireann, see J. A. Gaughan, *Scouting in Ireland* (Dublin, 2006), pt II; Marnie Hay, 'The foundation and development of Na Fianna Éireann, 1909–16' in *Irish Historical Studies*, xxxvi, no. 141 (May 2008), pp 53–71 esp. at pp 67–8; idem, 'Moulding the future: na Fianna Éireann and its members, 1909–1923' in *Studies*, c, no. 400 (winter 2011), pp 441–54. **28** Le Roux, *Clarke*, pp 102–3; Hay, 'Fianna Éireann', pp 55–7, 62. **29** *Ir. Indep.*, 25 Apr. 1910. **30** Hay, *Hobson*, pp 100–1. **31** For Constance Markievicz, see the article by Senia Pašeta in *D.I.B.* For the fracas, see *Ir. Indep.*, 5, 6 July 1911. Her surname was sometimes spelt 'Markiewicz'. **32** Le Roux, *Clarke*, pp 103, 149; Hay, 'Fianna

years later John Kenny recounted how, as a member of an offshoot of this group, he marched with fellow members from Blackhall Place in Dublin to Bodenstown churchyard. 'We marched openly through the streets of Dublin in uniform', he recollected, 'with dummy rifles to which were affixed French bayonets carried at the "slope" in true military fashion and dragging a hand-truck behind us in which our tent and other supplies were stored'.[33] The custom, which began in 1911, of Fianna units going on foot on Saturday evenings and pitching camp somewhere in Bodenstown on Saturday night continued until 1915.[34] It was to be resumed in 1917 or 1918. Fianna boys, orderly in their uniforms, energetic and hardy in their activities, readily joined, as they got older, the Irish Volunteers who, as will be shown, stole the scene at Bodenstown in 1914 and 1915.

The second pilgrimage of the new series took place on 23 June 1912.[35] Preparation had begun well in advance, as evidenced by the provision in instalments during preceding months of 1,607 dollars (or pounds?) for the 'Wolfe Tone excursion' by Joseph McGarrity, an Irishman prospering in the liquor trade in Philadelphia, where he was a pillar of Clan na Gael.[36] The procession that formed outside Sallins railway station was headed by the St Laurence O'Toole Pipers' Band, then came again the National Boy Scouts, or Fianna Éireann, some Irish National Foresters and other bodies. Amongst those near the grave were John MacBride, Countess Markievicz and Seumas O'Kelly, editor of the *Leinster Leader*. Clarke presided. The orators were Cathal Brugha (who spoke in Irish) and Bulmer Hobson (who had spoken the previous year). Brugha (also present in 1911) had co-founded a firm of candlemakers and was in the I.R.B.[37] It was at Bodenstown 'in the summer of 1912, on Wolfe Tone's grave', that a member of the Fianna, Éamon Bulfin, was sworn a member of the I.R.B. by Art O'Connor (who was to give an oration there in 1927).[38] After the speeches another *aeraíocht* was held in the field opposite, as there was to be in 1913 and 1918.

PATRICK PEARSE'S SPEECH

On 22 June 1913, Patrick Pearse made a speech at Bodenstown by which both he and the place are remembered. He had been put forward in I.R.B. circles as commendable, despite his lack of I.R.B. membership, by Clarke, who had known him since February 1911 for his nationalist sentiment and reputation as a speaker.[39] At that time, though qualified as a barrister, he was publicly known as the proprietor

Éireann', pp 60, 62, 64.   33 John Kenny, 6 Nov. 1957 (B.M.H., W.S. 1693, pp 1–2). He gives the impression it was in 1912, but it could have been later. Kenny was probably the old member, 'Jack K.', who wrote to a Dublin paper in 1966 recalling young marchers in 1913 'carrying dummy rifles at the slope' (*Evening Herald*, 21 Apr. 1966).   34 Séamus Kavanagh, 9 Sept. 1957 (W.S. 1670, p. 21.   35 The best report is in *Freeman's Jn.*, 24 June 1912.   36 N.L.I., McGarrity papers, MS 17,641.   37 James Quinn, 'Brugha, Cathal (1874–1922)' in *D.I.B.*   38 Éamonn Bulfin, 29 Mar. 1951 (B.M.H., W.S. 497, p. 1).   39 Le Roux, Clarke, pp 94, 120–22. Pearse (1879–1916) is much studied, e.g. by J. J. Lee in *D.I.B.*

of an experimental school for boys, St Enda's, noted for its progressive and nationalistic ethos. Later he was to achieve cult status comparable with Tone's. Pearse was introduced by Clarke. The *Freeman* summarised the speech for the general public. 'Wolfe Tone', asserted Pearse,

> was the greatest of Ireland's dead, and because he was the greatest of Irish Nationalists, they stood in the holiest place in Ireland, for what place could be holier than where the greatest of a nation's dead lay buried? In a sense they were all brothers of Tone, sharing his faith and his hopes, still unrealised, and they had come there not merely to pay their homage to the spirit of Wolfe Tone but to renew their cohesion to his faith.[40]

The *Leinster Leader* published the speech at great length, about one thousand words.[41] It was however an abridged version. Probably the *Leinster Leader* had a complete copy and reduced the number of words to fit it into the space available. The newspaper's editor from about 1912, until his arrest in April 1916, was Seumas O'Kelly's elder brother Michael (1873–1955), who at some time was a member of the I.R.B.[42] What must be regarded as the definitive version appeared in the I.R.B. paper, *Irish Freedom*, over a month later,[43] and was included in *Collected works of Pádraic H. Pearse: political writings and speeches*, published six years after his death.[44] It extends to nearly two thousand words and is repetitive, which suggests that it may not have been delivered in its entirety. It is possible that Pearse, like many a wordsmith, took the opportunity to revise his speech for publication. For want of a verifiable record of the exact words he spoke at Bodenstown, the version that appeared in *Irish Freedom* is relied upon here for discussion.

The speech is a true oration, delivered with great passion. 'We have come', Pearse began, 'to the holiest place in Ireland — holier to us even than the sacred spot where Patrick sleeps in Down. Patrick brought us life, but this man died for us. And though many before him, and some since him, have died in testimony of the truth of Ireland's claim to nationhood.' It pulsates with Catholic religious vocabulary and imagery: 'sacred'; 'this man died for us'; 'sharing in his faith'; 'we have come to renew our adhesion to the faith of Tone'; 'the gospel of Irish nationalism'; 'to come into communion with it is to come unto a new baptism, unto a new regeneration'; 'the evil thing against which he testified with his blood'. Even if Pearse lacked the brilliant eloquence of Sheil, he was no mean speaker: one contemporary remembered him as 'the most inspiring orator I have ever heard'.[45] Yet his famous Bodenstown speech has been dismissed by one of his biographers as

40 *Freeman's Jn.*, 23 June 1913. 41 *Leinster Leader*, 28 June 1913. 42 Michael O'Kelly, 9 May 1955 (B.M.H., W.S. 1155); James Durney, 'The brothers O'Kelly, writers, poets, editors and nationalists' (http://www.jamesdurney.com/the-brothers-okelly, accessed 7 Jan. 2016). 43 *Irish Freedom*, Aug. 1913. 44 The earliest posthumous publication of Pearse's *political* writings was by Maunsell & Roberts (Dublin, 1922, 372 pp, 10s.). This edition is knowledgeably reviewed by 'T. O'H.' in *Ir. Indep.*, 17 Apr. 1922. 45 Sydney Gifford Czira, alias John Brennan, *The years*

'no masterpiece',[46] and strangely ignored by two others.[47] This aspect of the speech, his mixing, his confounding, his religion and his politics, was, over fifty years later, discussed critically by a Jesuit priest, Francis Shaw.[48] It has been analysed too by another biographer, Sean Farrell Moran, who writes of 'Pearse's obsession with death' and his belief that 'in sacrificing himself for Irish freedom, the individual participated in a spiritual war that guaranteed him immortality'.[49] Pearse's purpose was to strengthen the ardour of his listeners — almost every one of them a practising Catholic — and to exhort them to self-sacrifice in pursuit of their political objective, which he defined vaguely as 'Irish freedom'.[50] After expressing regard for Tone at great length and in adulatory terms ('the greatest of Irish men'), Pearse, evidently versed in the *Life of Tone* or an abridged version, traces Tone's career: his 'boyhood and his young manhood in Dublin and Kildare', his political involvement, 'how he put virility into the Catholic movement, how this heretic toiled to make freemen of Catholic helots', his triple-concept that 'in Ireland there must not be two nations or three nations, but one nation — that Protestant and Dissenter must be brought into amity with Catholics, and that Catholic, Protestant and Dissenter must unite to achieve freedom for all', his exile to America, his presence on board French and Dutch fleets in attempts to invade Ireland. There are two significant omissions in Pearse's narrative. One is Tone's two-and-a-half-year residence in France during most of which he was an officer in the army of the French Republic. A possible explanation is that, in 1913, France was an ally of Great Britain and had a government that was strongly anti-Catholic. The other omission is the cause of Tone's death — Pearse depicts him as being 'dragged to Dublin and condemned to a traitor's death, then the last scene in Newgate and Tone lies dead'. The general belief among Catholics was that Tone died not by suicide but by the hand of government agents. This belief was expressed by successive Bodenstown orators: John Daly in 1880, George Lynch in 1894, Charles Doran in 1897 and P. T. Daly in 1902.[51] A possible explanation for Pearse avoiding the matter is that he was appealing for self-sacrifice in pursuit of Irish freedom; to have depicted Tone as taking his own life in this pursuit would have embarrassed his Catholic audience; to have depicted Tone as the victim of a murderer would have lessened his appeal for self-sacrifice.

The commemoration of 1913 was filmed by a newsreel cameraman and film exhibitor, James T. Jameson, whose footage was then shown thrice-nightly in Dublin at the Rathmines and Rotunda cinemas.[52] This too had been engineered by Thomas Clarke, this time under the auspices of the Wolfe Tone Memorial Committee, Clarke

flew by: recollections (Dublin, 1974), p. 18.   **46** Ruth Dudley Edwards, *Patrick Pearse: the triumph of failure* (New York, 1978), p. 174.   **47** Brian Murphy, *Patrick Pearse and the lost republican ideal* (Dublin, 1991); Joost Augusteijn, *Patrick Pearse: the making of a revolutionary* (Basingstoke, Hants, 2010). Murphy holds that 'the story of Pearse the revolutionary' begins with his joining the I.R.B. in December 1913 (ibid., p. 40). The Bodenstown speech suggests it began earlier.   **48** Francis Shaw, 'The canon of Irish history: a challenge' in *Studies*, lxi, no. 242 (summer 1972), pp 113–52.   **49** Sean Farrell Moran, *Patrick Pearse and the politics of redemption* (Washington, 1994), pp 139–40.   **50** *Irish Freedom*, Aug. 1913.   **51** *Freeman's Jn.*, 23 Aug. 1880, 25 June 1894, 21 June 1897, 23 June 1902.   **52** Kevin Rockett, Luke Gibbons and John Hill, *Cinema and Ireland* (London,

even persuading Jameson to give the committee a 'benefit' on 4 March.[53] An advertisement headed 'Pilgrimage to Wolfe Tone's grave at Bodenstown' promoting the film appeared in Dublin newspapers. Seats were at 3*d.*, 6*d.*, 9*d.*, 1*s.* and (with a reservation) 1*s.* 6*d.*[54] Clarke was impressed at the reception of the Bodenstown film at the Rotunda — the Dublin maternity hospital opened in the 1740s and which had a function room. 'No pictures he has ever shown...', Clarke wrote to John Devoy in America, 'ever received such tremendous applause. The old Round Room appeared to shake ... He is to show them next week in Galway, then Tralee, afterwards Queenstown, then Cork, then the Curragh, then back to Rathmines and the Rotunda.'[55] Clarke told John Daly that 'Jameson the picture show man was very reluctant to touch the pilgrimage — didn't think it would be so very popular. I went up and had a talk with him. The argument that carried weight with him was that I would be able to get an advertisement about the film in *Irish Freedom*, *Sinn Féin* and the *Gaelic American*.'[56] Seán MacDermott also watched the film at the Rotunda, significantly in the afternoon; he wrote on 1 July, also to Daly, that it 'got a great reception, although it was a time when the audience was almost exclusively respectable'.[57] Evidently, 'advanced' nationalism was taking the interest of people in higher social classes. And as Clarke noted in writing to Daly, Jameson had 'picture show places in a number of towns in Ireland'. Clarke's main regard for the film, or so he told Daly, was as a means of 'getting the memorial project well to the front at last' and 'before the minds of the younger element'.[58] It is more likely that 'memorial project' was a code for a much more ambitious project and that the 'younger element' were to be seduced into joining it.

The Bodenstown of this period was immortalised in drama as well as in cinema. In Sean O'Casey's *The plough and the stars* (1926), in act II, set in Dublin in November 1915, Peter Flynn, a labourer, boasts, 'there's not many that's talkin' can say that for twenty-five years he never missed a pilgrimage to Bodenstown'. When chided for his boasting and reminded that he is not the only one, he insists: 'I'm not blowin' about it; but there's not a year that I go there but I pluck a leaf off Tone's grave'. Did O'Casey know of the request Matilda Tone made of John Gray in 1843 and of Gray's sending her a shamrock plucked from Tone's grave? O'Casey went on a pilgrimage to Bodenstown on at least one occasion with the St Laurence O'Toole Pipers' Band, of which he was secretary from 1910 until, probably, 1914; he was secretary too of the Wolfe Tone Memorial Committee in 1913; he claimed twenty-four years later that he was the person who had 'first put the I.R.B. marching to Bodenstown on the cinema'.[59]

1987), p. 33.   **53** Clarke to John Daly, 5 Jan. 1913 (Le Roux, *Clarke*, p. 127).   **54** *Devoy's post-bag*, ed. William O'Brien and Desmond Ryan, ii (Dublin, 1948), p. 412.   **55** Clarke to Devoy, 25 June 1913, pr. in *Devoy's post-bag*, ii, 410–11. The Round Room was the function room. **56** Clarke to Daly, 18 June 1913, pr. in MacAtasney, *Clarke*, p. 264.   **57** MacDermott to Daly, 1 July 1913, Daly papers, Univ. of Limerick, cited in MacAtasney, *MacDiarmada*, pp 80, 195. **58** MacAtasney, *Clarke*, p. 264.   **59** Martin B. Margulies, *The early life of Sean O'Casey* (Dublin, 1970), pp 50–1, 61, 62; *The letters of Sean O'Casey, 1910–41*, ed. David Krause (London, 1975),

THE IRISH VOLUNTEERS

Pearse's speech was a fine prologue for two speeches that were more rousing, more militant, albeit very short, delivered by his patron, Thomas Clarke, at the Bodenstown pilgrimages in 1914 and 1915, the two preceding the 'Easter rising'. These took on a quasi-military character. During the second half of 1913 a politico-paramilitary movement, known as the Irish Volunteers,[60] had been created, in the spirit of the time, ostensibly at least to support the British government in its attempt to secure the passage of a third home-rule bill through a hostile House of Lords in the face of stubborn opposition from the Unionist party in Great Britain as well as Unionists in Ireland. In the north of Ireland a large number of unionists had already formed themselves into the Ulster Volunteers to resist home rule, thereby providing justification and a model for a similar body being formed by their opponents. The Irish Volunteers of 1913 might also have found warrant in the precedent of the Volunteers of the 1780s and 1790s. The Volunteer corps revived or formed in Ulster in the early 1790s were especially praised by Tone as progenitors and paragons of democracy; the Belfast regiment of National Volunteers admitted him as an honorary member on 10 June 1792 and he took part in its review on 14 July to commemorate the fall of the Bastille three years previously.[61]

Women whose nationalism and militancy were similar to the Irish Volunteers' joined an auxiliary organisation, Cumann na mBan ('Association of Women'). It came into existence in April 1914 and soon incorporated the Inghinidhe na hÉireann.[62] Its members were to prove the most faithful of pilgrims in the years that followed.

For the 'great pilgrimage' planned for June 1914 Clarke sought, in April, a loan from Clan na Gael in America 'to put the finishing touch upon the completeness of our arrangements'. He also sought (unsuccessfully, as it proved) the presence in Ireland, with Bodenstown in mind, of Ricard O'Sullivan Burke, famous for his connexion with the 'Manchester martyrs' and regarded in Clan na Gael circles in America as a fine orator. Clarke had got to know him there when both were members of Clan na Gael's military wing (also called 'the Irish Volunteers').[63] Another choice was Professor John MacNeill, head of the Irish Volunteers, formed the previous December. The increased presence of men and women of the middle class at Tone's grave in 1913, evident in Jameson's film and from its cinema success, must have enhanced its respectability. But MacNeill's invitation to speak, from the Wolfe Tone Memorial Committee ('all I.R.B. men'), was withdrawn after Clarke censured him

pp 29, 79, 163.   **60** 'Irish Volunteers' was the term used by Clarke, Pearse and Hobson in the early months of the existence of this body (*Devoy's post bag*, ii, 439–40, 444–5, 456–7). In press reports of the 1914 pilgrimage 'National Volunteers' appears.   **61** *Writings*, esp. i, 146, 159, 203–4, 207–8, 215–19, ii, 57, 329–30, iii, 439.   **62** Margaret Ward, *Unmanageable revolutionaries: women and Irish nationalism* (London, 1983), pp 88–93. See also Cal McCarthy, *Cumann na mBan and the Irish revolution* (revd ed., Cork, 2014).   **63** Le Roux, *Clarke*, pp 68–9, 138–9; Clarke to John Daly, 29 Apr. 1914, pr. in MacAtasney, *Clarke*, p. 274. For Burke, see James Quinn, 'Burke, Richard

for admitting nominees of John Redmond to the provisional committee of the Volunteers.[64] Now Redmond, leader of the Parnellite faction of Irish home-rulers in the House of Commons in the 1890s and by 1914 leader of the reunited home-rule party, was still regarded with gratitude by Clarke for his 'kindness' in paying him 'many a visit in prison'; he had also, after Clarke's release, supported him in applications for employment.[65] His party's strategy of relying on parliamentary pressure to bring about Irish independence was however contrary to that of the I.R.B., more so his latest strategy, connecting his party to the Volunteers, a connexion to which MacNeill with the majority of the Volunteer committee agreed on 16 June. Clarke's determination to make the pilgrimage a great success was no doubt strengthened by the possibility of armed resistance by the Ulster Volunteers to the imposition of home rule on Ulster. Some British army officers stationed at the Curragh declared in March that they would rather resign or be dismissed than enforce home rule on a hostile province, and towards the end of April the Ulster Volunteers acquired a large quantity of arms and ammunition from Germany. These were matters of concern in the three southern provinces, where Irish Volunteer units were proliferating.[66]

The demonstration at Bodenstown, on 21 June, was the largest and most impressive since 1898. It drew a crowd of 'many thousands', composed partly of contingents of Irish Volunteers and of allied bodies (some from as far away as Limerick, Galway and Belfast) who marched in military formation along the traditional route from Sallins to Bodenstown. In the detailed report in the *Freeman's Journal* eleven sections are listed.[67] At the head was 'a beautiful tricolour flag' (an early display of the green, white and orange flag of the future Irish Free State?); the second section was the O'Toole Pipers' Band; third was a youth body, 200 strong, the National Boy Scouts or Fianna Éireann, headed by Countess Markievicz; next were five companies of Irish Volunteers, their respective commanders named; after them were 'women and girls, 200 strong' (evidently Cumann na mBan, and perhaps also embryonic Clann na Gaedheal or Girl Scouts),[68] their leader unnamed; next, also 200 strong, the Irish Citizen Army (a workers' defence body formed during the Dublin 'lock-out' in 1913), among them their commander, the secretary of the Irish Transport Union, James Larkin. Present too were members of the provisional committee of the Volunteers, among them Pearse, MacDermott, Éamonn Ceannt, Con Colbert and Michael O'Rahilly.

Was this the earliest display of the Irish tricolour in a parade to Bodenstown? On reaching the graveyard the contingents, committee members and general public assembled in the field nearby. Clarke once more presided. Cables from Devoy and

O'Sullivan' in *D.I.B.*   **64** Kathleen Clarke, *Revolutionary woman*, ed. Helen Litton (Dublin, 1991), p. 46.   **65** Thomas J. Clarke, *Glimpses of an Irish felon's prison life*; intro. P. S. O'Hegarty (Dublin, 1922), p. 13; Le Roux, *Clarke*, pp 57, 59.   **66** People in Dublin could read of these events in *Sunday Independent*, 22 Mar., 26 Apr. 1914.   **67** *Freeman's Jn.*, 22 June 1914.   **68** Info. given on 3 Feb. 1949 by Molly Reynolds, who recalled being present among Cumann na mBan (B.M.H., W.S. 195, p. 2). The Clann na Gaedheal were first reported in 1917 but with their name spelt

Burke offering best wishes were read out by MacDermott; Devoy's political message — to be echoed by orators in years to come — was 'voice from that grave forbids partition'; Burke's was conciliatory, being addressed to 'National and Ulster Volunteers' with 'hopes for union of both' and the injunction 'Guard Ireland one and indivisible'.[69] The main oration, which seems to have been rather banal, was delivered (in the absence of Burke and MacNeill) by W. J. Ryan of Dublin. Ryan remains oddly obscure, despite his distinction of being the orator at Bodenstown in 1898, the centenary of the United Irish rebellion. By 1914 he was on the staff of the *Irish Independent*; he was known to Pearse as early as 1905, was remembered by Seán Fitzgibbon as a 'close friend' of Clarke and was proposed by Clarke as a house-guest of Daly at Limerick in 1913; he was officially regarded as a 'suspect' when in Britain in 1911, he was on the steering committee of the Irish Volunteers in November 1913 and less than a year later was suggested as 'chief editor' of a possible I.R.B.-sponsored daily newspaper; thereafter however Ryan was seemingly inactive in politics until his death in 1926.[70] It was decided that Clarke should make a speech himself, 'a thing he disliked', his wife Kathleen recalled, 'for he said he was no orator'.[71] It was the address given by Clarke that was significant. He observed, with *arrière pensée*, that 'the tramp of marching men, eager to grasp the rifle, was evidence that the spirit of Tone was abroad today. The drilling and arming of the Irish people was what was going to be the determining factor as to how much of their old ambitions would be fulfilled.'[72]

The circumstances and the importance of the Irish Citizen Army's participation in 1914 were recounted five years later by Sean O'Casey.[73] The Citizen Army was formed in November 1913 during a prolonged and violent 'lock-out' of 20,000 members or supporters of the militant Irish Transport Union. Its purpose was self-defence, its ideology the desirability of armies being composed of citizens serving part-time and led by progressive officers.[74] The commander of the 'army' in June 1914, James Larkin, expressed a desire to visit Tone's grave; the Citizen Army's council agreed to participate in the 1914 pilgrimage; the secretary duly 'visited the Wolfe Tone Committee to procure tickets'. At first the response was limited, as O'Casey recalled, for some of the committee 'doubted the wisdom of encouraging the Citizen Army to participate because of the differences between them and the Volunteers'. It must be stressed that the proletarian surge in 1913 had not universal approval amongst the sort of men who belonged to the I.R.B.; it was regarded by

Clan-na-Gael (*Ir. Times*, 26 June 1917); they are not to be confused with the Irish-American body of the same name.   **69** Le Roux, *Clarke*, p. 139.   **70** Sean Fitzgibbon, 20 June 1947 (B.M.H., W.S. 30, p. 4); Clarke to John Daly, 10 Oct. 1913, 20 Oct. 1914, pr. in MacAtasney, *Clarke*, pp 269, 281; Nat. Arch., Kew, CO 904/13, ff 137, 146, 223 (1911); see also above, chap. 4.   **71** Clarke, *Revolutionary woman*, ed. Litton, p. 46.   **72** *Freeman's Jn.*, 22 June 1914. The speech was reported in detail in *Irish Freedom*, July 1914, from which a long extract is reproduced in MacAtasney, *Clarke*, pp 78–9.   **73** Sean O'Casey, *The story of the Irish Citizen Army* (Dublin, 1919), pp 32–5. **74** For the Irish Citizen Army, see esp. D. R. O'C. Lysaght, 'The Irish Citizen Army, 1913–16: White, Larkin and Connolly' in *History Ireland*, xiv, no. 2 (Mar.–Apr, 2006), pp 16–21; Ann Matthews, *The Irish Citizen Army* (Cork, 2014).

some as conflicting with their economic interests or as an unnecessary distraction from the long-established Fenian objective of Irish independence. But Clarke 'warmly welcomed' the approach. When the day came, the 1st and 2nd companies of the Irish Citizen Army marched to Kingsbridge railway station to be met by Larkin, his son 'Seumas' (better known as James or Jim Larkin junior) and an unnamed 'orderly' appointed by Clarke to show them to their designated carriages. At Bodenstown the quasi-military units joined in the march-past in the field adjacent. 'It was', O'Casey concluded, 'a journey never to be forgotten, for it heralded the possibility of a closer unity and a fuller understanding between the Irish Citizen Army and the National Volunteers. It was the first time they had stood side by side, the first time they had received and taken orders from a common commander.' The full significance of this was to be seen two years later in the insurrection in Dublin of units of the Volunteers and the Irish Citizen Army. The elder Larkin left Ireland four months after his appearance at Bodenstown; he did not return until 1923.[75] It may have been in 1914 that Captain 'Jack' White, who was an admirer of Tone and who was prominent in the formation of the Citizen Army during the lock-out, led its contingent to Bodenstown; he recalled the occasion to some fellow pilgrims when on a return visit in the early 1930s.[76] It seems possible that, if the year was 1914, he marched with Larkin, as he resigned as commander of the Irish Citizen Army at the end of April to be succeeded by Larkin.[77]

On 20 June 1915, ten months into the First World War, the scene at Bodenstown was again spectacular. Again the O'Toole Pipers headed the procession;[78] at intervals came other bands including the Citizen Army Pipers and the Fianna Pipers; the contingent of Irish Volunteers, 450 strong, came next, marching in military formation; later came the Citizen Army (200), Cumann na mBan (several branches). the 'Boy Scouts of the Citizen Army' (50 strong) and the 'Hibernian Rifles Branch, Irish American Alliance' (about 80 marchers).[79] About 70 Volunteers or Citizen Army men leaving Dublin for Bodenstown by train were observed by the Dublin Metropolitan Police to be carrying rifles; 22 'extremists' were named as travelling, or at least 'taking an active part in the arrangements', among them Connolly, Pearse, Ceannt, Edward Daly and Michael O'Rahilly, Hobson and Countess Markievicz.[80] The women of Cumann na mBan had received 'foot drill' as part of their training.[81] The Hibernian Rifles were a small paramilitary group formed in Dublin in 1912 or 1913 by John Joseph Scollon and connected with the Irish counterpart of the Irish

75 For James Larkin senior, see Emmet O'Connor, 'Larkin, James (1874–1947)' in *D.I.B.*, and for James Larkin junior, Diarmaid Ferriter, 'Larkin, James (1904–69)' in ibid.   76 Unseann MacEoin, *The I.R.A. in the twilight years, 1923–1948* ([Dublin, 1997]), p. 521; Fearghal McGarry, 'White, James Robert "Jack" (1879–1946)' in *D.I.B.* He expresses admiration for Tone in his autobiography, *Misfit* (London, 1930), pp 181–2, 243.   77 *Evening Telegraph*, 4 May 1914, cited in Matthews, *Irish Citizen Army*, pp 38, 227.   78 There is a photo of the pipers, before or after the parade, in James Wren, 'Barney Murphy and the Abbey Theatre 1916 plaque' in *Dublin Historical Record*, li, no. 1 (spring 1998), pp 81–3.   79 *Freeman's Jn.*, 21 June 1915.   80 Nat. Arch., Dublin, CSO/JD/2/16. This D.M.P. report, endorsed by senior officials at Dublin Castle, states that altogether about 1,500 travelled by train from Dublin.   81 McCarthy, *Cumann na*

American Alliance wing of the Ancient Order of Hibernians.[82] The reporter of the *Leinster Leader* reckoned the attendance to be 'at least 9,000'.[83] One of those present, no doubt one of the Citizen Army contingent, was James Connolly; one member of the Socialist Party of Ireland and of the Dublin Brigade, Thomas Pugh, recalled of him, 'we sat on the grass there and ate our lunch together. We had a long conversation.'[84] Clarke, now described as 'president of the Wolfe Tone Committee', told the assembled Volunteers at Tone's grave 'that they were determined, if needs be, to go to the bitter end to realise Tone's ambition and the ambition of the Irish race for the last 700 or 800 years. His instructions from the Wolfe Tone Committee were that there was to be no oratory at Wolfe Tone's grave now, the time for oratory and resolution had gone by.' This was all the *Irish Independent* (full of war news) reported of Clarke's speech.[85] The *Freeman's Journal* stated only that he 'delivered a short address'.[86] The *Irish Times* ignored Bodenstown, just as it had done since 1876. The *Leinster Leader*, in contrast, was far from uninterested; its editor in 1915 was Michael O'Kelly, an I.R.B. man whose house at Naas was four months later the place used for the purpose of forming an organising committee of Volunteers for north Kildare.[87] It reported a quite long and very bellicose speech by Clarke, a few extracts from which better illustrate his mood and intentions. It began, 'Irishmen, Irishwomen, and Irish boys and girls. The world is at war. Where do we in Ireland stand now, today?' After referring to his 'instructions' that 'the time for words is past' he enunciated his vision to the gathered militants:

> The rifle is talking the world over today and it is going to talk in Ireland too … The men have the Irish Volunteers and the ladies have the Cumann na mBan who have done and who are doing a good work for Ireland. The boys have the Fianna and it delights the heart of an old man to see them all coming in such numbers to work for Ireland, The issue is knit. The time for oratory is gone (hear, hear). It is now action and action alone (hear, hear). That and that only is going to determine how far Ireland's ambitions are going to be satisfied … there is to be no more oratory – the time for action is here, and it is for each and everyone here to be up and doing.[88]

Clarke's reference to 'the Wolfe Tone Committee' — the Wolfe Tone Memorial Committee — was disingenuous. This body organised Bodenstown pilgrimages from 1899 until 1905, but from then on its ostensible function was to raise money for the erection of a monument to Tone in Dublin whilst in reality it was increasingly a front for the I.R.B. Not only Clarke but also several other members of that committee were members of the I.R.B. The import of his speech would not have

---

mBan, p. 46.   **82** John Joseph Scollon, 3 Nov. 1949 (B.M.H., W.S. 318, pp 1–2). It is remembered also in J. J. Walsh, *Recollections of a rebel* (Tralee, 1944), pp 35–7.   **83** *Leinster Leader*, 26 June 1915.   **84** Thomas Pugh, 19 June 1950 (B.M.H., W.S. 397, p. 22).   **85** *Ir. Indep.*, 21 June 1915.   **86** *Freeman's Jn.*, 21 June 1915.   **87** Michael Smith, 12 Nov. 1956 (B.M.H., W.S. 1531, p. 2); Michael O'Kelly, 9 May 1955 (B.M.H., W.S. 155, passim).   **88** *Leinster Leader*, 26 June 1915.

been lost on his hearers. Connolly was a case in point. He was impressed that Clarke 'was as full of fight and faith as ever' and 'we of the Citizen Army felt proud to be there'.[89] Clearly now to those in revolutionary circles, but not clearly to all Irish men and women when news of fighting on the European continent was the public preoccupation, Bodenstown had become the annual parade ground of the Irish Volunteers and allied corps where their I.R.B. leader could give his potentially fighting men and women the kind of pep-talk that would prepare them for action.

THE EASTER RISING

The insurrection that occurred in Dublin in Easter week of 1916 — officially, inaccurately, referred to at the time as the 'Sinn Féin rebellion', historically as the 'Easter rising' — was the work of the I.R.B. through its influence in the Irish Volunteers, the Irish Citizen Army, Cumann na mBan and Fianna Éireann. Clarke was at the head of the Dublin-based secret military council that organised and directed it. An 'Irish republic' was declared in a proclamation posted outside the General Post Office and elsewhere. Damage to buildings was caused in central Dublin and over five hundred lives were lost. Bodenstown was to have been the place of assembly for Kildare companies of the Irish Volunteers participating. On Wednesday, 19 April, some days before the planned outbreak, the military council's main agent in County Kildare, Thomas Byrne (1877?–1962), received instructions to mobilise all Kildare companies and order them to march to Bodenstown on the eve of the insurrection and assemble there, blow up a railway bridge and then march on Dublin to join the main body of insurgents.[90] The merits of Bodenstown as a place of assembly for local Kildare Volunteers in 1916 are obvious from any consideration of the pilgrimages there in preceding years. Suitable routes from villages round and about would have been well known to men of nationalist opinions, and the churchyard or adjacent fields used for assembly in June each year could be used again. Once again the proximity of the railway was an important factor. The reason for blowing up a railway bridge was to impede British army movements from the large camp at the Curragh. The likely target was the bridge over the canal at Sallins. Confusion arose owing to contradictory orders. Only one party of Volunteers reached Bodenstown on Easter Monday (24 April, the day the General Post Office was seized); it assembled in fact 'in a field at the back of the churchyard' and then proceeded to Maynooth. Michael O'Kelly, now a local Volunteer commander, arrived at the churchyard just before noon and found 'no

89 *Workers' Republic*, 26 June 1915, cited in Matthews, *Irish Citizen Army*, pp 59, 229.   **90** A good account of Bodenstown's part in the Easter rising is in James Durney, *Foremost and ready: Kildare and the 1916 rising* (Naas, 2015), pp 59–66. It relies mainly on accounts given to the Military History Bureau some forty years later by three Volunteers, Byrne himself (W.S. 564), Michael Smith (W.S. 1531) and Michael O'Kelly (W.S. 1155). See also Patrick Colgan (W.S. 850).

sign of anybody about'.[91] Other local commanders appeared on the same day only to be disappointed similarly. No order was received to proceed to Dublin.

The authorities were taken unawares. Between 1911 and 1915, in the monthly reports by the Kildare county inspector of the Royal Irish Constabulary, there was no recognition of the significance for the I.R.B. of the Bodenstown pilgrimages. Agrarian trouble was more concerning. Mention of the pilgrimage of July 1911 was interlined as if an afterthought: 300 attended from Dublin organised by 'Dublin Sinn Feiners'; 'locals took no interest'; the proceedings were 'rather flat'.[92] There is no mention at all in the report for June 1912.[93] Only a few words were considered sufficient for the well-publicised pilgrimage of June 1913 at which Pearse made his famous speech: 1,500 attended and the 'speeches were not violent'.[94] True, Pearse's speech was not overtly violent, but it was stirring and had bellicose undertones surely perceptible to many in his audience. In his report for June 1914 the county inspector mentioned 'numerous branches' of the Irish Volunteers being formed and drilling being 'regularly attended', he stated that the demonstration at Bodenstown was 'large', that 'speeches were made' and that 'some companies of the Volunteers marched but were very orderly'.[95] At Tone's grave in 1915, according to the same county inspector's report, 'the usual brothy addresses were made, but the meeting could not be described as pro-German; probably 1,500 people attended including the Dublin contingent'.[96] The chief secretary for Ireland, Augustine Birrell, away from Dublin Castle when the rebellion broke out and as much taken by surprise as most government officials, later told the royal commission of enquiry: 'I always thought that I was very ignorant of what was actually going on in the minds, and in the cellars if you like, of the Dublin population'.[97] Evidently he knew little of the Bodenstown pilgrimages and was not a regular reader of the *Leinster Leader*.

Of the seven signatories to the declaration of a republic, all of whom were executed after the suppression of the uprising, five (and perhaps six) are known to have gone on pilgrimages to Bodenstown before 1916: Clarke, MacDermott, Pearse, Ceannt, Connolly and (perhaps) Thomas MacDonagh. As well as these five (or six?), three other men known to have taken part in pilgrimages were executed for their parts in the insurrection: MacBride, who had addressed pilgrims in 1905 and 1911; Con Colbert, present in 1914 as one of the provisional committee of the Irish Volunteers; and Edward Daly, mentioned in the police report of pilgrims setting off by train in 1915. Daly was a nephew of John Daly and the only brother of Clarke's wife Kathleen. Another man, Michael Joseph O'Rahilly, known as 'the O'Rahilly', also present at Bodenstown as a Volunteer leader in 1914, was fatally injured during the fighting. Countess Markievicz (1912 and 1914) was sentenced to death but reprieved and lived to attend Bodenstown rallies again in 1917, 1920, 1922, 1926 and 1927. Significantly, six of the ten men named here as having forfeited their lives

91 Mentioned by O'Kelly but with little detail.   **92** Nat. Arch., Kew, CO 904/84, f. 469.
93 Ibid., CO 904/87, f. 268.   **94** Ibid., CO 904/90, f. 295.   **95** Ibid., CO 904/93, f. 599.
96 Ibid., CO 904/97, f. 304.   **97** Leon Ó Broin, *Protestant nationalists* (Dublin, 1985), p. 120.

in 1916 were present in 1914, the year that Bodenstown became a parade ground for the Volunteers. About the other four (Connolly, MacBride, Daly and MacDonagh) information is incomplete.[98]

The rising was to have lasting consequences for Irish politics and society. It had fatal (or near fatal) consequences for some of those who had been in Bodenstown churchyard. 'Nineteen-sixteen' quickly became a point of reference, and soon an inspirational foundation myth of a quickly growing republican movement resulting in an independent Ireland.

Close relations of the men who lost their lives were to be seen on later pilgrimages: Margaret Pearse, whose sons Patrick and William were both executed (each year from 1920 until 1927 except for 1924), later their elder sister, also Margaret (1923, each year from 1933 till 1939 and again in 1941 and 1946); the widows of Tom Clarke (1922, 1927, 1928, 1929, 1932, 1936 and 1942), of Éamonn Ceannt (1920 and 1922) and of James Connolly (1923); a son of the O'Rahilly (1932); the parents of Joseph Plunkett, another signatory executed in consequence (1922, 1932, 1934, 1935, 1938), one or the other separately (1925, 1928 and 1937) and his sister Fiona (surreptitiously in 1921, openly in 1935 and as late as 1967); a brother of Ceannt, David Rice Kent, was present in 1925; Connolly's son Roddy was present in 1967, 1971 and probably earlier. Clarke's widow, Kathleen, was a sister of Edward 'Ned' Daly, also executed. Another widow was Mrs MacBride, referred to romantically (because of her long residence in France) as Madame Gonne MacBride (1924, 1929, 1931, 1934, 1935, 1937 and 1938). She had first gone to Bodenstown in 1901. She married John MacBride in Paris in 1903, became legally separated in 1906 after a brief tempestuous marriage, remained in Paris until MacBride's execution in 1916, and one year later returned permanently to Ireland with their son Seán. Seán MacBride was to appear at Bodenstown in the 1930s and 1940s in his own right. These relations became a sort of 'republican nobility' gracing, after the nationalist split in 1922, the platforms of the anti-Treaty side.[99]

One of the most faithful pilgrims at Tone's grave in later years was sentenced to death for his part in the insurrection but was reprieved, which placed him on a slightly lower rank of the republican nobility. This was Éamon de Valera (1882–1975), who headed Irish governments for over twenty years (1932–48, 1951–4, 1957–9) and subsequently was president (1959–73). In June 1923 he sent a wreath; two years later he delivered a long oration at the Republican pilgrimage. De Valera subsequently went on a pilgrimage to Bodenstown on no fewer than 24 occasions between 1929 and 1958, missing only in 1932, 1941, 1943, 1952 and 1957; he spoke there again only twice, on 30 June 1929 and 22 June 1930; on all later occasions he laid a wreath on behalf of his party.

98 The names of those identified in this paragraph as participants in Bodenstown pilgrimages appear in contemporary newspaper reports, except for MacDonagh, recalled by Richard Mulcahy in 1923 as having been present in 1915 (*Freeman's Jn.*, 23 June 1923). Such is the nature of the evidence that the identifications are probably incomplete. 99 For a discussion of this phenomenon, see Caoimhe Nic Dháibhéid, 'Fighting their fathers' fights: the post-revolutionary

AFTER THE EASTER RISING

The history of the Bodenstown phenomenon after the Irish rebellion of 1916 and in independent Ireland is a cameo of much of the political history of Ireland in most of the twentieth century. Yet the phenomenon has received no treatment in print by historians other than in a few lines, or a few pages, in studies of wider subjects;[100] the only extensive treatment, by Kathleen Travers, remains unpublished.[101]

In June 1916, several weeks after the declaration of martial law and suppression of the Easter rising, there was only a small, almost unnoticed pilgrimage to Tone's grave. No report has been found in any of the Dublin morning papers, nor in the monthly return of the county inspector of the Royal Irish Constabulary. What did happen at Bodenstown in 1916, on 25 June, was reported sympathetically in one of the two local Naas weekly newspapers, the normally unsympathetic *Kildare Observer*, nearly two weeks after the event, under the heading 'Wolfe Tone anniversary':

> Never, perhaps, since the inauguration of the annual pilgrimage to Wolfe Tone's grave at Bodenstown was there such a mild display as on Sunday week. Indeed, but for the presence of a small crowd of people, mostly women and young girls and boys, with perhaps a dozen men, who travelled from Dublin by train, the event might have passed unnoticed even by a passer-by. Save for an occasional cyclist, who was attracted to the scene by the group of persons making the journey from Sallins to Bodenstown, there were few spectators. Of those who came from the metropolis many wore the Republican badge, but there was no demonstration, no panegyric, and no display such as we have been accustomed to for many years. Those who came to Tone's resting place knelt for a short time by the grave and recited a few prayers; a few women amongst the number wept; reproductions from photographs of many of the leaders in the recent rebellion were placed on the grave; tea was made by the pilgrims by the roadside, and having refreshed themselves they walked back to Sallins, where, before they entrained for Dublin, they drew up outside the station and sang 'God save Ireland', 'A nation once again' and 'Who fears to speak of '98?', with the very recent adaptation of the air and words to 'Who fears to speak of Easter week?'. Then they entered the station and awaited the train that carried them back to the city. Such was the 1916 celebration of the anniversary of Wolfe Tone.[102]

generation' in Senia Pašeta (ed.), *Uncertain futures: essays about the Irish past for Roy Foster* (Oxford, 2016), pp 148–60.   **100** Esp. Brian M. Walker, *Past and present: history, identity and politics in Ireland* (Belfast, 2000), chap. 2; Brian Hanley, *The I.R.A., 1926–1936* (Dublin, 2002), pp 50–52, 107–08; Peter Collins, *Who fears to speak of '98?: commemoration and the continuing impact of the United Irishmen* (Belfast, 2004), pp 54–7, 77.   **101** Kathleen Travers, 'The Tone of national commemorations: the annual Wolfe Tone commemorations at Bodenstown' (M.A., University College, Dublin, 2002).   **102** *Kildare Observer*, 8 July 1916.

It has to be considered that by the proclamation of martial law throughout Ireland on 29 April all political demonstrations had been prohibited.

In consequence of the rebellion, and particularly of its suppression and the authorities' treatment of participants, supporters and suspects, there occurred an unstoppable shift in the zeitgeist of Catholic Ireland. In the aftermath of the suppression of the insurrection, the Irish Volunteers were revivified and in later months reorganised. Sinn Féin, a movement begun by Arthur Griffith in 1904 to promote Irish self-reliance and separation from Great Britain, most particularly protection of Ireland's small industries from foreign competition and passive resistance to British rule and anglicisation, was in 1917 transformed into a modern political party of a decidedly republican tendency commensurately with the changing mood of the Catholic population.[103] Griffith's part in the revival of the Bodenstown pilgrimages in 1891, their success until 1905 and their second revival in 1911 has been mentioned above.

The Wolfe Tone Memorial Committee, a cover for the I.R.B. before May 1916, became a cover for its revival. George Lyons, a secretary of the committee in 1899 who had joined the I.R.B. the previous year, recalled that 'the I.R.B. borrowed a sum of money from the Wolfe Tone Fund', probably in 1913 or 1914, 'for the purchase of arms'.[104] Another I.R.B. man, Joseph O'Rourke, secretary from 1912 to 1917 of the 'circle' of the I.R.B. in Dublin, recalled that after the Easter rising 'the first sign of life in the organisation was a meeting of the Wolfe Tone Memorial Association. It was held in December 1916.' The committee held a fund from which money had been spent on munitions used during the rebellion.[105] Its stated aim of erecting a monunment in St Stephen's Green must have been considered by its members to be remote and unimportant. It did however continue to organise, or at least to sponsor, the annual pilgrimages to Bodenstown.

A sign of the changes was that the *Irish Times*, which since 1876 had ignored Bodenstown pilgrimages, reported under the headline 'Sinn Féin display' that of 24 June 1917. Evidently there was collaboration with the *Leinster Leader*, whose report was similar but longer. The graveyard, both reported, had been the destination of 'a big turn-out of the Sinn Féin organisations in Dublin, Kildare and many districts of the adjoining counties ... There was no organised demonstration or procession, but merely a spontaneous display.'[106] The *Irish Times*'s report appeared two days after the event, as did that of the *Irish Independent* (brief and mid-page). The *Kildare Observer* noted the presence of 'many thousands', among them a large contingent of 'Sinn Féin sympathisers', one of them, Countess Markievicz (recently released from prison), arriving by motor-car. There were references to 'the now familiar tricolour' and to 'wreaths and crosses beribboned with the Republican colours' being placed

103 Patrick Maume, *The long gestation: Irish nationalist life, 1891–1918* (Dublin, 1999), pp 48–59, 191, 193, 200–1.   **104** B.M.H., W.S. 104, p. 7. Lyons (whose deposition is undated) states 1914, but 1913 seems more likely. His position on the committee is stated in *Freeman's Jn.*, 16 June 1899. **105** Joseph O'Rourke, 16 Sept. 1955 (B.M.H., W.S. 1244, p. 15).   **106** *Ir. Times*, 26 June 1917; *Leinster Leader*, 30 June 1917.

on the grave.[107] The *Leinster Leader* reported that, as well as Sinn Féin people attending from Dublin and other places close to Bodenstown,

> people were also present from the more remote parts of the country. There was no organised demonstration or procession but merely a spontaneous display favoured by fine weather circumstances. Several contingents from the city however marched in orderly array, notably the Boy Scouts (the Fianna), Citizen Army and a corps of some hundreds of cyclists. A feature of the day, as a matter of fact, was the number of cyclists, although all kinds of other vehicles were employed conveying the crowds to the venue. Large numbers of young men and boys marched from the city, many of them during the night, while the ordinary 9.15 a.m. train was crowded. Cars, motors, cycles, pony traps etc. mostly carried Sinn Féin flags, while badges and miniatures of prominent leaders of the Sinn Féin movement were worn by nearly all. The profusion of flags and Sinn Féin colours and favours everywhere to be seen was remarkable. The grave in Bodenstown was decked with four or five beautiful flags while inside the railing surrounding the grave were placed many wreaths of varied and beautiful design from the Wolfe Tone Memorial Committee, Sinn Féin branches, the Clan na Gael [*sic*], Cumman na mBan and other National societies.

Countess Markievicz, the report continued, 'was received by a general doffing of hats by the men' and then made a short speech in which she alluded to 'dear friends' who were present with her at Tone's grave two years previously but were now 'in heaven', where they 'had gone to join Wolfe Tone and the great and glorious array of martyrs who had gone before them and given their lives for Ireland'. Cheers were given for 'an Irish republic' and for the countess.

In 1917, as in 1916, it was a Naas paper that was most informative. Several things stand out. One is the spontaneity of the pilgrimage. This is a confirmation of the easy accessibility of Bodenstown for ordinary people living in or near Dublin. Another is the presence, for the first time, of contingents of pilgrims from the Sinn Féin party, now revitalised, enlarged, republican and exuberant. Another is the ubiquity of the combination of green, white and orange as the colours of twentieth-century Irish nationalism. Striking, too, is that for the very first time a women addressed the crowd. Another novelty was the arrival of some pilgrims in motor-cars, the earliest such mention. Motor-car clubs had existed in Ireland for nearly twenty years, but motor-cars were within the means only of the rich and so their appearance at Bodenstown is an indication of a political as well as a social revolution.[108] Most significant is the invoking of the 'martyrs' of 1916 and placing them at Tone's right hand. Complementary to this invocation was the evoking of

---

107 *Kildare Observer*, 30 June 1917.   **108** Though she does not mention Bodenstown, see Miriam Daly, 'The return to the roads' (above, chap. 4, n. 156).

Tone's grave as the 'holiest place in Ireland', the appellation Pearse had given it in 1913. By inference its holiness was confirmed by the presence there, a few years before, of Pearse himself and other subsequent martyrs. These perceptions of Tone, his grave and the sacrifices of Pearse and other 1916 men were to be aired at many later pilgrimages.

The annual pilgrimage in 1918 took place a month after 150 men and women with republican tendencies were arrested under suspicion of being involved in an alleged 'German plot'. The *Freeman's Journal*, subjected like all newspapers to official censorship, reported 'contingents of men, women and young people to the number of between five and six thousand'. Of these, 2,000 travelled from Dublin, mostly, the weather being fine, on bicycles. 'Fifty members of the Fianna marched from the city to the graveyard, while a number of the Cumann na mBan from Dublin also reached the scene on foot. Though there was no regularly organised procession as in some other years, large bodies of men and women marched in formation to Bodenstown from centres ten miles away, carrying Sinn Féin flags, banners and other emblems.' Two brass bands played; the Rosary was recited in Irish, a Dublin pilgrim 'leading in the prayers, while the vast majority of the gathering on bended knees and with bared heads joined in the responses'. The Dublin papers made no mention of the Irish Volunteers, but Volunteers were present in strength again that year. One such man recalled 'almost the entire Dublin Brigade' being there, some or most of them cycling.[109] The *Leinster Leader*, partisan and exaggerating, put attendance at over 10,000, chiefly Volunteers and the two kindred bodies, and reported that several contingents marched from Dublin and camped overnight before joining the parade at Sallins.[110] A north of Ireland man, Cathal O'Shannon, delivered the oration partly in Irish and said, following Pearse five years before, that 'they stood on the holiest ground in Ireland' and repeated Clarke's advice in 1915 that 'the time for oratory had gone'.[111] O'Shannon (1890–1969), son of an engine driver on the Londonderry and Lough Swilly Railway, was employed for a while as a shipping clerk before becoming, in 1913, a full-time official of the Irish Transport and General Workers' Union in its Belfast office. As such he was the deputy of James Connolly. By June 1918, having shown talent as a contributor to the nationalist and socialist press, he was employed in Dublin on a labour newspaper, *Irish Opinion: the Voice of Labour*, which under his editorship showed his revolutionary leftist and pro-Bolshevic tendencies.[112] O'Shannon was, then, the first socialist to deliver an oration at Bodenstown.

By June 1919 the fighting on the Continent was over. Sinn Féin candidates elected to the British parliament in the general election of December 1918 were sitting not in London, but as 'deputies' in Dublin in an assembly with the name Dáil Éireann ('the Irish parliament', called for short 'the Dáil') in an attempt to revive

---

109 Michael Lynch, 24 Apr. 1951 (B.M.H., W.S. 511, p. 112); Jerry Golden, 30 May 1951 (B.M.H., W.S. 522, p. 7).   110 *Leinster Leader*, 29 June 1918.   111 *Freeman's Jn.*, 24 June 1918.
112 There is a detailed article on Cathal O'Shannon by L. W. White in *D.I.B.*

the republic declared in 1916. With increasing success, the Dáil, supported by the revived Volunteers, directed by the I.R.B., challenged royal officialdom for control of the country. This was the War of Irish Independence, or Anglo-Irish War, considered to have started on 21 January 1919, when Dáil Éireann assembled for the first time and Irish Volunteers ambushed a police vehicle in County Tipperary killing two policemen. There was a large turnout at Bodenstown on 22 June, over 5,000 according to the *Irish Independent*, very many from Dublin, others from Naas, Newbridge, elsewhere in Kildare and from places in adjoining counties; the 'tricolour flag was displayed generally, and Volunteers in uniform were on guard at the grave and entrance to the cemetery'; wreaths were laid by the Wolfe Tone Memorial Committee and other groups with I.R.B. or, probably, Sinn Féin connexions.[113] The *Leinster Leader* put the turnout at over 7,000 ('despite the inclemency of the weather') and enthused over 'Volunteers in uniform, Clann na Gaedheal Girl Scouts, Fianna Boy Scouts and members of Cumann na mBan in their picturesque costumes'.[114] The oration was given at the graveside by P. S. O'Hegarty. A son of a man who had been a member of the Fenian Brotherhood in America before returning to his native Cork, Patrick Sarsfield O'Hegarty (1879–1955) entered the civil service as a Post Office official in London and joined the I.R.B.; he had strong literary interests and within three years of delivering his oration was appointed to a senior post in the civil service of the infant Irish Free State. He was to be present at Bodenstown in his official capacity in 1929. Words he spoke on that day in 1919 were a neat summary of the changing situation: 'in previous years they assembled there a mere handful to keep alive the national principles in face of the majority of the people, who looked upon them as playboys; but now they came there in the name of the whole strength of the nation, and the principles for which Tone stood were justified before the world'.[115]

By June 1920, Ireland was eighteen months into a conflict that had become a guerilla war waged by the Irish Republican Army, better known by its initials, I.R.A., the paramilitary force into which the Irish Volunteers had metamorphosed. On the 21st, 'Bodenstown Sunday' (as reported in the *Freeman's Journal*), there was an impressively large number of pilgrims. They travelled from Dublin and environs 'by train, by cycle and motor'. The report continued:

> Five hundred Irish Volunteers left Parnell Square at eleven in the morning. Along the routes converging on the graveyard dust-stained Irish Volunteer companies and Fianna Éireann scouts tramped in a seemingly endless procession. In Sallins village, at Bodenstown cross roads, hundreds of cyclists rested beside their machines. Girl scouts in picturesque costumes bearing wreaths decked with tricolours and the Stars and Stripes passed the hedge-lined lanes.

113 *Ir. Indep.*, 23 June 1919.   114 *Leinster Leader*, 28 June 1919.   115 *Ir. Indep.*, 23 June 1919, 18 June 1929. For P. S. O'Hegarty, see Tom Garvin's article in *D.I.B.*; Frances Flanagan, *Remembering the revolution: dissent, culture and nationalism in the Irish Free State* (Oxford, 2015), chap. 3.

Margaret Pearse, the mother of Patrick and William Pearse, walked through the crowd as a sort of mascot. Prayers (in Irish) followed. At the end of the day pilgrims went 'back to the city in trains on the sardine-tin model, back on a thousand wheels and scores of motor cars'.[116] The report in the *Irish Times* was less romantic, but more perceptive and predictive of the developing political situation. The orator, Seán Ó Murthuile, an I.R.B. man and a member of the first Dáil Éireann, elected in December 1918,[117] said 'that the Irish people were not asked to establish a republic, because one was already established. They asked the people to maintain it, as there was now only one obstacle in their way — that was to say, they had to drive the British garrison out of Ireland, which could be done by unity and self-reliance.' The cyclists, most of whom wore raincoats rolled 'in bandolier fashion', returned to Dublin in 'military formation'.[118] The self-confidence of the pilgrims, no doubt supporters of, if not participants in, the guerilla campaign against the British military authorities, was manifest.

THE BANNED PILGRIMAGE IN 1921

In June 1921, the military authorities, just before the pilgrimage planned for the 19th, prohibited any 'assembly of persons' taking place at Bodenstown until further notice.[119] This prevented the customary parade and rally. It did not however prevent a raid by a group of women. Fifty years on, Máire Comerford, one of the women present, recalled names and events:

> Seán Ó Murthuile, top-ranking I.R.B. man and member of the Commemoration Committee, sent a note to Eilís Ní Riain, captain of Central Branch, Cumann na mBan: 'Eilis, the Big Fellow says you are to lay a wreath at Bodenstown on Sunday next. There will be a taxi at 41 Parnell Square at 10.30. There is seating accommodation for five people, and you can bring whom you wish — Seán.' Eilís brought her four section commanders. They were Fiona Plunkett, Emily Valentine, Margaret McElroy and myself. For a few hours we were the representatives of the nation. The taxi collected us at our headquarters, 25 Parnell Square, and we drove to No. 41. I saw the red face of Seán Ó Murthuile for a second when he opened a slit of the door to hand the wreath we were to lay to Eilís. The British were in occupation at Bodenstown alright. Some were in the graveyard and we passed through them without comment on either side. Eilís unlocked the gate and placed the wreath in position. Then we went back to Dublin. What force of troops was in ambush I do not know; but from the Republican aspect this was the smallest Bodenstown on record.[120]

116 *Freeman's Jn.*, 21 June 1920.   117 On Seán Ó Murthuile or Hurley (1881–1941), a travelling teacher of Irish, there is an article by Patrick Long in *D.I.B.*   118 *Ir. Times*, 21 June 1920. 119 *Freeman's Jn.*, 18 June 1921.   120 'Máire Comerford remembers' in *Ir. Press*, 11 Feb. 1971.

Eilís Ní Riain deposed a rather similar recollection in 1951. She recalled moreover that after laying a wreath they 'recited the Rosary in Irish' whilst 'enemy aeroplanes circled over our heads'.[121] The 'Big Fellow' mentioned was Michael Collins, another I.R.B. man and director of the I.R.A.'s operations against the British authorities.

Nor did the prohibition prevent a little-reported pilgrimage on 3 July at which wreaths were laid on the grave by members of the Wolfe Tone Memorial Committee and Cumann na mBan, and an address given by Mrs Margaret Pearse.[122] Probably the military authorities considered the women unthreatening, perhaps they knew that the war was almost over. Eight days later a truce was agreed. After five more months a formal agreement for independence was signed by the two sides — the Anglo-Irish treaty.

121 Eilís Ní Riain, 7 Aug. 1951 (B.M.H., W.S. 568, pp 59–60).   122 *Ir. Indep.*, 4 July 1921; photo (R.T.É. Archive, Cashman collection).

6

Rival pilgrimages, 1922–31

A CONSEQUENCE OF THE Anglo-Irish treaty, signed on 6 December 1921, was the phenomenon of rival pilgrimages to Bodenstown. The treaty divided Irish Catholic political opinion according to whether it was to be perceived as the achievement of the 'republic' declared by the insurgents in 1916 or as something insufferably less. Some, those who took office in the new 'Irish Free State' created in 1922, or who supported the new state as at least fulfilling their main expectations, were the Treatyites. Those who rejected the treaty on the ground that it was a betrayal of the republic already in existence since 1916 and reinforced by the first and second Dáils were the anti-Treatyites. The Dáils (more correctly Dáileanna) were the assemblies formed in Dublin by the Sinn Féin candidates elected to the British parliament in 1918 and the abortive parliament of the new 'Southern Ireland' in 1921. To the minds of the anti-Treatyites, the signing of the treaty was not merely betrayal of an ideal, an aspiration, it was the betrayal of a legitimate political and administrative entity validated by two general elections and backed by the Volunteers in 1914 — now the I.R.A. The quarrel started by the signing of the treaty was essentially about legitimacy, not about interests or policies to be pursued in an independent Ireland. It was to define Irish politics, and was to be the theme of successive orations at Bodenstown for the next fifteen years. It was to persist throughout the twentieth century, abating only gradually, and was still being vented at Bodenstown in the 1980s. Common to both parties, however, and consistent with their attitudes to the treaty, was a belief in both the legitimacy of the insurrection and the authority of the first and second Dáileanna.

THE ANTI-TREATYITES STEAL A MARCH

In the middle of June 1922 tension between the two parties was at a high. Negotiations to reunite the I.R.A. with the new 'national army' finally broke down on the 15th.[1] Pilgrimages to Bodenstown occurred a few days before the outbreak of violence between the parties — the Irish Civil War. The Wolfe Tone Memorial Committee had already fixed Sunday the 25th as the date of the annual pilgrimage.[2]

---

1 Maryann Gialanella Valiulis, *Portrait of a revolutionary: General Richard Mulcahy and the founding of the Irish Free State* (Dublin, 1992), pp 150–52. 2 *Freeman's Jn.*, 14 June 1922. This refers to the 'Wolfe Tone Memorial Association', but 'Association' must have been an error for

However, on the afternoon of the 20th (Tone's birthday), a Tuesday, under the direction of Oscar Traynor, commandant of the Dublin brigade of the I.R.A. based at the Four Courts,[3] some prominent anti-Treatyites, with 'practically all the units of the Dublin I.R.A.' and large units of the Irish Citizen Army (nearly all armed and deployed, younger Citizen Army men 'wearing the large slouch hats and dark green uniform'), stole a march on all others by going to Bodenstown and holding their own ceremony; among them were Traynor himself and three other I.R.A. commanders at the Four Courts 'garrison': Rory O'Connor, Liam Mellows and Harry Boland. This 'garrison' had been established at the Four Courts (the main judicial building in Dublin) on being commandeered, on 13 April, by units of the I.R.A. refusing to accept the treaty. It was the uncompromising O'Connor who, on 15 June, broke off the negotiations. The four I.R.A. commanders were accompanied by Countess Markievicz, Count and Countess Plunkett (parents of Joseph Plunkett, executed in 1916) and three other women, Margaret Pearse (mother of the Pearse brothers), Kathleen Clarke (widow of Tom Clarke and sister of Edward Daly, both executed in 1916) and Muriel MacSwiney (widow of Terence MacSwiney, a Volunteer officer who had died on hunger-strike in 1917).[4] In a passionate oration, Mellows said that 'that they did not assemble that day to sing the swan-song of Irish republicanism' and that while 'certain people had taken the road of expediency', the Republicans 'would not deviate one inch'. A detailed report appeared in the *Dublin Evening Mail* ('from our special representative') on the following afternoon. On Thursday morning the *Irish Independent* summarised this report and published four photographs of pilgrims: a large group of men at the graveside; O'Connor, Traynor, Countess Markievicz and Mrs MacSwiney together; 'Mrs Pearse laying a wreath', and, poignantly, Mellows (with 'an expression of grimness and pain')[5] delivering his prophetic oration.[6] These photographs were in fact stills taken from a 'movie' film by Pathé News and now accessible in the British Pathé archives.[7] Over two minutes in length, the film begins with a long file of men in flat caps headed by a piper walking through long grass from the entrance into the churchyard towards the grave, and features most or all of the pilgrims named in the two newspaper accounts. The second scene is of a woman in black (Mrs Pearse) laying a large wreath outside the railing surrounding the grave; then comes a caption, 'General Mellows declares that election results "do not mean the death of Irish republicanism"', to introduce Liam Mellows, coatless, his arms behind his back, making a speech at the grave; the next scene is of a group of two men and two women (O'Connor, Traynor, Countess

---

'Committee'.　**3** Oscar Traynor to Count Plunkett, 17 June 1922 (N.L.I., Plunkett papers, MS 11,374/25).　**4** All those named in this sentence, as well as Traynor, O'Connor, Mellows and Boland, are in *D.I.B.*　**5** C. Desmond Greaves, *Liam Mellows* (London, 1971), pp 51, 334. **6** *Dublin Evening Mail*, 21 June 1922; *Ir. Indep.*, 22 June 1922. Mrs Pearse appears only in the report in the *Independent*, which suggests another source was available or collaboration with the *Mail*. There was a photograph with a brief legend in the *Sunday Independent*, 25 June 1922, but no report in *Freeman's Jn.* or *Ir. Times.*　**7** 'Pilgrimage after the poll: prominent anti-treaty republicans at the grave of Wolfe Tone at Bodenstown' (www.britishpathe.com/video).

Markievicz and Muriel MacSwiney); it is followed by six more group scenes, one of which shows an older, bearded man (Count Plunkett), another, a younger man (O'Connor) in a homburg, looking confident, both close up. Evidently, this pilgrimage was well enough organised and its organisers sufficiently confident of support to be able to attract the attention of a commercial newsreel crew.

Mellows, one of the Fianna guard of honour for Pearse on the famous occasion at Bodenstown, in 1913, had been a negotiator in an attempt to reconcile the rival armies; he was now serving under O'Connor in the I.R.A. force holding the Four Courts.[8] The pilgrimage of 20 June 1922 was the one recalled many years later by another member of that force, Seán Prendergast.

> That assembly of armed I.R.A. men had more than sentimental reason in honouring the 'Father of Republicanism' whom Davis immortalised … It was the first 'spiritual communion' with the patriot dead, for some of us, since 1915, as, owing to the existence of the annual banning by the British authorities in the intervening years, few people made the pilgrimage. Small as the contingent was that June weekday, it was none the less impressive because it was an honest and sincere symbolic act of reverence to the best traditions of Irish separatism and the principles of Irish republicanism as upheld by Tone and appraised by Pearse as the 'greatest republican of them all' … Renewed in national vigour and by increased national inspiration, we returned to our respective duties, whether to man the military post, or, as in some of our cases, to watch and ward over our companies. Indeed it was always a case of watchfulness, wondering what was going to happen next.[9]

The motive stated by Traynor for the Dublin brigade of the I.R.A. organising its own pilgrimage in advance of that of the Wolfe Tone Memorial Committee was to avoid taking part in any pilgrimage 'in which troops other than Republican troops participate'. Could another factor have been anticipation of an assault on their positions at the Four Courts and elsewhere by forces of the pro-Treaty administration of Michael Collins? What happened to the Four Courts garrison, eight days after their appearance at Bodenstown, was that the building was attacked by artillery; O'Connor and Mellows were captured; six months later, on 8 December, they were executed by firing squad. Boland, who had been conciliatory, was not at the Four Courts; he lost his life sooner than the others, on 1 August, having been shot by pro-Treaty forces. Traynor, similarly not at the Four Courts, suffered only imprisonment for his part in the civil war; he reappeared at Bodenstown as minister for defence, laying wreaths on eleven occasions in the 1940s and 1950s, not dying until 1963.

---

8 Marie Coleman and William Murphy, 'Mellows, William Joseph ("Liam") (1892–1922)' in *D.I.B.* 9 Seán Prendergast, 3 Nov. 1952 (B.M.H., W.S. 755, pp 190–91). In fact the pilgrimage was banned only in 1921.

The demonstration organised by the Wolfe Tone Memorial Committee duly took place on 25 June 1922. Extensive coverage was given in the *Irish Independent* (with photographs), the *Kildare Observer* and the *Leinster Leader*.[10] The scene at Bodenstown was complex and a reflection of the political situation throughout the country.[11] Unlike earlier and later occasions, there were three or four bodies of pilgrims and apparently many individuals coming and going. The first group to visit the grave, in the morning, was the Fianna Éireann (anti-Treaty), 400 strong, many in uniform, under the command of Liam Mellows's younger brother, Barney, some (according to the *Irish Times*) attached to the Dublin brigade of the I.R.A.[12] These young men had marched from Dublin during the night and camped nearby at Ardclough. They were joined by Countess Markievicz, Mrs Pearse, Áine Ceannt and other members of the anti-Treatyite 'Executive'; a short address was given by Barney Mellows. They were succeeded by 450 or more members of Cumann na mBan (also anti-Treaty) who had arrived from Dublin by special train; these young and youngish women were joined by local units and marched into the cemetery led by Margaret Skinnider (a close associate of the Countess) to hear speeches by the three women named. Mrs Ceannt recited prayers and addressed the gathering emphasising 'the power which women wielded in furthering the national cause'; Countess Markievicz endorsed these remarks; Mrs Pearse recalled the words of her son Patrick 'who, standing beside the grave of Wolfe Tone, declared he was standing upon the holiest spot in Ireland'.[13] It seems that the women, unable to camp out and relying on a special train to reach Sallins, had to attend separately from the men. Next arrived soldiers, 'a very large body of Dáil troops' (pro-Treaty) — recruits of the incipient 'national army' — one contingent from the Beggar's Bush garrison in Dublin who had marched overnight and camped nearby, another, larger, from the Curragh, some of the latter having attended 12 o'clock mass en route at Naas, played to the church by their pipers.[14] At 2 o'clock a detachment entered the churchyard and formed a circle around the grave with arms reversed. Shortly afterwards arrived a party from the Wolfe Tone Memorial Committee headed by its chairman, Seán Ó Murthuile, who was in the I.R.B. and pro-Treaty, as was another in the party, P. S. O'Hegarty. In a short address, O'Hegarty stated, somewhat defensively, that 'they were there on behalf of all the nationalist people without distinction, and they stood for no party but Tone's party'. The mere presence of Ó Murthuile and O'Hegarty's

---

10 *Ir. Indep.*, 26 June 1922; *Kildare Observer*, 1 July 1922; *Leinster Leader*, 1 July 1922. The *Freeman* for the same date could not be found. The *Evening Herald*, 27 June, had a photo of 'Dinner being served to Dáil; troops' but no report.   11 For which see Michael Hopkinson, *Green against green: the Irish civil war* (Dublin, 1988), esp. chs 4, 7 and 9.   12 *Ir. Times*, 26 June 1922. For Herbert Charles 'Barney' Mellows (1896–1942), see obituary in *Ir. Press*, 25 Feb. 1942. Liam Mellows's biographer, who does not indicate his source, states that it was Liam who spoke on this occasion too and makes throughout mere passing mentions of Barney (Greaves, *Mellows*, p. 338). The *Irish Independent* reports 'B. Mellows' as one of those representing the Wolfe Tone Memorial Committee at Bodenstown in 1919, and in its report of the pilgrimage of 25 June 1922 identifies 'Barney Mellows' as commandant-general of the Fianna (*Ir. Indep.*, 23 June 1919, 26 June 1922). 13 *Leinster Leader*, 1 July 1922.   14 *Kildare Observer*, 1 July 1922.

speech warranted a report that Collins and Richard Mulcahy (Collins's minister for defence) were 'represented'.[15] As on previous such occasions, there was playing of music by bands — the St Laurence O'Toole Pipers' Band still prominent and the Irish National Foresters' Brass Band playing the 'Dead march in Saul' — as well as laying of wreaths. A novel practice, by both the incipient national army and the Fianna, was the sounding of the Last Post and the firing of volleys over the grave; but only in the National Army, later best known as the Irish defences forces, did firing of volleys become a custom.

The impression gained in reading these accounts of the Bodenstown pilgrimage of 25 June 1922 is that, while the pro-Treaty 'Dáil troops' were present in large numbers (some of them controlling civilian traffic), the anti-Treaty I.R.A. was invisible. The ratio of Treatyites to anti-Treatyites among the large and well behaved crowd is impossible to determine. Significant for the future was the presence early in the day of close to a thousand well-disciplined and highly-motivated members of Fianna Éireann and Cumann na mBan and a reminder in the form of a wreath from the 'officers and men' of the Four Courts garrison that they were a force to be reckoned with.[16] This pilgrimage in 1922 would prove to be the last pilgrimage of the Wolfe Tone Memorial Committee, for the previous quarter century the public face of the I.R.B. An irony was that the I.R.B., once the most militant of Irish nationalist organisations, was now pro-Treaty, because Collins controlled both it and the Irish government.

On 28 June 1922, three days after the turn-out at Bodenstown, the anti-Treaty I.R.A. garrison at the Four Courts in Dublin was attacked by pro-Treaty forces under the control and direction of Collins. The attack was the beginning of the civil war in the Irish Free State. By the time another commemoration was due, the fighting was over.

AFTER THE CIVIL WAR

Almost exactly a year later, on 24 June 1923, and almost exactly a month after the I.R.A. chief-of-staff, Frank Aiken, ordered a cease-fire, occurred the first official pilgrimage to Bodenstown. It was annouced in advance as 'a military display'.[17] One thousand officers and men of all the commands of the 'National Army', the defence forces of the Irish Free State, accompanied by army bands from the Curragh, Athlone and Kerry, took up positions before the parade in the field opposite the graveyard. By 1923 there were already several army bands; the historian of the Irish army, John P. Duggan, states that an army band was present at Bodenstown in June 1922.[18] Evidently from the countless accounts of Bodenstown pilgrimages since the

---

15 *Leinster Leader*, 1 July 1922.   16 For the Fianna, see Hay, 'Moulding the future: na Fianna Éireann and its members'; idem, 'The foundation and development of na Fianna Éireann' (see above, ch. 5, n. 27). For Cumann na mBan, see Ann Matthews, *Renegades: Irish Republican women, 1900–1922* (Cork, 2010), pp 312–29.   17 *Freeman's Jn.*, 22 June 1923.   18 J. P. Duggan, *A history*

earliest mass pilgrimage in 1873, bands were an indispensable feature. At noon General Richard Mulcahy, who was minister for defence and commander-in-chief, entered the churchyard and laid a wreath; the Last Post was sounded by twelve buglers. There was also a large civilian presence. W. T. Cosgrave, president of the executive council of the Irish Free State, arrived just before Mulcahy; he was accompanied by government ministers, by members of the third Dáil (the Irish parliament elected in June 1922) and the Senate (an appointed body), and by senior officials, among them the attorney-general, Hugh Kennedy, and the clerk of the Dáil, Colm Murphy; formally present also were the wives of Mulcahy and Kennedy. As in earlier years, special trains brought members of the public from Dublin and neighbouring districts; admittance to the graveyard, however, was by ticket only.[19] Mulcahy delivered a long oration in praise of Tone and asserted that 'Irishmen were now masters in their own country'.[20] Many of the Republicans present a year previously would not have agreed.

In fact, on the previous day, Saturday the 23rd, with little ostentation and one of the smallest of crowds, wreaths coming from Cumann na mBan, 'the Republican Army' and Éamon de Valera (president of Sinn Féin) had been laid on Tone's grave; those present heard a passionate address by Mary MacSwiney (a sister of Terence MacSwiney) deploring that the ministers of the new Irish government, having previously, like Pearse in 1916, pledged their allegiance to an Irish republic, were now 'the ministers of an English king, sworn to give him allegiance'.[21] This pilgrimage was, she said pointedly, 'composed almost entirely of women'. Beside herself, twelve women were named in press reports, among them Margaret the mother of Patrick and William Pearse — she said a few words about Patrick's famous speech on the same spot ten years before — and the widows of Connolly, Mellows and another casualty of the civil war, Cathal Brugha.[22] Mary MacSwiney (1872–1942) was a formidable speaker. As a member of the second Dáil, in the debate on the Anglo-Irish treaty, she had made a speech against it lasting 2 hours 40 minutes, and, when the vote went in its favour on 7 January 1922, protested sharply at what she regarded as a betrayal. She had been imprisoned during the civil war, twice on hunger strike, and finally released on 1 May 1923.[23]

The charge of pledge-breaking was the one that had been loudly made in 1890 and 1891 by Parnellites still loyal to their chief as a reproach to those who had 'thrown him over' in deference to English opinion. The dilemma of allegiance was deep in the Irish Catholic psyche. It stretched back to the closing years of the seventeenth century. Then, as a consequence of the flight of the Catholic king, James II, the catastrophe of the Jacobite defeat in the field at Aughrim, the decimation or exile of the Catholic upper class, and the imposition of legal disabilities on those of that class who remained, the burning, divisive issue among Irish Catholics was

of the Irish army (Dublin, 1991), p. 146.   **19** *Freeman's Jn.*, 25 June 1923; *Evening Herald*, 25 June 1923.   **20** *Ir. Times*, 25 June 1923; Ronan Fanning, 'Mulcahy, Richard (1886–1971)' in *D.I.B.* **21** *Ir. Times*, 25 June 1923.   **22** *Freeman's Jn.*, 25 June 1923; *Kildare Observer*, 30 June 1923. **23** *Ir. Times*, 2 May 1923; Margaret Ward, *Unmanageable revolutionaries: women and Irish*

whether, under pressure from England, to renounce allegiance to James and his son in return for some legal and economic advantage or whether to maintain their allegiance in the hope of a return and the restoration of a regime that was, as they envisaged, entirely to their liking. The faithfulness of some Irish Catholics to the republicanism of the 1916 rising and the subsequent war of Irish independence was to achieve a longevity comparable to their ancestors' faithfulness to the Jacobite cause, still enduring when Tone was born in 1763. It was to find annual expression at Bodenstown.

TREATYITE AND ANTI-TREATYITE RIVALRY, 1924–31

For the remainder of the 1920s, the graveyard at Bodenstown, the adjacent fields and the approach road from Sallins were to be places of contest between the personnel, both military and civil, of the Irish Free State and their Republican rivals and challengers, the latter deeply reproachful and at times threatening. Remarkably, from 1924 until 1928 they all assembled on the same day, the official ceremony usually beginning at 1 p.m., the Republicans' about an hour and a half later. The schedule in 1924 was for Cosgrave to lay a wreath at 1.30 p.m. and then proceed to the saluting base nearby, review the troops and deliver a speech; meantime Republicans were to have left Kingsbridge by a 11.30 train to arrive at Sallins at 12.30 and then to proceed to Bodenstown in time to hear a Sinn Féin orator deliver his speech at 3 o'clock.[24] In one account of the interval between the two pilgrimages in 1925, the first addressed by the minister for defence, the second by the president of Sinn Féin, it was stated that

> aeroplanes were still circling overhead and battalions marching off the parade ground when the approach of Republican pilgrims was observed. Departing staff officers making for their cars rubbed shoulders with uniformed women of the Cumann na mBan. Around a bend of the road leading to the cemetery one had here and there a glimpse of marching men in civilian attire and military formation. It was a confused jumble, Free Staters and Republicans, dust and music, soldiers and aeroplanes, 'hacks' and motor-cars. But out of it all eventually came the Republican pilgrimage.[25]

Such forbearance may have been what Tim Pat Coogan had in mind in commenting that 'unlike either the Russian or Spanish civil wars, the Irish affair differed in the degree of magnanimity shown by the victors towards the losers'.[26] Obviously, 'magnanimity' is an inappropriate word in any of these three cases, but 'forbearance' is admissible in the Irish case. This forbearance, not easily explained when the deaths, destruction and consequent bitterness of the civil war are considered, may

nationalism (London, 1983), pp 167–9; Brian Murphy, 'MacSwiney, Mary' in *D.I.B.* **24** *Ir. Indep.*, 18, 21 June 1924. **25** *Ir. Times*, 22 June 1925. **26** Tim Pat Coogan, *The I.R.A.* (revd ed.,

perhaps have been due to the absence or paucity of economic, social and ideological differences between the pro- and anti-Treaty factions, and, in comparison with Russia and Spain, the small loss of life and damage to property. The civil war in Ireland was not between Reds and Whites or Blacks and Reds. Another factor may have been the close family connexions between political enemies. One example will suffice. Mulcahy's politically minded wife 'Min' (née Ryan) had politically minded sisters, Mary Kate and Phyllis, who successively married his anti-Treatyite foe Seán T. O'Kelly; another sister, Agnes, was married to a Treatyite, Denis McCullough; their brother James was an anti-Treatyite.[27] (O'Kelly was to speak at Tone's grave in 1933, just ten years after Mulcahy.) The tenor of the Bodenstown orations in the 1920s is indicative that differences were over symbolism and loyalty, that the Treatyites were more pragmatic, the anti-Treatyites more idealistic.

In 1928 (as will be shown) there were, for the first time, *three* rival pilgrimages to Tone's grave, a consequence of a split between Sinn Féin and the I.R.A. And in 1929 and 1930 (as also will be shown), there were three pilgrimages, again because of a split among Republicans.

THE IRISH FREE STATE'S OFFICIAL PILGRIMAGES

The core element of the Irish Free State's official demonstration in 1924 and subsequent years consisted of large, seemingly well-equipped units of the National Army which put on a martial display, even more impressive owing to overhead support from the army's air corps; other important elements were Cumann na nGaedheal government ministers, deputies, senior civil servants, once even district justices. Members of the general public were there too but in uncertain numbers. Missing from the official pilgrimages, however, were 'republican nobility' — men and women bearing the names of fallen heroes — whose presence might have confirmed and enhanced the authenticity of Cosgrave's Dáileanna (the fourth, fifth and sixth Dáils) as the legitimate successors to the distinctly republican first and second. The usual routine was that the military would proceed from Sallins to Bodenstown, reform shortly after midday and give a display; the minister for defence would appear and place a wreath on Tone's grave after which three volleys would be fired over the grave and the Last Post sounded by buglers; all would move to a temporary parade ground where the army band would play, the minister would review the troops, take the salute and then make an address, always referring to Tone's character and career, on occasion in some detail.

W. T. Cosgrave himself, perhaps in his capacity as acting minister for defence, gave the oration at the official demonstration on 22 June 1924, for the most part a military one; he spoke mainly about Tone, citing him as a preacher of unity and calling upon Ireland's citizens 'to help in the rebuilding of the nation', before going on, less convincingly, to compare Tone with Collins.[28] The flamboyance of other

London, 2000), p. 41.   **27** Foster, *Vivid faces*, esp. pp 65–7, 257, 303, 320–21, 427–8.   **28** *Ir. Times*,

Bodenstown orators was lacking in Cosgrave, but he was an earnest, effective speaker with credentials as a Volunteer combatant in the Easter rising, while some Dubliners may have remembered him as the Sinn Féin city councillor who, with Griffith and other nationalists, had agreed in March 1911 to form a committee to oppose the royal visit later that year, a decision that brought about the revival of Bodenstown pilgrimages.[29] Behind Cosgrave were members of his Cumann na nGaedheal party in Dáil Éireann and the Senate; on parade were 800 troops from the Curragh, whilst flying overhead were four airplanes of the new Irish military air corps. Only four years before, hostile British planes had overflown the vicinity of Bodenstown on the evening before the commemoration when Volunteers were camping to be in readiness for the next day, and again when it was in progress.[30]

A very large number of pilgrims appeared at Bodenstown in 1925, as many as ten thousand 'from all parts of the country' (reported the *Irish Independent*). Not all were there for the official ceremony, to be addressed by the unpopular and untalented minister for defence, Peter Hughes. A more obvious attraction was a controversial figure, Éamon de Valera, who gave the oration at the Republican ceremomy that followed. The custom was confirmed of the minister for defence taking the stand. Hughes did so in this and the next two years, Desmond FitzGerald from 1928 until 1931; both drew on the Tone legend, characterising Tone's career as exemplary for citizens of the Irish Free State.[31]

The official commemoration at Bodenstown in 1926 was probably the largest of its kind. Notice was given the previous day in the *Kildare Observer* and in the *Evening Herald*. The latter gave much detail of the army's programme. The ceremony was to begin at 1 p.m. with the placing of a wreath by the minister for defence, the firing of three shots over the grave and the sounding of the Last Post; next the reception of the minister on the 'parade ground' by assembled troops; at 1.30 the minister was to review troops accompanied by the 'Defence Council and general officers commanding'; at 1.50 the minister was to address the troops; at 2 o'clock (subject, one supposes, to the politician's brevity) it would be over. Deployed were to be an infantry brigade, a mounted infantry troop, units of transport, air, medical and military police corps, and the No. 3 Army Band. In charge was the officer commanding the Curragh Military Camp.[32] The No. 3 Army Band, attached to the Curragh, was to play at Bodenstown many times in years to come. Although there was no mention of other ministers, Dáil deputies, government officials, other civilians or the general public, a good number of each attended. At the graveside were Cosgrave, his finance minister Ernest Blythe, several Cumann na nGaedheal deputies and a high court judge, John O'Byrne. A veteran I.R.B. man

---

23 June 1924. The speech and whole ceremony are also reported at length in *Freeman's Jn.* and *Ir. Indep.*, 23 June 1924, and in *Leinster Leader*, 28 June 1924.   **29** *Freeman's Jn.*, 25 Mar. 1911; Eunan O'Halpin, 'Cosgrave, William Thomas (1880–1965)' in *D.I.B.*   **30** *Ir. Indep.*, 21 June 1920. **31** *Ir. Times*, 22 June 1925, 21 June 1926, 20 June 1927, 18 June 1928. Hughes's speech in 1925 is reported in *Ir. Indep.*, 22 June 1925.   **32** *Kildare Observer*, 19 June 1926; *Evening Herald*, 19 June

and pilgrim, George Lyons, represented 'the Old Dublin Brigade, I.R.A. Association', presumably men who had accepted the Treaty. The *Irish Times* put the number of pilgrims at several thousand. Its figure of some 4,000 troops from the Curragh is probably an exaggeration, 1,400 was the figure in the *Leinster Leader*. A highlight was a squadron of Bristol fighters from Baldonnel.[33] This is a military airfield 15 kilometres to the north-east of Bodenstown. Perhaps the reason for the increased scale of the official pilgrimage in 1926 was the rise of the I.R.A. and the Cumann na nGaedheal government's need to challenge it.

In 1927 the official pilgrimage was on the same model. The crowd was large and over a thousand troops were drawn up.[34]

In 1928 the official commemoration, on 17 June, was reported as 'large'; the minister for defence, Desmond FitzGerald spoke of 'the tradition of Tone and Emmet, of Griffith and Collins, and of Kevin O'Higgins'.[35] The last of these was the minister for justice murdered by Republicans eleven months previously. In 1928, FitzGerald and three other dignitaries (one of them Blythe) standing to attention at the grave, FitzGerald making his speech and other scenes at the ceremony were captured on seventy-one seconds of silent film by British Pathé. Other scenes are soldiers in a field firing their rifles into the air, a group of officers saluting, and the whole troop marching, rifles raised upright.[36]

There were two departures from strict custom at the official commemoration on 17 June 1929: it was held on a Monday (owing to the funeral in Dublin of John Devoy the previous day) and, though FitzGerald reviewed the troops as before, there was apparently no oration. The attendance was smaller, but it included more government ministers and also visitors from America.[37]

In 1930, on 22 June, the routine established in 1923 by Cosgrave's government — a military and civilian presence with the usual formalities — was followed once more except that again there was no address by the minister.[38]

On 21 June 1931 the routine was followed, hurriedly, for the last time. FitzGerald arrived shortly after 1 o'clock accompanied by Blythe, at least five government deputies and a civil servant, Kevin Sheil, secretary of the Department of Justice; the minister declined again to address the troops, the ceremony lasted less than half an hour. The main event of that day at Bodenstown was to be the pilgrimage of Cumann na nGaedheal's self-confident rivals for power.[39] On 9 March 1932, before the next 'Bodenstown Sunday', a new government, headed by Éamon de Valera, entered office.

1926. **33** *Ir. Indep.*, 21 June 1926; *Ir. Times*, 26 June 1926; *Leinster Leader*, 26 June 1926. **34** *Ir. Indep.*, 20 June 1927. **35** *Ir. Indep.*, 18 June 1928. **36** 'Wolfe Tone anniversary: Mr D. Fitzgerald, minister for defence, places a wreath on the grave and takes salute at the march past at Bodenstown' (www.britishpathé.com/video, viewed 17 Dec. 2014). **37** *Ir. Times*, 17, 18 June 1929. **38** *Ir. Indep.*, 23 June 1930; *Ir. Times*, 23 June 1930. **39** *Ir. Indep.*, 22 June 1931.

THE REPUBLICANS' PILGRIMAGES

On 22 June 1924, the day on which Cosgrave made his speech at Bodenstown, a thousand and more Republicans (anti-Treatyites) succeeded in making a pilgrimage to Tone's grave. It had been advertised in the *Evening Herald* as the annual pilgrimage of Sinn Féin with the instruction that 'Republicans' should begin parading at 2 o'clock.[40] Some travelled by special train to Sallins (at a return fare of 2s. 6d.) to be joined by others who had arrived by road. The pilgrims formed into military formation at about 2.45 p.m. and marched to the grave. This was a revival of the custom of the Irish Vounteers, perforce discontinued after 1915, followed again in 1919 and 1920. The parade, headed by the Fintan Lalor Pipers' Band, included representatives of Fianna Éireann, Cumann na mBan, Sinn Féin Clubs and an organisation described as the 'Irish Republican Soldiers' Federation'. It arrived almost immediately after the departure of the official party. The oration was delivered by Brian O'Higgins.[41] At Bodenstown ten years previously he had read an ode to Tone of his own composition.[42] O'Higgins (1882–1963) was an obsessive devotee of Tone — he was founder and editor of the *Wolfe Tone Weekly* (1937–9) and the *Wolfe Tone Annual* (1932–62). This devotion to Tone, who was hostile to religion, was irrational, even perverse, if considered with O'Higgins's fervent devotion to catholicism — he became a daily mass-goer. A factor in his being chosen to be Bodenstown orator in 1924 was no doubt his recent release from internment for subversive activity.[43]

Republicans gathered again at Bodenstown in 1925, just as the official party and supporters were departing. A young Irishman wrote to a friend in Australia how at 12 noon 'the minister of defence with 2,000 Free State troops' entered Bodenstown churchyard and told them 'that they had got the freedom for which Tone died' and at 2 p.m. Éamon de Valera with 'some thousands of Republicans took up the position' and told his audience 'that they had not got the freedom which Tone fought for'.[44] The irony of the situation was not lost in the report in the *Irish Times* (reproduced more fully above) of 'a confused jumble' of 'Free Staters and Republicans' and of 'departing staff officers' of the defence forces 'making for their cars' rubbing shoulders 'with uniformed women of the Cumann na mBan'.[45] De Valera had to pass through 'surging crowds' sporting 'miniatures' of himself to reach Tone's grave, which he referred to in his long speech (made in a field nearby) as a 'shrine' at which vows were to be renewed; he imagined Clarke, Pearse, Connolly, Brugha and Mellows as present in spirit; and (like other Bodenstown orators before and after him) he quoted Tone on England being 'the never failing source of Ireland's political evil' and on a need 'to abolish the memory of all past

40 *Evening Herald*, 21 June 1924.   41 *Ir. Indep.*, 18, 21, 23 June 1924; *Freeman's Jn.*, 23 June 1924.
42 *Leinster Leader*, 27 June 1914.   43 For Brian O'Higgins, see Patrick Maume's article in *D.I.B.*
44 Billy Judge to Liam Corrigan, 24 June 1925, Corrigan papers, National Library of Australia, quoted in David Fitzpatrick, 'Commemoration in the Irish Free State' in Ian McBride (ed.), *History and memory in modern Ireland* (Cambridge, 2001), pp 184–203 at pp 188–9.   45 *Ir. Times*,

dissensions and substitute the common name of Irishman' for 'Protestant, Catholic and Dissenter'.[46] It was passionate and clever. He invested 'Tone and his cult', one historian has written, 'with a mythical significance, freely employing religious imagery in the manner of Pearse' before facing 'the demands of present-day reality' and invoking Tone's teaching to justify the Republicans' position.[47] The Dublin paper's allusion to 'marching men in civilian attire and military formation' was made more explicit in the *Leinster Leader*, which referred to 'several hundred Irish Volunteers marching in military formation' — no doubt men of the I.R.A. The significance of the Republican pilgrimage in 1925 was anticipated by Jack B. Yeats, who made sketches of a group of pilgrims at Kingsbridge Railway Station about to set off on their journey to Sallins; he later painted the scene, in impressionist-style, as 'Going to Wolfe Tone's grave'.[48]

In November 1925 the I.R.A. separated itself from Sinn Féin in order to throw off the authority of the second Dáil. This Dáil, elected in May 1921 shortly before the truce that preceded the Anglo-Irish treaty, had been replaced by later Dáileanna, elected in June 1922 and August 1923, and so was little more than a chimera, though still regarded by Sinn Féin as the legitimate Irish parliament. In the spring of 1926 a split developed in the Sinn Féin party. De Valera, its president, resigned and formed a new party, Fianna Fáil, willing to enter the fourth Dáil if the impediment of the oath of fidelity to George V were removed. The rump of Sinn Féin drifted away from the I.R.A. and went into decline; in 1930 it attracted only 40 to its annual conference.[49] It became, as one historian has observed, 'a shadow political party which took no part in practical politics'.[50] Apparently a few adherents of the new party were present at the Republican demonstration at Bodenstown in 1926; it was formally represented by seven members in 1927, among them Robert Brennan, then a lieutenant of De Valera's and during the Second World War the accredited minister of Éire in Washington.[51]

The Republican pilgrimage in 1926 was of the traditional 'processional' type. Countess Markievicz was present for the last time. The orator was John Madden (1896?–1954). Madden, a physician and a member of Sinn Féin, was elected to the fourth Dáil for his native Mayo in a by-election in November 1924, but, respecting his party's policy, refused to take his seat; he was also in the I.R.A., from which he was expelled in 1927 for standing for election contrary to orders; he later practised in Dublin and became sympathetic to Fianna Fáil. Harking back to the 1790s, he criticised 'the bishops and priests' for being 'more concerned with getting money

22 June 1925. **46** *Leinster Leader*, 27 June 1925, which gives the speech at great length. The text in *Speeches and statements by Eamon de Valera, 1917–73*, ed. Maurice Moynihan (Dublin, 1980), pp 118–21, is taken from *An Phoblacht*, 26 June 1925. **47** Patrick Murray, 'Obsessive historian: Éamon de Valera and the policing of his reputation' in *Proceedings of the Royal Irish Academy*, ci (1999), sect. C, no. 2, pp 37–65 at p. 47. **48** Hilary Pyle, *Jack B. Yeats: a catalogue raisonné of the oil paintings* (3 vols, London, 1992), i, 351, iii, 167. The painting was first exhibited in 1929; it is now in private ownership. **49** Brian Feeney, *Sinn Féin: a hundred turbulent years* (Dublin, 2002), p. 171. **50** Richard English, *Armed struggle: the history of the I.R.A.* (London, 2003), p. 45. **51** *Ir. Indep.*, 21 June 1926, 20 June 1927.

out of England for Maynooth College' than with establishing 'an Irish republic';
addressing in his audience men belonging 'to the army of the Republic', he bid
them, 'do all in your power to organise yourselves for defence and offence'.[52]

In 1927 the orator was Art O'Connor, De Valera's successor as president of Sinn
Féin. O'Connor (1888–1950) was a native of Celbridge, County Kildare, which
county he represented in the first and second Dáileanna; he was one of those present
at the Volunteer meeting at Naas in October 1915 and was an energetic organiser,
but he took no part in the Easter rising; he was also a fine speaker and had a
knowledge of Tone's career above the ordinary, which he expounded to the pilgrims
in a very long speech. Obliged to abandon his career as a county engineer and
imprisoned during the civil war, he later abandoned politics too for a successful
career in law.[53] His father, also Arthur (1835–1907), of Elm Hall, Celbridge, for
many years a member of the Celbridge Board of Guardians, was at Bodenstown in
1893 as president of the Celbridge and Hazelhatch Gaelic Athletic Association.[54] By
all accounts the pilgrimage was large. Sinn Féin, Fianna Éireann, Cumann na mBan,
Republican Girl Scouts and Irish National Foresters participated (the last of these
perhaps for the last time), as did representatives of Fianna Fáil, notably the 1916
next-of-kin Margaret Pearse and Kathleen Clarke; the I.R.A. was not accounted for,
but its involvement may be inferred from the favourable report in its newspaper, *An
Phoblacht*.[55]

The Republican pilgrimage on 17 June 1928 is significant for the participation
of one of De Valera's closest lieutenants, Seán Lemass, and for the explicit
recommendation of the I.R.A. by the orator, George Gilmore. Lemass and other
Fianna Fáil deputies processed from Sallins with 'Irish Volunteers' (no doubt I.R.A.)
and uniformed Cumann na mBan.[56] Gilmore (1898–1985), reputedly of left-wing
opinions, had recently been released from prison; he had been arrested in November
1926 and convicted of assisting in the escape of nineteen I.R.A. prisoners from
Mountjoy Jail one year before; in the early 1920s he and Lemass had been close
associates in the I.R.A.[57] Gilmore was still in the I.R.A., as evident in his telling his
audience: 'I am not going to appeal to the young men present to join the Republican
Army. I expect most of you are already members of that organisation. If any of you
are not, then (subject to the regulations governing recruiting) you are offered the
privilege of membership of the Army of Independence.'[58]

Sinn Féin, regarding Fianna Fáil as renegades, and perhaps scornful of Fianna
Fáil participating so openly with the I.R.A., held its own pilgrimage three days later,

52 *Ir. Indep.*, 21 June 1926; *Ir. Press*, 29, 30 Sept., 2 Oct. 1954; Hanley, *I.R.A.*, pp 93, 111, 209.
53 The text of O'Connor's speech is given at length in *Kildare Observer* and *Leinster Leader*, both
25 June 1927. For his career, see William Murphy, 'O'Connor, Arthur' in *D.I.B.* For his part in
the Volunteers, see Patrick Colgan (B.M.H., W.S. 850).   54 *Leinster Leader*, 1 July 1893; *Kildare
Observer*, 9 Feb., 19 Oct. 1907. For more on the O'Connor family, see Lena Boylan, *Of whistlers
and runners-in: an historical and archaeological survey of Celbridge*, ed. Catherine Boylan (Celbridge,
2016), pp 391–403.   55 *An Phoblacht*, 24 June 1927.   56 *Ir. Indep.*, 18 June 1928.   57 *Ir. Indep.*,
9 June 1928; Diarmaid Ferriter, 'Gilmore, George' in *D.I.B.*   58 *An Phoblacht*, 23 June 1928.

on the evening of Wednesday the 20th; Madden was the orator, buglers of Fianna Éireann sounded the Last Post; the arrangements were made by a veteran of the Easter rising, Joseph Clarke (1882–1976), a regular Bodenstown pilgrim until the mid 1970s.[59] Thus in 1928, for the first time, there were three quite separate pilgrimages.

In the report in the *Irish Times* of the Republican pilgrimage on 16 June 1929 mention was made of the 'Óglaigh na h-Éireann'. This was the name in Irish of the Irish Republican Army — the I.R.A. It was the first specific mention of that body in a report from Bodenstown since 1922. The I.R.A.'s newspaper, *An Phoblacht*, referring to the event as having been held 'under the auspices of the Republican organisations', reported that the various contingents in the procession 'fell in' at Sallins and that 'Óglaigh na h-Éireann', headed by a pipe band, 'made a fine muster'; the main body 'was drawn from the Dublin City Brigade and the South Dublin Battalions, there were 'contingents' from Kildare and adjacent counties and 'officers were present who represented units as far distant as Belfast and Clare'.[60] Unmistakably now, the 'Republican' pilgrimages were the pilgimages of the I.R.A. The oration, rather banal, was given by Seán Buckley of Cork, who cited Tone on the desirability of uniting 'Protestant, Catholic and Dissenter'. Buckley (1870?–1963), a builder by trade, was active in the I.R.A. during and after the war of independence, he quit in the mid 1930s, joined Fianna Fáil and was a Dáil deputy for a Cork constituency from 1938 to 1954.[61] He was introduced by one Proinnsias Ó Riain, obviously Frank Ryan (1902–44), editor of *An Phoblacht*. Ryan, after a controversial career in the I.R.A., went to Spain in 1936 to fight on the Republican side in the civil war.[62]

In 1929, on 30 June, Fianna Fáil made, for the first time, its own, separate pilgrimage. At Tone's graveside, De Valera devoted his oration to praising Tone to an audience of 400 or so who, keeping up the tradition, had travelled by special train to Sallins (tickets 2s. 6d. at the party's office at 13 Upper Mount Street) and processed to Bodenstown headed by a band (the Fintan Lalor Pipers'). Among the pilgrims were seven Dáil deputies, including Seán Lemass, Frank Aiken and James Ryan (Mulcahy's brother-in-law) and two senators, one of them Kathleen Clarke.[63]

Again in 1930, Fianna Fáil made a separate pilgrimage, this time on the same day as the official ceremony. The army began its proceedings at 1 o'clock in the presence of the Cumann na nGaedheal minister for defence, Desmond FitzGerald (a strong critic of Fianna Fáil); as planned, De Valera and his party moved in immediately afterwards; the purer, die-hard Republicans had their ceremony a week later.[64] Accompanying De Valera were ten deputies, among them Aiken (again) and Seán T. O'Kelly (a future president of Ireland). De Valera's speech on this occasion is discussed below.

59 *Kildare Observer*, 23 June 1928. For Clarke, see Anne Dolan's article on him in *D.I.B.* **60** *Ir. Times*, 17 June 1929; *An Phoblacht*, 22 June 1929. **61** *An Phoblacht*, 22 June 1929; *Cork Examiner*, 2 Dec. 1963; Hanley, *I.R.A.*, p. 186. **62** Brian Hanley, 'Ryan, Frank' in *D.I.B.* **63** *Evening Herald*, 29 June 1929; *Ir. Indep.*, 1 July 1929. **64** *Ir. Indep.*, 23, 30 June 1930.

Interestingly, for the Republican pilgrimage to be held in 1930, on 29 June, full details of arrangements made for marching groups at Sallins were published in *An Phoblacht*: first to move off were units of the I.R.A. (still referred to as 'Óglaigh na hÉireann'), next Cumann na mBan, then Sinn Féin, Fianna Éireann, Republican Girl Guides and so on.[65] On the day, over 500 travelled by special train from Dublin. As usual, there were contingents from surrounding districts. The main oration was delivered by 'Tom' Maguire of Cross, County Mayo. Maguire indignantly rejected the advice of Michael Price (secretary of the Wolfe Tone Commemoration Committee) to draw parallels between the French, Russian and Irish revolutions, but instead made rather banal observations on Tone and Pearse.[66] Interest in Maguire, earlier in life a coachbuilder (like Peter Tone) and by 1930 an employee of the Irish National Insurance Company, now lies in his tenacity and longevity. Born in 1892, he was active in the I.R.A. in the independence and civil wars, he was elected to the Second Dáil in 1921 and continued to regard it as solely authoritative; he died aged 101 in 1993, by then a patron of the new Republican Sinn Féin.[67] It is evident that as late as 1930 the pilgrims, whether members of the I.R.A. or affiliated bodies, or just members of the public, were still drawn from no further away than Kildare, adjacent counties and the Dublin metropolis, with the exceptions only of senior I.R.A. personnel.

The Republican pilgrimage on 21 June 1931 was freely reported as the I.R.A.'s pilgrimage. A few hours before the event, the Cumann na nGaedheal government attempted to prevent it. This it did by ordering the arrest (on a charge of organising an unlawful army) of the appointed orator, Seán Russell, by prohibiting the usual special trains to Sallins, and by commandeering the usual assembly field there. In *An Phoblacht* the previous Saturday appeared a sketch-map of Sallins ('Mobilization at Sallins for Bodenstown Pilgrimage, Sunday, 21st June 1931') showing the assembly field and the positions in that field to be occupied by the various contingents before setting off on the march.[68] The Republican pilgrimage was not banned in that year, it took place under these constraints on the appointed day. On that day (as the *Irish Times* was to report), to replace the trains (cancelled overnight and guarded at Kingsbridge terminus by soldiers) the organisers secured from the Irish Omnibus Company thirty buses to transport pilgrims from Kingsbridge to the assembly field at Sallins. The field (rented by the Wolfe Tone Commemoration Committee and with marquees in place) was occupied by the military, who denied access; meantime, 'at intervals of a few minutes, special buses came from all parts of the country' — including Belfast; large crowds formed in the village, while 'continuous streams of pedestrians and cyclists dodged between the motor-cars as best they could. Large contingents of I.R.A. were present, as well as Fianna Éireann and many girls in Cumann na mBan uniform.' These 'contingents' were in truth

---

65 *An Phoblacht*, 21 June 1930.   **66** *Ir. Indep.*, 30 June 1930; *An Phoblacht*, 5 July 1930; Uinseann MacEoin, *Survivors: the story of Ireland's struggle as told through some of her outstanding living people recalling events* (Dublin, 1980?), p. 391.   **67** Marie Coleman and Michael MacEvilly, 'Maguire, Tom (1892–1993)' in *D.I.B.*   **68** *An Phoblacht*, 20 June 1931.

'battalions'. At the head of the procession was Seán MacBride and the 1st battalion of the Dublin Brigade of the I.R.A. When it moved forward, at about 2.30, 'military commands' were given by men in charge.[69] It was due to the overbearing manner of MacBride and the efficiency of his organising committee that the buses were hired at such short notice.[70] MacBride (1904–88) was the son of John MacBride, who had addressed pilgrims in 1905, again in 1911, and who had been executed for his part in the 1916 rising.[71] Another participant recalled that 'every vehicle that could move, taxed or untaxed, was put on the road ... Cyclists poured out from boreens everywhere following on the radio announcement of the night before.' This was Peadar O'Donnell, Russell's replacement as orator. He had a reputation as an agitator and writer of left-wing tendencies.[72] Russell, early on the day of the pilgrimage, had been found in possession of '183 military training books'; he was later tried at the Dublin Circuit Court and acquitted.[73] Just before the Republicans arrived at Bodenstown, the Irish defence forces, in the presence of FitzGerald and several other Cumann na nGaedheal deputies, held their ceremony as usual; an army band played; troops were reviewed; aeroplanes swooped down close to the ground as they passed the saluting base. But it was all over within half an hour. The I.R.A.'s ceremony was a grander affair. Its newspaper claimed an attendance of 'close to 10,000'; an *Irish Times* reporter at Kingsbridge claimed to have seen drawn up 'about 100 carriages which had been got ready to take the 2,400 passengers who were expected to travel to Sallins' and thirty relief buses taking on board ticket-holding passengers refused admission; in Dáil Éireann a Fianna Fáil deputy, Thomas Mullins, claiming to have information 'from a reliable source', stated that as many as 17,000 persons had purchased tickets expecting to travel by one of the special trains to Sallins, some of which he said, citing the *Cork Examiner*, were to run from Cork, Kerry, Waterford, Limerick, Galway, Sligo or Belfast.[74] It is likely, from this, that two thousand or so pilgrims reached Bodenstown by the relief buses, that individuals living convenient enough to Bodenstown managed by other means and that only intending pilgrims relying on trains were prevented from going. In 1930 'over 500' had reportedly travelled by special train from Dublin.[75] Contrary to the government's intentions, the I.R.A.'s pilgrimage in 1931 was the most successful so far. This trend was to continue to the mid 1930s.

In that procession to Bodenstown in 1931 was a Fianna Fáil contingent. All branches of the party had received a message stressing the importance of a large turn-out.[76] The contingent, led by De Valera himself ('bareheaded'), consisted of

69 *Ir. Indep.*, 22 June 1931; see also *An Phoblacht*, 27 June 1931.   **70** Caoimhe Nic Dháibhéid, *Seán MacBride: a republican life, 1904–46* (Liverpool, 2011), p. 94.   **71** For Seán MacBride (1904–88), see also the article on him by Ronan Keane in *D.I.B.*   **72** Peadar O'Donnell, *There will be another day* (Dublin, 1963), p. 125. For O'Donnell, see Fearghal McGarry, 'O'Donnell, Peadar (1893–1986)' in *D.I.B.*   **73** *Ir. Indep.*, 11 July 1931.   **74** *An Phoblacht*, 27 June 1931; *Ir. Times*, 22 June 1931; *Dáil Éireann debates*, xxxix, cols 948–9 (24 June 1931).   **75** *Ir. Indep.*, 30 June 1930.   **76** Donnacha Ó Beacháin, *Destiny of the soldiers: Fianna Fáil, Irish republicanism and the I.R.A., 1926–1973* (Dublin, 2010), pp 105–6.

fourteen Dáil deputies and, no doubt, many other party stalwarts. Among the deputies were Frank Aiken (an I.R.A. chief-of-staff during and after the civil war, and a future minister for defence), Seán Lemass (who was to succeed De Valera as party leader in 1959) and Gerald Boland (a younger brother of Harry and a future minister for justice).[77] Evidently the participation of Fianna Fáil was not a last-minute decision, as its position had been indicated on the sketch-map drawn at least 10 days previously. The party joined the parade in spite of the risk of disorder. Somewhat undignified, Fianna Fáil came well behind the large number of I.R.A. battalions — each identified in the I.R.A. newspaper, *An Phoblacht*, by county and number — and immediately in front of the Irish Friends of Soviet Russia.[78] The importance of Fianna Fáil's defiance of the ban in collaborating with the I.R.A. is stressed by Kathleen Travers, who argues that the ban threatened to give the Irish Free State government 'the opportunity to claim the Tone tradition all for themselves' and cites the defiance as substantiation of Lemass's claim that Fianna Fáil were a 'slightly constitutional party'.[79]

For its part, Sinn Féin, on the ground of Fianna Fáil's participation, reversed its own decision to participate on 21 June; a group of about 40 Dublin members of Sinn Féin did go to Bodenstown on the preceding Friday evening.[80] Another (unadmitted) reason for Sinn Féin's going alone may have been the party's acute numerical weakness.[81]

A secret report compiled by the Department of Justice in August 1931 states how the I.R.A. 'asserts itself to be the government of the State', with its 1,300 'officers' and 3,500 'rank-and-file', its 'military nomenclature and military order'. The report continues, referring to the I.R.A. demonstration at Bodenstown: 'the Government's decision to prevent this open breach of the law was criticized in certain circles as if authorized Defence Forces of the State and the I.R.A. were merely rival bodies equally entitled to parade in public and between which it was unfair for Government to draw any distinction'.[82] This report no doubt gave the government stronger ground for introducing a new public safety bill two months later.

Why did De Valera and Fianna Fáil participate, in 1931, in a pilgrimage organised to all appearances, and in reality, by the I.R.A.? There were several reasons. The late Ronan Fanning perceived Fianna Fáil's participation as simply a continuation of a custom that survived the split of 1926.[83] But he did not mention that Fianna Fáil went on its own, separate pilgrimage in 1929 and again in 1930. Another explanation is implicit in Tim Pat Coogan's concept of a renewed dalliance between De Valera

77 *Ir. Indep.*, 22 June 1931.   **78** *An Phoblacht*, 27 June 1931.   **79** Travers, 'Tone of national commemorations', p. 26.   **80** *Ir. Indep.*, 17 June 1931; *Sunday Independent*, 21 June 1931; *Irish Freedom*, July 1931. Sinn Féin's change of mind is explained in Mary MacSwiney to — — , 25 June 1931 (Univ. Coll., Dublin, Mary MacSwiney papers, 480a/48 (25)).   **81** Hanley, *I.R.A.*, pp 94, 240.   **82** Quoted in Ó Beacháin, *Destiny of the soldiers*, p. 109.   **83** Ronan Fanning, '"The rule of order": Eamon de Valera and the I.R.A., 1923–40' in J. P. O'Carroll and John A. Murphy (eds), *De Valera and his times* (Cork, 1983), pp 160–72. Fanning states that in 1931 'Fianna Fáil and the I.R.A. still made a joint annual pilgrimage to Wolfe Tone's grave at Bodenstown' (p. 162).

and the Republicans. He holds that Fianna Fáil at that time were heavily indebted to the rank-and-file of the I.R.A., the latter being mostly 'united in outlook and social background with Fianna Fáil supporters' and naturally impressed by Fianna Fáil's promise to release I.R.A. men serving prison sentences.[84] He argues that De Valera also had a 'constituency' in the United States where he was expected to hold to a 'republican' position to earn the money Irish Americans were sending him, and he shows elsewhere how Irish Americans, even De Valera's patron Joseph McGarrity and his Clan na Gael, sometimes failed to understand De Valera's true position.[85] These factors may explain Fianna Fáil's reluctance to yield to pressure from the government to dissociate itself from politically motivated crimes committed by Republicans: murders and woundings, intimidation of witnesses and juries, physical attacks on members of the police force — the Garda Síochána. Such crimes were increasingly common in 1931.[86] Another factor, of immediate concern, was a by-election in Kildare, due a few days after the pilgrimage. By defying the government, particularly after the arrests of the secretary of the Wolfe Tone Commemoration Committee, Michael Price, and the quartermaster-general of the I.R.A., Seán Russell, the night before the pilgrimage, Fianna Fáil believed it could motivate all Republicans to turn out and cast their votes favourably.[87] Conspicuous association with the I.R.A. and reluctance to denounce murders might have alienated Kildare electors unsympathetic to 'physical force'; but in the event, Fianna Fáil won the vacant seat.

ORGANISATION

Because of the split between Treatyites and anti-Treatyites in 1922, the Wolfe Tone Memorial Committee, the organisers of the pilgrimages since 1898, became dormant. One reason for the *démarche* of Traynor in summoning anti-Treatyites to Tone's grave five days before the pilgrimage arranged by the committee for 25 June 1922 was probably that the committee was under the influence of Collins. Its function of organising annual pilgrimages was from 1923 onwards undertaken in rivalry by the authorities of the Irish Free State and the leadership of the various anti-Treatyite bodies. The committee's other function, its original function, of erecting a memorial to Tone in St Stephen's Green, was all but forgotten. Its long-serving treasurer, Stritch (who became anti-Treaty), safeguarded its funds and remembered it in writing his will by a bequest of £100.[88] It seems that Kathleen Clarke, whose husband Tom had been joint-treasurer with Stritch before 1916, had custody of the funds after Stritch's death in 1933 until they were put to their original purpose in 1967 (see above, chapter 4).

84 Tim Pat Coogan, *The I.R.A.* (revd ed., London, 2000), p. 60.   85 Coogan, *De Valera*, p. 414; idem, *I.R.A.*, pp 99–107.   86 Coogan, *I.R.A.*, pp 47–51.   87 Cf. Ó Beacháin, *Destiny of the soldiers*, pp 103–07.   88 *Ir. Press*, 23 Apr. 1934.

The organisation of the official pilgrimages in 1923 and subsequent years was a duty of the Irish defence forces. The first was advertised in a Dublin evening paper in June 1926 as 'the annual military commemoration ceremony in honour of Theobald Wolfe Tone'.[89] In this and later years the military played essential roles in the ceremonies inside and outside the churchyard. The minister for defence did have a formal role: he would be received by the commanding officer, be accorded a guard of honour and be invited to inspect the troops; but other civilians were observers, albeit in some cases distinguished ones in places of honour. These pilgrimages differed from the earlier, unofficial pilgrimages and from the contemporaneous Republican pilgrimages in logistics as well as innovation. The location of the main Irish army base at the Curragh, situated about 15 kilometres south-west of Naas, and, like Sallins, on the main railway from Cork, made it easy for regular military units to assemble at Bodenstown before noon. A local newspaper reported how, for the official demonstration in 1924, 'the troops taking part in the review were drawn from the Curragh Training Camp ... They entrained at the Curragh Siding at 10 a.m. ..., detrained at Sallins and marched from the railway station to Bodenstown'.[90] The Irish Volunteers to be seen marching from Sallins in 1914 and 1915 and officially regarded after 1921 as the linear predecessors of the Irish defence fores had no such local base and arrived separately from Dublin or from elsewhere via Dublin. Another difference was aerial support, which came from Baldonnel to raise the enthusiasm as well as the heads of Treatyite pilgrims; in 1920 a hostile aeroplane had flown overhead. There was no difference in one respect: the defence forces had use of the field at Bodenstown where Volunteers had been in 1914 and 1915.

Who were the organisers, what were the logistics, of the anti-Treatyites' pilgrimages to Bodenstown? In 1923, 1924 and 1925, newspapers tended to use the word 'Republican' to refer to anti-Treaty pilgrimages. The pilgrimage addressed by Mary MacSwiney in 1923 was probably organised by Cumann na mBan, if not a scratch affair. That held in 1924 advertised as the annual pilgrimage of Sinn Féin was organised, at the request of Éamon de Valera, by Joseph O'Connor, aided by Éamon Donnelly.[91] O'Connor (1882?–1959) had been taking part since about 1900; he was a dependable ally of De Valera, having been a comrade in the 3rd battalion of the Dublin Brigade of the Irish Volunteers and his second-in-command in the Easter rising; he had been on hunger strike whilst interned for his anti-Treaty I.R.A. activities; he was to be chief marshal at Fianna Fáil pilgrimages in the 1930s and to be seen standing near his chief at the party's pilgrimage in 1956.[92] Donnelly (1877–1944), another close associate, and apparently in 1924 secretary of Sinn Féin, had a flair for organising; he was a founder of Fianna Fáil in 1926 and director of elections for the party in its victorious contest in 1932.[93] Quite likely Donnelly had an

89 *Evening Herald*, 19 June 1926.   **90** *Kildare Observer*, 28 June 1924.   **91** *Evening Herald*, 21 June 1924; Joseph O'Connor, 28 June 1951 (3rd statement, B.M.H., W.S. 544, p. 33).   **92** Joseph O'Connor, 13 Oct. 1948 (B.M.H., W.S. 157, pp 1–3); *Ir. Press*, 25 June 1934, 14 June 1937, 18 June 1956, 24 Feb. 1959.   **93** *Newry Reporter*, 2 Jan. 1945, repr. 25 Jan. 2008; Pauric J. Dempsey,

organising role in 1925 when De Valera was the orator, as he was present with other De Valera loyalists.[94]

At the end of 1925 the I.R.A. broke away from Sinn Féin and in March 1926 there was a split in Sinn Féin that soon reduced it to a rump. In a report of the Republican pilgrimage the following June it was stated that the procession was 'organised by the Wolfe Tone Commemoration Committee'.[95] Unlike the old Wolfe Tone Memorial Committee (defunct after 1922), its sole purpose was to organise annual pilgrimages to Bodenstown. Presumably its members were all sympathetic to, if not members of, the I.R.A., Sinn Féin, Cumann na mBan, Fianna Fáil or a kindred body. Essentially, this organising entailed chartering special trains to run from Dublin and, in the 1930s, from more distant towns; renting the field opposite the railway station at Sallins for pilgrims to assemble and form; franchising a refreshment tent in the field; engaging suitable bands to play; publicising the event in advance by advertising it on posters and in newspapers, most particularly the I.R.A.'s newspaper, *An Phoblacht*.[96] The committee could expect to draw on greater goodwill and wider support than the I.R.A., particularly from unattached Republicans. It is a fair guess that some of the old hands of the Wolfe Tone Memorial Committee got involved.

The pilgrimage addressed by Gilmore in 1928 was reported in the *Irish Times* as having been 'organised by the Republican and the Fianna Fáil political parties'.[97] Even if this ignored the Wolfe Tone Commemoration Committee, it does indicate the collaboration of Fianna Fáil with the I.R.A. And yet, whilst Fianna Fáil were rising politically, the detail of the arrangements published in *An Phoblacht* before the event leaves little doubt that the I.R.A. was paramount. The annual commemoration at Bodenstown was, as Brian Hanley says, in his study of the I.R.A. during the years 1926–36, 'the I.R.A.'s most important public event'.[98] Certainly, all the orators after 1925 (with the likely exception of Art O'Connor in 1927) are identifiable as members of the I.R.A.

The I.R.A. were regularly able to assemble in the field at Sallins before processing in formation, flags flying, to the graveyard, just as pilgrims had done since the 1870s; indeed they could freely maintain all Bodenstown customs. They did not however have use of the field opposite the churchyard. Was the owner unwilling to let them use it while allowing the Irish defence forces to do so? It is hard to believe there were no trespassers. An exception was made in 1925, when clearly from the published notices the organising body was Sinn Féin, not the I.R.A. Public space in the graveyard was, because of its nature, restricted. The side road leading to and beyond the graveyard was, and remains, a mere country lane. It can only be supposed, from the success of the Republican pilgrimages, that the experience of being in a large crowd of like-minded people, close to the railing around the grave of one's hero, was

'Donnelly, Eamon' in *D.I.B.*; Frank Donnelly, 28 Apr. 1954 (B.M.H., W.S. 941, pp 13–14). **94** *Ir. Indep.*, 22 June 1925. **95** *Ir. Indep.*, 21 June 1926. **96** Hanley, *I.R.A.*, pp 50–52. **97** *Ir. Times*, 18 June 1928. **98** Hanley, *I.R.A.*, pp 50–52.

uplifting. It is likely, though evidence is thin, that contingents would afterwards return to Sallins to disperse, flags flying en route and spirits high.

Undoubtedly, the Republicans' greatest organisational success during this period was in 1931 when, on the eve of their annual pilgrimage, an attempt was made by Cosgrave's government to prevent it by cancelling trains. The organisational genius was Seán MacBride, who succeeded in hiring large numbers of buses within a few hours of to make up the loss. In his memoirs he recalls in a pilgrimage in 'the year I was running it': there were 'about thirty-five special trains coming from all over the country', it was 'a vast operation'.[99] This must have been a year in the first half of the 1930s. The power of the I.R.A. over the Wolfe Tone Commemoration Committee is evident from incidents at the pilgrimage in 1934 and 1935. Peadar O'Donnell and George Gilmore, aggrieved at their Irish Republican Congress contingent — a splinter group — being manhandled by stewards and their banners seized in 1935 (as in the previous year), complained publicly that whilst 'the Bodenstown Commemoration was advertised as a national commemoration and national bodies were asked to participate, the arrangements are in the hands of the I.R.A., who allot places, choose the speaker and determine the content of the speech'.[100]

ULSTER AND BODENSTOWN

During Cosgrave's ten years in office, one historian of twentieth-century Ireland, Eunan O'Halpin, has stated, 'Northern Ireland was forgotten, the quest for unity abandoned'.[101] Support for this statement can be found in the accounts of Bodenstown pilgrimages until 1930, in which year De Valera took the opportunity of the Fianna Fáil pilgrimage to raise the Ulster question, live on the eve of, during and just after, the First World War, alluded to in Ricard O'Sullivan Burke's cable read out there in 1914, but otherwise absent from the accounts. Some consideration of Ulster's constitutional position is necessary here. Under the Government of Ireland Act of 1920 (which predated the Anglo-Irish treaty), six Ulster counties (Antrim, Armagh, Down, Fermanagh, Londonderry and Tyrone) were constitutionally separated from the other twenty-six Irish counties; the new province (*de facto*) was granted a form of home rule and the name 'Northern Ireland'. This act established separate parliaments and administrations for Northern Ireland and, with very little effect, for 'Southern Ireland'. It also provided for the creation of a 'council of Ireland' consisting of equal numbers from both parliaments to deal with matters of common interest. A provision of the Anglo-Irish treaty was for a boundary commission that would redraw rationally the common border. The treaty also confirmed the provision of a council of Ireland. The commission was not finally

---

99 Seán MacBride, *That day's struggle: a memoir, 1904–1951*, ed. Caitríona Lawlor (Dublin, 2005), p. 121. 100 *Ir. Press*, 24 June 1935. 101 Eunan O'Halpin, 'Politics and the state, 1922–32' in *A new history of Ireland*, vii (Oxford, 2003), p. 87.

appointed until October 1924. After much wrangling it was effectively abolished, and with it the council (which never met), by an agreement between the British, Northern Ireland and Irish Free State governments in December 1925. This perpetuated 'partition'.[102]

The Ulster Catholics, whose situation as a detached minority subject, as they could expect, to an unsympathetic, often hostile regime made them lament the constitutional division of Ireland, might have been unquestioning anti-Treatyites, natural Republicans. In fact, they were in 1922 pro-Treaty and remained so until the mid-1920s. They regarded Collins as their protector. His death in August 1922 was a shock that brought on feelings of exhaustion and disillusionment; their general awareness was of being now helplessly isolated from their co-religionists and of being in a political situation peculiar to Northern Ireland.[103] Those living near the border did find hope in the promise given in the treaty for redrawing the boundary, which they supposed would result in their districts being transferred to the Irish Free State, where they would be among their coreligionists. Catholics in Belfast and its hinterland had the small hope that an intergovernmental council would redress some of their grievances. The decision taken in 1925 removed those hopes. Cosgrave's subsequent indifference to their concerns was the disillusionment that made them turn to the anti-Treaty parties, as would eventually become evident at Bodenstown.

Before 1914 wreaths for Tone's grave had been received from Belfast. In that year contingents of Irish Volunteers arrived at Bodenstown from Belfast, Derry and Newry.[104] But, with one small exception, no contingent from Belfast or elsewhere north of the border delineated in 1921 is mentioned in reports between 1914 and 1930. In the Bodenstown speeches examined for the 1920s there is no advocacy of reunion or any specific mention of the north of Ireland. No orator was from Ulster. De Valera made no allusion to Ulster in the long speech he delivered at the grave in 1925. Whether the absence of Ulster contingents in the 1920s was a cause or an effect of the absence of concern for Ulster in orations, or vice versa, would be *une question mal posée*. Throughout the 1920s the provenance of Bodenstown pilgrims was very largely Dublin and the Bodenstown hinterland, just as it had been before 1914. On the evidence of the rarity of special trains arriving at Sallins from distant parts of Leinster or from Munster or Connacht, pilgrims seldom travelled far. Not until the 1930s were there special trains, buses and lorries to transport pilgrims from afar to Sallins and back in a single day. As for the silence of the orators on 'partition', their concerns were with the politics of the Irish Free State and, at that, very largely with the treaty of 1921, the oath of fidelity to the king and other links to Great Britain. The quarrel between Treatyites and anti-Treatyites over formalities must have been remote from Ulster Catholics' concerns. The Northern I.R.A. had, in the

102 A very lucid account is Michael Laffan, *The partition of Ireland, 1911–25* (Dundalk, 1983).
103 Marianne Elliott, *The Catholics of Ulster: a history* (London, 2000), pp 377–9.   104 *Freeman's Jn.*, 22 June 1914.

words of one of its commanders, 'no interest in the civil war, as their concern was the protection of their kith and kin in the six counties and the eventual unity of the country'.[105] Another consideration is that before and after 1922 Sinn Féin (and by extension the I.R.A.) never achieved the same degree of popularity in Ulster as in the other provinces; independent-minded and strong-willed nationalist politicians, most famously Joseph Devlin in Belfast, had large personal followings.[106] Only in Belfast, in the Catholic districts, was there significant Republican sentiment. According to one authority, some Belfast Republicans, lacking prospects, moved south of the border for employment with the consequence that the I.R.A. became almost extinct in Belfast.[107] One such migrant was Eunan O'Halpin's grandfather, who joined the new police force.[108] There was one man from Northern Ireland who had an important role in organising the Republican pilgrimages in 1924 and 1925 — Éamon Donnelly, whose home was at Newry, just north of the border. In June 1924 he apparently had some fellow 'North of Ireland Republicans' join him at Bodenstown.[109] In April 1925, standing as a Republican, he was elected to the Northern Ireland parliament as one of the M.P.s for Armagh and so in June he was uniquely an elected representative of Ulster Catholics at Bodenstown; about this time however he moved south and threw himself into Fianna Fáil politics, trying unsuccessfully to persuade De Valera to extend the party's organisation into Northern Ireland.[110] No report has been found earlier than 1929 of the Northern I.R.A. being represented at Bodenstown, and then it was a vague mention in *An Phoblacht* of 'officers' representing 'units as far distant as Belfast'; there are no allusions to Ulster at all in 1930; not until 1931 did *An Phoblacht* allude to pilgrims arriving from Belfast (as did the *Irish Independent*), but it was left unclear whether they formed an I.R.A. contingent.[111]

There was an alternative to Bodenstown for Belfast Republicans. Some in the late 1920s and into the 1930s commemorated Tone at McArt's Fort on Cave Hill.[112] This was the place on the north-western outskirts of the city where, a few days before Tone left Ireland for America on 13 June 1795, he and half a dozen political associates assembled and solemnly undertook 'never to desist in our efforts until we had subverted the authority of England over our country'.[113] In 1898, the centenary of the Irish rebellion, a wreath of heather gathered near McArt's Fort had been laid on Tone's grave on behalf of the organising committee at the annual commemoration.[114]

105 Robert Lynch, *The Northern I.R.A. and the early years of Partition* (Dublin, 2006), p. 171. **106** Esp. Eamon Phoenix, *Northern nationalism: nationalist politics, partition and the Catholic minority in Northern Ireland, 1890–1940* (Belfast, 1994).   **107** Ronnie Munck and Bill Rolston, *Belfast in the thirties: an oral history* (Belfast, 1987), pp 166–7.   **108** Eunan O'Halpin, *Defending Ireland: the Irish state and its enemies since 1922* (Oxford, 1999), p. viii.   **109** There is a passing mention of this group in *Leinster Leader*, 28 June 1924.   **110** Brian Walker, *Parliamentary election results in Ireland, 1918–92* (Dublin, 1992), p. 47; Ó Beacháin, *Destiny of the soldiers*, p. 139. **111** *An Phoblacht*, 22 June 1929, 27 June 1931; *Ir. Indep.*, 22 June 1931.   **112** *An Phoblacht*, 22 June 1929; *Irish News* (Belfast), 23 June 1930, 22 June 1931.   **113** Tone, *Writings*, ii, 333. **114** *Freeman's Jn.*, 20 June 1898; *Ir. Daily Indep.*, 20 June 1898.

The 'alternative' pilgrimage to McArt's Fort was intended to coincide with the Republicans' annual pilgrimage to Bodenstown; it was a feeble imitation but drew opposition from the authorities.

THE NATIONAL GRAVES ASSOCIATION

Tone's grave was being looked after by local people when Davis and Gray paid their visit in 1843. At that time and until the coming into effect on 1 January 1871 of the Irish Church Act of 1869, Bodenstown churchyard was part of the property of the established Protestant church and as such was a public graveyard. Under that act ownership passed to the state and by the 1890s the property was vested in the Naas Board of Guardians. From the early 1920s the graveyard (as distinct from the graves) seems to have been vested in Kildare County Council as a result of the effective abolition of the Boards of Guardians in 1922, formalised in 1923 by the Local Government (Temporary Provisions) Act.[115] None of these changes prevented private individuals, typically family members, from looking after graves. In 1908 a 'committee of local Gaels' was formed to take charge of Tone's grave, for which purpose they would raise money for 'necessary renovation' and collaborate with the Wolfe Tone Memorial Committee.[116] But the state of the churchyard in the mid 1920s appalled some. In June of 1925 the Dublin correspondent of the *Fermanagh Herald* complained that 'long grass, briars and nettles are in abundance everywhere, and, were it not for the little iron railing surrounding the grave of Tone, it too would be covered over. ... Nothing has been done for many years to make the place worthy of the noble heart that lies there.'[117] Late spring and early summer are periods of aggressive growth and so by mid June mowing and trimming would have been imperative. The presence of pilgrims also had an adverse effect. In a report of the pilgrimages in 1926, held in 'glorious summer weather', the *Irish Independent*, under the heading 'Unedifying scenes mar ceremonies', noted that a new wall and new paths gave the place 'a greatly-improved appearance', which however was spoilt after the military and official parties in the first ceremony withdrew to the parade ground at some distance:

> the gates of the graveyard were thrown open, and no one was in charge. Amongst the first to enter were vendors of fruit, ice cream and liquid refreshments with their hand-carts and baskets, and they proceeded to establish 'stands' in all parts of the sacred ground. They numbered between 30 and 40, and at least half-a-dozen of them stood shouting their wares within a few feet of the grave of the patriot ... There was no order, and the refreshment vendors and itinerant photographers seemed to be doing a

115 Brian Donnelly, 'Local government in Kildare, 1920–1970' in William Nolan and Thomas McGrath (eds), *Kildare history and society* (Dublin, 2006), pp 672–711 at pp 677–8. 116 *Freeman's Jn.*, 13 July 1908. 117 *Fermanagh Herald*, 27 June 1925.

thriving trade. Orange peels, apple skins, papers, fragments of food, bottles broken and whole, were strewn all around. Some wreaths were smashed ... Graves were trampled on and fresh flowers placed on some of them were crushed to pulp. Such was the condition of the place shortly before the beginning of the second ceremony. Fianna boy scouts and volunteers, after some trouble, succeeded in restoring something like order when the procession arrived ... the grave of a hero to become the temporary stand for a vendor of fruit and refreshments. One would expect that some responsible body would undertake the control and regulation of such a historic spot on the day of the commemoration of the patriot whose remains it contains.

The report of the scene concluded, 'it is to be hoped that next year some method of control and organisation will be adopted to prevent a recurrence'.[118] The maintenance of the 'holy place' at other times (as distinct from the organising of pilgrimages) was soon to be a matter for another body: the National Graves Association.

The first meeting of the National Graves Association took place, according to its official history, on 21 August 1926, presided over by Kathleen Clarke, at 41 Parnell Square — the address of the Wolfe Tone Memorial Committee. Its treasurers were Mrs Clarke and James Stritch; the more active of its two secretaries was Seán Fitzpatrick; the stated purpose of the association was to locate and mark graves of 'known patriots of any period' and renovate and preserve them in good condition.[119] To judge from the lack of any mention of the association in the newspapers in 1926 and 1927, it either made slow progress or the year given is wrong. It was not mentioned in any report of Bodenstown pilgrimages until 1934. Tone must have qualified as a patriot (a term not defined), as the association 'turned its attention' to his grave in 1930, cleaning the inscription on the stone erected in 1895.[120] The National Graves Association is mentioned often in this study, as is Seán Fitzpatrick (1887–1963), a Dublin Corporation employee and old I.R.A. man, who remained secretary until 1962, in which year he was succeeded by his son, also Seán (d. 1986).[121] It is described by Anne Dolan, an historian of Irish republican commemorations, as a 'shadowy body' that 'no one knows or cares to find out very much about'.[122] Neither Professor Dolan, nor Dr Peter Collins (one who does give the National Graves Association attention), nor any other historian of Irish republicanism, explains the legal basis for its reappropriation of a family grave and its monuments in a public cemetery.[123]

---

118 *Ir. Indep.*, 21 June 1926.   119 National Graves Association, *The last post* (2nd ed., Dublin, 1976), pp 13–14. More information about the association is given by Seán Fitzpatrick in a letter to the *Irish Press*, published on 17 May 1933, and in his article, 'Lest we forget' in *Irish Press*, 6 June 1940, p. 6. For Fitzpatrick himself, see *United Irishman*, Apr. 1963.   120 *The last post*, p. 16.
121 *Ir. Press*, 8 Mar. 1966, 2 May 1986.   122 Anne Dolan, 'An army of our Fenian dead' in Fearghal McGarry (ed.), *Republicanism in modern Ireland* (Dublin, 2003), p. 134.   123 Collins, *Who fears*, p. 55. Brian Hanley, generally thorough in his *I.R.A.* (2002), is silent on this point.

Stritch's treasurership of the National Graves Association, jointly with Tom Clarke's widow, was the final episode of the story of his association with the Irish republicans which began in Manchester in the 1860s. He had been treasurer of the Wolfe Tone Memorial Committee since 1905 (if not before) and remained custodian of its funds, no longer being drawn down for pilgrimages after 1922. In or after 1924 he retired from his position with Dublin Corporation and in 1931 was in receipt of a pension of £256; he probably derived an income too from the eight houses he owned at Drumcondra, a salubrious suburb.[124] According to an account of his career published at the time of his death in 1933, he 'never missed the annual pilgrimage to Bodenstown, held in June, since its inception'. Certainly eight months before, he took part in a small Sinn Féin pilgrimage.[125]

OFFICIAL AND UNOFFICIAL

Nationalist or Republican pilgrimages were unofficial until 1923. From that year, when the revolution was virtually completed but the ultras not subdued, there were rival official and unofficial pilgrimages, until 1928 on the same day. The continuation of the custom of annual pilgrimages to Tone's grave after the achievement of Irish independence, and the gravity and scale of the officially-organised pilgrimages in the middle years of the 1920s, can be explained by the intention of the pro-Treaty party now firmly in power not to be upstaged by the anti-Treaty party as had happened in 1922. For their part the anti-Treatyites had every reason to keep up appearances. The greater strength of the official party lay in its ability to display conventional military might and to parade at the same time members of its administrative and judicial establishment. The greater strength of the Republicans lay in their ability to continue the custom of volunteering begun in 1913 as well as the ritual, oratory and pastime dating from the 1870s, thereby drawing large crowds. They had strength too in the size and demeanour of the participants in their rallies: their crowds were more impressive, more enthusiastic, probably (though unstated) more proletarian. During the first few years after 1922 the official demonstrations, essentially military displays, attracted large numbers of the general public; by 1931 this interest seems to have waned. But the Republicans' demonstrations were increasingly large; that of 1931 larger than before in spite of all special trains to Sallins being cancelled by order of the government. Despite all this posturing, comparisons can be made of the rivals.

Demonstrations at Bodenstown from 1923 until 1931 were assertions of legitimacy by both the Cumann na nGaedheal government of the infant Irish Free State and its Republican challengers, who regarded any connexion with the British monarchy as incompatible with the declaration of a republic in 1916, and with the principles on which the war of independence was waged until 1921. Republicans

---

124 *Ir. Times*, 2 Jan. 1931; *Ir. Press*, 23 Apr. 1934.   125 *Ir. Press*, 28 June 1932, 25 Feb. 1933.

who were in the I.R.A. would imitate the National Army (the Irish defence forces) in their formation and discipline; members of Fianna Éireann ('the Fianna', the Republican Boy Scouts) would, like army cadet buglers from the Curragh, sound the Last Post. Laying of wreaths on Tone's grave was, for both parties, *de rigueur*, as before. Assertions of legitimacy were made all the more strongly when the two groups assembled on the same day. Cumann na nGaedheal and Republican orations alike were long in rhetoric and aspiration. All did at least include a mention of Tone — rather as public speeches in Soviet Russia invariably included a mention of Lenin. Most orators referred to Tone's career, quoted one or two apt dicta, and earnestly drew lessons for the present; they showed familiarity with Tone's writings rather as a Protestant preacher would show familiarity with the Bible. The core text — the Gospel — was the Autobiography.[126] Just the same, the dispassionate listener might have asked, 'what have the pilgrimages to do with Tone?'

126 Usually, most likely, *The autobiography of Theobald Wolfe Tone, 1763–1798*, ed. R. Barry O'Brien (2 vols, London, 1893). It was mentioned by a speaker at Bodenstown on 25 June 1893 (*Leinster Leader*, 1 July 1893). There were reprints in 1910 and 1912.

7

Rival pilgrimages, 1932–9

O**N 9 MARCH 1932**, Fianna Fáil, led by De Valera, strong-minded and capable, replaced Cumann na nGaedheal in office; by June the new government had taken measures to abolish the oath of fidelity obnoxious to Republicans, thereby removing one of the main grievances hitherto aired by Republicans at Bodenstown.

In 'Orders of the day', published in *An Phoblacht* to give advance notice of the I.R.A.-sponsored pilgrimage to be held on 19 June 1932, provision was made, under 'Order of procession', for 'members of Fianna Fáil'.[1] It proved to be, as in 1931, a grand affair: some fifteen thousand participants arriving by train, bus and lorry from all parts of the Irish Free State; fourteen bands; a procession of thirty-seven I.R.A. battalions and of associated bodies, a newcomer among them the Revolutionary Workers' Party (or Group), the communist party created by the Comintern eighteen months before.[2] Except for the large Belfast battalion, no battalion was from any of the six Ulster counties that remained attached to Great Britain. It was the first Bodenstown pilgrimage to be reported in the Fianna Fáil daily newspaper, the *Irish Press*. The first issue had appeared the previous September; the new paper was avant-garde in design; unlike the established papers that it rivalled, it had news on the front page. In the issue for the day after the I.R.A. pilgrimage to Bodenstown the glaring front-page headline read: 'Twelve thousand more pilgrims'. But they were not pilgrims to Tone's grave, they were participants in the Eucharistic Congress, a mammoth Catholic prayer-meeting in the Phoenix Park. A report of Bodenstown appeared on page seven. It stated, in bold type, that Kathleen Clarke and two others had 'laid a wreath on Tone's grave on behalf of the National Executive of Fianna Fáil'. Mrs Clarke had been a Fianna Fáil member of the Senate since 1928. Only three Fianna Fáil members of the Dáil, all back-benchers, were named as present: John Flynn, elected a deputy for Kerry three months before; Richard Walsh, a deputy for Mayo South since September 1927; and Stephen Jordan, a deputy for Galway since that date.[3] Another member of Fianna Fáil was named in the report in the *Irish Times*: Donal Buckley who, first elected to the Dáil as a Fianna Fáil candidate in Kildare in June 1927, had suffered the ignominy of

1 *An Phoblacht*, 18 June 1932; repr. in Hanley, *I.R.A.*, pp 205–06. 2 *Ir. Times*, 20 June 1932; *Ir. Indep.*, 16, 20 June 1932; Emmet O'Connor, *Reds and the green: Ireland, Russia and the communist internationals, 1919–43* (Dublin, 2004), pp 155, 158. It had in Nov. 1930 been renamed Revolutionary Workers' Group. 3 *Ir. Press*, 20 June 1932; Walker, *Ir. parlty election results, 1918–92*

being defeated badly in the Fianna Fáil landslide election of 1931.[4] As, unlike in the previous year, neither De Valera nor any of his close associates was present, it is a safe assumption that Fianna Fáil were not being represented officially; and unlike in 1929 and 1930, the party did not have its own pilgrimage in 1932. At Bodenstown on that June day in 1932, Seán Russell, who twelve months previously had been arrested a few hours before he was to give the oration, lauded Tone, castigated the authorities of the Irish Free State and urged young people listening to join the I.R.A. or Cumann na mBan.[5] Russell was later, like Tone, to seek military support from Great Britain's enemy during time of war and to return to Ireland in an enemy vessel; unlike Tone, he was to die, of natural causes, before being able to set foot again on Irish soil. More on him is to come below.

Nine days later, on 28 June 1932, a Tuesday (perhaps to avoid clashing, if only metaphorically, with the prayer meeting in the Phoenix Park on the previous Sunday), members of the new government were at Bodenstown taking part in what was a military ceremony lacking the conspicuous civilian presence in the official pilgrimages of the mid 1920s. Headed by an army band, two infantry battalions followed by an armoured-car detachment and contingents from the Army Medical Service and Signals Corps marched in review past the new minister for defence, Frank Aiken; overhead appeared a flight of three planes dipped in salute. Accompanying Aiken were the ministers for justice and education, James Geoghegan and Thomas Derrig respectively. After the display, Aiken addressed the troops, complimenting them on having 'played their part so well in making a huge success of the great Eucharistic festival which took place during last week' and surmised that Tone, 'looking down on us today, must feel glad to see us here'.[6] Now Aiken (1898–1983), chief-of-staff of the I.R.A. from the last months of the civil war until the end of 1925, had not left the organisation until May 1927; he had marched with the I.R.A. to Bodenstown in 1931; moreover, three days after polling in the general election of February 1932 which put Fianna Fáil into office, he had written to the I.R.A.'s chief-of-staff, Maurice Twomey, arguing for a merger between their organisations.[7] In speaking effusively of the role of the defence forces of the Irish Free State at the Eucharistic Congress he was able to ignore its deployment against the I.R.A. during the civil war. In so publicly recognising and respecting the defence forces he antagonised his former comrades in the I.R.A. and brought upon himself charges of hypocrisy. One criticism was advertising the defence forces' ceremony as 'the annual commemoration in honour of Wolfe Tone'. If he had in mind the annual commemoration by the defence forces when Cumann na nGaedheal were in office, from 1923 until 1931, it was at least, as one historian of the party has pointed out, 'a curious description considering that Fianna Fáil had never attended it before'.[8]

(Dublin, 1992), pp 128, 129, 134, 136. 4 *Ir. Times*, 20 June 1932; Marie Coleman, 'Ó Buachalla, Donal (1866–1963)' in *D.I.B.* 5 *Ir. Times*, 20 June 1932; *Ir. Indep.*, 20 June 1932. 6 *Ir. Times*, 29 June 1932. A similar report is in *Ir. Indep.*, 29 June 1932. 7 Hanley, *I.R.A.*, pp 113–14, 126, 248. There is a long article on Aiken by Ronan Fanning in *D.I.B.* See also Bryce Evans and Stephen Kelly (eds), *Frank Aiken, nationalist and internationalist* (Dublin, 2015). 8 Ó Beacháin,

Only twelve months before, Aiken and other members of the party had taken part in the annual Bodenstown pilgrimage of the Irish Republican Army, arguably a seditious organisation.[9] He could have had in mind this pilgrimage and earlier Republican pilgrimages and not the defence forces' ceremonies. In 1927, Fianna Fáil's own newspaper, the *Nation*, advertised the Republicans' commemoration (which members of the party were to, and did, attend) as 'the Annual Pilgrimage to Bodenstown'.[10] It could also be pointed out that the defence forces' ceremony in 1932 was held on a weekday and that, to judge from press reports, the general public were largely and inevitably absent.

De Valera was not with Aiken at Bodenstown on that working day in 1932, perhaps because he had to be present in the Dáil and also to receive visitors from overseas.[11] A more likely reason was a wish that Aiken should be the one to deflect expected criticism of Fianna Fáil's *volte face*. But he was not to be absent from Bodenstown again until 1941. Missing from the front page of the Fianna Fáil newspaper, the *Irish Press*, on the following day was any report of the defence force's ceremony; it was hidden away on page 5 and brief; the main item on the front page was an adulatory report of the progress north of the papal legate.[12] A few days earlier it had reported a million people gathered in the Phoenix Park to hear a message from the Pope, the high point of the Eucharistic Congress, some devotees having waited all night.[13] Such reports put adulation of Tone and pilgrimages to his grave into perspective.

Of less importance, the remnant of Sinn Féin made its own pilgrimage to Tone's grave on the evening before Aiken and the defence forces. The *Leinster Leader* reported 'a considerable number' arriving 'in motor-cars and specially chartered buses'. One was James Stritch. Part of the proceedings was the reciting of a decade of the Rosary by a maverick priest and dedicated supporter, Michael O'Flanagan.[14] The orator was Peadar McAndrews, who kept a grocery in Dublin; he was sentenced to imprisonment in 1940 for refusing to account for his movements and was later interned at the Curragh; he was free by 1946 when he presided at Bodenstown; he seems to have died in 1961.[15] It was a sequel to the hastily-organised Sinn Féin pilgrimage of 1931. Whether more were organised annually in the 1930s has not been ascertained. In August 1936, after the I.R.A. and its planned pilgrimage were banned, Sinn Féin did organise a demonstration at Bodenstown to compensate Republicans for their loss, as will be shown.

FIANNA FAIL'S MOST SPECTACULAR PILGRIMAGE

In 1933 the governing party's pilgrimage, on 25 June, was a spectacular display of organisational ability and eagerness by its supporters to appear in large numbers.

Destiny of the soldiers, p. 131. **9** A point discussed in ibid., chap. 4. **10** *Nation*, 18 June 1927. **11** *Ir. Times*, 29 June 1932. **12** *Ir. Press*, 29 June 1932. **13** *Ir. Press*, 27 June 1932. **14** For O'Flanagan (1876–1942), see Patrick Maume's article on him in *D.I.B.* **15** *Leinster Leader*, 2

The report in the *Irish Press* was long, detailed, enthusiastic and uniquely enhanced by one of its reporters witnessing the scene from a low-flying aeroplane. 'What', he asked, 'would Tone have thought could he have seen it thus? Bodenstown, its churchyard and its pilgrims stretched out below like a patterned patchwork quilt, the tomb no bigger than a thumbnail, the long procession now like a dark river through the grass, now like a string of coloured beads.' As the plane approached, this reporter had observed that

> Naas passed under, its streets empty. Along the railway lines flashed a special train from Dublin. The white dresses of children could be seen in the dark carriages. Over Sallins. Sallins! ... The streets of the village itself were thronged. As we passed over the assembly field the sections of the procession had begun to take their places ... We circled and flew on ... a gray mortuary chapel just beside the grave. The railings marked it out ... There were already many in that high field and, as in Sallins, to the South, more came hurrying across the meadows, singly and in twos, little rivulets of pilgrims. Over a platform ... a tricolour was taut in the high wind ... we could just pick out the tall figure of the Fianna Fáil president. In front of them moved the pilgrims, each as he went keeping his face in homage towards the tomb. Along three sides of the field the slow procession moved, passing thence into the big parade ground where a thousand or so had already taken their places in long files by the platform. Outside the field the road was packed with pilgrims waiting to enter. To the left were many motor cars grouped in a parking field ... The white caps of the bandsmen, the saffron capes of the pipers, the long green hooded cloaks of girl processionists, the gay summer colours of the women's frocks and children's dresses, the flashing band instruments, the cream white catering-tents, the white banners with the lettering too far below to read which caught the sun, and beyond the ever filling big field ... we turned ... At Sallins the streets were still crowded as people from late trains and busses hurried towards Bodenstown to pay homage.

The 'Fianna Fáil president' was Éamon de Valera, a very tall man. Heralded by the St James's Brass and Reed Band, he headed a procession of members of the Executive Council (his cabinet), the party's National Executive, the Dáil and the Senate, after whom came county contingents of ordinary members. Wolfe Tone souvenir papers and badges were sold. De Valera placed a wreath on the grave beside that placed earlier by Aiken; he then 'paused for a few moments in prayer'. An oration was given by the deputy leader, Seán T. O'Kelly. The *Irish Press* estimated the attendance to have been fifteen thousand.[16] The *Irish Times*, which named eleven bands, put it at ten thousand, the *Irish Independent* at eight thousand; both had

July 1932; *Ir. Press*, 12 Jan. 1940, 5 Feb. 1941, 5 Dec. 1961; Uinseann MacEoin, *The I.R.A. in the twilight years, 1923–1948* ([Dublin, 1997]), pp 433, 487, 720, 768–9; Nat. Arch., Dublin, JUS 8/900 (1946).   16 *Ir. Press*, 26 June 1933. In the same issue was an aerial photograph.

estimated the attendance at the I.R.A.'s pilgrimage the previous Sunday as over five thousand, the *Irish Press* as 'between ten and fifteen thousand'.[17] Comparison could be made with the Cumann na nGaedheal government's display at Bodenstown ten years previously. In both cases the new government had only recently secured its hold on power; Bodenstown in the month of June was an opportunity to show its popularity and its adhesion to a nationalist tradition. At Bodenstown in 1933 Tone became, as one writer has put it, 'affiliated to Fianna Fáil as a mascot'.[18]

SEPARATE COMMEMORATIONS BY THE IRISH DEFENCE FORCES

An important and lasting difference in 1933 was the separation of the party's commemoration from the army's. From then on the army appeared at Bodenstown about midday, the party and its followers in the afternoon. This practice was to continue into the 1940s, with two exceptions, until Fianna Fáil left office in 1948. At the military ceremony the minister for defence would be present, he would lay a wreath, three volleys would be fired, the Last Post would be sounded, and then he would inspect a guard of honour, as in the 1920s. In 1932 and in the four following years, the minister, Aiken, addressed the troops; this practice was dropped in 1937 'in view of the inclement weather'.[19] It was never resumed. Aiken's last appearance at Bodenstown in this ministerial capacity was in 1939. It was a spectacular affair in 1932: infantry, artillery, armoured cars, transport, medical and signals corps, cadets from the Military College sounding the Last Post, finishing with a flight of aeroplanes dipping in salute; two thousand troops participated in 1933 and 1934; there were 1,400 men 'from all units' on parade in 1935; there were, as variously stated, between 1,000 and 3,000 reviewed in 1936; three battalions, several armed or ancillary corps and an air squadron appeared in 1937, though no composite figure has been found; a report for 1938 states that 'about 50 officers, 35 cadets and the No. 3 Band composed the entire parade' and that 'in contrast to the pageantry of other years' there was 'a simple ceremony lasting twenty minutes'; similarly in 1939 the ceremony was simple.[20] Evidently for the Fianna Fáil minister's first three appearances a great effort was made to impress; it was increased in the mid-1930s, perhaps to challenge the I.R.A.; it decreased noticeably in 1938, the I.R.A. much less a threat, and became little more than a customary formality.

REPUBLICANS AND FIANNA FÁIL APPEAR ON ALTERNATE SUNDAYS

Another difference was that during the 1930s the Republicans' pilgrimage was never on the same day as that of the government party. In 1933 and 1934 it was on the Sunday preceding, in 1935 on the Sunday following. So on 18 June 1933 (a week

17 *Ir. Times*, 19, 26 June 1933; *Ir. Indep.*, 19, 26 June 1933; *Ir. Press*, 19 June 1933.   **18** Travers, 'Tone of national commemorations', p. 25.   **19** *Ir. Times*, 14 June 1937.   **20** *Ir. Times*, 29 June

before the large Fianna Fáil pilgrimage) a spectacular I.R.A. commemoration was held at Bodenstown, drawing, according to a long and detailed report in the *Irish Press*, between ten and fifteen thousand people, from 'all parts of Ireland', some arriving on one of ten special trains and thirty or more long-distance buses; others in motor-cars or on bicycles — ten men cycling from Waterford overnight; probably a couple of hundred making up the 22 bands.[21] 'In a very large measure', reported the *Irish Times*, 'the gathering bore the character of a turn-out by the Irish Republican Army and its leaders ... About 45 named units, companies and battalions of I.R.A. members marched in the procession, together with members of the Cumann na mBan, Republican Girl Guides and boys of Fianna Éireann.' Its reporter was taken by the 'interesting spectacle' of 'the variety of uniforms, especially those of children from about 12 years of age, who were exemplars in their ready response to drill commands. Most of the women and girls were in uniform.'[22] Some of these 'children' and 'girls' were members of the Cumann na gCailíní formed a few years before.[23] The main purpose of the orator, Maurice ('Moss') Twomey, chief-of-staff of the I.R.A., was to reject accusations made by Catholic ecclesiastics of his organisation 'being anti-religious' and 'aiming at the subversion of religion in Ireland'; to dissociate it from communism and 'the Communist movement'; and to deny 'that the I.R.A. was secret', that an 'oath of secrecy was demanded' and that its leadership was clandestine. 'In the face of the attacks which are being made on us', he said, 'we will be careful to distinguish between the moral law, the law of the church, and the politics of the Church dignitaries and the clergy'.[24] Twomey himself was a practising Catholic whose political opinions were, except for his attitude to the Irish Free State, conventional. The same was probably true for the large majority of the members of the I.R.A. Despite this, there were a few members whose perceived tendencies were secular and even socialist. The best known were George Gilmore, a Protestant, and Peadar O'Donnell, who had given the orations in 1928 and 1931 respectively and were present in 1933. Embarrassing to Twomey must have been the 80 men and women who 'marched at the rear of the procession behind a banner bearing the inscription "Communist Party of Ireland, Dublin Local"', likely as it was that many of the men were also in the I.R.A.[25] Certainly, the publicity given by the I.R.A. in *An Phoblacht* to the Bodenstown pilgrimages that it sponsored, and which it used to promote itself, told against the charge that it was a secret society. The I.R.A. did, however, require of its members an oath, something never mentioned by its orators at Bodenstown.[26]

1932, 26 June 1933, 17 June 1935, 15 June 1936 (over 2,000), 14 June 1937, 27 June 1938, 19 June 1939; *Ir. Press*, 25 June 1934, 15 June 1936 (1,500), 17 June 1940; *Ir. Indep.*, 15 June 1936 (about 3,000).   21 *Ir. Press*, 19 June 1933. The attendance figure was given as 'over 5,000' in *Ir. Indep.*, 19 June 1933, and 'between 5,000 and 6,000' in *Ir. Times*, 19 June 1933.   22 *Ir. Times*, 19 June 1933.   23 Ann Matthews, *Dissidents: Irish Republican women, 1923–1941* (Cork, 2012), p. 202. Girls in Cumann na gCailíní were aged from 8 to 16.   24 *Ir. Times*, 19 June 1933.   25 *Kildare Observer*, 24 June 1933; Adrian Grant, *Irish socialist republicanism, 1909–36* (Dublin, 2012), p. 205. 26 Some of these points and more are discussed in Hanley, *I.R.A.*, pp 36, 64–7.

The Fianna Fáil demonstration at Bodenstown of 1934 was reported in the *Irish Press* under the headline 'Nation's homage at grave of Tone' and described as 'All-Ireland Pilgrimage' led by De Valera. Attendance was estimated to be 'between eight and ten thousand'; there, as well as expected Fianna Fáil dignitaries, ordinary members from the provinces including 'Monaghan, Cavan, Donegal, Derry and other Ulster counties'; more curiously still there were at the graveside 'members of the Dublin Brigade, I.R.A.'. The last mentioned were no doubt members of what, in Fianna Fáil circles, came to be known as 'Old I.R.A.', men who had fought on the anti-Treaty side in the civil war and later followed Lemass and Aiken out of the I.R.A. The chief marshal at the assembly field at Sallins was one such man, Joseph O'Connor, formerly commanding officer of the Dublin Brigade. The 'official Fianna Fáil Wolfe Tone badge' was generally worn. The orator, Patrick Ruttledge, minister for education, repeated Tone's statement of the United Irishmen's mission: 'to abolish the memory of past dissensions', and asserted that 'the task of Fianna Fáil today was the task which Tone set himself to accomplish ... the uniting of the people'.[27] This endorsement of national unity echoed that made by Cosgrave at Bodenstown ten years before. Fianna Fáil's pilgrimage in 1934 was less spectacular than in 1933; it did not compare in size with a religious pilgrimage in Belfast on the same day. This was another 'eucharistic congress', this one organised by the Catholic Truth Society of Ireland and reported to have attracted 120,000 devotees and required 2,500 stewards.[28]

THE I.R.A.'S LEGENDARY PILGRIMAGES

The Republican pilgrimage of 17 June 1934 is legendary. It came at a time when some Republicans, already dismissive of both Sinn Féin and Fianna Fáil, were becoming disillusioned with the I.R.A. As well as for its great size, it was important for several new factors: the reappearance of the Irish Citizen Army; the persistence of the Communists in returning; the appearance of a new party, the Irish Republican Congress; the participation of a Protestant contingent from Belfast; and physical conflict between different contingents. The *Irish Times* reported a turn-out of 30,000, half of them in the I.R.A. and in 42 units drawn from all thirty-two counties of Ireland.[29] The number recorded by the police is still impressive: over twenty thousand, 4,000 of them onlookers, 17,000 participants.[30] The *Irish Independent* reported that

> the procession included a contingent of 500 representing the James Connolly Workers' Republican Club, a body formed by the Republican Congress Party. The members of this contingent were composed largely of Protestants and Presbyterians drawn in the main from the Shankill, Newtownards Road and

27 *Ir. Press*, 25 June 1934.   28 *Ir. Indep.*, 25 June 1934.   29 *Ir. Times*, 18 June 1934.   30 Hanley, *I.R.A.*, pp 51, 226.

other Orange districts of Belfast. Earlier in the day members of this contingent visited the grave of James Connolly in Dublin.

The reporter was informed that 'this was the first occasion ... on which a body from purely Orange areas of Belfast took part in the commemoration at Tone's grave'.[31] Undoubtedly it was. Two 'lorry loads' had made their way south led by Bill McMullan; nine or ten of them have been identified by Raymond Quinn; no doubt they were republican socialists encouraged by Peadar O'Donnell and, unlike most Republican pilgrims, motivated by concern about economic and social matters, not about shortcomings in the Anglo-Irish treaty; several of them were to die in the Spanish civil war.[32]

What was most divisive arose from the presence of the Republican Congress, a group of a socialist tendency which two months before, led by O'Donnell, Gilmore and Frank Ryan, had broken away from the I.R.A. Just before the customary procession began moving off from the assembly field at Sallins there was an ugly scene. Pilgrims in the Republican Congress contingent, which included the Shankill Connolly Workers' Club (the Protestant body), were ordered by stewards to fold their banners 'as permission for their display was not given by the Pilgrimage Committee'; an exchange of words between leaders followed; then 'fifty or sixty' members of the Tipperary Battalion of the I.R.A. near the scene were called upon to aid the stewards; they responded by tearing down flags of the Irish Republican Congress and the red flag of the Communist Party of Ireland; men of the Republican Congress retaliated with blows and were joined by some men of the Irish Citizen Army. The brawl lasted several minutes. It seems that the flags of the Belfast Connolly clubs and the Communist Party of Ireland were similarly not permitted. The torn flags were displayed on the parade, but some of the Congress and Citizen Army men refused to enter the churchyard, instead returning with the Workers' Union of Ireland Band to the assembly field and holding a protest meeting.[33] What was upsetting to the organisers, fearful of being tainted with socialism, was wording on the banners such as 'Break the connection with capitalism'.[34] The affair became 'an established part of left-wing republican folklore'.[35] The experiment of Protestant working men taking part in a pilgrimage to Tone's grave was not repeated. Gilmore was later given to remarking, 'It'll be a long time before "Come on Shankill!" will be heard at Bodenstown again'.[36]

The oration, delivered by Patrick McLogan, was aggressive and made no allowance for the Protestant contingent. 'In the name of all Ireland and their kin beyond the seas', he trumpeted, 'they of the I.R.A. and of kindred revolutionary organisations declared their intention to make another effort to end English rule in

31 *Ir. Indep.*, 18 June 1934.   32 R. J. Quinn, *A rebel voice: a history of Belfast republicanism, 1925–1972* (Belfast, 1999), pp 19–26. This includes a photo of Belfast men holding their banner aloft in the parade. See also Munck & Rolston, *Belfast in the thirties*, pp 181, 183.   33 *Ir. Press*, 18 June 1934; *Ir. Indep.*, 18 June 1934.   34 Nic Dháibhéid, *Seán MacBride*, p. 117.   35 Hanley, *I.R.A.*, p. 107.   36 Peter Hegarty, *Peadar O'Donnell* (Cork, 1999), pp 219–20.

Ireland'.[37] McLogan (1898?–1966), an Armagh man running a public house south of the Irish border in County Leix, was then chairman of the I.R.A. army council; he was in the 1940s interned at the Curragh and in the 1950s president of Sinn Féin; he was remembered by Seán MacBride as 'rather narrow-minded in his outlook but an extremely fine person himself'.[38] It has been stated that after the demonstration in 1934 was over, a group of Fianna Éireann led by Brendan Behan, who was to achieve literary fame in the 1960s, reached Sallins to find that they had over an hour's wait for a train back to Dublin; Behan, aged only eleven, entered a public house and became drunk, for which he was court-martialled.[39] This is questionable. Behan's great youth combined with his tempestuousness would have barred him from a leadership role and from admittance to a public house. Perhaps it was later.

The Republicans' pilgrimage in 1935 was almost a repeat performance, but without the Protestants and without the Irish Citizen Army. The organising committee announced that there were to be twenty-two special trains arriving from all parts of Ireland, those from the north direct to Sallins via the Loop Line.[40] After the event it was reported that the trains carried 4,517 passengers, more pilgrims arrived in about 50 buses (particularly from the north) while others made their way in lorries, in motor-cars and on bicycles; some 7,000 took part in the procession watched by hundreds at the assembly point and along the route.

Near the assembly field at Sallins there was an incident, a brawl, similar to the previous year's. A section of the I.R.A. attempted to seize a banner inscribed 'Republican Congress'; resistance was offered by the Republican Congress men, by Communists and by Workers' Union of Ireland bandsmen; wooden marker posts were used as cudgels; the two hundred or so resisters succeeded in breaking into the field, forming up with the main body and starting to march. A few hundred yards outside Sallins they stopped and returned. An impromptu protest meeting was addressed by Sean Murray, Barney Conway, George Gilmore and Peadar O'Donnell. Conway spoke of the 'disgraceful scene' as having been 'caused by a Hitlerite section of the I.R.A.'.[41]

The orator was Seán MacBride (1904–88). Several times he has been mentioned above, and his father, John, over twenty times. John MacBride led an Irish unit against the British in the Boer War, for which he became known as 'Major MacBride'; he made a somewhat seditious speech at Bodenstown after his return to Ireland in 1905, presided when the pilgrimages were revived in 1911, and was executed for commanding insurgents in 1916. Seán MacBride's mother, Maud, was an English heiress, independent-minded and a convert to Irish nationalism and catholicism. Seán, of the 'republican nobility', educated by Jesuits in France and by a nationalistic Benedictine priest in Ireland, had been in the Four Courts garrison

---

37 *Ir. Press*, 18 June 1934. 38 *Ir. Indep.*, 22 July 1964; Hanley, *I.R.A.*, p. 194 et passim; Seán MacBride, *That day's struggle: a memoir, 1904–1951*, ed. Caitríona Lawlor (Dublin, 2005), p. 124. See also Coogan, *I.R.A.*, pp 257–8. 39 Michael O'Sullivan, *Brendan Behan: a life* (Dublin, 1999), p. 27. The author gives no source. A variant of this story, where the year is 1935 (when Behan was 12), is in MacEoin, *I.R.A.*, p. 566. 40 *Ir. Indep.*, 17 June 1935. 41 *Ir. Press*, 24 June

in 1922 and was to be chief-of-staff of the I.R.A. the year after delivering his oration at Bodenstown.[42] He was the superior of other orators in wealth, education and talent. On the platform he took Tone's name in objecting to the Anglo-Irish treaty, to the institutions set up in consequence, to partition and to any association with Great Britain; he also asserted, no doubt to appeal to socialists present even if going beyond the usual objections to socialism, that the governments north and south of the border 'were based on a system which gave unlimited power to the possessors of wealth over the lives and destinies of those who either possessed no wealth or possessed a lesser degree of wealth'.[43] MacBride closed his remarks by stating, overconfidently, 'today the Republican movement was on the rising tide, and was gathering strength rapidly'.[44] His confidence was to be confounded, as events would show.

The Irish Citizen Army is not mentioned in 1935. Its action in going to the aid of the Republican Congress at Sallins in 1934 was probably its last in public. The part it played at Bodenstown in 1914 and 1915 before the insurrection and again in 1917 and 1922 has been stated above. Its appearance at Bodenstown on 20 June 1922, as reported in the *Dublin Evening Mail*, is evidence that it was still vigorous in that year: 'as vehicles approached there was a shout of "Hands up", and half a dozen revolvers were presented menacingly by young men wearing the large slouch hats and dark green uniform of the Irish Citizen Army'; the men of the I.R.A. were in mufti.[45] But from then on the Irish Citizen Army was out of the public eye, more a Dublin social club than a revolutionary organisation; it is not mentioned again in any report of a pilgrimage until that of 1934, when it was present 'under the command' of Séamus McGowan, who was attempting, ineffectually, a revival. Its refusal to participate in 1935 was on the ground, as it argued, that the I.R.A. was neglecting social injustice. By 1936 one of its best-known members, Roddy Connolly (son of James Connolly), was in the Labour Party persuading it to adopt as an aim a 'workers' republic'.[46] The last mention of it found in a report of a Bodenstown pilgrimage is in 1970 when Laurence McLoughlin, 'a veteran of the Citizen Army', laid the wreath at the so-called 'Official' Sinn Féin ceremony.[47] Roddy Connolly was to appear at Bodenstown in April 1971 for the dedication of a new Tone memorial, by which time he was the party's chairman and politically in the centre.[48]

The Irish Republican Congress, forthright and muscular in June 1935 but weakened by internal disputes, was almost defunct by the time another pilgrimage was due twelve months later. An application was made to the Republicans' organising committee by Frank Ryan and George Gilmore for their group to take part, but the pilgrimage was banned.[49]

1935; *Ir. Times*, 18 June 1935. **42** For Seán MacBride (1904–88), see also the article on him by Ronan Keane in *D.I.B.* **43** *Ir. Press*, 24 June 1935. **44** *Ir. Times*, 24 June 1935. **45** *Dublin Evening Mail*, 21 June 1922. **46** *Ir. Times*, 18 June 1934; Brian Hanley, 'The Irish Citizen Army after 1916' in *Saothar*, xxviii (2003), pp 37–47. **47** *Ir. Press*, 22 June 1970. **48** L. W. White, 'Connolly, Roderic James (1901–80)' in *D.I.B.* **49** Hanley, *I.R.A.*, pp 108, 244.

DE VALERA'S GOVERNMENT TURNS AGAINST THE I.R.A.

By the mid-1930s the Fianna Fáil government's administrative successes had won it greater popular support and much respectability. Fianna Fáil's dalliance with the I.R.A., manifest in the party's participation in the I.R.A.'s parade in 1931, was ending. The Fianna Fáil pilgrimage on 16 June 1935 was impressive even though attendance was down to two thousand; De Valera led the procession, eight bands played, so-called 'Old I.R.A.' formed his guard of honour. In an oration in the field nearby, Seán Lemass made an appeal for an end to the discord and violence that was increasingly common. He did not name the I.R.A. but clearly had it in mind. 'For any person to come here to the graveside of Wolfe Tone and there to preach that national policy should be dictated by a faction would', he said, 'be a monstrous insult to the patriot's memory and a repudiation of his teaching'. He pledged Fianna Fáil 'to serve loyally the cause of Irish republicanism' and pleaded 'to all those who have fallen out or held aloof from the ranks of the main body of the national forces to lend their aid to Fianna Fáil in another great effort to seep away the last trappings of foreign domination so that the oldest man around this platform may live to see the proclamation of 1916 made effective and the unity and independence of Ireland completely established'.[50] The appeal was to have limited immediate effect.

Throughout 1935 and into 1936 the I.R.A. was causing acute embarrassment to the government by carrying out high-profile murders and giving muscular support to striking transport workers; moreover the I.R.A. was denounced by Catholic bishops, as was the Republican Congress and the Communist Party. De Valera, a pious man (evident in his deep solemnity at Tone's grave), always wished to avoid ecclesiastical censure. The government's patience with the I.R.A. finally snapped on 19 June 1936. Late in the evening it issued a proclamation declaring 'the organisation styling itself the Irish Republican Army, also the I.R.A. and Óglaigh na hÉireann', to be 'an unlawful association' and consequently prohibiting the Bodenstown demonstration planned for the following Sunday, 21 June, and to be addressed by Mary MacSwiney.[51] The banned demonstration, like all Republican pilgrimages during the previous ten years — except, obviously, for Fianna Fáil's — was being organised by, or under the auspices of, the I.R.A. On the day after the intended event, Bodenstown was reported as having been an 'armed camp' with 500 police and about 1,000 troops being deployed to prevent Republicans arriving. 'From night-fall on Saturday', the report continued,

> military with full war kit, trench helmets, armoured cars, machine guns and all the other paraphernalia of active service were in camp in a field near the little churchyard … In all about a thousand troops, equipped with gas masks and tear gas bombs, were encamped in the vicinity of Sallins and Bodenstown, whilst the police on duty numbered well over 500. The bulk of the troops were

---

50 *Ir. Press*, 17 June 1935. **51** *Ir. Press*, 20 June 1936.

quartered in a large field close to the graveyard ... Military aeroplanes
reconnoitred the surrounding area and communicated by wireless with the
forces on the ground.[52]

The 'special branch' of the Garda Síochána made great efforts to prevent pilgrims
from reaching their destination. One daring I.R.A.-man, Pierce Fennell, boarded a
Galway-Dublin train intending to pull the communication cord and stop it near
Sallins; he was spotted before it left Galway.[53] After one young man, Seán Glynn,
was arrested on his way from his home in Limerick and subsequently held in a
prison cell, where he killed himself, McGarrity in Philadelphia, who had sponsored
the pilgrimage organised by Clarke in 1912, finally broke with De Valera, explaining,
'it was the last straw for me'.[54] The Fianna Fáil government's banning of the I.R.A.'s
pilgrimage in 1936, unlike the Cumann na nGaedheal government's attempt to ban
it in 1931, was entirely effective. The tryst that De Valera had made with the
Republicans before entering office was emphatically, irreparably broken.

Sinn Féin were not affected by the prohibition and so were able to hold their own
demonstration at Bodenstown in compensation. On 10 July, the party issued from
its headquarters at 9 Parnell Square a brief statement that 'the Republican
pilgrimage to Bodenstown, under the auspices of Sinn Féin, will take place on
Sunday, 9th August. There will be a procession from Sallins to Wolfe Tone's grave,
where an oration will be delivered. Citizens of the Republic are invited to avail of
the occasion to assert their right to honour publicly the Father of Irish
Republicanism.' It was published not in the *Irish Press*, the Dublin daily preferred
by Republicans, but in the *Irish Independent*.[55] The reference to 'citizens of the
Republic' was a reproach to the I.R.A. as well as to Fianna Fáil, as the I.R.A. had
broken with Sinn Féin in 1925 over the matter of continuing to recognise the
republic declared in 1916 as still *de jure*, which the I.R.A. considered futile and
counterproductive. Two weeks later Sinn Féin advertised a special train to Sallins
on 9 August, tickets at 2s. 6d. at Sinn Féin headquarters, with Mary MacSwiney
(now aged 64) as orator of the day.[56] It was she who was to have addressed the banned
I.R.A. demonstration. She had in 1934 resigned from Sinn Féin, unable to
countenance its new president, Michael O'Flanagan, taking employment with the
Irish Free State — he accepted a commission to compile Irish-language county
histories for use in schools. Her opportunity to taunt the government by addressing
a crowd at Bodenstown in spite of the ban may have reconciled her to the party. On
9 August a mere 300 pilgrims travelled to Bodenstown to hear her praise the I.R.A.
— surreptitiously by referring to it as Óglaigh na hÉireann. She referred to the new
constitution approved a month before in a referendum. While insisting that the
republic declared in 1916 and confirmed by the first Dáil in 1919 still existed, she
asserted that 'if Mr de Valera produced a constitution for the whole of Ireland and

52 *Ir. Indep.*, 22 June 1936. Most detailed is *Leinster Leader*, 27 June 1936.   **53** MacEoin, *I.R.A.*,
p. 551.   **54** Ó Beacháin, *Destiny of the soldiers*, p. 139.   **55** *Ir. Indep.*, 11 July 1936.   **56** *Ir. Indep.*,
25 July 1936. It was readvertised in ibid., 8 Aug. 1936.

having no connection with England, Republicans would support him'.[57] But so insignificant was Sinn Féin by 1936 that the police could dismiss the rally as harmless.[58] Her oration was her swan-song.

In June 1937, the Republicans were back at Bodenstown in much smaller numbers than two years previously — a mere 1,140 to the reckoning of the police.[59] There was no interference by the authorities. Pilgrims travelled from all parts of Ireland, 'by special train and 'bus, motor cars, taxis, bicycles and on foot'; they marched from Sallins in military formation; at their head, led by a Belfast pipe band, were 200 northerners under a banner, 'Óglaigh na hÉireann, Belfast Battalion'. Some were from Sinn Féin, some were from 'labour bodies'; the 'great majority', however (according to one report), 'marched openly under the banners of the proclaimed military organisation' — the I.R.A. When the pilgrims assembled in the graveyard, messages received from imprisoned Republicans were read out by the chairman, Michael Fitzpatrick; one was from Maurice Twomey, serving a sentence imposed by a military tribunal.[60] The orator was Tom Barry, who, after ritually praising Tone, rejected the new constitution as 'merely a new-fangled Free State constitution maintaining the connection with England, based on the legislation crowning George VI, King of England, as King of Ireland, legalising Partition, and', he added, with his usual bellicosity, 'without a clause which would enable the people of this nation to drive out the invader and to end the conquest'.[61] Barry, who had served with distinction in the British army during the First World War before becoming, in the War of Irish Independence, a very effective leader of an I.R.A. 'flying column' in west Cork, held from 1927 a senior position with the Cork Harbour Commissioners. Twomey had been chief-of-staff of the I.R.A. from June 1926 until his arrest in May 1936, at which Seán MacBride succeeded him; Barry succeeded MacBride some time in 1937 and Fitzpatrick succeeded Barry in the same year.[62] Thus, whilst the I.R.A. were not as assertive at the Republican pilgrimage of 1937 as a few years previously, their presence was evident to perceptive observers.

The complexion of the Republican pilgrimage in 1938 was no different. Some 4,000 pilgrims from all over Ireland assembled; the procession was led by 'big contingents of Óglaigh na hÉireann from Belfast and Armagh'; Sinn Féin, 'ex-I.R.A.', Cumann na mBan, Fianna Éireann and Cumann na gCailíní were there too. Twomey, released from prison, was one of the orators; he and another, Michael Conway of Clonmel (who referred several times to Tone), dwelt on the question of 'partition'. A wreath was laid by Seán Russell 'on behalf of the I.R.A.'.[63]

57 *Ir. Press*, 10 Aug. 1936. **58** Hanley, *I.R.A.*, p. 95. **59** Ibid., p. 52. **60** *Ir. Times*, 21 June 1937.
61 *Evening Herald*, 21 June 1937. **62** Hanley, *I.R.A.*, pp 191, 194. Twomey (1897–1978) and Barry (1897–1980) are subjects of articles in *D.I.B.* (by Brian Hanley and M. A. Hopkinson respectively); some details of the career of Michael Fitzpatrick (1893–1968), who followed MacBride into Dáil Éireann in 1948, are in *Ir. Indep.*, 9 Oct. 1968, and Brian Hanley, 'The I.R.A. and trade unionism, 1911–72' in Francis Devine et al. (eds), *Essays in Irish labour history: festschrift for Elizabeth and John W. Boyle* (Dublin, 2008), pp 161–2. **63** *Ir. Indep.*, 20 June 1938.

Significantly, Russell (1893–1940), a Dubliner, had the previous April become chief-of-staff and was colluding with elements in Northern Ireland to take over the organisation; he planned a bombing campaign in Britain and made contacts in Nazi Germany, resulting in seven civilian deaths in 1939, the execution of two I.R.A. men and his own death in a German submarine. Russell had been due to give the oration at the Republican demonstration at Bodenstown in 1931, but had been arrested on its eve.[64] Conway (1910?–97), said to be a motor mechanic, had in 1935 been sentenced to three months' imprisonment for illegal possession of ammunition; in 1936 he been convicted by a military tribunal of murder and sentenced to death, a sentence reduced to life imprisonment, from which he was soon released, on 4 May 1938;[65] he gave practical support to the I.R.A. bombing campaign in Britain which began in January 1939, was interned from 1940 to 1944, and was imprisoned again in 1946 for his I.R.A. activities; he was chairman at Bodenstown in 1949, led an I.R.A. contingent in the parade in 1950, and later that year entered a Cistercian monastery in County Louth, dying there aged 87 on 23 December 1997 to be honoured by Republicans at his funeral mass. In an obituary in the newspaper of Republican Sinn Féin (which broke away from 'Provisional' Sinn Féin in 1986), it was stated that 'shortly after his death … he told the abbot of the monastery, "I have lived a long life and have no regrets. If I had to live it all over again, I would change nothing"'.[66]

   The Fianna Fáil pilgrimage on 14 June 1936 attracted (at the highest estimate) three thousand people who, led by De Valera and party associates including Mrs Kathleen Clarke and Miss Margaret Pearse, walked from Sallins to the accompaniment of five bands.[67] The oration, by Thomas Derrig, minister for education, was largely about Tone; Derrig quoted large extracts from Tone's autobiography and drew the counsel that 'it was necessary to forget all former feuds'.[68] The minister's speech contained no hint of any plan for the crack-down on the I.R.A. that occurred five days later when the Fianna Fáil minister for justice issued a proclamation banning both the I.R.A. and its pilgrimage announced for the following Sunday. There were, however, protests from Republicans, women, against the suppression of *An Phoblacht*.[69] Nineteen thirty-six proved to be the last of the mass pilgrimages of Fianna Fáil.

   In 1937, De Valera again led the procession from Sallins. Five bands took part. It was the turn of Seán MacEntee to deliver the oration. Unlike previous orators, MacEntee drew from the earlier parts of Tone's writings in speaking of 'his merry jesting about the Clerk of the Parish and Gog and Magog' (Tone's friend Russell and the Catholic Committee men John Keogh and Richard McCormick) and of Tone's association with William Jackson who was arrested for high treason; 'this we know', MacEntee said, 'from his diaries and other contemporary documents' and

64 Hanley, *I.R.A.*, pp 197–8; idem, 'Russell, Seán' in *D.I.B.*   65 *Ir. Indep.*, 13 May, 3, 16, 17, 22, 25 July 1936, 5 May 1938.   66 *Saoirse*, Jan. 1998; Coogan, *I.R.A.* (revd ed., 2000), pp 60, 148, 225, 254–5; Nat. Arch., Dublin, JUS 8/900 (1949, 1950).   67 The figure given in *Ir. Times*, 15 June 1936. The longest report is in *Ir. Press*, 15 June 1936.   68 *Ir. Press,* 15 June 1936.   69 *Ir.*

also from Seán O'Faolain's recently-published 'abridged edition of Tone's auto-biography'.[70] But he may have had few listeners in the heavy rain. 'So small was the attendance of the general public', it was reported, 'that when leaving Sallins there were more bandsmen than processionists'.[71] If the party planned a demonstration on the grand scale of its earlier ones, there must have been disappointment. It was not so much that, as asserted by one historian of the Fianna Fáil party, its alternative to the I.R.A.'s pilgrimages had 'failed to catch on'[72] — the attendance figures from 1933 until 1936 suggest otherwise — as that there was no longer any need to compete with the I.R.A.

A year later De Valera was at Bodenstown again with Ruttledge, MacEntee and a few Fianna Fáil associates. The ceremony 'was a simple one and lasted but a few moments'. The party arrived at the graveyard by 10.30 a.m. (before the army); about a hundred civilians watched De Valera lay his wreath. There was no parade, no oration.[73] The ceremony in June 1939 was similar; De Valera was however given a guard of honour — by the South Dublin Battalion of the 'Old I.R.A.'.[74]

If any doubt remained about De Valera's tryst with the I.R.A. being broken, its broken state was emphasised in 1939, painfully to the latter. On 23 June, five days after De Valera's brief appearance at Bodenstown, the commissioner of the Garda Síochána, acting under a new Offences against the State Act, declared the Irish Republican Army to be an unlawful organisation and prohibited the Republican pilgrimage planned for the 25th. The area was sealed off on the appointed day by a force of 250 police with a back-up of 50 armed soldiers; parties of intending pilgrims were turned back from Bodenstown at some distance; the *Irish Times* was able to report the scene under the headline 'All quiet around Tone's grave'.[75] But the centre of Dublin was not quiet. The scene was described in the *Irish Press*:

> A contingent of over 500, including young men, young women in Cumann na mBan uniform, Girl scouts and Fianna boys, arrived at Amiens Street Station from Belfast about noon. On leaving the train they got into military formation on the platform. As they marched out of the station carrying a banner, they were met outside the carriageway by Gardaí, who ordered them to disperse. The party marched on and a struggle then took place which lasted for some minutes. The party continued their march into the city and after a fight of several minutes ... the Belfast party, who had been joined by about 300 others on the way, made a circuit of O'Connell Street and then drew up outside the G.P.O., where they were joined by a considerable number of spectators.

Outside the G.P.O. — headquarters of the insurgents in 1916 — protests were made against the bans imposed on the Republicans. There was 'some liveliness' but no

Indep., 15 June 1936. **70** *Ir. Press*, 14 June 1937. **71** *Ir. Indep.*, 14 June 1937. **72** Ó Beacháin, *Destiny of the soldiers*, p. 137. **73** *Ir. Times*, 27 June 1938. **74** *Ir. Times*, 19 June 1939. **75** *Ir. Times*, 26 June 1939. The headline echoes the title of Erich Maria Remarque's novel, *All quiet on the Western Front* (1929), very popular in the 1930s.

serious disturbance.[76] Little did the Ulster Republicans realise that there was not to be a pilgrimage for the next two years and that their like would not reappear in strength for another fifteen years.

THE DUAL ROLE OF THE IRISH DEFENCE FORCES

It has been asserted, ironically, that while the Irish defence forces under the Fianna Fáil government were deployed at Bodenstown to prevent commemorations, their role under the Cumann na nGaedheal government in the 1920s had been as a guard of honour.[77] A further consideration is that the large scale of the new Irish army's presence at the official demonstrations at Bodenstown in the years after 1922, and particularly its ostentatious display of heavy military equipment, suggests, in view of the continuing challenges to the legitimacy of the infant Irish state, that its role was more as a reminder to subversives of the state's capacity to defeat them if civil war were resumed. On one occasion — in 1931 — the Cumann na nGaedheal government did deploy troops to contain Republicans going to Bodenstown. To enforce its cancellation of special trains to Sallins, as the *Irish Independent* reported, 'a detachment of troops in full service kit' was placed outside the Kingsbridge terminus; moreover, to prevent I.R.A. units forming at Sallins, 'a field which had been rented by the Wolfe Tone Commemoration Committee near the station, where the procession was to be assembled, was occupied by the military, who denied civilians access'; and at the graveyard it was hinted to the organisers by a police superintendent that if they could not 'quieten the crowd' he might 'have to call for the assistance of the military', which he said after pointing to a large force of troops who had taken part in the official review earlier, one company of which was equipped with rifles, bayonets and steel helmets.[78] In 1936, to enforce its prohibition of the planned I.R.A. demonstration at Bodenstown, the Fianna Fáil government deployed a thousand soldiers there (as stated above) 'with full war kit, trench helmets, armoured cars, machine guns and all the other paraphernalia of active service'. The army at Bodenstown was down to a mere guard of honour in 1938. The field opposite the churchyard was no longer needed. But in 1939, after the banning of the I.R.A. pilgrimage, there was another deployment of the military for law enforcement at Bodenstown. At some distance from the graveyard 'fully armed troops equipped with tear gas bombs stood to during the day, ready to relieve any strain that might be imposed on the police force'.[79] This was a much smaller deployment than in 1931 and 1936 and is indicative that, even when the I.R.A. was engaged in a bombing campaign in England and a major European war was threatening, the Fianna Fáil government could rely on the police to enforce a ban with only a lightly-armed military unit in reserve.

76 *Ir. Press*, 26 June 1939.   **77** Brian M. Walker, *A political history of the two Irelands: from partition to peace* (London, 2012), pp 18–19.   **78** *Ir. Indep.*, 22 June 1931.   **79** *Ir. Times*, 26 June 1939.

MORE ON ULSTER AND BODENSTOWN

The Ulster question was raised at Bodenstown in 1930 by De Valera. It had been ignored there since 1922. He declared at the Fianna Fáil pilgrimage on the Sunday before that of the I.R.A. that 'today a new barrier to national unity had been created. Ireland had been united in territory, as well as in sentiment, and a multitude of selfish interests'. Her people, he argued,

> never willed the partition of their country ... Differences of religious belief, of tradition and of race, made the achievement of national unity a difficult task even with general good will, but it could be done. They who claimed to be followers of Tone had a special duty in this manner. They should resist all temptation to bitterness. They should show themselves as sensitive ... to the rights and feelings of other Irishmen as in regard to their own.[80]

Except for these words, there was nothing eirenic about De Valera or his party. He and his followers had broken with political associates in 1922 and turned against them in armed conflict; he had split with more recent associates in 1926; he had never shown any empathy with the Protestant two thirds of the population in Northern Ireland who resolutely objected to incorporation into the Irish Free State. He had towards the end of 1924, when president of Sinn Féin, attempted to intervene in elections to the Northern Ireland parliament by getting 'Republican' candidates nominated; he was arrested on 25 October for entering the province illegally; none of his candidates was elected other than himself (for County Down). This intervention 'united all sections of northern nationalism in their hostility'.[81] He presided over a meeting in Dublin on 7 December 1925 attended by an intransigent Ulster priest, Eugene Coyle, to denounce the abolition of the boundary commission and council of Ireland.[82] De Valera alluded to Ulster when addressing followers at the inaugural meeting of Fianna Fáil on 16 May 1926: they were all, he was reported as saying, 'no parties to partition, and felt themselves free to use any means God gave them to win back the lost province'; but 'that could only be done by the people of the South regaining their sovereignty in the 26 counties'.[83] The response amongst Ulster Catholics to this speech has not been ascertained, nor has the response to his Bodenstown speech in 1930. Their newspaper, the *Irish News*, did report the speech made by De Valera at Bodenstown in 1929 which however made no allusion to Ulster; it made in 1930 only a passing mention of 'a Dublin pilgrimage' to Tone's grave on 22 June without even distinguishing between the official one and the Fianna Fáil one or alluding to De Valera's mention of partition.[84] Ulster Catholics were no doubt impressed by his accession to power in 1932. Coyle

80 *Ir. Indep.*, 23 June 1930. **81** Walker, *Ir. parlty election results, 1918–92*, p. 48; Phoenix, *Northern nationalism*, pp 308–9, 320. **82** Phoenix, *Northern nationalism*, p. 333. **83** *Ir. Indep.*, 17 May 1926. The text in *Speeches and statements by Eamon de Valera, 1917–73*, ed. Maurice Moynihan (Dublin, 1980), is a later, amplified version. **84** *Irish News*, 1 July 1929, 23 June 1930.

had joined the national executive of Fianna Fáil by 1927, and several nationalist members of the Northern Ireland parliament played an active role in Fianna Fáil's electoral campaign in 1932, without however receiving any significant benefits.[85]

De Valera's public stance when in office in the 1930s was irredentist; he was more willing to exploit the propaganda value of the plight of Catholics in Northern Ireland than to seek the redress of their grievances.[86] Even in June 1940 (and again in December 1941), during the Second World War, when it was made known to him that the British prime minister, and one Northern Ireland cabinet minister (more in 1941), were willing to agree to reunion in return for 'Éire' (a name superseding 'Irish Free State' after 1936) co-operating fully with Britain, he rejected the prospect, preferring to keep Éire neutral.[87] Why then did he raise the question in 1930? By his speech at Bodenstown he perhaps thought 'partition' could be made a live issue again, one that would draw support to his party. In turning attention to the partition of Ireland (a provision of the Government of Ireland Act of 1920 and so pre-Treaty), he may have believed that the issue would excite others and so gain his party more votes in the forthcoming general election. More than most Irish nationalists living south of the border and so concerned mainly with 'southern' affairs, De Valera had strong feelings about Northern Ireland and no doubt much sympathy for the Catholic minority there even though his entry into its politics in 1924 was brief and ineffectual.[88] But however unfailingly De Valera revisited Bodenstown each June until 1959, never again did he deliver an oration.

As if prompted by De Valera's oration at Bodenstown in 1930, allusions to Ulster were made at pilgrimages of the I.R.A. in the following years. In 1931, Peadar O'Donnell referred to 'Imperialists in Ireland both North and South'.[89] In 1932, Seán Russell, after referring to 'two regiments of the British Army, one dressed in khaki in the North and the other dressed in green in the South', pointed out that there was 'a representative of the English king in both places'.[90] In 1933, Twomey referred to 'partitioning this ancient nation into two statelets' and asserted that they were 'not free' and so 'could not be recognised as legitimate governmental authorities'. All three were alluding to the partition of Ireland chiefly to make once more the Republicans' fundamental objection to the Irish Free State — its connexion with the British crown. They said nothing about the political situation in Northern Ireland. The Republican orator in 1934, McLogan, who had recently been elected M.P. for South Armagh (though he declined to sit in the House of Commons), was slightly more explicit in asserting that in Northern Ireland 'the interests of Imperialism were served by sectarian organisations which fostered

85 Phoenix, *Northern nationalism*, pp 370, 353.   86 T. Ryle Dwyer, 'Eamon de Valera and the partition question' in J. P. O'Carroll and John A. Murphy (eds), *De Valera and his times* (Cork, 1983), pp 74–91 at p. 89.   87 Paul Bew, *Ireland: the politics of enmity, 1789–2007* (Oxford, 2007), pp 469–73.   88 De Valera's views on Ulster and partition have been examined by different historians too; none mentions his speech at Bodenstown in 1930. See also John Bowman, *De Valera and the Ulster question, 1917–1973* (Oxford, 1982); Stephen Kelly, *Fianna Fáil, partition and Northern Ireland, 1926–71* (Dublin, 2013).   89 *Ir. Indep.*, 22 June 1931.   90 *Ir. Indep.*, 20 June

bigotry', but his main message was that 'there must be no palliation of the treaty of surrender or of partition. We want not a better or a less humiliating treaty, but the repudiation of that infamous instrument.'[91] Similarly in 1935, Seán MacBride, who was to be the prime mover in the Irish government's anti-Partition campaign thirteen years later, lamented that 'the country was partitioned' and 'bound to the British crown'.[92] In 1938, Twomey referred twice (at least) to partition, though in the context of denouncing the Fianna Fáil government.[93] There was no specific mention of partition in the Fianna Fáil orations delivered between 1933 and 1937 — by O'Kelly, Ruttledge, Lemass, Derrig and MacEntee. One reason was that they did not share De Valera's obsession. In 1938, MacEntee (an Ulsterman) was privately very critical of De Valera's stance and would have resigned but for De Valera eventually being persuaded to exclude partition from negotiations for a series of accords with Great Britain.[94]

The paucity of mention, in Bodenstown speeches in the 1930s, of the situation of the Catholics in Northern Ireland, and the emphasis placed on the relationship between the Irish Free State and Great Britain, is surprising when it is considered that during the same period contingents from Belfast and other places north of the Irish border regularly participated in Bodenstown pilgrimages. In 1931, despite the Irish Free State government's attempt to prevent the I.R.A.'s pilgrimage, buses arrived at Bodenstown from Belfast. In the parade in 1932 was the Belfast Battalion of the I.R.A.[95] In 1933, the *Irish Press* reported 350 persons arriving at Sallins by train from Belfast for the I.R.A. pilgrimage, and more on the twenty-two buses coming

> from the Six Counties, fourteen of them from Belfast and four from Lurgan ... The voices of the North were everywhere and a general comment was that Ulster was the most strongly represented province. Exciting stories were told, by men and women from the North, of Belfast contingents leaving under the close scrutiny of the R[oyal] U[lster] C[onstabulary] ... Among the contingents were strong bodies from Belfast, Armagh and South Down. The Newry Republican Club also attended.[96]

In the Fianna Fáil parade from Sallins a week later the contingents from 'Monaghan, Cavan, Donegal and from the six partitioned counties' were placed immediately after the members of the party from the Dáil and Senate and ahead of all the other county contingents.[97] Grouping all nine Ulster counties together when Fianna Fáil now had the power of office over three though not even any party organisation in the other six may seem no more than a gesture from the leadership. The Northerners would have remembered that in the two previous years Fianna Fáil

---

1932. **91** *Ir. Press*, 18 June 1934. **92** *Ir. Press*, 24 June 1935. **93** *Ir. Indep.*, 20 June 1938. **94** Brian Girvin, 'The republicanisation of Irish society, 1932–48' in *A new history of Ireland*, vii (Oxford, 2003), pp 146–8. **95** *Ir. Times*, 20 June 1932. **96** *Ir. Press*, 19 June 1933. **97** *Ir. Press*,

deputies, I.R.A. men and Northerners had marched in the same parade. At the Republican pilgrimage in 1934, when the orator was the Armagh I.R.A. man Patrick McLogan and when a contingent of Protestant working men from Belfast marched in the parade, as many as 1,400 arrived by three special trains from across the border; four buses brought pilgrims from Dungannon, four from Derry, others from Armagh and Down. In its report of these the *Irish Press* claimed that 'it was the first large organised pilgrimage from the Northern counties since 1913'.[98] (In fact the first such pilgrimage was in June 1914, a few months after the formation of the Irish Volunteers.) Again in the Fianna Fáil pilgrimage, on 24 June 1934, there were members from 'Monaghan, Cavan, Donegal, Derry and other Ulster counties'.[99] Merely 'Ulster' (with no breakdown) is mentioned in the *Irish Press* report of the Fianna Fáil pilgrimage in 1935; Belfast, 'Derry city and county' and Counties Tyrone, Donegal and Armagh are named as provenances of participants in the Republican pilgrimage a week later.[100] In 1936 the I.R.A. was prevented from gathering at Bodenstown; its support was probably weakening. But remarkably at its demonstration in 1937, there was in the parade, at a distance behind the Belfast pipe band and the banner reading 'hÓglaigh na Éireann, Belfast Battalion', a 'group of little uniformed girls who marched under a banner embossed with the Red Hand of Ulster' and who 'were cheered as they tramped cheerily along the road'.[101] Even after the banning of the I.R.A. pilgrimage in 1939, Belfast Republicans made such a determined attempt to reach Bodenstown that they almost caused a riot in Dublin streets.

Why did Bodenstown orators say so little about the six Ulster counties? One possible reason is that of the thirty or so who gave an oration between 1922 and 1939 only four were natives of one or another of the six. The four were Gilmore from County Tyrone (1928), Aiken from County Armagh (1933), McLogan from County Armagh (1934) and MacEntee from Belfast (1937). Only one had much personal experience of the Belfast industrial heartland of Ulster, and all were living in the Irish Free State by the time they were delivering orations. The primary concerns of all Bodenstown orators in the 1920s and 1930s were with the Irish state under which they lived. Their indifference in most cases may have been, as stated by Roy Foster in referring to a prevalent attitude among Republicans on both sides of the border in the 1970s, 'an indifference based on difference'.[102] Until about 1930 the crowds who descended on Bodenstown were from Dublin, Kildare and counties adjacent to Kildare. Not until 1932 were there special trains, buses and lorries to transport pilgrims from distant counties there and back in a single day. Bodenstown orators may have 'denounced partition' in the 1930s (if never in the mid- and late 1920s), but, as Brian Hanley observes, the I.R.A. 'remained very much an organisation focused on the overthrow of the southern rather than the northern state'.[103]

26 June 1933.   **98** *Ir. Press*, 18 June 1934.   **99** *Ir. Press*, 25 June 1934.   **100** *Ir. Press*, 17, 24 June 1935.   **101** *Ir. Times*, 21 June 1937.   **102** R. F. Foster, *Luck and the Irish: a brief history of change, c.1970–2000* (Oxford, 2008), p. 121.   **103** Hanley, *I.R.A.*, p. 27.

THE TREATYITES FORSAKE BODENSTOWN

The observation was made in the *Irish Times* at the time of Bodenstown pilgrimages in 1933 that 'since the present government came into office the Cumann na nGaedheal party have not concerned themselves with the celebration'.[104] It was prescient. Never again did Cumann na nGaedheal, or Fine Gael (its name after absorbing other parties in 1933), participate as a party, whether in or out of office, in which respect it differed sharply from Fianna Fáil. At the military ceremony four months after Fine Gael gained office in February 1948, the Fine Gael minister for defence did appear formally and he was accompanied by two other Fine Gael deputies; but by then the military ceremonies were brief and it was accepted by both parties that ministers for defence had a purely ceremonial role at Bodenstown.

Instead of going every June to Bodenstown, members and followers of the party that left office in 1932 went every August to Bealnablath, the place in County Cork where Michael Collins had met his death in an ambush in August 1922. They had done so since 1924, when commemorating Collins had been a somewhat grand occasion, with ministers and officials in attendance and troops lined up, as at Bodenstown but less formal and on a smaller scale. 'It was', writes Anne Dolan, 'a desolate place, … a place evocative purely of a man … , a place of pilgrimage of a morbid fascination'. In these characteristics it resembled Bodenstown, the pilgrimages to which Professor Dolan hardly mentions. But the remoteness of Bealnablath — on a minor road, 30 kilometres west of Cork, nearly 300 kilometres from the metropolis — 'had always', in her words, 'contained the crowd, limiting it to locals' and 'to those willing and financially able to make the journey'.[105] Its appeal was further limited to Treatyites, as Collins, despite his membership of the I.R.B. and his cunning and ruthlessness during the war of Irish independence, was ill remembered by anti-Treatyites for having signed the Anglo-Irish treaty and headed the provisional government of the nascent Irish Free State. Therefore after Fianna Fáil entered office in March 1932 the new government ordered the Irish defence forces not to participate in the commemoration at Bealnablath the following 21 August. On the day 3,000 supporters of the previous government assembled there to hear an address by Richard Mulcahy, who had addressed Treatyites at Bodenstown nine years before when minister for defence. In 1933 the Bealnablath commemoration was banned by the new government, in 1934 and 1935 there were again large attendances; the custom continued throughout the century.[106] Bodenstown had the advantage of place that had brought about the early success and popularity of its pilgrimages; it appealed to all strong nationalists, not just to self-proclaimed Republicans but to all politically-minded Irish Catholics who perceived Tone to have died a martyr for the cause of their empowerment and as ultimately the founder of the modern Irish state.

---

104 *Ir. Times*, 6 June 1933.   **105** Anne Dolan, *Commemorating the Irish civil war: history and memory, 1923–2000* (Cambridge, 2006), pp 57–68, 191.   **106** Dolan, *Commemorating*, pp 192–8.

Just as the I.R.A.'s successful defiance of the Cumann na nGaedheal government's attempts to prevent its pilgrimage in 1931, and its further success in drawing large numbers of pilgrims to Bodenstown during the first half of the 1930s, showed that organisation's effectiveness, so the Fianna Fáil government's success in preventing its pilgrimages in 1936 and 1939 showed a rather more rugged determination to suppress it as well as an ability to draw off some of the popular sentiment that in the 1920s attached itself to Sinn Féin and the I.R.A. Fianna Fáil found itself unchallenged at Bodenstown by Cumann na nGaedheal and its successor, and in a position to prevent its access to its alternative place of pilgrimage at Bealnablath. None the less, refrains at Republican rallies of pledge-breaking, of betrayal of the 'republic' proclaimed in 1916, persisted throughout the period.

8

Bodenstown during the Emergency and after, 1939–59

T HE SECOND WORLD WAR, known in independent, neutral Ireland as 'the Emergency', caused interruption to the mass Republican pilgrimages, but none to the commemorations at Tone's grave by the Irish defence forces and Fianna Fáil. The pilgrimage planned by the I.R.A. for 25 June 1939, when a major war in Europe was threatening, was prohibited under the Offences against the State Act, a prohibition enforced by a large police and military presence at approaches to Bodenstown. The act had become law on 14 June and had been brought in more on account of the I.R.A.'s activities in Ireland, and its direction from Ireland of a bombing campaign in England, than on account of the international situation.[1] In 1940 plans by Sinn Féin for a pilgrimage on 23 June were well advanced — a veteran member of the party, J. J. O'Kelly ('Sceilg'), was expected to speak — when, four days before the event, it was prohibited, partly perhaps because Belgium and France were being invaded by Germany.[2] An even more important consideration for De Valera's government was that the I.R.A. was jeopardising Irish neutrality by its contacts with German army intelligence. But in the years that followed, Sinn Féin were able to hold a pilgrimage each June and for their commemoration to be reported. The statement by an historian of the Fianna Fáil party that 'only reporting of the official Fianna Fáil commemoration was permitted' is incorrect, but it may well have been that reports from Bodenstown were shortened by official censors.[3] On 22 June 1941, after the defence forces' ceremony, the Sinn Féin party's president, Mrs Margaret Buckley, laid a wreath and made a short speech.[4] It has been plausibly argued that her gender and her age (she was in her early sixties) exempted her from internment with other Republicans during this period.[5] Another consideration is that in the early 1940s Sinn Féin, few in number, were not controlled by the I.R.A. and were relatively harmless. In 1942 two small Sinn Féin pilgrimages were reported: on 7 June, a Sunday, members from Dublin, Cork and Belfast, supported by two dozen locals, laid wreaths, heard a speech by Seán

---

1 Coogan, *I.R.A.*, p. 132. 2 *Ir. Indep.*, 28 May, 20, 24 June 1940. For O'Kelly (1872–1957), known as 'Sceilg', see Brian P. Murphy's long article in *D.I.B.*, which however ignores this period. 3 Cf. Ó Beacháin, *Destiny of the soldiers*, p. 162. 4 *Ir. Indep.*, 23 June 1941. 5 Brian Feeney, *Sinn Féin: a hundred turbulent years* (Dublin, 2002), pp 177–8. She had a similar escape in July 1957 at 78 (Sinéad McCoole, *No ordinary women* (Dublin, 2015), pp 142–3).

MacGloin of Belfast and recited the Rosary in Irish; on the 17th, a Wednesday, Mrs Buckley, part of another group, laid a wreath and spoke briefly.[6] Apparently it was in 1942 that a body calling itself the Young Ireland Association but otherwise unidentified held a demonstration at Bodenstown at which a reference was made to 'Ireland's real National Army, the I.R.A.'.[7] There were very brief reports of a Sinn Féin event at Bodenstown in 1943, on the evening of Friday, 18 June, and again in 1944, apparently on 19 June, a Monday; no details of either have been found.[8]

THE NATIONAL GRAVES ASSOCIATION INTERVENES

Much more significant, and separate from these, were the pilgrimages organised in 1942, 1943 and 1944 under the auspices of the National Graves Association. The public were informed in May 1942 that the association had set up a Wolfe Tone commemoration committee 'representative of various shades of opinion' to organise a pilgrimage on 21 June. Named as officers were Seán Fitzpatrick (chairman), Kathleen Clarke (vice-chairman), Seán MacBride and Luke Duffy (joint secretaries), and Seán Dowling and Donal O'Donoghue (joint treasurers).[9] This new Wolfe Tone committee was hardly a very representative group. Its membership appears to have been carefully and cleverly selected with regard to possible repercussions in the potentially volatile situation existing during the Emergency. Fitzpatrick was an obvious choice, being secretary of the association and so precluded (if its rules were strictly regarded) from membership of any political party. Whilst Mrs Clarke was a member of the governing party, Fianna Fáil, she had for several years been critical of the government's policies, increasingly since 1940 when she had objected to its allowing I.R.A. prisoners to die on hunger strike; her great strength was that, as the widow of Tom Clarke, she was 'republican nobility'. For these reasons she was in 1942 tolerable to the government and acceptable to Fianna Fáil rank-and-file and Republicans alike. A year later she resigned from the party.[10] MacBride, as the son of 'Major' MacBride, a rebel commander executed in 1916, was similarly 'republican nobility' and so virtually untouchable whilst Fianna Fáil were in office; he was qualified doubly as a Republican by being chief-of-staff of the I.R.A. in the mid-1930s; he had achieved even greater respect by qualifying as a barrister in 1937 and subsequently defending, with some success, I.R.A. men brought before a court. Luke Duffy was secretary general of the Irish Labour Party and, unusually for a Labour official, of Republican sympathies. His respectability in the Labour Party would have enhanced considerably the respectability of a committee composed largely of Republicans well known for their rebelliousness. Naturally, he took part in the pilgrimage on 21 June 1942 organised by the

6 *Ir. Indep.*, 9, 18 June 1942; *Ir. Times*, 9 June 1942.   7 Typescript 'issued by the Young Ireland Association', n.d., but 'Bodenstown 1941' hand-written on verso (N.L.I., Seán O'Mahony papers, MS 44,079/2).   8 *Ir. Times*, 19 June 1943; *Ir. Indep.*, 20 June 1944.   9 *Ir. Indep.*, 25 May 1942.
10 For her resignation, see Kathleen Clarke to Éamon de Valera, 3 May 1943 (N.L.I., Clarke

'representative' committee on which he served. The question of how much Labour people took part in Bodenstown pilgrimages is considered below in chapter 11. Seán Dowling had been in the I.R.A. after 1923; he presumably was officially considered harmless by 1942 or he would have been interned with many others.[11] O'Donoghue (1897–1957), an accountant by profession, had been a member of the Dublin brigade of the I.R.A. and a member of the I.R.A.'s staff; he too must have been considered harmless.[12] In spite of the stated intention of organising resumed pilgrimages under the auspices of a broadly-based committee, responsibility was, in reports examined, always attributed to the National Graves Association. The names of Kathleen Clarke and Luke Duffy did not recur.

The National Graves Association's first pilgrimage took place, without objection by the authorities, on 21 June 1942, shortly after the pilgrimages of the defence forces and Fianna Fáil. It received much advance notice and publicity in Dublin newspapers. The *Dublin Evening Mail*, warning that special trains were unavailable, stated that many planned to travel to Sallins 'by horse-drawn conveyances' as 'in former years', but recognised that the chief mode would be cycling, on which it gave advice on route and times — 'even by cycling slowly, the journey can be covered within two hours' — and reported that some cycling parties were expected from as far away as Carlow and Limerick.[13] Evidently it was to be a popular social occasion. Perhaps for some it was a rare opportunity during the Emergency for an excursion. The event proved as usual very political. In charge at Bodenstown was Seán MacBride; present as usual were the women's groups Cumann na mBan, Girl Scouts and Cumann na gCailíní; in newspaper reports there was no mention of Fianna Éireann, the I.R.A. or Sinn Féin, but a police report stated that of the 130 in the procession from Sallins, 22 appeared to be of the I.R.A. and 45 of the National Graves Association; a statement from the committee deploring that 'the connection with England was still unbroken' and asserting that it was 'still the source of evils, social and political' was read by James Killean and then in an Irish version by Donal O'Donoghue.[14] Killean (sometimes spelt Killeen) joined the Volunteers in 1914, was in the post-Treaty I.R.A., spent six months in prisons in London and Dublin in 1926, was a regular at Bodenstown in the early 1930s, and from 1936 to 1941 was a prisoner in Belfast.[15] There was a passing mention (in the *Irish Press*) of a newcomer to Bodenstown, a newly-formed, decidedly quasi-Fascist and pro-Nazi political party, Ailtirí na hAiséirghe ('Architects of the Resurrection'). It had its heyday in 1945 and joined Republicans at Bodenstown again in 1946, 1947 and 1948 before vanishing in the 1950s.[16]

papers, MS 49,356/14/3). **11** For Dowling, see Uinseann MacEoin, *Survivors: the story of Ireland's struggle* (2nd ed., Dublin, 1987). **12** For O'Donoghue, see the article on his wife Sheila Humphreys by Patrick Maume in *D.I.B.* and esp. HumphrysFamilyTree.com, accessed 4 Feb. 2016. **13** *Dublin Evening Mail*, 12 June 1942. **14** *Ir. Indep.*, 22 June 1942; *Ir. Press*, 22 June 1942; Nat. Arch., Dublin, JUS/8/900 (1942). **15** For Killean (1893?–1974), a native of Rathowen, Co. Westmeath, see Hanley, *I.R.A.*, pp 20, 193 et passim; *Ir. Press*, 23 Jan., 20 Dec. 1974; *Ir. Indep.*, 23 Apr. 1974 (sports and deaths pages); N.L.I., Seán O'Mahony papers, MS 44,071/3. **16** For this party, see R. M. Douglas, *Architects of the Resurrection: Ailtirí na hAiséirghe*

The Wolfe Tone Commemoration Committee's pilgrimage in 1943, referred to as the National Graves Association's commemoration in police reports, again attracted the women's groups; it also attracted Fianna Éireann, 'Old I.R.A.', three bands (one the Irish Transport and General Workers Union's) and, again, Ailtirí na hAiséirghe; Michael Fitzpatrick was in charge; O'Donoghue gave the oration, exhorting pilgrims 'to keep Wolfe Tone's ideas'.[17] The twenty men observed by police at the front of the procession of 250 or so were probably I.R.A. One man present was Maurice Twomey, who had left the I.R.A. in 1938 to open (like Tom Clarke) a tobacconist's shop in Dublin; he remained influential in I.R.A. circles.

In 1944 there were close to 500 pilgrims, some 60 of them 'Old I.R.A.', a few Fianna Éireann; the orator was MacBride himself, whose spectacular success as a barrister had brought him a call to the inner bar in 1943.[18] He was to form on 6 July 1946 a new political party, Clann na Poblachta, which O'Donoghue and Killean joined, as did Kathleen Clarke.[19] The content of his speech will be discussed below. It is safe to infer that these war-time pilgrimages were acceptable to the authorities for being, nominally at least, independent of both the I.R.A. and Sinn Féin.

In the usual newspaper reports of Bodenstown speeches there were no allusions at all to the war raging outside Ireland. Probably this was because of official censorship, thought necessary to preserve Éire's neutrality and in force during the Emergency until lifted in May 1945.[20] More significantly the police reports contain no mention of the war. Any silence was hardly due to indifference among Republicans, as shown by an incident that shocked Seán Mulready, an I.R.A. man interned with hundreds of other Republicans at the Curragh Camp. When in June 1940 news reached them of the collapse of the French Third Republic and its submission to the German Third Reich 'the whole camp just went berserk. The prisoners ran around in sheer delirious joy that the Germans had defeated, and were about to occupy, the cradle of militant republicanism.'[21] The camp was a few kilometres distant from Bodenstown, where Tone lay buried 142 years after dying, honourably, an officer in the service of the first French republic; the incident must have occurred a few days after 16 June 1940, on which day 'a wreath of laurels tied with tricolour ribbons' was laid on Tone's grave by De Valera, a republican with credentials that were impressive even if (to the minds of his Republican opponents) not impeccable. On the morning that De Valera set off for Bodenstown, a Dublin Sunday newspaper reported that 'the Irish Minister in France' — an official position once coveted, jocularly, by Tone — had left Paris in the entourage of the

and the fascist 'New Order' in Ireland (Manchester, 2009); idem, 'Ailtirí na hAiséirghe: Ireland's fascist New Order' in *History Ireland*, xvii (2009), pp 40–4. For a nervous encounter with Ailtirí na hAiséirghe in the early 1940s, see R. B. McDowell, *McDowell on McDowell* (Dublin, 2008), p. 98. **17** *Ir. Indep.*, 21 June 1943; *Ir. Press*, 21 June 1943; *Ir. Times*, 21 June 1943; Nat. Arch., Dublin, JUS/8/900 (1943). **18** *Ir. Press*, 19 June 1944; *Ir. Indep.*, 19 June 1944; Nat. Arch., Dublin, JUS/8/900 (1944). **19** For Clann na Poblachta, see Eithne MacDermott, *Clann na Poblachta* (Cork, 1998). **20** Brian Girvin, *The Emergency: neutral Ireland, 1939–45* (London, 2006), pp 84–95, 278–80. **21** Brian Hanley, *The I.R.A.: a documentary history, 1919–2005* (Dublin, 2010), p. 105.

fleeing French government.[22] After the rally of Republicans at Bodenstown on 18 June 1944, when Dublin newspapers were full of news of the Allies' invasion of Normandy, begun twelve days earlier, there was no report of the orator of the day referring to the drama unfolding on the Continent. Yet one aim of the invaders was to oust the régime of Marshal Pétain which had abrogated the Third Republic and restricted the playing of the 'Marseillaise', the French revolutionary anthem so beloved by Tone.[23] The reason could simply have been press censorship. Perhaps some concern for France might have been expected from the orator, MacBride, who was born and brought up in France. Although MacBride did not move to Ireland until 1917, in his early teens, and spoke English with a pronounced French accent (which he never lost), he was not in the usual French sense a republican. His mother, Maud Gonne MacBride, his lone parent, had during her long period of residence in France associated closely with politicians who were on the radical right, clericalist, even monarchist, principally Lucien Millevoye, a confederate of General Boulanger and Paul Déroulède and a publicist of the anti-Dreyfusards. His father, John MacBride, one of the rebels executed in 1916, he hardly ever knew. His half-sister, Iseult, his mother's daughter by Millevoye, was held in prison in 1942 for aiding a German agent parachuted into Ireland to liaise with the I.R.A., by then pro-Nazi; Iseult's husband, Francis Stuart, was in Germany employed by the government there as a propagandist.[24] Had Seán MacBride sympathies with Pétain's régime? It would not be fanciful to see the Pétainistes as spiritual and intellectual successors of the Boulangistes. In a review of MacBride's memoirs sixty years later it was asserted that George Gilmore 'was convinced that he was in line for the job of "quisling" taoiseach (prime minister) had the Germans landed in 1941'.[25] What greatly agitated MacBride at Bodenstown in June 1944 was that 'a portion of Ulster was occupied by foreign troops and ruled by an autocratic government'.[26] What inspired him was irredentist nationalism, the inspiration of Boulangistes intent on France recovering Alsace-Lorraine. Could alarm at the prospect of British forces overturning Pétain have been a reason MacBride articulated such hostility to Britain at that moment in 1944?

Brian Hanley holds that numbers attending 'during the war years point to the steady decline of militant republicanism'.[27] Another consideration is that the official prohibition, effectively enforced, of Republican demonstrations in 1939 and 1940 and the restrictions on travel and transport throughout the war years make it difficult to infer from the paucity of pilgrims that militant Republican *sentiment* was in decline. The number of Republicans held in military custody at the Curragh and elsewhere during the Emergency — close to two thousand[28] — implies that they

22 *Sunday Independent*, 16 June 1940; *Ir. Indep.*, 17 June 1940. For Tone's wish to be Irish ambassador to France, see *Writings*, ii, 59–60, 224. 23 Tone, *Writings*, ii, 50, 137. 24 Adrian Frazier, *The adulterous muse: Maud Gonne, Lucien Millevoye and W. B. Yeats* (Dublin, 2016). Iseult Stuart (née Gonne) was at Bodenstown in 1923; an article on her by Deirdre Toomey is in *Oxford dictionary of national biography* (Oxford, 2003). 25 Review by Roy Johnston in *Irish Democrat*, lvi, no. 2 (Apr.–May 2006), p. 14. 26 *Ir. Press*, 19 June 1944. 27 Hanley, *I.R.A.*, p. 52. 28 Girvin, *Emergency*, p. 84.

were a body of men otherwise to be reckoned with. Severe shortages of petroleum removed almost completely private cars and motor-cycles from the roads; by early in 1941 registrations of motor vehicles had fallen by two-thirds, and most motor vehicles remaining on the roads were buses or lorries; by mid-1942 the crisis was severe. Poor quality coal necessitated reduction in passenger services on the railways; passenger trains were few, slow and unreliable; 'specials' for such events as pilgrimages to Bodenstown were prohibited. Horse-drawn vehicles were common again and bicycles the norm. The situation began improving in April 1944.[29] On the advice of the National Graves Association, conveyed in advertisements in Dublin newspapers, some pilgrims made their way to Bodenstown in 1942 by forming 'cycling parties' to assemble at Aston Quay at 10.30 a.m., whilst others 'arranged to go by horse-drawn conveyances'; similar cycling plans were made in 1943 and 1944.[30] Could Killean, who was to be for 23 years president of the National Cycling Association, have had a role in such plans? Certainly the City of Dublin Road Club made Burgh Quay their meeting point and Bodenstown their destination on 20 June 1942 specifically for the 'Wolfe Tone commemoration'.[31] As late as 1948 an English visitor to Ireland, travelling by bus from Tralee to Limerick, observed that between Glin and Limerick, a distance of 50 kilometres, no motor-car passed.[32] Until well into the 1950s, people of the lower social classes to which Bodenstown pilgrims generally belonged would have depended heavily on bicycles and buses.

During the winter of 1944–5, the National Graves Association removed the Tone gravestone erected in 1895 to Farrell's Monumental Yard at Glasnevin for a decision to be made about repair or replacement.[33] What follows in this episode in the history of the stones will appear below. A question that needs to be put here, considering that the war on the Continent was still raging and emergency legislation in Ireland still in effect, is whether the timing of the association's decision to move the stone was determined by political considerations as well as by a need for stonemasons' attentions. Was it intended, perhaps like the decision to sponsor revived pilgrimages in 1942, to soften misgivings about radical republicanism? Whatever the case, its care for Tone's grave must have been appreciated by the Fianna Fáil party and by the minister for defence in the Fianna Fáil government.

THE I.R.A. REVIVES

The Republican pilgrimage held on 24 June 1945, six weeks after the surrender of Germany, can be considered to have been a success. The *Leinster Leader* reported that 'contingents of the I.R.A. from various counties' took part in the parade as well

---

29 Clair Wills, *That neutral island: a cultural history of Ireland during the Second World War* (London, 2007), pp 250–2; Peter Rigney, *Trains, coal and turf: transport in Emergency Ireland* (Dublin, 2010), esp. chap. 8.   30 *Evening Herald*, 10 June 1942; *Ir. Press*, 13, 19 June 1942, *Dublin Evening Mail*, 18 June 1942; *Ir. Indep.*, 8 June 1943, 14 June 1944.   31 *Dublin Evening Mail*, 20 June 1942.   32 S.P.B. Mais, *I return to Ireland* (London, 1948), pp 245–6.

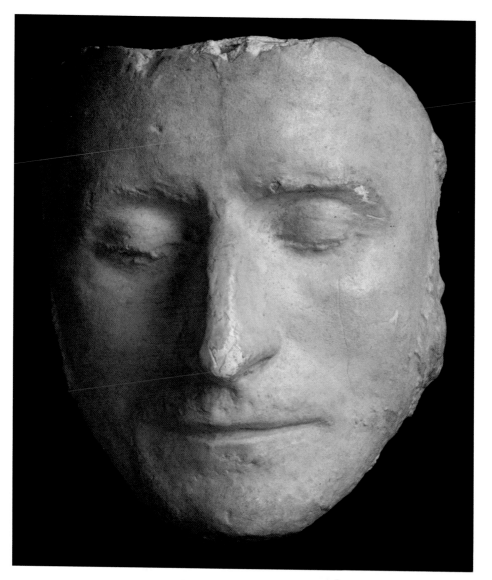

1a Death mask of Theobald Wolfe Tone said to have been made by James Petrie, November 1798 (courtesy of Board of T.C.D.).

1b No. 46 (formerly No. 65) High St., Dublin, where on the second floor Tone's body was laid out (Henry Shaw's *Dublin pictorial guide & directory of 1850* (facs. ed., Belfast, 1988)). William Dunbavin's name is shown engraved over the front as a previous occupant.

JOHN DILLON,
LATE WM. DUNBAVIN,
SOAP BOILER, TALLOW CHANDLER,
AND
CHEMICAL MOULD CANDLE MANUFACTURER.

2a Fragment of Young Irelanders' memorial slab laid in the autumn of 1844 (courtesy of N.M.I.).

2b Portrait of Michael Cavanagh, early 1860s (courtesy of N.L.I.). Cavanagh took part in rebellions in Ireland in 1848 and 1849 before moving to the United States, where he became active in the Fenian Brotherhood; he returned briefly in 1861 and was in a small group who visited Tone's grave on 9 November 1861; later he served in the New York National Guard.

3a Dublin Wolfe Tone Band's gravestone within its railing rebuilt by Peter Clory, 1870s or 1880s? (courtesy of N.L.I.). Clory took part in pilgrimages in 1892 and 1896.

3b This gravestone lying flat and chipped, with William Tone's gravestone upright, *c.* 1890 (courtesy of County Kildare Archaeological Society).

This Burial Place Belongs
to Wm Tone & his Family Here
lieth the Body of the above
who Departed this Life ye 24
of April 1766 aged 60 years
also 3 of his Children

The original Slab
been accidentally broken
the Members of the Dublin
Wolfe Tone Band
in respect to the memory of their
Noble Patron
erected this Slab 14 Sept. 1873

GOD SAVE IRELAND.

4a Kildare Gaelic Association's upright gravestone erected in 1895 (courtesy of Wikipedia). The picture dates from its renovation in 1945.

4b This stone as damaged and uprooted, October 1969 (*Irish Independent*, 1 Nov. 1969; courtesy of N.L.I.). It is largely intact, its inscription complete and Round Towers visible.

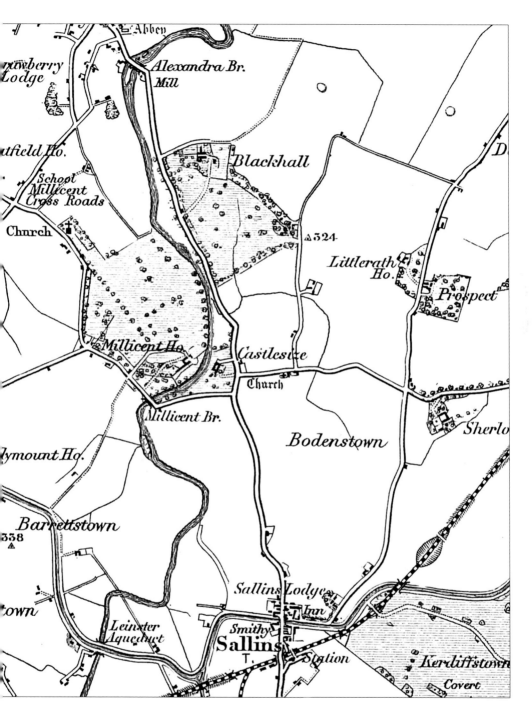

5 Extract from Ordnance Survey one-inch map, 1901, showing the route from Sallins to Bodenstown churchyard (courtesy of Matthew Stout). It is not here to the same scale; from Sallins railway station to Bodenstown church is approx. 2 km. Directly to the north of the church was the house where Tone's parents lived in the 1780s; Tone's 'cottage' was probably at Castlesize.

6a John MacBride, *c.*1906 (courtesy of N.L.I.). He addressed pilgrims in 1905 and 1911. For his part in the Easter rising he was executed in 1916.

6b (*below, left to right*) John Daly, Tom Clarke and Seán MacDermott, *c.*1912 (courtesy of N.L.I.). All three had parts in the revival of the pilgrimages in 1911.

7a Tom Clarke (*on right*) on the way to Bodenstown with Diarmuid Lynch, *c.*1913 (courtesy of N.L.I.). Lynch, like Clarke, was in the I.R.B.

7b (*below*) Fianna Éireann marching to Bodenstown, 1912 or 1913, Pádraic Ó Riain leading Countess Markievicz (courtesy of N.L.I.). The two were elected joint secretaries of the nationalist scouting organisation in 1909.

8a Tom Clarke and St Laurence O'Toole Pipe Band, *c*.1913 (courtesy of N.L.I.). This band played occasionally at Bodenstown until the late 1950s.

8b Patrick Pearse with Fianna Éireann at Tone's grave in 1913 or perhaps 1914 (*An Phoblacht*, 1930s). Pearse's oration in 1913 is the most famous and controversial.

13 Maurice Twomey addressing Republicans at Bodenstown, 18 June 1933 (courtesy of late Maurice Twomey, junr). It was a wet day. Probably the girls in the foreground are members of Cumann na gCailíní, the older ones to the rere Clann na Gaedheal Girl Scouts.

The Irish Press

Vol. III., No. 151. — MONDAY, JUNE 26, 1933. — The Truth in the News. — PRICE ONE PENNY

GREAT BODENSTOWN PILGRIMAGE FROM THE AIR

FIFTEEN THOUSAND AT TONE'S GRAVE

"We Shall See His Dream Fulfilled"—Mr. O'Kelly

MR. AIKEN'S REMARKABLE SPEECH

BELOW our representatives at Bodenstown describes yesterday's great pilgrimage. One description is as it was seen from the air.

From 12,000 to 15,000 are estimated to have gathered at Tone's grave. For hours before the time fixed for the ceremony of laying the wreath the people began to assemble, and when Mr. Sean T. O'Kelly, T.D., delivered the oration the gathering was of great dimensions.

Mr. O'Kelly in his speech said: "We share the political faith of Tone, and we of this generation cherish the hope that it will be our privilege to see his dream fulfilled."

Earlier in the day Mr. Frank Aiken, having reviewed the troops at the graveside, made a remarkable speech:

"ABOLISHING AS HE MADE IN THE MEMORY OF PAST DISSENSIONS, WE," SAID MR. AIKEN, "STAND SHOULDER TO SHOULDER AS THE ADVANCE-GUARD OF THE PEOPLE IN THEIR STRUGGLE FOR POLITICAL, ECONOMIC, AND FINANCIAL INDEPENDENCE. THE STRONGEST CHAIN BINDING US IN SUBSERVIENCE TO ENGLAND HAS BEEN BROKEN BY THE PEOPLE ACTING CONFIDENTLY IN THE SURE KNOWLEDGE THAT THEY HAD AT THE COMMAND OF THE REPRESENTATIVES A WELL-DISCIPLINED ARMY."

An aerial view of a section of the pilgrims filing past Tone's grave at Bodenstown and beginning to assemble in the field beyond.

Sun Lights Great Scene

(By Our Special Representative.)

WHAT would Tone have thought could he have seen it thus? Bodenstown, this churchyard and its pilgrims stretched out below like a patterned patchwork quilt, the tomb no bigger than a thumbnail, the long procession now like a dark river through the grass, now like a string of coloured beads. He would surely have jested about it in his letters to "my dearest love."

The long grass swished against the body of our 'plane as it raced along Kildanan aerodrome before rising into the air, wheeling and facing to Bodenstown.

The rich Co. Dublin lands were brilliant in summer green, deep in the varied colour of trees, black in the shadows of woods and hedges. Still cattle grazed. Away the mountains were silver in a heat haze.

Here and there the hay was already cut, lying golden in the sun in careful layers. In one field a farmer was busy turning it. Locust went by in smoke. Jleas passed under, its streets empty. Along the railway lines flashed a special from Dublin. The white dresses of children could be seen in the dark carriages.

OVER SALLINS.

Sallins! so road to leave it. From the air it was like the hub of a wheel, and along every spoke little people hurried to the centre. The streets of the village itself were thronged. As we flashed over the assembly field the sections of the procession had begun to take their places. The white cards were visible from above, but not the numbers on them: the flags and standards threw glorious colours into the sky.

We circled and flew on. Many broad meadows away, about a bare hill, toil-tan yellow by the many shutters of Sunday last. On its crest were the gray ruins of a mortuary chapel, and just beside them the grave. The grave ruling marked it out. The chapel threw a noble shadow of mourning over it. Yet bright wreaths could be seen.

There were already many; in that field and, as in Sallins, to the South, more came hurrying across the meadows, singly and in twos, little threads of pilgrims. Over a platform a stream played the tricolour was lost in the high wind.

ABOVE TONE'S GRAVE.

We flew on and an hour later were again circling above the grave of Tone. Crammed now that hare, square hilly field. At the ruins stood a group of dark clothed men, the leaders probably, for we could just pick out the tall figure of the Fianna Fáil President. In front of them moved the pilgrims.

TO-DAY'S WEATHER

IRELAND—Moderate northerly wind, local showers, moderate temperature.

Mr. Seán T. O'Kelly, Minister for Local Government delivering the oration at Bodenstown yesterday.

bands, the saffron capes of the pipers, the long green hooded cloaks of girl processionists, the gay summer colours of the women's frocks and children's dresses, the flashing band instruments, the cream-white catering tents, the white banners with the lettering too far below to read which caught the eye, and beyond the ever filling big field where men and women waited in long ranks to hear Tone's ideal re-stated.

From that strange scene we turned to the Dublin which, as stirred by Tone to-day, remained mute and marrow while he lay panting on his pallet. At Sallins the streets were still thronged. The special trains and buses moved towards Bodenstown in gay homage.

FROM ALL IRELAND

HOW THE GREAT PROCESSION WAS MARSHALLED

(By Our Staff Reporters.)

Members of Fianna Fáil, coming together from the four parts of Ireland, united yesterday in another great act of homage to the memory of Tone.

From noon, the town of Sallins was the mustering point. Every possible conveyance—the donkey cart as well as the motor car brought the pilgrims. Men from the land, their dusty boots telling of many miles walked along the roads, their colours and ties in their hands and their old spare-figured woman rushed forward and dropped on her knees in front of the tomb.

The procession proceeded to the field at the other side of the laneway to hear Mr. Sean T. O'Kelly deliver the oration and re-pledge fidelity to the cause for which Tone gave his life. The procession then re-formed and made the supreme sacrifice. Behind him was Mr. de Valera and on the platform, too, were the Attorney-General, members of the Executive Council, Mr. Oscar Traynor, Mr. Gerald Boland, Mr. Hamon Roes, Mr. Tadhg Crowley, Mr. James Victory, Mr. Michl. Kilroy, Dr.

(Continued on Page 2.)

BOMB OUTRAGE IN ST. PETER'S

OUR CROSSWORD

IN pursuance of our policy of making THE IRISH PRESS the complete paper, we begin to-day the publication of a daily cross-word puzzle. Turn to Page Five.

(Continued from preceding column.)

four houses in the town were prepared to minister to the hungry.

Newsboys dashed hither and thither with the Wolfe Tone Souvenir. Commemoration badges were sold by the ten thousand. Vendors of unofficial favours sold nearly as many more.

When Mr. de Valera arrived, stewards and Gardaí had a struggle to clear his car of the surging crowds.

As he took his place at the head of the procession, St. James's Brass and Reed Band played the National Anthem, all uncovering and standing to attention.

Three members of the Cabinet were absent from the march to Bodenstown—Mr. Seán Lemass, Senator Connolly, who is in London, and Mr. Tomás O Deirg, who was in Carlow at the Feis. Then came the members of the National Executive of Fianna Fáil and the members of the party from the Dáil and Senate walking in ranks of four.

AT THE CHURCHYARD.

After them were the contingents from Monaghan, Cavan, Donegal, and from the six partitioned counties; then Longford and Westmeath, Mayo, Roscommon and Leitrim, and so to the rearguard. The ranks of well-known Cumainn passed by in banners, and the streamer carried by the members of Roscru Cumainn caught the eye. As each of American soldier from Clonsilla carried the Stars and Stripes.

Bands were there—St. James's Brass and Reed, Fintan Lalor, New Ireland, Dalkey Pioneers, St. Kevin's, Sheriton, Robert Emmet's Pipers, Roscrea, Nenagh and Palmerstown.

In twenty-eight minutes the churchyard was reached. Along the roads hundreds of amateur photographers clicked their cameras as they cheered the leader.

They cheered, too, as the Easter Week veterans, Denis Dunne and Stephen O'Brien, from Rathmines-Pembroke Comhairle Ceanntair, walked past carrying the wreath which was to be the symbol of their fidelity to Tone's ideals.

At the churchyard the stewards had again to press hard to keep the throng from surrounding Mr. de Valera as he stood in front of the grave.

LAYING OF THE WREATH.

Mr. de Valera was handed the wreath and he advanced with it to the iron railings, entered the wicket and placed it in position beside that laid a few hours before by Mr. Aiken.

Mr. de Valera paused for a few moments in prayer when he had finished the ceremony, and as soon as he left his place an old spare-figured

(Continued in next column.)

FOUR INJURED IN EXPLOSION

"CASE" LEFT IN CLOAKROOM: ONE MAN DETAINED

POPE SHOCKED

VATICAN CITY, Sunday.

A BOMB exploded in the main entrance of St. Peter's to-day, injuring four persons, states a United Press message. Entrances to the Vatican were closed immediately to permit the Papal police to assist the Italian police in a search for the culprit among the crowd.

The bomb had been left in a suitcase, which was placed in a kind of cloakroom situated beside the huge bronze gate at the main entrance to St. Peter's.

Only slight damage was caused by the explosion, but there was a panic among the persons who were in the neighbourhood at the time.

The Pope was shocked to learn of the explosion, saying:—"It is an outrage against God and Man."

His Holiness inquired about the condition of the injured and was relieved to learn that no one was in a serious condition. He said he would offer up prayers for their recovery.

MAN DETAINED

After an hour the Vatican was re-opened to the public, and it was stated that no arrest has been made yet.

It has been ascertained that the suitcase which contained the bomb was left by men who entered the Basilica of St. Peter's with a group of persons.

The bomb, which was equipped with a time device, contained only black powder and no metal. Had it been more powerful there might have been serious loss of life, as several hundred pilgrims were entering the Basilica when the explosion occurred.

The injuries to the victims were caused by the metal fittings of the suitcase in which the bomb was placed.

After Mr. de Valera had placed the wreath a suitcase similar to that in which the bomb exploded has been detained by the Papal gendarmes and handed over to the Italian police on suspicion.

SWEEPS AIR PLAN

The wing of the International Air Race prepared to advertise the Irish Sweepstakes published exclusively in THE IRISH PRESS on Saturday has since been denied in statements given to other Irish papers.

Before publishing this news we sought and secured its confirmation in a fully authoritative quarter and we adhere to it.

SUDDEN END OF RAIL STRIKE

DECISION AT MEETING ON SATURDAY

MEN BACK AT WORK

THE sectional strike on the G.N. Railways in Dublin ended on Saturday afternoon.

Representatives of the sections on strike—Midland and point sections, North Wall and Broadstone sections—held meetings at 33 Parnell Square, and met Mr. C. D. Watters and other N.U.R. officials, following which it was announced that all men were to report to their depots immediately for work.

The men's representatives would not disclose the conditions on which re-sumption of work had been agreed to, but it was understood that their demands was taken pending to-morrow's conference between the Strike Committee and representatives of the Railway Co., Ministry and the N.U.R.

All the sections of the G.N.R. affected by the recent strike were working normally on Sunday.

Mr. C. D. Watters told an IRISH PRESS reporter that he was gratified the trouble had been settled. He could not, he said, make any statement on the merits of the dispute at the moment.

Mr. Watters added that the Government had been most helpful and he thanked them for their interest in the matter.

It was stated at the hospital at mid-night that their condition was not serious.

The bus was not seriously damaged and the occupants escaped injury. The car was towed away from the scene.

Mr. Murphy in his official capacity accompanied Mr. de Valera on his recent visit to Rome.

Mr. O'Hegarty is the former Secretary to the Congress Cabinet and has been it dissolved was appointed a Commissioner for Public Works.

CO. DOWN TRAGEDY

Man Struck While Picking Flowers

HOLIDAY TRAIN

(IRISH PRESS Staff Reporter.)

BELFAST, Sunday.

A FEW moments after picking a bunch of flowers by the railway track near Holywood, Co. Down, this afternoon, a 24-year-old deaf mute, John Gilpin, Thorndyke Street, Belfast, was dashed into by a train and killed instantaneously.

The train drew to a standstill within a few yards, and a train full of city passengers, bound for Bangor, were horrified to learn of the tragedy.

The body was disvened, lying huddled against the embankment, where it had been buried by force of the impact.

The police were notified immediately, and the corpse was removed to Holywood, where an inquest will be held.

A bunch of flowers, evidently gathered from the grassy slope of the embankment, was found grasped in the hand of the victim.

TWO INJURED

HIGH CLASS OFFICIALS IN DUBLIN CRASH

Two higher officials of the Free State Civil Service, Mr. Seán Murphy, of 3 Palmerston Road, Dublin, Assistant Secretary, Department of External Affairs, and Mr. Diarmuid O'Hegarty, 9 Seaview Road, Dunbreoin, Commissioner of Public Works, were injured last night at the junction of the Malahide and Clontarf Roads near Fairview, Dublin, when a saloon car in which they were travelling collided with a Dollymount 'bus.

The collision took place at about 8.30 o'clock. It appears that the saloon car driven by Mr. O'Hegarty was coming down the Malahide Road on to the main Dublin road when it collided with the 'bus, which was proceeding in the Dollymount direction. The windscreen of the car was smashed and the radiator damaged.

The occupants were rushed to St. Vincent's Hospital in a semi-conscious condition, where Mr. O'Hegarty was found to be suffering from a head injury and Mr. Murphy from injury to the leg.

PARIS MOVE TO ADJOURN CONFERENCE

Vote on Chamber Resolution To-day

AMERICAN ACTION

MOVES to adjourn the World Economic Conference immediately are reported both from France and the United States, the two countries whose policy has clashed over the vital question of a currency truce.

The representative of the French Chamber have, according to Reuter, tabled a motion demanding the suspension of the Conference until the de facto stabilisation of currencies has been accomplished. The voting on the motion will take place to-day.

France has insisted throughout that stabilisation of the pound and dollar is the only foundation on which the Conference can build.

A message from Paris adds that there is no possibility of the French delegation withdrawing, but the economic discussions will, in French view, remain merely theoretical unless and until the dollar is pegged.

The opinion was expressed at an informal meeting in New York of the American Economic Conference until some time later, the present being an inopportune time for the Conference.

PRESIDENT "HOPEFUL."

The Conference enters on its third week to-day—a third week which the President, Mr. Ramsay MacDonald, has declared that he is resolved "with a very buoyant and hopeful heart."

According to a statement made to Reuter by one of those most closely in touch with the French delegation yesterday, statements in the French Press prophesying that the Conference will shortly adjourn in no way express the views of the French delegation or the French Government.

These conversations have been proceeding during the week-end between the principal Conference delegates interested in the wheat question. While an agreement is still far from being reached, it is stated on good authority that a definite advance has been made towards that desirable end.

A meeting of the Wheat Committee will be held early this week, but no date has yet been fixed.

"BLOW TO CONFERENCE"

FRENCH CHAMBER PASSES AGRICULTURE BILL

PARIS, Sunday.

When the French Chamber of Deputies voted the Government's new Agricultural Bill yesterday after an all-night sitting, it dealt a severe blow to the World Economic Conference, states the United Press.

After this Bill become law not a single bushel of foreign wheat will be allowed to enter France. The effect is to place a strong barrier round France since it abolishes the temporary right allowing for the import of wheat.

KERRY TEAM BEATEN

THE Kerry Gaelic football team was beaten by New York yesterday by 16 points to 5 points, a most interesting match played before 8,000 spectators.

Type of wheat for blending with the French wheat.

In addition the export of wheat is to be encouraged by a subsidy of about 6s. a bushel for every bushel exported. The Government proposes a minimum credit of 400,000,000 francs (£2,500,000 at par) for financing the scheme. It is expected that this will be raised by the taxation of certain agricultural processes.

The new Bill particularly hits the Canadian exporters who have exported considerable quantities of wheat to France.

RUSSIAN PROTEST.

MOSCOW, Sunday.—A Russian Note, protesting against Dr. Hugenberg's Memorandum to the World Economic Conference, has been handed to the German Foreign Office by M. M. Khinchuk, the Russian Ambassador to Germany.

It will be recalled that Dr. Hugenberg, who is the German Minister of Agriculture and Economics, suggested "planting" German colonies in Russia. The Russian protest Note describes the Memorandum as a violation of the Russo-German trade treaty.

ON OTHER PAGES.

	Page
Literary Corner	3
Rugby Fixtures	3
The Log Diary	3
Dublin Occurrences	3
Radio Programmes	3
Weather for the Week	9
Markets	11
Births and Deaths	

Mr. de Valera at Wolfe Tone's grave at Bodenstown, yesterday.
(Other Pictures on Back Page.)

15 Cork Volunteers' Pipe Band passing through Sallins for Bodenstown, 15 June 1958 (*United Irishma*n, July 1958; courtesy of Mick Healy and Jim Lane). The instruments were borrowed, their own having been lost in a fire. The band played at Bodenstown in the early 1930s and following decades; it took part in the Workers' Party pilgrimage in 1977.

16 Aerial view of Bodenstown churchyard and Provisional Sinn Féin pilgrimage, 11 June 1972 (*Irish Times*, 12 June 1972; courtesy of Irish Times). The National Graves Association's structure, completed in April 1971, abuts the south wall of the ivy-covered church.

as Cumann na mBan, Fianna Éireann, Clann na Gaedheal and Sinn Féin, and that present (again) were Seán MacBride, Maurice Twomey, Patrick McLogan and Donal O'Donoghue (all men with I.R.A. credentials).[34] The Dublin dailies were less informative, none mentioned the I.R.A., but the *Irish Press* did give much space to the oration of Brian O'Higgins.[35] O'Higgins, affectionately regarded now for his manufacture of brightly coloured and oversentimental greetings cards and calendars, had previously given the oration in 1926; he was a propagandist for the I.R.A. by means of his *Wolfe Tone Annual* (suppressed in 1944), but apparently not a member since the civil war. The police reported '125 present-day I.R.A.' and named several including a local I.R.A. member, Frank Driver, who gave commands.[36] The choice as orator of the popular and relatively innocuous O'Higgins suggests caution by the I.R.A. leadership. Whatever the case, if Tim Pat Coogan was reliably informed, three current I.R.A. leaders, Michael Conway, Anthony Magan and Seán McCool, all recently released from prison, took the opportunity to confer secretly in an assembly field and discuss how they might reinvigorate their organisation.[37]

At Bodenstown in 1946 the I.R.A. appeared in greater strength. The Garda Síochána had reason to expect trouble. Garda observers counted 184 members of the I.R.A. together with 16 Cumann na mBan and 40 Fianna Éireann. The crowd in the graveyard were surprised by the sudden appearance of a man who read out, falteringly, a statement he said was from the I.R.A.'s army council urging the youth to train, arm and equip; it had been handed to him by Michael Conway, who afterwards seized it back; the man was identified by Gardaí as a twenty-year old unemployed road-sweeper named Edward Quinn, not suspected of being in the I.R.A. but a 'dupe' not worth prosecuting. Also walking in the parade, but distancing himself from the I.R.A. contingent, was Seán MacBride.[38] As if to confirm that Sinn Féin were still in good standing with the other Republican bodies, Margaret Buckley laid a wreath. The orator was Frank Driver, who had commanded I.R.A. men at Bodenstown the previous year. Driver (1903?–81) lived at Ballymore Eustace, a village further up the Liffey; he was at the Republican pilgrimage in 1933 and seems to have been recently in prison; he was on the 'Provisional' Sinn Féin pilgrimage shortly before his death.[39] Another group mentioned in the Garda report was Ailtirí na hAiséirghe, 40 in strength.

In 1947, according to the Garda Síochána, there were 216 members of the I.R.A. in the parade and the orator, Seán McCool, spoke mainly of 'the history of Wolfe Tone' and 'did not at any time' refer to 'the use of force or the joining of illegal organisations'.[40] The size of the I.R.A. presence would have made such a reference superfluous. Two newspapers reported only tendentious remarks he made on the Ulster question.[41] McCool (1900?–49) was a Donegal man who in his youth had

33 *Ir. Press*, 9 Feb. 1945.   34 *Leinster Leader*, 30 June 1945.   35 *Ir. Press*, 25 June 1945.   36 Nat. Arch., Dublin, JUS/8/900 (1945).   37 Coogan, *I.R.A.*, p. 254. The police report of the pilgrimage names only McCool.   38 Nat. Arch., Dublin, JUS/8/900.   39 *Ir. Indep.*, 24 June 1946. For Driver, see *Ir. Press*, 19 June 1933; *Leinster Leader*, 14 Nov. 1981.   40 Nat. Arch., Dublin, JUS/8/900.   41 *Ir. Indep.*, 23 June 1947; *Ir. Press*, 23 June 1947.

been a schoolmaster and who during the Emergency was briefly chief-of-staff of the I.R.A; he died less than a year after making his speech.[42] For the first time in the reports examined the sounding of the Last Post was followed by Reveille, a subtle Christian allusion to the expected resurrection.[43]

The Bodenstown pilgrimages of 1948 were held four months after the formation of a new government, a coalition of Fine Gael, Labour, Clann na Poblachta and minor parties. For the first time the Republicans participated under the auspices of a new organisation, the National Commemoration Committee. From Sallins there was a parade, 1,500 strong, of 'units' of Sinn Féin and 'kindred Republican organisations' — the estimate of the *Irish Times*, though the police reckoned 800 marching in columns of four; the rally was addressed by Tomás Mac Curtáin, who praised Tone for his acceptance of 'the policy of force of arms'.[44] Mac Curtáin (b. 1915), important in the leadership of the I.R.A. until April 1959 but long forgotten by the time of his death in 1994, had been released from prison on 9 March after serving seven years' imprisonment for a politically motivated offence. The circumstances were that during the Emergency he was sentenced to death by a special court for the murder of a policeman in January 1940; the sentence was (at the eleventh hour) commuted to imprisonment, no doubt because of the mitigating factor of his famous name — his father and namesake, commandant of the Cork No. 1 brigade of the I.R.A. during the war of independence and prominent as the Sinn Féin lord mayor of Cork, had been sensationally murdered by another policeman.[45] The defence counsel in the case was Seán MacBride. MacBride was in June 1948 a leading member of the coalition government, being founder-leader of Clann na Poblachta and minister for foreign affairs. Also present at Bodenstown were three Dáil deputies from the government side: Con Lehane, Michael Fitzpatrick and Patrick Kinane, all of Clann na Poblachta.[46] Lehane was the deputy leader of the 'Clann', which prided itself on being a Republican party; he was close to MacBride and with him had taken part in Bodenstown pilgrimages in 1937, 1942, 1944 and 1945; as a practising solicitor he supported MacBride in cases before special courts during the Emergency.[47] No doubt the three deputies, and any other 'Clann' members present, optimistically sought to reassert their republicanism or, at least, to preserve their republican credentials in the face of republican criticism of Clann na Poblachta for entering office with Fine Gael, led, as it was, by Richard Mulcahy — minister for defence during the civil war and so a *bête noire* of

42 *Derry People and Tirconaill News*, 7 May 1949. He features in J. Bowyer Bell, *The secret army: the I.R.A., 1916–1979* (new ed., 1979), pp 217–25. **43** *Leinster Leader*, 28 June 1947. I am grateful to Dr James McCafferty for explaining Reveille. **44** *Ir. Indep.*, 21 June 1948; *Ir. Times*, 21 June 1948; Nat. Arch., Dublin, JUS/8/900. **45** *Ir. Times*, 2 Feb. 1940, 10 Mar. 1948; *Cork Examiner*, 17 Apr. 1994. For more on Mac Curtáin, see Caoimhe Nic Dháibhéid, 'Fighting their fathers' fights: the post-revolutionary generation' in Senia Pašeta (ed.), *Uncertain futures: essays about the Irish past for Roy Foster* (Oxford, 2016), pp 155–7, 158. He is not mentioned in the *D.I.B.* article on his father. **46** *Ir. Indep.*, 21 June 1948; *Ir. Press*, 21 June 1948. **47** *Ir. Press*, 21 June 1937; *Leinster Leader*, 30 June 1945. For more generally on Con Lehane (1911–83), see Proinsias Mac Aonghusa's appreciation in *Ir. Times*, 27 Sept. 1983; Terry Clavin, 'Lehane, Con' in *D.I.B.*,

Republicans. MacBride absented himself in 1948. Whatever his reason, general awareness of his official position was perhaps conducive to greater permissiveness at Bodenstown than had been evident since the mid 1930s.

At the Republicans' pilgrimage to Bodenstown in 1949 the enthusiasm and militancy of the early and mid-1930s were evident once more. The I.R.A. was freely reported again. 'Southern Ireland' had become a republic — the Republic of Ireland — on 18 April 1949 under legislation introduced by the government in which MacBride was a senior minister.[48] As one close observer of the scene recalled, so-called 'hardline' Republicans 'were ready to welcome the new name as a step in the right direction achieved by their friends in office'.[49] Another innovation owing something to MacBride's influence and supported publicly, universally and enthusiastically by all parties in the nascent republic was the Anti-Partition Fund created in January to aid anti-Partition candidates in forthcoming elections in Northern Ireland, some of whom were Republicans.[50] On 19 June a special train from Dublin and 'buses from many places, including Belfast, Cork, Limerick, Clare, Tipperary, Galway, Waterford and Wexford' brought (the *Irish Press* reported) 'several thousand people' to form the parade from Sallins.[51] The police estimate was, as usual, much smaller at a little over a thousand, but it specified 650 members of the I.R.A., 80 of Fianna Éireann, 30 of Cumann na mBan and 40 of Cumann na gCailíní.[52] This could have been the largest attendance since 1938. Present again, representing Clann na Poblachta, were Con Lehane and other party members.[53] Again the Last Post was followed by Reveille.[54] The principal speaker was named as Criostóir O'Neill. This was Christopher O'Neill, 'clerk', who was sentenced to 18 months' imprisonment by a special court in 1941 for 'membership of an unlawful organisation' (i.e. the I.R.A.) and possession of 'illegal documents'; better known as Christy O'Neill (1919–93), he was born into poverty in Dublin; between 1965 and 1980 he was an official of the Irish Transport and General Workers' Union, retiring as secretary to the Dublin No. 11 (Railways) branch; Christy and his younger brother Mattie (first secretary of the Irish Labour History Society) were friends of Brendan Behan, Christy and Behan having been imprisoned together during the Emergency.[55] The most detailed and sympathetic report of his speech appears in a provincial newspaper, the *Leinster Express*. O'Neill conceded that 'there was a republic of sorts in being in part of Ireland today' while insisting that it should be based 'on the proclamation of 1916' and include the six counties of Northern Ireland. He explained that 'the republican movement was divided into the military

xi (Cambridge, 2018). **48** Republic of Ireland Act, 1948 (1948/22). 'The description of the state shall be the republic of Ireland' (State Paper Office, 14387 A-B, as cited in Ronan Fanning, *Independent Ireland* (Dublin, 1983), p. 175). **49** Conor Cruise O'Brien, *Memoir: my life and themes* (Dublin, 1998), p. 161. **50** *Ir. Indep.*, 28, 31 Jan. 1949. **51** *Ir. Press*, 20 June 1949. **52** Nat. Arch., Dublin, JUS/8/900. **53** *Ir. Press*, 20 June 1949. **54** *Ir. Indep.*, 20 June 1949. **55** *Ir. Indep.*, 17, 27 Mar. 1941; Francis Devine, 'Mattie O'Neill' in *Saothar*, xvii (1992), pp 7–9; MacEoin, *I.R.A.*, pp 721, 736; Michael O'Sullivan, *Brendan Behan: a life* (Dublin, 1999), pp 113–14; info. Karen Hackett, SIPTU. Matt O'Neill was among the I.R.A. contingent at Bodenstown

and civil arms — the Irish Republican Army and Sinn Féin' and held that 'the work of one was as important as the work of the other … Men or women not suited to military organisation by reason of age or sex should join the republican civil organisation — Sinn Féin'.[56] As reported in the *Irish Press*, he 'appealed to all young men present to join the "I.R.A." and said that all those who were unable to do so should join Sinn Féin'.[57] O'Neill's linking the two bodies confirms that they were now united, as suggested above by the change of name of the committee organising the pilgrimages. Tim Pat Coogan (without stating his sources) reproduces another part of O'Neill's speech which is more aggressive: 'the aim of the Army' — by which O'Neill meant the Irish Republican Army — 'is simply to drive the invader from the soil of Ireland … To that end, the policy is to prosecute a successful military campaign against the British forces of occupation in the Six Counties'. Coogan sees O'Neill as the herald of a new era of conservative republicanism: violent resistance to any degree of British presence in Northern Ireland; refusal to recognise the authority of the 'Free State' (despite 'Southern Ireland' having become a republic); acceptance of the social policies enunciated by the Papacy and rejection of the 'welfare state'.[58] One likely factor making Bodenstown particularly enticing in 1949 and allowing the I.R.A. to parade so openly, and its orator to speak so frankly, was the prominence in the government of a man with impressive Republican credentials and only five years previously himself the orator. Another was that government's embrace of the Republican ideals of complete separation from Great Britain and of a united, hostile attitude to Northern Ireland. The choice of O'Neill as orator is puzzling. He seems not to have been in the senior ranks of the I.R.A. Could he have been put forward for this very reason?

In 1950 there was an attendance of a thousand or more, to judge from the arrival of two special trains from Dublin and special buses, even lorries, from elsewhere; a hundred or so men of the I.R.A. marched, as did contingents of Cumann na mBan, Cumann na gCailíní and Fianna Éireann; present too were Con Lehane, Michael Fitzpatrick and James Killean of Clann na Poblachta. Police reported that the orator, Gearóid Ó Broin, 'reiterated the Sinn Féin policy of physical force and advised those present to train as soldiers'.[59] Ó Broin was a member of the I.R.A.'s army council during the Emergency and was one of those who in December 1944 damaged badly Ireland's only equestrian statue, Foley's magnificent Gough monument in the Phoenix Park; he was national organiser of Ailtirí na hAiséirghe until December 1947, and the following June led its contingent in the procession.[60] One of Ó Broin's audience was a young man beginning to achieve literary fame, Brendan Behan.[61]

In June 1951 the Garda Síochána at Dublin Castle were expecting a large display by the I.R.A. On the day the local Naas force counted 840 in the parade, of whom

in 1945 (Nat. Arch., Dublin, JUS/8/900). **56** *Leinster Express*, 25 June 1949. **57** *Ir. Press*, 20 June 1949. **58** Coogan, *I.R.A.*, pp 256–9. He is not mentioned in Bowyer Bell, *Secret army* (1979), which is anecdotal in method; he seems not to have been important in the I.R.A. **59** *Ir. Press*, 19 June 1950; Nat. Arch., Dublin, JUS/8/900 (1950). **60** Douglas, *Architects of the Resurrection*, pp 168, 213, 256, 279, 285; Nat. Arch., Dublin, JUS/8/900 (1948). **61** Nat. Arch.,

close to 500 were members of the I.R.A., the others of the usual kindred associations and of a body not recently named as participating: the Irish Workers' League, which was connected to the Communist Party of the Soviet Union. The Communist contingent was said to have been 168 strong (perhaps an exaggeration) and to have been led by Seán Mulready (who had been interned during the Emergency). Other Communists named were Michael O'Riordan (a veteran of the Spanish Civil War) and Éamonn Smullen (who was to speak at Bodenstown in 1977). Fitzpatrick and Lehane, no longer Dáil deputies, also appeared.[62] The orator was Anthony Magan who announced that 'he was speaking on behalf of the I.R.A.'.[63] 'Tony' Magan (1921–81), a single-minded, disciplined, hard man who had sold his farm in County Meath and moved to Dublin in order to devote himself to the I.R.A. whilst making a living as an accountant and small businessman, had been chief-of-staff since 1948.[64]

Bodenstown in June 1952 attracted, according to the *Irish Times*, 1,000 pilgrims, of whom 500 marched; four bands and the usual Republican contingents (the I.R.A., Sinn Féin, Cumann na mBan and Cumann na gCailíní) were present; police from Naas and Dublin Castle reckoned about 758 marching behind the 'colour party', of whom about 587 were in columns of four as I.R.A. units and of the latter 200 were from Northern Ireland led by James Steele; they recorded also 40 adherents of the Anti-Partition League led by Eoin O'Mahony (an engaging and eloquent eccentric); but the Irish Workers' League (whose paper, the *Irish Workers' Voice*, was sold before the parade) accounted for only 20 marchers.[65] The orator, Joseph McGurk (or McGuirk), a clerk from Belfast, reading out his oration, warned De Valera and other party leaders in what he would have called 'the South' that 'the Republican tradition is still alive in the North' and that a determination to fight existed there.[66]

In 1953, over 400 people and three bands (one from Newry) took part in the parade; by the police count, 174 led by Steele, Manus Canning and Joe Cahill came from Northern Ireland (obviously all in the I.R.A.). The orator was again Tomás Mac Curtáin, who, according to police reports, claimed to be 'a true follower of Wolfe Tone' and 'a soldier of the Irish Republican Army'. By the same account a mere seven members of the Irish Workers' League were present.[67]

The Dublin brigade of the I.R.A. made in June 1954 an audacious and successful raid on the British military barracks at Armagh only eight days before the Republican pilgrimage planned for the 20th. No doubt because of the excitement

Dublin, JUS/8/900 (1950). **62** Nat. Arch., Dublin, JUS/8/900 (1951). **63** *Ir. Press*, 25 June 1951 (where he is named as 'Anthony McCann'); *United Irishman*, July 1951 (where he is 'A. MagCana'). Perhaps it was intended to disguise his name. Magan is stated to be the orator in 1951 in Bowyer Bell, *Secret army* (1979), p. 251. **64** For Magan, see Bowyer Bell, *Secret army* (1979), pp 245–85. There is an obituary of Magan in *Meath Chronicle*, 11 July 1981. **65** *Ir. Times*, 23 June 1952; Nat. Arch., Dublin, JUS/8/900 (1952). **66** *Leinster Leader*, 28 June 1952. The Dublin morning papers ignored his speech. McGurk, who lived off Divis St., had trained for teaching; he was a senior I.R.A. man by 1932 and was an associate of Joe Cahill (MacEoin, *I.R.A.*, pp 422–3; Brendan Anderson *Joe Cahill: a life in the I.R.A.* (Dublin, 2002), pp 119, 121). **67** *Ir. Press*, 22 June 1953; Nat. Arch., Dublin, JUS/8/900 (1953).

the raid caused, Bodenstown drew large numbers of pilgrims, at least 3,000 according to the *Irish Independent*. Contingents arrived from Belfast, Derry and Armagh as well as from distant places in the new republic. The orator of the day, Gearóid Ó Broin, now president of Sinn Féin, was cheered after saying that 'the arms captured at Armagh were for use against the British occupation forces in the Six Counties and would be used against them in due course'. Police reports put the attendance at under 1,000, but the number was still formidable, as 650 or so were said to be members of the I.R.A. or kindred bodies. A separate report was made by Dublin Castle on 'known Communists' present, 14 of whom were identified. (The police from Naas counted 28 but could not identify them.) A few people, among them Roy Johnston and his wife, sold copies of the *Irish Workers' Voice* at Sallins; another, George Dearle (a future orator), was however seen removing Communist posters from the walls of Bodenstown churchyard.[68] Evidently the small number of Communist propagandists were of greater concern to Dublin Castle than an armed and menacing I.R.A., perhaps because of the evident deep-seated anti-communism of the latter.

The threat made in Ó Broin's statement was made again at Bodenstown, more forcefully, twelve months later, when the orator, Éamonn Thomas, declared that 'they of the republican movement were training, preparing and fighting for nothing else but to break the connection with England'.[69] Thomas, or Mac Thomáis (1927–2002), was to be interned at the Curragh from July 1957 until March 1959 for his I.R.A. activities; he was imprisoned in 1961 and again (when editor of *An Phoblacht*) in 1973 and 1974; he was also distinguished for his antiquarian knowledge of Dublin and in 1967 defended the Irish Georgian Society against criticism from Republicans.[70]

The Republicans' pilgrimage in June 1956 was only briefly reported in the Dublin morning papers. Their monthly, the *United Irishman*, depicted it as 'one of the largest and most inspiring rallies', pilgrims arriving from 'north, south, east and west' and showing 'the new spirit of advance'.[71] The orator was George or Seoirse Dearle (d. 1989), a Dublin I.R.A. man and a Sinn Féin candidate in Dáil elections in 1957, but by the 1970s active in the Labour Party and hostile to Sinn Féin.[72] On a visit to Bodenstown, no earlier than 1951, Dearle 'met someone he knew and joined the I.R.A. On his way home in the train he met a girl who became his wife.'[73]

THE 'BORDER CAMPAIGN' OF THE I.R.A.

The Republican demonstrations at Bodenstown during the next five years were held when the I.R.A. was waging war. Its activities in the preceding ten years, in the

---

68 *Ir. Indep.*, 22 June 1954; Nat. Arch., Dublin, JUS/8/900 (1954).   69 *Ir. Times*, 20 June 1955.   70 *United Irishman*, Aug. 1967; *Ir. Times*, 10 Aug. 1973, 9 Oct. 1974, 24 Oct. 2002.   71 *United Irishman*, July 1956.   72 *Ir. Times*, 7 Oct. 1970, 11 Mar., 8 Sept. 1972, 12 Sept. 1989; Walker, *Ir. parlty election results, 1918–92*, pp 194, 223.   73 Michael McInerney, 'Dublin boy reached Labour

opinion of one authority, 'did not amount to much' and the annual pilgrimage was (with occasional street meetings) its main means of keeping up the 'public flame of republicanism'.[74] Its new campaign began on 12 December 1956 when guerrilla units called 'flying columns' crossed the Irish border into Northern Ireland and attacked police posts and personnel. It became known as the I.R.A.'s 'Border campaign', and also as 'Operation harvest'.[75] Three months later Fianna Fáil re-entered office and were to remain undisturbed until the mid 1970s. The new government was from the beginning, like all the main parties in the Dáil, hostile. The reports in the three Dublin morning newspapers of the Republican pilgrimages were, until after the campaign ended in 1962, briefer. This was especially to be seen in the *Irish Press*, which, while anti-Treatyite in its genesis and the preferred daily paper of the republican-minded, did represent the government interest, as was generally evident in its pages.

On 23 June 1957 were held the usual pilgrimages of the defence forces, the Fianna Fáil party and the National Commemoration Committee. The *Irish Press* devoted twice the amount of space to the Fianna Fáil ceremony, a larger affair than in previous years, than to the I.R.A.'s. Perhaps as a timely reminder of Fianna Fáil's republican credentials, the national flag was raised again (as in 1956 and 1958) by Joseph O'Connor, referred to as commandant of ther 3rd Battalion, Dublin Brigade, I.R.A. It was he who had organised, at De Valera's request, the Sinn Féin pilgrimage in 1924.[76] The *Irish Times* was more generous to the present I.R.A., noting special trains and buses bringing, it estimated, some 3,000 pilgrims from all parts of the Irish island, 'many' from Northern Ireland. Alluding to the Border campaign, the orator, Seán Dougan, said 'that so long as part of Ulster was occupied, there could be no freedom, democracy or peace in Ireland. The people in the North were now speaking in the only language that the British understood, appreciated or listened to.'[77] It appears that Dougan, or Duggan, a native of Dunloy, County Antrim, was living in Dublin whilst working as an insurance agent; he was believed by detectives at Dublin Castle to be on the run from the police in Northern Ireland for his I.R.A. activities. Dublin Castle reported to the minister for justice that as many as two thousand marched in the parade, a larger number than for many years.[78]

In June 1958 the Republicans' pilgrimage was held on the 15th, one week before the other ceremonies. It was a grand affair. The *Irish Independent* reported marching from Sallins more than 2,000 'young men', a good number of veterans of the war of independence and uniformed Cumann na mBan and Fianna Éireann, headed by colour parties and accompanied by seven bands. The police similarly reported 2,000 marchers, none however displaying their origins or allegiance to the I.R.A.[79] The

via boy scouts and I.R.A.' in *Ir. Times*, 24 Feb. 1973. Dearle corrected some small points in a letter (ibid., 26 Feb. 1973).　**74** Eunan O'Halpin, *Defending Ireland: the Irish state and its enemies since 1922* (Oxford, 1999), p. 298.　**75** Barry Flynn, *Soldiers of folly: the I.R.A. Border campaign, 1956–1962* (Cork, 2009). See also Brian Hanley and Scott Millar, *The lost revolution: the story of the Official I.R.A. and the Workers' Party* (Dublin, 2009), pp 14–21.　**76** *Ir. Press*, 18 June 1956, 24 June 1957, 23 June 1958.　**77** *Ir. Times*, 24 June 1957.　**78** *Ir. Indep.*, 26 Sept. 1959; Nat. Arch., Dublin, JUS/8/900 (1957).　**79** *Ir. Indep.*, 16 June 1958; Nat. Arch., Dublin, JUS/8/900 (1958).

orator, John Joseph McGirl, referring to the 'partition question' and the Border campaign, said that 'every generation since '98 had taken up Tone's teaching that the connection with England must be broken' and, knowing his audience would be aware of I.R.A.'s losses, to 'the seven who had died'.[80] Two of these had been shot dead when attacking a police barracks at Brookeborough, County Fermanagh. One of the two, Seán South, was known to be a very pious Catholic as well as a republican martyr and so was even more highly esteemed by the pilgrims.[81] McGirl (1919?–88), of Ballinamore, County Leitrim, was briefly chief-of-staff of the I.R.A. in 1958; he had been elected deputy for Sligo–Leitrim in 1957, but refused to take his seat in the Dáil; he was imprisoned three times for his subversive activities.[82]

The Republican pilgrimage on 21 June 1959 attracted, at the count of the Special Branch of the Garda Síochána, 3,460 persons, 1,860 of them marchers, 79 of these members of the I.R.A. and named. One of those named, Cathal Goulding, had been released from prison a month before.[83] The only mention of Bodenstown in any Dublin morning paper was in the *Irish Times*, under 'Sun sent crowds to the beaches', reporting three 'specials' carrying about 1,400 individuals to Sallins 'for the Wolfe Tone commemoration'.[84] It was given a few lines, under 'Wolfe Tone remembered', in the *Leinster Leader*.[85] The *United Irishman*'s claim of a parade of 15,000[86] is hardly credible. A report in the *Meath Chronicle* also gave the attendance as 15,000; it stated that 40 members of Navan Sinn Féin club travelled by special bus and that.[87] Obviously this was supplied by a local Republican and the attendance wildly exaggerated. The orator was a deputy for Longford-Westmeath, Rory Brady. The local paper, the *Longford Leader*, gave ample space, reckoning the attendance to be between eight and ten thousand and reporting the speech at length and also the fact that the chairman, Tomás Mac Giolla, read a statement from 250 men in Belfast jail (no doubt in connexion with the Border campaign) expressing confidence in the I.R.A. leadership.[88] Rory Brady was to be better known under the Irish form of his name, Ruairí Ó Brádaigh. Both he and Mac Giolla were again to be prominent at Bodenstown. An indication of the degree of interest in participating and the degree of religiosity of one likely party of pilgrims was a notice in the *Kerryman* advertising a special train departing from Listowel at 7.45 a.m., calling at Tralee and Killarney, arriving at Sallins at 1.40 p.m. and departing on the homeward journey at 7.10 p.m. A dining car would be provided and 'ample time' allowed at Killarney 'for attendance at Holy Mass'.[89] It is likely that this interest in politics had been generated by a veteran local Republican, John Joseph Rice, who in March 1957 had been elected as Sinn Féin deputy South Kerry after undertaking not to take his seat in the Dáil. He was to address Bodenstown pilgrims in 1961.

---

80 *Ir. Times*, 16 June 1958; *United Ireland*, July 1958.   81 For this episode, see Flynn, *Soldiers of folly*, pp 120–29.   82 *Ir. Times*, 23 June 1952, 9 Dec. 1988; Hanley & Millar, *Lost revolution*, p. 7. 83 Hanley & Millar, *Lost revolution*, pp 19, 620; Nat. Arch., Dublin, Jus8/900 (1959).   84 *Ir. Times*, 22 June 1959.   85 *Leinster Leader*, 27 June 1959.   86 *United Irishman*, July 1959.   87 *Meath Chronicle*, 27 June 1959.   88 *Longford Leader*, 27 June 1959.   89 *Kerryman*, 13 June 1957.

RELATIONS BETWEEN SINN FÉIN AND THE I.R.A.

Bodenstown was the main annual public event of Sinn Féin and the I.R.A. from the mid 1940s until 1969, after which both split. Unlike in the 1930s, they rallied jointly. Whilst Sinn Féin was always lawful, the I.R.A. remained under a ban. It was prudent and practical therefore to advertise the pilgrimages as 'Republican'. The organising of these pilgrimages was attributed by the Garda Síochána during the Emergency to the National Graves Association, from 1945 until 1951 to the Wolfe Tone Commemoration Committee, and from 1952 until 1959 to the I.R.A. or the I.R.A. and Sinn Féin jointly.[90] Newspapers referred to the Wolfe Tone Commemoration Committee until 1947, after which, and throughout the 1950s and 1960s, responsibility was assigned to the National Commemoration Committee. Particulars of the composition of this committee are hard to find beyond the names of pilgrims placing wreaths on its behalf.[91] In 1957 it was described as 'a national committee of various organisations', and after the pilgrimage in 1959 it had to be made clear that the 'National Commemoration Committee were solely responsible for the arrangements' and 'not the National Graves Association'.[92] Despite the paucity of information, there can be little doubt that it was one of the 'civil wings' of the I.R.A. alluded to by Seán Garland, who joined in 1953, in a revealing speech he made at Bodenstown in 1968. 'The traditional policy of the I.R.A. up to the present', he said, 'has been to prepare the army for an armed struggle and use the civil wings of the movement simply as support groups for publicity, finance, recruits and suppliers of transport and friendly houses'.[93] Other 'civil wings' had regularly paraded at Bodenstown in the 1920s and 1930s and resumed doing so only two or three years into the Emergency: Cumann na mBan (the Republican women's association) and Fianna Éireann (the Republican youth movement).

On the evidence of the pilgrimage in 1945, reunion of Sinn Féin and the I.R.A. was a *fait accompli* in that year even if it was not formalised until the end of the decade. The pilgrimage of 1946 leaves very little doubt. Clearest evidence of their reunion is the speech of Christy O'Neill at Bodenstown in 1949 in which he stated that 'the republican movement was divided into the military and civil arms — the Irish Republican Army and Sinn Féin'.

THE DEFENCE FORCES AND FIANNA FÁIL AT BODENSTOWN

During the 1940s and 1950s, on the precedent created by W. T. Cosgrave in 1924 and respected by Aiken in 1932, there was an annual June ceremony at which the minister for defence, supported by a contingent of military officers and men, would lay a wreath on behalf of 'the Army' — the Irish defence forces. From 1940 until 1947 (when Fianna Fáil were in office) the minister was Oscar Traynor; in 1948,

90 Nat. Arch., Dublin, JUS/8/900.　91 E.g. Seán Dunne in 1953 and 1955 (*Ir. Press*, 22 June 1953, 20 June 1955).　92 *Ir. Press*, 24 June 1957, 27 June 1959.　93 *United Irishman*, July 1968.

1949 and 1950 (when Fine Gael were in office with other parties) it was Thomas O'Higgins; in 1951, 1952 and 1953 (another period of Fianna Fáil government) it was again Oscar Traynor; in 1954 and 1955 (years of another coalition government led by Fine Gael) the minister for defence was Seán Mac Eoin; in 1956 the wreath was laid by Liam Cosgrave, acting minister for defence (Mac Eoin having left office); in 1957 the minister was Kevin Boland, who, as a Fianna Fáil defence minister, was to lay wreaths until 1961.[94] The ceremony began with the minister being met by the chief-of-staff and then inspecting a guard of honour. From 1942 the local companies of the Local Defence Force (the L.D.F., a corps formed during the Emergency) participated; in 1946 three provided a guard of honour for the minister and, under its new name, Fórsa Cosanta Áitiúil (F.C.Á.), and again in 1947; there was similar participation on later occasions. The F.C.Á. units were almost always drawn from the Kildare or North Kildare Battalion. One company participating on occasions was based at Clongowes Wood College.[95] From 1955 until 1959 the chief-of-staff was Patrick Mulcahy, a brother of Richard Mulcahy. Next the minister would lay a wreath. The custom of cadets firing three volleys over the grave preceded or followed by the sounding of the Last Post, begun in 1922, seems to have died out after 1951; a new custom began, apparently in 1952, of buglers following the Last Post with Reveille, a custom already adopted by the I.R.A. in 1947 if not earlier.[96] The ceremony would terminate with the playing of the national anthem, 'The soldiers' song', by the No. 3 Army Band.

There were, however, by the 1940s three important reductions of the scale of the 1920s. Aiken in 1932, no doubt with De Valera's full approval, made the defence forces' ceremony an entirely military occasion with no formal civilian participation other than that of the minister for defence. After 1936 the minister no longer made an address to the troops and after 1937 the size of the military deployment was reduced to what can only be guessed, in the absence of figures in newspaper reports, as no more than a hundred or two. There were no longer orations and military reviews in the field opposite the churchyard. None of these changes was reversed after Fine Gael entered office in 1948.

During the two decades under consideration the Fianna Fáil party, more precisely its national executive, held its own annual pilgrimage. Only in 1943, when there was an election campaign in June, was there none. De Valera, as president of the party, would almost invariably be present to lay a wreath for the party, doing so for the last time in 1958.[97] Exceptions were 1941, when the wreath-layer was Seán T. O'Kelly, 1952 (Oscar Traynor), 1957 (James Ryan) and 1959 (Seán Lemass).

94 These details of ministerial attendance are to be found in newspaper reports appearing on the day after the army ceremonies.   95 *Ir. Press*, 22 June 1942, 21 June 1943, 26 June 1944, 18 June 1945, 17 June 1946, 16 June 1947, 21 June 1948, 20 June 1949, 19 June 1950, 18 June 1951, 23 June 1952, 22 June 1953, 21 June 1954 etc.   96 In the newspaper reports examined the last mention of firing volleys over the grave is in *Ir. Press*, 19 June 1950, the first mention of Reveille at a defence forces ceremony at Bodenstown is in *Ir. Press*, 23 June 1952. For the I.R.A. adopting Reveille, see above, p. 152. No instance of the I.R.A. or Fianna Éireann firing a volley has been found after 1922.   97 My source throughout is the *Irish Press*, the Fianna Fáil newspaper.

Lemass laid the wreath on 21 June, the day before he succeeded De Valera as taoiseach. Whenever Fianna Fáil were in office — except for 1941, 1951 and 1955 — the party's ceremony in Bodenstown churchyard would immediately follow that of the defence forces, a custom that began in 1933.[98] This was practical and sensible for the party, as it ensured (one can presume), that not only was the grass mown by the caretaker but the churchyard was inspected by an army detail and any hazard removed, all reliably a few hours previously. The two ceremonies were however distinctly and formally separate, the first official, the second a party national executive matter. De Valera's predecessor in government, Cosgrave, had in 1923 and successive years combined the two elements in having the minister for defence make a partisan political speech in the presence of military men, government ministers and party members. De Valera broke with this policy on entering office. When Fianna Fáil were out of office, a slightly different routine was adopted. In 1948, 1949 and 1950, the military and Fianna Fáil ceremonies were held on successive Sundays. When Fianna Fáil re-entered office on 13 June 1951 it was only four days before the defence forces were due to be at Bodenstown and so the party held a brief ceremony on the 24th, an hour or two before the arrival of the Republicans. Fianna Fáil were able to keep to their old routine in 1952 and 1953. Another period of their opponents being in office was from early June 1954 until mid March 1957. On 26 June 1954, the Fine Gael minister for defence and Fianna Fáil's president were at Bodenstown on the same Sunday, perhaps because Fianna Fáil party officials had weeks previously arranged their party's pilgrimage to coincide with that of the defence forces as usual. In 1955 Fianna Fáil appeared, more diplomatically, on the following Sunday. In 1956 the rival parties were again present on the same day. From June 1957 the custom of Fianna Fáil doubling up with the defence forces was to continue unbroken until 1973.

From 1937, Fianna Fáil's pilgrimages were usually quiet affairs compared with the ostentation of the Republicans. There was no need for the field opposite the churchyard. During the Emergency only a few senior party members would attend; by 1948 small crowds of supporters were appearing and in that year there was what the *Irish Press* (which tended to exaggerate Fianna Fáil's successes) reported as 'a large gathering' that included young men and women from Dublin, Kildare and parts of the Midlands as well as veterans; in 1954, when the party was out of office, the paper reported 'a large representation' of Fianna Fáil *cumainn* (branches) in Dublin, Kildare, Wicklow and elsewhere; they were able to hear Eoin Ryan, son of James Ryan, a party stalwart, read an extract from the writings of Pearse 'on the character of Wolfe Tone and his influence on the ideals which led to the national resurgence'.[99] There were never orations. De Valera, hardly ever absent in the 1940s and 1950s, was uncharacteristically unpartisan in remaining silent, but characteristically pious in laying a wreath and standing pensively at Tone's grave.

98 In 1941 the army's ceremony was on 22 June, Fianna Fáil's on the following Friday; in 1943, after the army's ceremony on the morning of 20 June, the National Graves Association's ceremony was held in the afternoon.   99 *Ir. Press*, 28 June 1948, 21 June 1954.

And Fianna Fáil pilgrims no longer marched from Sallins, as they had done until 1936. De Valera and his lieutenants, young men in 1916, were now well into middle age; moreover they were, even with young recruits, too few to create a strong impression. In 1959, at least acknowledging the old custom, Lemass, in De Valera's retirement, led a march of members of the government and party organisation along the road beside the churchyard followed by members of the general public.[100] The reports of Fianna Fáil pilgrimages in the *Irish Press* suggest that they never attracted the very large crowds seen at the party's pilgrimages in the early and mid 1930s.

One reason for Fianna Fáil continuing to go on pilgrimage to Bodenstown year after year was perhaps De Valera's devotion to Tone. Another was the political need to maintain the party's republican profile in its eternal contest with the I.R.A. Perhaps there was another reason too, the opportunity for party officials, county councillors and local party activists to meet ministers and Dáil deputies on what was, as in the early years of Bodenstown pilgrimages, an outing to a pleasant rural spot. It was a morale booster. It was also, as in the early years, a largely Dublin affair, it did not attract pilgrims from afar. This allowed the party leadership to reassert that it cared as much for metropolitan as for rural interests. A novelty at Fianna Fáil's ceremony in 1954 was the sounding of the Last Post followed by Reveille in imitation of the defence forces and the I.R.A.[101] No doubt the buglers added a frisson of militarism to the occasion. After the I.R.A. began its militarily aggressive Border campaign in December 1956, there was an increase in Fianna Fáil's need to display its own militancy, relatively harmless as it was. This seems to have been about the time that a special effort was made by Seán Lemass to increase the profile of Fianna Fáil at Bodenstown.[102] Certainly in 1957 the party got a large turn-out of senior party members, presumably in an attempt to reassert Fianna Fáil's republicanism at the 'holy place' where an hour or two later was due the ceremony of I.R.A. and Sinn Féin, activists in and apologists for (respectively) the Border campaign.[103] In 1958 eight deputies and three senators turned out.[104] Fianna Fáil were even more impressive in 1959 when Lemass led to the graveside, seemingly marching, three cabinet ministers, four other parliamentarians, the entire National Executive, sundry party members, 'I.R.A. veterans' and general public; a wreath was laid, buglers sounded the Last Post and Reveille and the Irish tricolour was hoisted.[105] These stirring effects were repeated throughout the 1960s but in the presence of much smaller crowds.

An astonishing aspect of the Bodenstown phenomenon was the presence there on the very same day of units of the Irish defence forces and units of the I.R.A. This began in 1925. It happened in 1948, 1949 and 1950, in each year from 1952 to 1957, again in 1959 and throughout the 1960s. (The exceptions were 1929, the years 1932 to 1938 and 1944.) To give a single illustration, in 1956, on 17 June, the defence forces had their ceremony at 11.30 a.m., Fianne Fáil at noon, and in the afternoon

---

100 *Ir. Press*, 22 June 1959.   **101** *Ir. Press*, 21 June 1954.   **102** Bryce Evans, *Seán Lemass, democratic dictator* (Cork, 2011), p. 189.   **103** *Ir. Press*, 24 June 1957.   **104** *Ir. Press*, 23 June 1958.   **105** *Ir. Press*, 22 June 1959.

the I.R.A. (under the auspices of the so-called 'National Commemoration Committee').[106] The I.R.A. was officially and widely perceived as threatening the legitimacy and security of the state. The bearing of the various contingents at Republican demonstrations at Bodenstown was manifestly militaristic even if the letters 'I.R.A.' (or the Irish name 'Óglaigh na hÉireann') were seldom to be seen on banners. Contingents identifying themselves as Sinn Féin, Fianna Éireann and Cumann na mBan, though lawful, connected themselves with the I.R.A. The symbiotic relationship between Sinn Féin and the I.R.A. was stated openly by Criostóir O'Neill at Bodenstown in 1949. In some instances the orator of the day had recently been in prison for subversive activities, in the case of Tomás Mac Curtáin for murder. Such proximity of place and time is strikingly incongruous. It is hard to imagine in other countries the lawful army being ostentatiously challenged, on the same day, in the same place, by an unlawful army. Incongruous too is the proximity of ministers of the government at the military and Fianna Fáil party commemorations held an hour or two before Republican commemorations at which well-known subversives were present. A clue is to be found in Marianne Elliott's remark in 1989 about this separation symbolising 'that ambivalence towards armed resistance which lies at the heart of Irish nationalism'.[107] In fact 'constitutionalists' and the 'physical-force element' (her words) were usually separated by a mere two hours, not by one week as she supposed. It is the proximity of the two armies that signifies ambivalence.

Was there any need for co-operation between the Irish military authorities and whatever organisation was organising Republican pilgrimages? Were mutual agreements made informally between the Irish defence forces and the Irish Republican Army? There might have been benefits for both. The National Graves Association, though a lawfully- and legally-constituted albeit shadowy organisation, was, to judge from its representatives laying wreaths at I.R.A. pilgrimages (though never at those of Fianna Fáil), linked directly or indirectly to the I.R.A. It could at least, one supposes, be relied upon to maintain the Tone family grave throughout the year leaving the maintenance of the churchyard to Kildare County Council and inspection early on the morning of the pilgrimages to 'details' of the army units due for deployment at Bodenstown, usually before noon. The National Graves Association could, one also supposes, be relied on again to tidy up after the dispersal of the I.R.A., kindred bodies and followers early in the evening. In fact the Irish defence forces' ceremony was always shortly after midday and brief; the I.R.A. in six years during the 1940s and 1950s years appeared on the previous or following Sunday; on those Sundays when both 'armies' had their ceremonies (in 1942–3, 1948–1950, 1952–7 and 1959) an interval of about two hours would separate them. If an intermediary was ever needed to avert conflict, it might have been the ostensibly neutral National Graves Association. That the churchyard was shared without conflict between foes does suggest some sort of understanding if not collaboration.

106 *Ir. Indep.*, 13 June 1956; *Ir. Times*, 18 June 1956.   **107** Marianne Elliott, *Wolfe Tone* (London, 1989), p. 417. It is not in the 2nd edition (2012).

THE GRAVESTONE REFURBISHED, THE RAILINGS REPLACED

By 1945 the gravestone erected fifty years before by the Kildare Gaels was considered to be in need of repair, as Seán Fitzpatrick, the secretary of the National Graves Association, reported after inspecting the grave in the summer of 1944.[108] Damage to one of the figures 'evidently effected by means of a hammer' had been noticed in 1920.[109] At some stage after its formation in 1926 the association took charge of the Tone family grave. It made the arrangements for the Republican pilgrimage in 1942 and each year until 1948, after which a body calling itself the National Commemoration Committee (known also by its Irish name, Coisde Cuimhneacháin Náisiúnta) was in charge.[110] No doubt the members of the two committees were kindred spirits whether or not any of them was a member of both. In any case, as all those prominently involved organising Republican pilgrimages after 1921 were known for their membership of Sinn Féin or the I.R.A (or both), it would be safe to state that the members of both committees were close to Sinn Féin and the I.R.A. Their purpose, whether it was caring for the plot and the graves, or organising the pilgrimages, was surely to facilitate Sinn Féin or the I.R.A., not the Fianna Fáil party, nor the 'national army', the defence forces of the Irish state. In February 1945 the *Irish Press* reported somewhat light-heartedly but with serious intent that

> the limestone wolfhound that guarded Wolf [*sic*] Tone's grave at Bodenstown has lost his head, tail and legs. It would be hard to tell his breed from all that is left of him. This is not due to any single act of vandalism, nor to the weather, but to the loving attention of visitors over forty-seven years. Bits of the carving off Tone's tomb must now be scattered over the world, with a preponderance in the U.S.A. So great is the destruction that some sympathisers must have come armed with hammers. Otherwise it would be hard to explain how solid chunks of practically indestructible limestone could have been separated from their base. Having chipped away all the more vulnerable parts of the dog, they then started on the rest of the ornament, flattening out the shamrock wreath with harp in middle, blunting the mountain tops, carrying off the upper stonework of the carved Abbey and taking a storey off the tops of the flanking Round Towers. The National Graves Association has now moved the headstone to Farrel's Monumental Yard in Glasnevin, where the sculptors are considering whether they can recondition the old dog or carve and insert an entirely new one. Tone would have got a great kick out of that.

It was Farrell & Sons, stonemasons, who had cut the stone in 1895. A few months after the report, not long before the annual pilgrimages, the association issued an

---

108 *Dublin Evening Mail*, 25 July 1944.   109 *Ir. Indep.*, 21 June 1920.   110 After the pilgrimage of 1949 was reported in the *Irish Press* to have been 'under National Graves Association auspices', a further report stated that the 'National Commemoration Committee were solely responsible for

appeal for subscriptions for 'repairs to the Wolfe Tone Memorial Stone and to the grave at Bodenstown'.[111] In 1950, according to information supplied to the same newspaper twenty years later (probably by the secretary of the National Graves Association, Seán Fitzpatrick the younger), the Tone memorial stone erected by the Kildare Gaelic Association was 'completely renovated' in 1945 and in 1950 'completely re-lettered'.[112] Old photographs show this stone with the plinth inscribed 'Renovated by the Irish National Graves Association ...'. When it was moved back to Bodenstown from Farrell's yard in Glasnevin has not been ascertained.

The railings too needed repair or even replacement. Fitzpatrick on his visitation in 1944 found them to be so rusty that they barely held together. In March 1949 the National Graves Association adopted a design by an architect for a new railing and appealed for subscriptions.[113] The architect was Donal O'Dwyer (1908–99), who was head of the building department at the Bolton Street Institute, Dublin, from 1940 until he became principal in 1952.[114] Manufacture was eventually carried out by 'advanced students' at the institute; the railings were described as 'an intricate ornamental surround for Wolfe Tone's grave' and in a later report as being 'in Celtic mode'.[115] Some of the expense was borne by the Kildare Gaelic Athletic Association and by local people in the county.[116] According to the account given in 1969 and referred to above, there were to be two keys for the gate into the railed area: one in the possession of the secretary, Seán Fitzpatrick the elder, the other in the keeping of the caretaker and gravedigger, Dan Hegarty.[117] (Hegarty, aged 65 in 1969, became caretaker in 1946 and was still in office in 1979.)[118] By 24 June 1951 the new railings were in place for the Republicans' rally at Bodenstown on that day, where they were generally praised. There was a discordant voice. John Dunphy, a member of the Kildare county board of the G.A.A., expressed the opinion that the old railings, broken in several places, 'could have been repaired, thus preserving their historic value.' and objected that 'no permission for their removal had been given by the board'. The secretary of the National Graves Association retorted that 'the railings were now only scrap'.[119] Dunphy's point was well made, but he was mistaken in thinking, as he did, that the old railings had been erected by the Kildare G.A.A. — they had in fact been erected by 'the men of Kildare' in 1874, before the foundation of the G.A.A.; still, he made a valid point about their historic value and might have added that their market value as a former fixture on Tone's grave could have been higher than their scrap value.

the arrangements' (*Ir. Press*, 20, 27 June 1949). **111** *Ir. Press*, 9 Feb., 4 June 1945. **112** *Ir. Press*, 1 Nov. 1969. **113** *Ir. Press*, 23 Mar. 1949. **114** Irish Architectural Archive, Dictionary of Irish Architects, 1720–1940 (on-line). **115** *Ir. Press*, 8 Feb. 1951. **116** Nat. Arch., Dublin, JUS/8/900 (1951). **117** *Ir. Press*, 1 Nov. 1969; *Ir. Indep.*, 25 June 1979, photo. **118** *Ir. Times*, 3 Nov. 1969. **119** *Ir. Press*, 8 Feb., 25 June 1951.

9

The 1960s: the leftward shift and the National Graves Association's monument

IRELAND WAS IN A TIME WARP when the 1960s opened. Fianna Fáil had been in office almost continuously since 1932, with only two intervals in opposition (1948–51 and 1954–7), and were to remain in office uninterrupted from then until 1973. The annual, separate pilgrimages to Bodenstown by Fianna Fáil and Sinn Féin — rival republicans or republican rivals — were routine. Throughout the 1960s the Fianna Fáil pilgrimage was little more than a wreath-laying ceremony. It was always preceded by a similarly formal ceremony of the Irish defence forces. The minister for defence would lay a wreath on behalf of the officers and men, and shortly afterwards the president of Fianna Fáil, or another senior party member, would lay a wreath on behalf of the party organisation. When Fianna Fáil were in office the senior party members laying wreaths were also senior government ministers: Seán Lemass, taoiseach or prime minister (in 1960, 1961 and 1962), Seán MacEntee, tanaiste or deputy prime minister (1963 and 1964), Frank Aiken, minister for external affairs (1965 and 1966), Jack Lynch, who in November 1966 succeeded Lemass as taoiseach (1967 and 1968) and Michael Hilliard, minister for defence (1969). Hilliard, 'wearing two hats', laid two wreaths. In 1960 the military ceremony was enlivened by the presence of French naval officers and men from two vessels on a courtesy visit to Dublin; the Curragh army band played the French and Irish national anthems, the 'Marseillaise' and the 'Soldiers' song' respectively.[1] This was the only instance of participation by French defence forces notwithstanding Tone's status as a French army officer.

In 1968, in changing times, Fianna Fáil departed from its custom since 1938 of not having an oration. The orator, Ruairí Brugha, whose father Cathal had made a speech in 1912, fastened upon Tone's belief in 'the ultimate unity of the nation. The unity of our country is a natural right. We are too small.'[2] Brugha had been interned for I.R.A. activity during the Emergency and did not join Fianna Fáil until 1962.[3] Lynch, laying a wreath on the occasion, lacked not only a strong power basis in his parliamentary party but also the Republican credentials normally expected of a Fianna Fáil politician, for which reasons he continually was threatened by ambitious

1 *Ir. Times*, 20 June 1960; *Ir. Indep.*, 20 June 1960.   2 *Ir. Press*, 24 June 1968. This Fianna Fáil pilgrimage is also recounted by Tim Pat Coogan (*I.R.A.*, pp 221–4).   3 Ruairí Brugha (1917–2006) was married to Máire MacSwiney, daughter of Terence MacSwiney and so a niece of Mary

166

and staunchly republican rivals.[4] Probably he felt more secure with the man beside him who had a famous name and Republican credentials to boot. The following June, Brugha returned to lead a decade of the Rosary in Irish for the three hundred or so Fianna Fáil faithful; after him Frank McDonnell, like Brugha a member of the party's national executive, made another departure by delivering again Pearse's famous oration heard at Bodenstown in 1913.[5] This Fianna Fáil commemoration occurred eight months after the outbreak of disturbances in Northern Ireland.

CONSERVATIVE REPUBLICANISM IN THE EARLY 1960S

At the beginning of the 1960s the I.R.A.'s 'Border campaign', was all but over and was to be called off publicly on 26 February 1962. The hubris evaporated but the campaign was not forgotten. Seventeen men imprisoned for their parts in the campaign were to deliver in the 1960s or 1970s the usual oration at Bodenstown: Seán Stephenson, alias Seán Mac Stiofáin (1960), Tomás Mac Giolla (1962, 1969, 1973, also 1982), Thomas Mitchell (1963), Martin Shannon (1964), Tony Meade (1965), Séamus Costello (1966, 1975, 1976), Cathal Goulding (1967, 1975), Seán Garland (1968, 1972), Dáithí Ó Conaill (1970), Joe Cahill and Malachy McGurran (both in 1971, for rival factions), Seán Keenan (1972), Liam McMillen (1973), Michael 'Mick' Ryan (1974), Proinsias Mac Airt (1975), Des O'Hagan (1976, also 1981), Jimmy Drumm (1977). An eighteenth man, Proinsias de Rossa, barely 16 when arrested in 1956, was an orator in 1983. Another Border warrior, Gearóid Ó Broin, had been the Republican orator in 1954, and another, Mac Thomáis, in 1955. Of the seventeen, eight spoke for the 'Official' faction after the Republican split in 1969, five for the 'Provisional' faction; De Rossa spoke for the Officials.

Stephenson, the orator in 1960, was said to be of Cork, but in fact was a rather strange Englishman born, in 1928, John Edward Drayton Stephenson in Essex to parents of no verifiable Irish ancestry and not Catholics. No doubt because he attended a Catholic school in Islington and worked in the building trade he fell in with working-class Irish Catholics; he became in 1949 commander of an I.R.A. unit in London, which led to his imprisonment in 1953 for stealing guns from an army cadet school in his native county. Not long before his arrest he laid a wreath at Bodenstown on behalf of a London branch of Sinn Féin. On his release in 1959 he joined his wife in her native County Cork; they moved to County Meath in 1966; he was to be the first chief-of-staff of the so-called 'provisional' wing of the I.R.A. in 1969, as such proving ruthless until his arrest three years later. An uncompromising Catholic and enthusiast for the Irish language, he gaelicised his name to Seán Mac Stiofáin; he died in 2004, long after ceasing to be militarily active.[6] A large number travelled by train from Cork to hear his oration.[7] It was ignored by the Dublin and Cork morning papers.

MacSwiney.   **4** For Lynch's travails within his party, see Ó Beacháin, *Destiny of the soldiers*, chap. 13.   **5** *Ir. Times*, 23 June 1969; *Ir. Press*, 23 June 1969.   **6** *Ir. Press*, 22 June 1953; Patrick Maume, 'Mac Stiofáin, Seán' in *D.I.B.*   **7** *Ir. Indep.*, 20 June 1960.

In 1961 the oration was given by John Joe Rice who during the war of independence had commanded the Kerry No. 2 Brigade of the I.R.A.; Rice (1893?–1970), who later in life managed a branch of a mineral water company at Tralee, was little known outside his county until elected a Dáil deputy for Sinn Féin in 1957.[8] The politics of Seán Mac Stiofáin and Rice could only be described as 'nationalist' and 'militarist' and, with regard to the legitimacy of the republic declared in 1949, 'uncompromising'. Tomás Mac Giolla (who was destined to become lord mayor of Dublin), giving the oration in 1962, was less so, but instead lauded the 'courage' of Tone and paid tribute to 'the young soldiers of the Republic', the I.R.A. men who had engaged in the Border campaign. The pilgrimage was barely mentioned in the three Dublin morning papers, perhaps to starve the I.R.A. of publicity; the *United Irishman*, expansive, referred to the presence of 'thousands of Republicans from all over Ireland'.[9] Unusually, it was reported in a provincial paper, the *Southern Star*, according to which there was 'the largest attendance for many years' (10,000), numerous pipe bands and a colour party formed by '6-County men'.[10] But in the stated opinion of the minister for justice, Charles Haughey, the I.R.A. was at its lowest ebb since 1922, lacking popular support and American money; its Border campaign had petered out long before being called off; Sinn Féin was 'largely moribund'.[11] And in 1960 the Special Branch of the Garda Síochána had dismissed the leadership of the I.R.A., with one or two exceptions, as 'non-descript persons in lower middle-class and working-class families who make no particular impact on persons outside that organisation'.[12]

The twentieth of June 1963 was the two hundredth anniversary of Tone's birth. The bicentenary was marked by De Valera, as president of Ireland, opening formally on the day a commemorative exhibition at Trinity College (Tone's alma mater).[13] Sinn Féin organised various unmistakably republican celebrations in Dublin for the week beginning Monday the 17th, called 'Wolfe Tone week'.[14] Bodenstown on the following Sunday was the culmination of these events. Early on the army was present, and a wreath laid by the defence minister, Gerald Bartley, to be followed, after the army's departure, by a ministerial colleague, MacEntee, who laid a wreath for the party. In the afternoon over 5,000 people paraded from Sallins to the accompaniment of six bands in a commemoration said in the *Independent* to have been 'under the auspices of the Republican Movement'. The orator was Thomas Mitchell.[15] A Dubliner, a bricklayer by trade, a veteran of a successful I.R.A. raid on a military barracks at Omagh in 1954 which landed him in prison, Mitchell (b. 1931) was by 1963 already famous for four attempts to win the Mid Ulster seat in the British parliament which he had no intention of taking up if elected; he was

8 *Ir. Times*, 19 June 1961, 25 July 1970; *Kerryman*, 25 July 1970.   9 *United Irishman*, July 1962. There seem to be two different editions, one reporting Mac Giolla's remarks on Tone, the other his remarks on the 'Border campaign'.   10 *Southern Star* (Skibbereen), 30 June 1962. 11 Hanley & Millar, *Lost revolution*, pp 22, 27, 70.   12 Quoted in Matt Treacy, *The I.R.A., 1956–69: rethinking the republic* (Manchester, 2012), p. 13.   13 *Ir. Times*, 21 June 1963.   14 *Ir. Press*, 17 June 1963; *Ir. Indep.*, 18 June 1963.   15 *Ir. Indep.*, 24 June 1963.

to make two more attempts.[16] He claimed almost forty years later that his oration in 1963 was socialistic.[17]

Despite all the commemoration of Tone at the bicentenary of his birth, the pilgrimage organised by the National Commemoration Committee a year later was reported only briefly in the three Dublin morning papers. As many as 2,000 attended; there were seven bands, and an oration was given by Martin Shannon (a connexion of Ó Brádaigh, who appears above and below).[18] Not stated publicly was that Shannon was a member of the I.R.A. and had played an important organising role in the Border campaign; he was now editor of the *United Irishman*, since 1948 the mouthpiece of Sinn Féin and the I.R.A.[19]

The National Commemoration Committee's pilgrimage on 20 June 1965 was reported only in the *United Irishman*. The oration was given by one 'Antoin Ó Midheach' — no doubt Tony Meade, editor of the paper in 1966 and 1967 and previously an I.R.A. operative in the Border campaign. Meade spoke of a need for Republicans to engage in popular struggles, a hint of what was to come.[20] There was no allusion to the turnout, which must have been small if only because of a transport strike that weekend. This did not prevent ceremonies at Tone's grave on 20 June organised by the Irish defence forces and Fianna Fáil, nor did it prevent afterwards, the *Irish Times* reported, 'visits' being made to the cemetery by mysterious 'uniformed young men'. Other Republicans, feeling confined to Dublin by the strike, joined a ceremony organised by Sinn Féin — a march led by a band, a wreath laid in the street where Tone had lived as a boy and speeches by Mac Giolla and others.[21]

'A MORE RADICAL, LEFT-WING REPUBLICANISM'

In the mid-1960s there developed an increasingly socialist tendency in Sinn Féin under the leadership of Tomás Mac Giolla and in the I.R.A. under the leadership of Cathal Goulding. In this they were closely supported by Seamus Costello and Seán Garland. At Bodenstown in June 1966 and in June of the three following years the orations were delivered by these men, representatives of the left-wing of Sinn Féin and the I.R.A.: Costello (1966), Goulding (1967), Garland (1968) and Mac Giolla (1969). Early signs of this socialist tendency could be detected in 1964 and 1965 when the *United Irishman* gave much publicity to striking workers and the I.R.A. engaged forcibly on their behalf.[22] These developments have received much scrutiny from historians.[23] Kathleen Travers has written of 'a change of image for

16 Hanley & Millar, *Lost revolution*, pp 13, 74.   17 Treacy, *I.R.A.*, pp 40, 44.   18 *Ir. Indep.*, 22 June 1964; *Ir. Press*, 22 June 1964.   19 Sean Swan, *Official Irish republicanism, 1962 to 1972* ([London]: Lulu.com, 2008), pp 81, 106.   20 *United Irishman*, July 1965; Treacy, *I.R.A.*, pp 51–2. For Meade, see Bowyer Bell, *Secret army* (1979), p. x, 320–21, 346; Hanley & Millar, *Lost revolution*, pp 88, 96; Swan, *Official Irish republicanism*, pp 134, 156.   21 *Sunday Independent*, 20 June 1965; *Ir. Indep.*, 21 June 1965; *Ir. Times*, 21 June 1965.   22 Hanley, 'The I.R.A. and trade unionism', pp 168–9.   23 Swan, *Official Irish republicanism* (as above, n. 19); Hanley & Millar,

Wolfe Tone ... It was now a more radical, left-wing republicanism, as opposed to the physical force republicanism' attributed to Tone in previous decades.[24]

Seamus Costello in 1966 referred to 'the workers', claimed that 'the profits which accrued from their labours were invested abroad', recommended 'a virile co-operative movement among the farming community' and urged trade-unionists 'to organise a militant trade-union movement with a national consciousness ... There should be a limit to the amount of land owned by any single individual.' The policy of Sinn Féin, he said, 'was to nationalise the key industries with the eventual aim of co-operative ownership by the workers ... nationalisation of the banks, insurance, loan and investment companies'. But he did not abandon physical-force republicanism, he warned his listeners that 'to think that they could establish a republic solely by constitutional means was folly. They must organise, train and maintain a disciplined armed force'.[25] Of Costello himself more will be stated below. This move to the political left, detectable in successive Bodenstown speeches after 1965, was evident in 1966 from the presence of vendors of socialist literature and of a delegation, for the first time, from Belfast Trades Council.[26] Another sign of the times in 1966 was the appearance of two Communist-influenced bodies, Scéim na gCheardchumainn (a group of trade-unionists speaking Irish) and the Connolly Youth Movement (members of which held a camp at Bodenstown over the weekend).[27] The leftward shift is evident too in a handbill issued in 1967 to members of the I.R.A. This stated that the leadership wanted members and republicans generally to become more socially active by infiltrating trade unions and small farmers' bodies, and by exploiting housing and civil-rights issues. In the words of one historian surveying the period, the leadership, in Dublin at least, were 'almost ignoring the issue of partition in their political programme'.[28]

In 1967 the orator was Goulding. The Republicans' pilgrimage of that year was the largest since the 1930s, between fourteen and fifteen thousand at the estimate of Costello, the chief marshal; Goulding in his speech objected to a new Irish free-trade agreement with Great Britain as no less 'disastrous' than in Tone's day.[29] It was Goulding, who in 1966, before Costello's speech, had laid a wreath 'on behalf of the I.R.A.', this four days after his release from prison.[30] A painter and decorator by trade from a working-class part of Dublin, Goulding (1922–98) was described many years later by a younger admirer as having been 'very much a man of times — the sixties was that burgeoning period, it seemed as if the left was going to sweep the world in front of it'.[31] The year of his speech was a year when members of the

Lost revolution (2009); Treacy, *I.R.A.* (2011). Swan gives a succinct and clear survey of other books. 24 Travers, 'Tone of national commemorations', pp 17–18.   25 *Ir. Indep.*, 20 June 1966.   26 *Ir. Times*, 20 June 1966.   27 Matt Treacy, *The Communist Party of Ireland, 1921–2011*, vol. i (Dublin, 2012), p. 325.   28 Diarmaid Ferriter, *The transformation of Ireland: 1900–2000* (London, 2004), pp 566–7.   29 *Ir. Times*, 19 June 1967. A newspaper report put the attendance at 'close on 10,000', still larger than any reported since the 1930s (*Ir. Indep.*, 19 June 1967).   30 *Ir. Times*, 16, 20 June 1966.   31 Dessie O'Hagan, 5 Mar. 2002, quoted in English, *Armed struggle*, pp 84, 400; L.W. White, 'Goulding, Cathal' in *D.I.B.*   32 Treacy, *I.R.A.*, pp 124–5.

Irish Workers' Party and the Communist Party of Northern Ireland were present; it was well received by the Communists' paper, *Unity*.[32]

In 1968, the year of youth revolt in Paris, it was the turn of Garland. He began by testifying that 'Theobald Wolfe Tone was a Republican, a democrat and above all a revolutionary ... The first manifesto of modern Irish democracy as Pearse called it was issued by Tone, Neilson and the United Irishmen in 1791.'[33] The faithful among his large audience — he thought it close to ten thousand — were then reminded that their purpose was to 'build a strong, militant political organisation in every part of Ireland'. His new message was that

> the fight for freedom is a class struggle. It cannot be divorced from the fight for better housing or working conditions any more than it can be divorced from the fight for the land. Our objective is, and must be, a socialist republic in which the producers of wealth can exercise complete control over the means of production, distribution and exchange. This is our definition of Irish Republicanism in 1968.

In seeking the continuance of economic, political and military action to achieve the aims of the 'republican movement', he said that he wished to make the movement's 'army' the army of 'the people' and 'the vanguard of all revolutionary movements in the country'.[34] He then acknowledged what his listeners either knew or guessed but which was not stated publicly: 'the traditional policy' of that army — the I.R.A. — was to 'use the civil wings of the movement simply as support groups for publicity, finance, recruits and suppliers of transport and friendly houses'.[35] Garland, born into a poor Dublin working-class family in 1934, had the additional pedigree (to his listeners' minds) of having been the comrade-in-arms of Seán South and Fergal O'Hanlon on the I.R.A.'s Border campaign in which he was wounded and the other two were killed; his political opinions (his Irish nationalism apart) were unambiguously socialist.[36] By his speech at Tone's grave, which he finished predictably with repeating Tone's appeal to 'that most numerous and respectable of classes, the men of no property', he qualified himself further as an Irish *soixante-huitard*.

In 1969 came the turn of Mac Giolla, who used words and expressions that show this shift of emphasis by Sinn Féin ideologues. A particular concern was Irish entry into the European Economic Community. He feared Ireland becoming 'a province of Britain' and so 'subjected to even greater foreign incursions in our economy'. He gave a minatory reminder that 'the Republican movement had already pointed out to potential purchasers of our national assets that they risk incurring the wrath of the Irish people' and proudly proclaimed, 'a Republican is both a socialist and a

---

33 *United Irishman*, July 1968. Samuel Neilson was a Belfast United Irishman. Garland seems to have in mind 'Declaration and resolutions of the Society of United Irishmen of Belfast'; see Tone, *Writings*, i, 133, 140–41. **34** *Ir. Times*, 24 June 1968. **35** *United Irishman*, July 1968. **36** Hanley & Millar, *Lost revolution*, esp. pp xi–xii, 9, 14–18, 66.

separatist'. Mac Giolla also referred to 'the people of Vietnam' and 'all other peoples fighting for their freedom'. Just as significant was the presence among the 4,000 pilgrims of obviously left-wing bodies: Young Socialists of Belfast and the Connolly Youth Movement. Just the same, the usual contingents, Sinn Féin, Cumann na mBan, the I.R.A. and Fianna Éireann were in the parade headed by 'an advance guard dressed in green battle dress' and wearing 'black berets'.[37]

Tomás ('Tom') Mac Giolla (1924–2010), untypically of Republicans, was of the middle class; an accountant, and a nephew of a member of Parnell's parliamentary party and promoter of industrial development, Thomas Gill, after whom he was named. Mac Giolla was from 1964 both president of Sinn Féin and chairman of the I.R.A. army council.[38] In contrast to the speech he made at Bodenstown in 1969, his oration there in 1962 contained no hint of socialism, it was firmly traditionalist, anti-Treatyite. 'No man' he said then,

> can claim to be a Republican and a Separatist while he accepts and works with the very institutions of government which were designed by Britain to keep Ireland divided and sundered and under her domination. Let us then reaffirm our determination never to accept the Treaty of Surrender or the assemblies arising from it, but to work constantly and determinedly to re-establish the sovereign Irish Republic with one parliament elected by the universal suffrage of all the Irish people.[39]

But by the end of the decade Mac Giolla's fixation on the Anglo-Irish treaty had given way to other concerns and socialism had become a theme at Bodenstown. What in retrospect is astonishing is that, while Mac Giolla made a 'review' of the failure of the Border campaign of 1956–62, he made no reference to the violent confrontations between demonstrators and counter-demonstrators that had occurred in different parts of Northern Ireland and the political crises there since the previous year's pilgrimage. What could have been the thoughts of the chairman, Liam McMillen, a well-known Belfast I.R.A. man?

The Republican pilgrimage of 1969 was recorded for posterity by an amateur film-maker, Séamus Murphy; his film, eight minutes long, in colour but silent and now grainy, depicts, parading through Sallins and then in Bodenstown churchyard, various contingents, some in uniform, with their banners aloft, several colourful marching bands, and numerous activists and adherents, some of them identifiable to *cognoscenti* as Republican leaders of whom more was to be heard in following decades.[40] Little did those to be seen on the film know that the Republican pilgrimage of that year was to prove the last before an explosion that damaged the Tone plot and the last before a bitter split in the Republicans' movement.

37 *Ir. Press*, 23 June 1969.   38 Hanley & Millar, *Lost revolution*, pp 22, 25, 70–71; Brian Hanley, 'Tomás Mac Giolla' in Emmet O'Connor and John Cunningham (eds), *Studies in Irish radical leadership: lives on the left* (Manchester, 2016), pp 214–24.   39 *United Irishman*, July 1962, quoted in Swan, *Official Irish Republicanism*, p. 80.   40 I am grateful to Brian Hanley for sight of and

RECREATION AT BODENSTOWN IN THE LATE 1960S

The important recreational aspect of Republican pilgrimages at about this time is well described by Tim Pat Coogan, who first joined a crowd there in 1967:

> The Bodenstown marchers form up in assembly fields beside the shabby old limestone village of Sallins and then march out to the graveyard itself. All around the area there are encampments of various groups. Stalls do a roaring trade selling teas and ices and people go through the crowds selling booklets with the biographies of various patriots or distributing Republican literature. But the processional route is dotted at intervals by Special Branch cars with walkie-talkies and reputedly more lethal weapons. Special Branch photographers in plain clothes with miniature cameras normally mingle with the crowd taking pictures of those present.
>
> Most of the marchers I have seen at Bodenstown were young men, generally from country districts, but there were also fathers and mothers wheeling prams, and elderly people. Behind the Republicans marched sympathetic groups. A contingent of Communists marched openly on at least one occasion. Here and there an American was to be seen, taking part in a pilgrimage. I once met one very fat old lady, barely able to walk, who had been coming for nearly fifty years. Although there were political tones to her gesture she was making it in much the same spirit as any other woman of her generation would pay a visit to a noted shrine.
>
> Even on my first visit men with wives and families chatted quite freely with me and, although the fact of my writing a book about the I.R.A. had aroused controversy within the movement (and throughout the day I was shadowed by two young men detailed to watch me by a senior member of the movement who objected to my writing), no one offered me anything other than friendly conversation and the hope that, whatever my views, I would put their case fairly.[41]

The scene became rather less relaxed in later years. Coogan's book, entitled *The I.R.A.*, was first published in 1970.

AN EXPLOSION AND SO A NEW MONUMENT

As the 1960s closed, on 31 October 1969, at about 5 o'clock in the morning, the Tone memorials, situated within railings on the outside of the south wall of the ruined church, were damaged by an explosion. An anti-I.R.A. terrorist group, the

information on this film in DVD. Séamus Murphy, who was from Kildare and an I.R.A. activist in the 1950s, died in Nov. 2015 (*Ir. Times*, 28 Nov. 2015).   41 Coogan, *I.R.A.* (revd ed., London, 2000), pp 240–41. I am grateful to Tim Pat Coogan for permission to reproduce this passage.

Ulster Volunteer Force, claimed the next day to have been the perpetrators.[42] The U.V.F., based in Northern Ireland and active mainly in Belfast and parts of County Armagh, had already made bomb attacks in the Republic of Ireland; fifteen months later, on 8 February 1971, it did damage to the Wolfe Tone statue in St Stephen's Green, Dublin.[43] The reports in the *Irish Times* the day after the explosion at Bodenstown, a Saturday, and the following Monday, were detailed, remarkably well informed on the history of the site and accompanied by photographs of the scene. The headstone marking the burial place of William Tone and his family was stated to have been 'destroyed'; it was certainly badly damaged; it was years later still to be seen, with other remnants, on the inside of the south wall. One remnant was described as a 'piece of sculpted limestone' with a 'chiselled inscription' beginning 'Theobald Wolfe Tone — Born 20th June, 1763 — Died 19th Nov., 1798 — For Ireland'. This could only have been part of the gravestone erected by the Wolfe Tone Band in 1873, though no other evidence for its survival has been found. The wrought-iron railings surrounding the graves erected by the National Graves Association in 1951 (to replace the railings erected by 'the men of Kildare' in 1874) were reported to be undamaged 'except for a few dents'.[44] In photographs of the scene after the explosion published in all three Dublin morning dailies the gravestone erected by the Kildare Gaelic Association in 1895 can be seen torn from its base, the seated wolfhound at the foot obscured or missing, but the stone otherwise intact: the inscription honouring Theobald Wolfe Tone is clearly visible (albeit not legible) and the two Round Towers are still in place.[45] The local Naas paper, the *Leinster Leader*, stated that, while the 'family stone' was 'shattered', the explosion having apparently gone off underneath it, 'the six-foot memorial to Wolfe Tone was uprooted' — no more than this.[46]

Only hours after the explosion the National Graves Association intervened. On the evening of the same day its secretary, Seán Fitzpatrick the younger, promised, 'our association will repair the damage done to these memorials and will have it once more as a fitting tribute to the memory of the father of the Irish Republic'.[47] On the following Monday morning the *Irish Press* mentioned, in a report concerning culpability for the explosion, that 'only slight damage was caused to the memorial'. Fitzpatrick's use of the word 'repair' must have seemed apt. But on the Tuesday after the explosion, all three Dublin morning papers published a formal appeal from the National Graves Association for donations apparently to *replace* the damaged structure; the names of seventeen men and women of a certain age respected in Republican circles were given in support.[48] One of them, Thomas Mullins, who had in 1931 raised Bodenstown in the Dáil, was a former general secretary of Fianna Fáil and a participant in that party's pilgrimages since 1929; he had been in his youth a

42 In a 'communiqué' headed 'Ulster Volunteer Force, November 1st, 1969. Hdqtrs N.I.', signed 'Capt. Wm Johnston … 1st Belfast Batt. U.V.F.', reproduced in *Ir. Times*, 3 Nov. 1969.   43 Jim Cusack and Henry McDonald, *U.V.F.: the endgame* (Dublin, 2008), pp 73–8.   44 *Ir. Press*, 1, 4 Nov. 1969.   45 *Ir. Press*, *Ir. Indep.*, *Ir. Times*, 1 Nov. 1969.   46 *Leinster Leader*, 8 Nov. 1969. 47 *Ir. Press*, 1 Nov. 1969; see also *Leinster Leader*, 8 Nov. 1969.   48 *Ir. Press*, *Ir. Indep.* and *Ir.*

member of Fianna Éireann, active in the I.R.A. during the civil war and a close friend and collaborator of De Valera.[49] Another was Michael Mullen, general secretary of the Irish Transport and General Workers' Union, who had been interned during the Emergency for I.R.A. activity and was from 1961 until 1969 a Labour member of Dáil Éireann. His Republican sympathies remained latent.[50] Five other signatories to the appeal, George Gilmore, Peadar O'Donnell, Tom Barry, Maurice Twomey and James Killean, had addressed pilgrims many years before. The association's purpose was not altogether clear, the relevant wording was clumsy and ambiguous — 'to restore [*sic*] an even more worthy memorial than that so wantonly destroyed'. Fitzpatrick's statement at a special commemoration ceremony at Bodenstown on 23 November 1969 (said by another man present, Éamonn Mac Thomáis, to be the 171st anniversary of Tone's burial) did not clarify the matter: in referring to 'the restoration fund', he said that 'it was hoped to have a suitable memorial erected at the grave prior to the national commemoration ceremonies in June'.[51]

Five months later, on 16 April, the National Graves Association was able to announce its plans at a press conference (said to be only its second such event in 44 years of existence). These were for, as reported in the *Irish Times*, 'the renovation of the grave'. The architect for the 'restoration' was named as Hugo Duffy, of Peppard and Duffy, and the 'main theme of the restoration plans' was said to be 'the blending with nature of the grave and its surroundings'. The report was accompanied by a photograph of the architect's model. This shows the 'green grave' of Davis's poem transformed into a sort of plaza. To the south of the old church and almost completely covering the Tone family graves is an area as large as that of the church having the appearance a huge chess-board with five pillars along the east side. The damaged gravestones and the surrounding railing seem to be incorporated within the north side of the 'chess-board' adjacent to the south wall of the church and yet still in their original position over the grave.[52]

On the same occasion the association's chairman, Séamus Mac Ciarnáin, made a statement, published in the *Irish Press* eleven days later, which adds to the mystery of its purpose. A typescript survives. He referred to Tone's grave as

> a holy spot, in perfectly natural surroundings, and although the grave of this great man was modest, it was acceptable by a large majority of those who visited it. Let it be stated emphatically, most emphatically, that the National Graves Association would prefer that the grave remained unmolested forever than that it should be improved as a result of dastardly desecration. However it must be restored.

Times, 4 Nov. 1969.   **49** For Mullins (1903–78), see Marie Coleman, 'Mullins, Thomas Lincoln' in *D.I.B.*   **50** For Mullen (1919–82), see Marie Coleman, 'Mullen, Michael' in *D.I.B.*; Hanley & Millar, *Lost revolution*, p. 133.   **51** *Ir. Indep.*, 24 Nov. 1969. In fact the anniversary was the 21st (see above).   **52** *Ir. Times*, 17 Apr. 1970. A similar report, with photo, was in *Ir. Indep.*

Then he left it to Duffy 'to outline his plans and to enlarge on his designs'.[53] The grave was not to be restored, the site was to be flattened and to be built upon. No explanation was given.

On 13 February 1971, again as reported in the *Irish Times*, a contract was signed at Sallins for 'the reconstruction of Tone's grave and memorial in the Bodenstown Churchyard' and a little later that day 40 people gathered there to witness the vice-chairman of the National Graves Association 'turn the first sod of the reconstruction work'. The continuation of the report would have made it increasingly evident to any reader familiar with the grave that what was planned would be very much larger than what had existed and would be very different:

> This memorial has been left as it was found on November 1st, 1969, when an explosion shattered the gravestones and blasted the old church wall which backs on to the grave … The new grave and memorial, the association's secretary, Mr Seán Fitzpatrick explained, is to be a much more impressive construction than the old one. On the church wall overlooking the grave there will be a bronze plaque with an image of Tone and a quotation from Pearse. The grave is to be raised about three feet, surrounded with paving stones, and with steps leading up on either side. In front of the grave and stretching down to the poplar trees in the heart of the graveyard will be an assembly ground, paved with cobble stones from Patrick Street in Dublin.[54]

Now in the aftermath of the explosion the *Irish Times* reported that the Tone 'family headstone' had been 'destroyed', whilst showing in a photograph that the stone headed 'THEOBALD WOLFE TONE' erected by the Kildare Gaelic Association in 1895 and renovated by the National Graves Association in the mid 1940s had been uprooted and damaged but was largely intact.[55] Photographs in the *Independent* and the *Press* are similar. The *Irish Times* provided some financial details and the future prospect for the graveyard: the contract signed, requiring expenditure of £4,000, was 'only for the grave memorial'; another £1,500 would be required 'to complete the architect's design'. The National Graves Association intended 'to continue the entrance path which leads in from the gate on the left of the grave around in a semi-circle and build another gate on the right-hand side'. The ruined church was to be 'turned into a museum, where the old memorial stones will be stored'.[56] The figure of £4,000 'only for the grave memorial' should have seemed very high — a newly-built semi-detached three-bedroomed house at Bray, County Wicklow, could be purchased for £4,000 in 1970 — but it did not arouse any comment in the newspapers seen. When, three months later, the memorial was completed, it was reported that it had cost £5,000.[57]

---

53 Seán O'Mahony papers (N.L.I., MS 44,236/1). See also *Ir. Press*, 27 Apr. 1970. **54** *Ir. Times*, 15 Feb. 1971. **55** *Ir. Times*, 1 and 3 Nov. 1969. **56** *Ir. Times*, 15 Feb. 1971. **57** *Ir. Times*, 26 Apr. 1971.

On the site of the Tone family's grave a gigantic and jarring limestone platform was erected. In commanding positions were a flagpole and a dais from which political discourses could be delivered. The new structure was formally 'unveiled' on 25 April 1971 by Maurice Twomey, chief-of-staff of the I.R.A. forty years before, in the presence of Mrs Katherine Dickason (sole representative of Tone's descendants), some minor dignitaries and a thousand members of the general public (including the present writer as a curious observer).[58] The dedication of the new memorial was performed by the Protestant archdeacon of Kildare, the Venerable Brian Handy; present too were the local Presbyterian minister, two Catholic priests of the local Kill parish, and a Capuchin friar from Dublin. A Methodist minister and Jewish rabbi had also been invited. Such a mixed gathering of clergy at Tone's grave was hitherto unimaginable. The attendance of the president of the 'Provisional' faction of Sinn Féin, Ruairí Ó Brádaigh, was reported, as was that of a representative of the rival 'Official' faction, the aforementioned Roy Johnston. The split in Sinn Féin in January 1970 is treated of below. Nowhere in the newspaper reports examined is any other person from the 'Official' faction mentioned. Remarkably, the *United Irishman*, hitherto effusive in its reports of ceremonies at the grave and in 1971 the organ of the Official faction, reported the latest ceremony only briefly, limiting itself to 83 words and naming only Tone, Twomey and Handy.[59] Even more remarkably, *An Phoblacht*, the organ of the Provisional faction, which had interviewed Fitzpatrick about its project in its very first issue, in February 1970, carried no report at all. Two well-known members of the Irish Labour Party were present: Michael Mullen and Roddy Connolly. But there was no representative of the Fianna Fáil party, nor of the Irish government, nor of the Irish defence forces. It is likely that the leadership of Fianna Fáil, which was in government in 1971, would have feared the ceremony proving to be an I.R.A. demonstration and so would have refused to allow the party, the government or the defence forces to be represented. After the dedication of the new memorial, the French and Irish national anthems were played by the band of the Irish Transport and General Workers' Union. A minor sensation occurred when one man present, Yann Goulet, a Breton nationalist, protested on hearing the French anthem — the *Marseillaise*; he complained of 'treatment by the French of the Algerian nationalists and the Basque and Breton people'.[60] If Goulet was invited by the organisers, it was insensitive, as Tone refers in his Brittany diary to Breton particularists — 'brigands' — as enemies of the French Republic.[61] There seems, however, to have been no representative of the French government. None of the three Dublin morning papers included photographs in their reports other than one of Mrs Dickason and her husband (in the *Irish Press*). The report in the *Irish Independent* did at least describe the new monument — as having 'as the focal point of a large paved area a silhouette

58 The ceremony was reported in all three Dublin morning papers the next morning and in the *Leinster Leader* the following Saturday. An advance notice in *Ir. Indep.*, 21 Apr. 1971, mentions the Methodist minister and the rabbi.   59 *United Irishman*, May 1971.   60 *Ir. Press*, 26 Apr. 1971.   61 Tone, *Writings*, ii, 315.

of Tone in bronze, side by side with a bronze tablet bearing a quotation from Pádraig Pearse';[62] that in the *Irish Times* (usually a newspaper of record) was obsequious to the organisers, lacked perspicacity and ignored the significance of its earlier reports. The *Leinster Leader* must be credited with naming more participants than the morning papers and with the best description of the new monument: 'fifty feet by thirty feet, it surrounds the original green grave which has been elevated about three feet and enshrined in a tomb of Irish limestone. Overlooking it on the ruined church walls is a bronze plaque with a silhouhetted image of Tone and a quotation from Pádraig Pearse.'[63] None of the reports mentions the railing erected in 1951 by the National Graves Association.

Thus the promise of the secretary of the National Graves Association in the immediate aftermath of the explosion — 'our association will repair the damage done to these memorials' — was altered to 'restore' when a 'restoration fund' was set up three weeks later. Next came the plan for 'renovation of the grave' and appointment of an architect. In February 1971, sixteen months after the damage was done, the vice-chairman of the National Graves Association was seen in a newspaper photograph to 'turn the first sod of the reconstruction work'. The result was far from being repair or restoration or renovation of a damaged gravestone, it was the actual removal of all the stones from a family grave, as well as the railing protecting them, and their replacement with a raised platform obviously intended for political rallies complete with rostrum and engraved slogans. The railing erected in 1951 by the National Graves Association must have been moved from its location outside the south wall of the ruined church to a new location inside the church and abutting the south wall, which is where it encloses now (2018), as it did outside the wall before the explosion in 1969, the Kildare Gaels' stone erected in the 1890s and repaired in the mid 1940s. This stone is still intact except for the loss of the tops of the two Round Towers. The gravestone naming Tone's grandfather William Tone, part of the historical evidence for the patriot's grave, seen by six generations of pilgrims and visible in its fragmentary state beside the Gaels' stone in the 1990s, is now to be seen only in fragments. Long vanished is the 'green grave' of Davis's poem, the area of the grave is now an arena, the old church, once under threat of being turned into a museum, is now deprived of its ivy and its east wall demolished.

The new memorial showed also the proprietorial attitude of the National Graves Association, its assertion of rights over a family grave in a public graveyard, an attitude previously evident in 1951 when it removed and scrapped the railings erected by the 'men of Kildare'. The assertion of ownership made by the Tone family, read by generations of visitors — 'This burial place belongs [to] William Tone & his family' — was disregarded and the stone on which it appeared was not repaired but its fragments cast aside. There was a disregard too for the wish of Matilda Tone for her husband's grave, expressed to John Gray in 1843, that 'the spot where he lies' be marked. The 'unveiling' and 'dedication' ceremony on 25

April 1971 showed the exclusive nature of the National Graves Association despite its public appeal for funds 18 months previously, none of the regular pilgrim groups taking part except for one faction of Sinn Féin.

A question neither put nor answered in reports of the affair was, 'what part was played by the owners of the graveyard, Kildare County Council?'. Its predecessor, the Naas Board of Guardians, gave permission for the erection of the Gaels' stone in 1895, the National Graves Association had in 1944 to seek permission from the Board of Health at Naas (an adjunct of Kildare County Council?) to carry out improvements.[64]

Under 'Bodenstown' the first edition of the *Shell guide to Ireland* (1962) noted 'the remains of a small, medieval, nave-and-chancel church with simple Romanesque windows and w[est] doorway. In the churchyard is the grave of Theobald Wolfe Tone (1763–98), Protestant father of Irish Republicanism'.[65] Curiously, in the second edition, published in 1967, when the gravestone erected by the Kildare Gaelic Association in 1895 was still intact, the words 'vulgar memorial' were waspishly inserted (between parentheses) after 'grave'.[66] Perhaps the motifs — shamrocks, Round Towers, a wolfhound — were dismissed as late Victorian kitsch. This severe judgement was repeated in the third edition (1989) without any reference to the memorial that had replaced the Gaels' stone in 1971.[67] It was an oversight. One wonders what the editors' judgement of the edifice erected by the National Graves' Association would have been. In an obituary-type appreciation in the *Irish Times* of its architect, Hugo Duffy, a cultured man with literary and artistic interests, and a published authority on Gandon, no mention was made of the Tone memorial at Bodenstown.[68]

As the plot of the Tone family graves was flattened and slabbed over beyond recognition, and any archaeological evidence was destroyed, it seems unlikely now that the remains of Theobald Wolfe Tone, his grandfather William, his father Peter, his uncle Jonathan, his sister Fanny, his brother Mathew, his little son Richard or any other member of his family could ever be identified by the forensic procedures, archaeological excavation and scientific analysis of finds, by which the remains of Richard the Third were positively identified in Leicester in 2012 — unless only the modern structure could gently be removed. Turning the old church into a museum of Tone paraphernalia, as envisaged by the National Graves Association, also now seems unlikely. Such procedures are subject to stricter official control than required in the early 1970s.

64 Above, chap. 4; *Dublin Evening Mail*, 25 July 1944.   **65** Lord Killanin and M. V. Duignan, *The Shell guide to Ireland* (London, 1962), p. 327.   **66** Ibid. (1967), pp 328–9.   **67** Lord Killanin and M. V. Duignan, *The Shell guide to Ireland*, revised and updated by Peter Harbison (Dublin, 1989), p. 209.   **68** *Ir. Times*, 19 Aug. 2002.

10

The 1970s: the Split and the Ulster dimension

TWO MONTHS AFTER the U.V.F. bomb exploded at Bodenstown, the I.R.A. split in two; Sinn Féin split soon afterwards. Just as the attack on the Tone gravestones was a consequence of the intensification of inter-communal conflict in Northern Ireland in the summer of 1969, so also was the dissension in the I.R.A. and Sinn Féin. The main difference in the I.R.A. was over the strategy of pursuing economic and social matters, even to the extent of carrying out violent attacks on business premises south of the Irish border whilst seemingly paying less attention to the grievances of Catholics north of the border, and most particularly to the desire of Belfast I.R.A. men for firearms for defence from, or use against, 'the other' — police, military, Protestants and uncompliant Catholics. Some of the I.R.A. on both sides of the border were willing to accept arms through the intervention of members of the Fianna Fáil government, a *quid pro quo* of which would be the cessation of the attacks on business premises. The dissension in Sinn Féin was not a simple matter of a north–south divide, it was a matter also of how much Republicans should concern themselves with social and economic issues, how much they should resort to armed force; it was also a matter of whether they should give up their traditional policy of 'abstention' and in future to engage in electoral politics like other political parties. Like earlier disagreements among Republicans they were not everywhere clear cut. In the late 1960s there were already signs of serious disagreement affecting Bodenstown. For example, in 1968 the National Commemoration Committee invited the Irish Workers' Party (whose orientation was to Moscow) to join the parade, displaying their own banner, and in so doing antagonised traditionalists and especially members of Cumann na mBan; consequently the majority of the women refused to join the march; the presence of the contingent with its banner also brought hostile resolutions at Sinn Féin's annual convention the following December.[1] The differences became more serious and grew in the last months of 1969 with opposition by I.R.A. men in Belfast to the I.R.A. leadership in Dublin.[2]

The disagreement eventually resulted in splits and in the emergence of two separate paramilitary bodies and two rival Sinn Féin parties. The rupture in the I.R.A. occurred immediately after a special convention held late in December 1969. Ó Brádaigh and Mac Stiofáin broke away and formed a new army council and

---

1 *Ir. Times*, 24 June 1968; Hanley & Millar, *Lost revolution*, p. 68; Treacy, *I.R.A.*, pp 137–9; idem, *The Communist Party of Ireland, 1921–2011*, vol. i, *1921–1960* (Dublin, 2012), pp 347–8.
2 Hanley & Millar, *Lost revolution*, chap. 4.

established a new I.R.A. organisation. Similarly, Sinn Féin split in two at its annual *ard-fheis* (national conference), held on 11 and 12 January 1970. The larger of the two factions retained the party's Dublin headquarters in Gardiner Place and the party's newspaper, the *United Irishman*; Mac Giolla remained as president. For this reason the party became known for some time as 'Official' Sinn Féin, though obviously not official in the sense of being a statutory body. The break-away faction at first was referred to as 'Provisional' Sinn Féin (implying a temporary arrangement, or perhaps echoing the proclamation by the 'Provisional Government of the Irish Republic' in 1916) and opened offices in Kevin Street on the south side of Dublin. These may have been just 'names that were more the invention of the media than the choice of their leaders'.[3] Somewhat absurd as these designations may be, they became used generally and are used here for brevity and clarity. Confusingly both factions called themselves 'Sinn Féin'; sometimes they were distinguished by reference to the addresses of their headquarters. By the time of the pilgrimages in June 1977, 'Official' Sinn Féin had been renamed south of the border as Sinn Féin the Workers' Party and north of the border as the Republican Clubs the Workers' Party, the new name incorporating a slogan that first appeared on banners and posters. By June 1982 it was known simply as the Workers' Party. Consequently its rival was referred to thereafter simply as Sinn Féin. Similarly the two factions of the I.R.A. came to be distinguished as 'Official' and 'Provisional'.[4] There was another split in the winter of 1974–5. A dissident group at the Official Sinn Féin *ard-fhéis* on 8 December 1974 broke away, led by Costello, to form the Irish Republican Socialist Party; at the same place Costello set up new paramilitary body eventually known as the 'Irish National Liberation Army'.[5] These Republican splits have been much studied.[6]

OFFICIALS' AND PROVISIONALS' RIVALRY IN JUNE 1970

Rivalry between political factions holding demonstrations at Bodenstown was intense throughout the 1970s and into the 1980s. The first to be at Tone's grave after the split were the break-away Sinn Féin group — the 'Provisionals'. Their parade on 14 June 1970, 3,000 strong, formed at Sallins with Ó Brádaigh at its head.[7] This faction was to grow in strength and largely to displace Mac Giolla's; its I.R.A. associate was to be much more proactive, more destructive, than Goulding's. One week later, on the 21st, after the ceremonies of the Irish defence forces and Fianna

---

3 Ed O'Moloney, *Voices from the grave: two men's war in Ireland* (London, 2010), p. 14. 4 Hanley & Millar, *Lost revolution*, pp 144–9, 327, 367–8, 376. 5 Ibid., pp 283–4. Beyond the scope of this study is a split from Sinn Féin in 1986 when a group broke away objecting to the party's decision to take seats in Dáil Éireann. The dissident group became Republican Sinn Féin. 6 For a succinct and clear survey of what has been published in book form of the splits in the I.R.A. and Sinn Féin in 1969 and 1970, and for an argument that the analyses are almost as numerous as the analysts, see Sean Swan, *Official Irish Republicanism, 1962–1972* ([London]: Lulu.com, 2008), pp 7–29. 7 *Ir. Press*, 15 June 1970.

Fáil were over, the group that the *Irish Times* vaguely called 'the Republican Movement' held theirs.[8] This was the Sinn Féin faction still considered to be the republican main stream, the 'Officials'. Mac Giolla (who was to remain president until 1988) and Cathal Goulding (the chief-of-staff of the associated I.R.A.) headed their 3,000–strong procession from Sallins. There too were two trade-union leaders from Belfast and the union committee of some cement workers engaged in a strike. The wreath was laid by a veteran of the Irish Citizen Army.[9] In the words of Roy Foster, 'the I.R.A. were splitting into new-look socialist persuaders and old-style bomb-and-bullet militants'.[10]

THE LAWFUL IRISH ARMY AT BODENSTOWN

The Irish defence forces' annual ceremony at Bodenstown continued routinely in the early 1970s, on each occasion an hour or two before ceremony of the 'Official' wing of the I.R.A. but barely noticed. It received unusual publicity in 1972 when scenes of soldiers parading and an army band playing appeared in a TV documentary on Bodenstown presented by Proinsias Mac Aonghusa.[11] But their commemoration in 1973, with its evocative sounding of the Last Post and Reveille, was their last for many years. It was not resumed until after the period under consideration. In 1974 the defence forces were present at Bodenstown only to back up the Garda Síochána in an attempt to arrest suspected members of the Provisional I.R.A. including (unsuccessfully) Dáithí Ó Conaill; in 1975 and 1976 they were again present in strength at the Provisionals' commemoration.[12] There were precedents in 1931, 1936 and 1939. A likely factor in a decision to discontinue the Irish army's ceremony after 1973 is that the Fine Gael and Labour coalition government formed in March of that year may have considered its presence in troubled times to be unwise on the same day as the I.R.A. In fact the government decided that only St Patrick's day (17 March) would in future be celebrated officially as a day of national commemoration.[13] But at the ceremony of the Fianna Fáil party in 1974 the Last Post and Reveille were heard again, as it was in successive years.

FIANNA FÁIL'S REVIVAL AT BODENSTOWN

Fianna Fáil's annual pilgrimages continued throughout the 1970s. Of these the most significant was on 21 June 1970 when the party was bitterly divided. Jack Lynch's leadership of the party and so of the government was under threat from colleagues intent on taking them in a direction similar to that of the more militantly nationalist

8 *Ir. Times*, 20 June 1970. 9 *Ir. Press*, 22 June 1970; *Ir. Times*, 22 June 1970. 10 In his review, 'Partnership in loss' in *London Review of Books*, xxixx, no. 24 (13 Dec. 2007), of Paul Bew, *Ireland: the politics of enmity, 1789–2007* (Oxford, 2007). 11 'In Bodenstown churchyard there is a green grave' (R.T.É. Archives). It features also Neville Keery's oration at the Fianna Fáil pilgrimage on

'Provisional' faction of Sinn Féin, spurred to armed action on the side of Catholics in Northern Ireland. Both sides regarded Bodenstown as an opportunity to express their differences. Some 400 persons were present, about 250 of them 'insiders'. After Lynch's arrival, political enemies appeared, among them Kevin Boland, Neil Blaney and Paudge Brennan, all members of his government until dismissal or resignation seven weeks before. Blaney, dismissed by Lynch on 6 May and arrested on 26 May, was on trial on a charge of conspiracy to import arms. Boland, on positioning himself beside Lynch, received prolonged applause and handshakes; after Lynch placed a wreath on the grave there were taunts of 'Judas Lynch'. Perhaps to ease tensions, the organisers had prudently invited a local little girls' accordion band to play martial airs such as 'Roddy McCorley'. The choice of orator was also inspired. This was Senator Neville Keery, a thirty-year-old Quaker, who had been appointed by Lynch to the senate in 1969 and whose career was to be in the European Economic Community. After referring to Tone and 'the spirit of the French Revolution, liberty, equality and fraternity', Keery linked Tone and Pearse as founders of the Irish 'national movement'; he looked forward to membership of the E.E.C. as a reconnection to France as well as to Britain; he cited Tone's *Argument on behalf of the Catholics* (1791) as 'the classic statement of brotherly love'; and before concluding, as was the custom, with the United Irishmen's enjoinder to forget 'all past dissensions' and 'substitute the common name of Irishmen' for 'Protestant, Catholic and Dissenter', he warned against seeing 'simple solutions to the complexity of our time', and held that 'in both parts of our island there are men and women who demand more liberty and greater equality' — controversial statements for a Fianna Fáil audience.[14] Before dispersal, the Last Post and Reveille were sounded. Keery's oration was more conciliatory than Brugha's two years before. As time would tell, Lynch succeeded in keeping his party together; the split that was significant in the long term was the split that had occurred in Sinn Féin and the I.R.A. six months before Lynch's fraught appearance at Bodenstown.

In 1971 it was the turn of Ruairí Brugha's son Cathal, grandson of the Cathal Brugha killed in the civil war, to deliver the oration.[15] By then Lynch, again present, had overcome the adversaries in his party. In 1972, when only a hundred were present, among them Lynch to lay a wreath, Keery was again the orator. 'The strength of aspiration of the party', he said,

> should not be judged by the numbers present ... Respect for democracy was central to Republicanism. Respect for Tone, his achievements and virtues is one thing. Recognition of the reality of changing times another. No one familiar with the detailed narrative of 1798 would have history repeat itself ...

the same day, 19 June 1972.   **12** *Ir. Indep.*, 17 June 1974; *Ir. Press*, 16 June 1975, 14 June 1976. **13** *Ir. Times*, 14 June 1974; *Dáil Éireann debates*, cclxxiii, col. 1737 (27 June 1974).   **14** All three Dublin morning papers reported Fianna Fáil's pilgrimage at length on 22 June 1970. The fullest account of Keery's oration is in *Ir. Times*.   **15** *Ir. Press*, 21 June 1971; *Ir. Indep.*, 21 June 1971, incl. photo.

Tone had sought help from France because he was impatient with the progress of reform. His inspiration had been the vision of brotherhood.[16]

Evidently, the Fianna Fáil leadership, in summoning back Keery, a 'civic' republican, wanted to tell the robustly republican element in its rank-and-file to accept Lynch's policy of moderation. By June 1973 the party formed the opposition in the Dáil after many years in office; its pilgrimage was a small, wreath-laying affair. In contrast, its pilgrimage, on 23 June 1974, was on a larger scale than in previous years. Buglers sounded the Last Post and Reveille, and a local girls' choir rendered the national anthem. The party's national vice-president, Joseph Groome, made a speech asserting that Fianna Fáil were the only real republican party in Ireland and paying tribute to Tone as the father of republicanism.[17] Groome, an old I.R.A. man and a founder of Fianna Fáil, first reported at Bodenstown in 1948 and supportively at Lynch's side there in 1970, was well known for his Dublin hotel, much frequented late at night in the 1960s and 1970s by Fianna Fáil ministers and deputies; he died in June 1977.[18] The occasion was reminiscent of the late 1950s when Fianna Fáil, challenged in office by an I.R.A. engaged in a guerilla campaign in Northern Ireland, asserted its republicanism by appearing at Bodenstown ostentatiously and in strength. It was out of character. Jack Lynch summarised its attitude to Tone at Bodenstown in 1975 in saying 'that the party always paid a silent and dignified tribute to Wolfe Tone, one of the fathers of republicanism'.[19] During the seven preceding years an oration had been given at six Fianna Fáil pilgrimages; it was not however the party's custom: between 1936 and 1967 there had been none. The attendance in 1975 was put at about 400.[20] At the ceremony on 18 June 1978 of the Fianna Fáil party (by then back in government), the Last Post and Reveille were sounded by two members of the Curragh Command Band of the Irish defence forces 'who attended unofficially'.[21]

Charles Haughey, who succeeded Lynch in December 1979, made his first appearance at Bodenstown as party leader on 22 June 1980 and simply laid a wreath.[22] But on the morning of 21 June 1981, the future of his government in doubt because of losses in Dáil Éireann elections ten days before, a dozen or so Fianna Fáil supporters waited in vain at Bodenstown for the expected arrival of Haughey and other Dáil deputies for the party's commemoration; the party's general secretary had to inform the party's newspaper, the *Irish Press*, that 'nothing had been planned for Bodenstown yet'.[23] A commemoration was held instead three months later, on 27 September, by which time Haughey was leader of the opposition. He led a procession of two hundred into the cemetery, laid a wreath at Tone's grave, but again made no speech. It was explained that the party's leadership 'had apparently

16 *Ir. Times*, 19 June 1972.   **17** *Ir. Press*, 24 June 1974.   **18** *Ir. Press*, 28 June 1948; *Ir. Times*, 30 June 1977; Tim Pat Coogan, *Ireland in the twentieth century* (London, 2003), p. 774; Gerry McElroy, 'Goome, Joe (*c.*1908–77)' in *D.I.B.*   **19** *Ir. Press*, 23 June 1975.   **20** *Ir. Times*, 23 June 1975; *Ir. Indep.*, 23 June 1975.   **21** *Ir. Times*, 18 June 1973, 19 June 1978.   **22** *Ir. Press*, 23 June 1980.   **23** *Ir. Press*, 13, 15, 22 June 1981.

forgotten about their annual commemoration ceremony at Bodenstown in June in the aftermath of the general election defeat'.[24] From then on until 1991, Haughey regularly made a speech at Fianna Fáil's pilgrimages. These were held not in June but in the autumn. For Haughey they were opportunities for photographs and for policy statements. On 26 September 1982 (in office again) he criticised the British government for its policies in Northern Ireland.[25] He did so on several subsequent occasions at Bodenstown. On 16 October 1983, when as many as 700 responded to the party leadership's call for a good turn-out, Haughey (out of office once more) devoted his speech to the Ulster question.[26] Spectacularly, on 30 September 1984, hundreds of Fianna Fáil supporters, led by a colour party in black berets and headed by Haughey himself, marched a hundred yards to the gate of the churchyard and to the auditorium at the grave, a pipe band playing 'Let Erin remember' and a large banner proclaiming 'Fianna Fáil the Republican Party'; on a roll of drums, Haughey laid a wreath and delivered an oration castigating the British government and calling in effect for the annexation of Northern Ireland (by agreement with that government) to form 'an Irish unitary state'.[27] His speeches at Bodenstown in 1985 and 1986 were in the same vein.[28]

Thus there were similarities and dissimilarities between Fianna Fáil's political purposes at Tone's grave under Lynch's leadership in the early 1970s and under Haughey's a decade later in a political situation that was essentially unchanged. Both men, and the party they led, would have perceived a need to challenge the two Sinn Féin parties at Bodenstown and have been aware of the model followed by early cohorts of Republicans. A purposeful walk to the churchyard, flags and banners, stirring music, wreaths, sounding the Last Post, followed by passionate orations defining and affirming republican principles —this was the model. The Fianna Fáil pilgrimage was a miniature version of Sinn Féin and I.R.A. pilgrimages since 1924. But Lynch's attitude was eirenic, Haughey's was hostile. For Haughey the auditorium erected by the National Graves Association was a place for 'grand-standing'. Kathleen Travers explains Haughey's attitudes by referring to his indebtedness to the more nationalistic wing of his party for his election as leader, to his fear of losing support to Sinn Féin, and to his belief in 'the national issue as the key to his future fame'.[29] Yet for Éamon de Valera, the founder of the party and no mean nationalist himself, the Tone family grave had been, whenever he laid wreaths on behalf of the party in the 1940s and 1958s, a place of silent reflection, not of speechifying.

24 *Ir. Times*, 28 Sept. 1981.   **25** *Ir. Times*, 27 Sept. 1982; *Ir. Press*, 27 Sept. 1982.   **26** *Ir. Press*, 17 Oct. 1983.   **27** *Ir. Times*, 1 Oct. 1984. The speech is reported more fully in *Ir. Press* and *Ir. Indep.*, 1 Oct. 1984, but without details of the ceremony.   **28** *Ir. Times*, 14 Oct. 1985, 13 Oct. 1986. Haughey's first speech at Bodenstown after regaining office again in March 1987 was conciliatory (*Ir. Times*, 12 Oct. 1987).   **29** Kathleen Travers, 'Tone of national commemorations', pp 35–98.

THE OFFICIALS METAMORPHOSE AT BODENSTOWN

The Officials, who were at first generally but soon decreasingly perceived to be the main-stream Republicans, continued to hold pilgrimages during the same period. On 21 June 1970 (six months after the split) they attracted over 3,000 to Bodenstown, a number which, according to the *Irish Times*, equalled 'the number that attended the Provisional ceremony the previous Sunday'. Mac Giolla, president of Official Sinn Féin, and Goulding, chief-of-staff of the Official I.R.A., headed the parade; Jim Sullivan, a senior Belfast I.R.A.-man and chairman of the Belfast Central Citizens' Defence Committee (a broadly based Catholic 'rights' association), was the chief steward; another Belfastman, Malachy McBurney, delivered a one-hour oration in which, again according to the *Irish Times*, he alleged 'agents of Fianna Fáil' had been supplying Provisionals in Northern Ireland with money 'under the catch-cry of "national unity"'. Two senior Belfast trades-union officials, Betty Sinclair and John Freeman (both apparently from Protestant districts),[30] were present too, as were leaders of workers at a County Dublin cement factory engaged in a strike.[31] The presence of representatives of men described as 'workers' (not as 'republicans') was a sign of the times. Missing again were women of Cumann na mBan. On 25 January their executive had issued a statement of allegiance to the Provisionals and rejection of 'an extreme form of socialism'.[32]

In June 1971 there were, the *Irish Times* estimated, between four and five thousand at the Officials' demonstration; the orator was a Northerner, Malachy McGurran; another Northerner, Frank McGlade, laid the wreath. The parade from Sallins, reported the *Irish Press* (which put the turn-out at 7,000), was 'led by the northern contingents, 50 Republican clubs with their banners, 400 members of Na Fianna Éireann, the Connolly Youth Movement and the Communist Party of Ireland'.[33] This was the first time since 1935 that the Communist Party had under this name (readopted in March 1970) formally paraded at Bodenstown. When there in the 1950s it was disguised as the Irish Workers' League. In 1968, when it was known as the Irish Workers' Party, its participation in the Republicans' parade, displaying its own banner, had antagonised members of Cumann na mBan to the extent that the majority of the women refused to join the march. The party was not to hold, for the first time, a separate pilgrimage until 1984, on 10 June, a few years before the collapse of communist parties all over Europe. Its intention was to mark the half-centenary of the pilgrimage of 1934 in which working-class Protestants

---

30 Miss Sinclair (1910–81), a member of the Communist Party since its formation in 1933, in which year it joined the Republican pilgrimage, was secretary of the Belfast Trades Council 1946–75 (Maurice Cronin, 'Sinclair, Elizabeth' in *D.I.B.*); Freeman (1934–2011) became in 1974 regional Irish secretary of the Amalgamated Transport and General Workers' Union (*Union Post*, Apr. 2011, p. 13).   31 *Ir. Times*, 22 June 1970; *Ir. Press*, 22 June 1970.   32 Treacy, *I.R.A.*, p. 182. 33 *Ir. Times*, 21 June 1971; *Ir. Press*, 21 June 1971.   34 *Ir. Times*, 11 June 1984. It was followed an hour or two later by the annual pilgrimage of the Officials, with whom it had a fraternal association.

from Belfast participated. The organisers 'claimed an attendance of between 400 and 500 people from all over the country'.[34]

Official Sinn Féin's pilgrimage in 1972 was reported in the *Irish Times* under the heading 'Socialist strategy of Officials'. In appearances the pilgrimage kept to tradition: 'thousands' marched from Sallins, bands played and there was 'a colour party of six men in paramilitary uniform'. The orator, Seán Garland, made what the reporter, Eileen O'Brien, described as 'one of the most revolution-conscious speeches delivered at Bodenstown for many years'. Garland was now national organiser of the party and adjutant-general of the Official I.R.A., which in May 1972 declared a 'cease-fire'. By the end of the decade he was claiming not to know of even the existence of this organisation.[35] He had given the oration in 1968; he called in 1972 for 'the establishment of an alliance of the Left, which would embrace those who were now struggling within the Labour Party … those genuine representatives of the working class … the only possible alliance of the Left'. His vision was a 'struggle' that 'would be all-embracing and would be carried on in the schools, the churches, the factories, the fields, the shops and the streets'. Censuring the Provisionals without naming them, he condemned 'terrorism' and stated that 'the Republican Movement' — meaning the Officials — 'did not wish to bomb a million Protestants into a united Ireland'.[36]

In 1973 representatives of the French Communist Party and 'a contingent' from the Irish Labour Party took part in the pilgrimage of the Official faction. Mac Giolla denounced the 'sectarianism' of the Provisionals; another speaker, Liam (or Billy) McMillen from Belfast, attaching great importance to the revival of the Irish language, incongruously proposed 'a kind of Gaeltacht soviet'.[37] Attendance was estimated at 5,000, of whom 500 came from Belfast.[38] In 1974, similarly, there was a left-wing tenor. Among the pilgrims were members of the Connolly Youth Movement and the Labour Liaison of the Left; the orator of the day, Michael Ryan of Dublin, denounced what he saw as a 'sinister evil in the boardrooms of Dublin, Belfast, London, Brussels, wherever men conspired to change the future of the masses', and 'control of Irish wealth by multinational corporations' and even — hitherto unthinkable at Bodenstown — 'the domination of the Catholic hierarchy'.[39] The *Irish Press* put the audience at almost 4,000.[40] 'Mick' Ryan, not yet forty, had a long career in the I.R.A. since joining in 1954; in the year that he spoke at Bodenstown he also produced a sort of manual, *A reporter's guide to Ireland*, on counter-intelligence techniques.[41]

---

35 Hanley & Millar, *Lost revolution*, pp 9, 18, 400, 406–9 et passim. **36** *Ir. Times*, 19 June 1972. **37** *Ir. Times*, 15, 18 June 1973. A picture of McMillen speaking on this occasion is in Hanley & Millar, *Lost revolution*, facing p. 211. **38** *Ir. Press*, 18 June 1973. **39** *Ir. Times*, 24 June 1974. **40** *Ir. Press*, 24 June 1974. **41** Hanley & Millar, *Lost revolution*, esp. pp 194.

AN ATTEMPTED BOMB ATTACK ON PILGRIMS

On the morning of 22 June 1975 a bomb was planted on the railway at Baronrath bridge, six kilometres north-east of Sallins, in an attempt to derail a train, a 'special' carrying Bodenstown-bound pilgrims.[42] After the closure of Sallins railway station to regular passenger traffic in 1963, it continued to be used for Bodenstown specials. A local man on his Sunday walk, Christopher or Christy Phelan, on surprising the bombers at their work, was beaten, stabbed and killed. On board the train when it left Dublin at 1.32 p.m. were 281 or so Officials on their annual pilgrimage; it passed under the bridge about 3 or 4 minutes before the bomb exploded at 1.55 or 1.56 p.m. and so none of the passengers suffered injury — one of them was May 'Bean' Mac Giolla (née McLaughlin), wife of Tomás Mac Giolla and herself a Republican activist since the 1940s. There was some suspicion that the perpetrators were members of the rival Irish Republican Socialist Party, six of whom, one of them the party's leader, Costello, were afterwards arrested. There is little or no doubt, however, that the perpetrators were men associated with the U.V.F., the body that in 1969 had set off a bomb on Tone's grave.[43] According to an investigating journalist, the leader of the gang who planted the bomb at Baronrath bridge was Robin Jackson, a ruthless U.V.F. operative who died in 1998 of natural causes.[44] Despite the intense rivalry between the several parties claiming descent from the original Sinn Féin, this was the only case of a violent death on a pilgrimage to Bodenstown. One likely reason for the long record of personal safety is that policemen were always on duty close to the scene and prepared to intervene. Usually they coolly observed — I have been reliably told of investigative Special Branch men in the 1950s concealing themselves in a hay-barn to watch for wanted I.R.A. men. Another reason is that the Republican managers themselves, well disciplined and not wanting trouble, kept good order. An exceptional case at a pilgrimage was in 1979, when Provisionals attacked policemen with flag-poles, stones and bottles.[45] The case of Christopher Phelan was a special case, as the victim was not a pilgrim, the attackers were not Republicans, and the death occurred early in the day and beyond sight and sound of the scene of the pilgrimage.

The Officials' commemoration took place despite the murder. It appears that the news of the fatality and the rail passengers' brush with death was not generally known among the five thousand present at Bodenstown. There were seven bands, a colour party, and a guard of honour for the orator of the day, Cathal Goulding. Pilgrims from Ulster were numerous and Goulding was probably representative of some of them in voicing a demand for 'the removal of the British Army of

---

42 The station reopened for a new north Kildare passenger service in 1994.   43 *Ir. Times*, 23 June 1971; *Ir. Indep.*, 23 June 1975; *Houses of the Oireachtas: Joint Committee on Justice [etc.]: interim report ... of the independent commission of inquiry* (Prn A6/1091, July 2006), pp 161–4; Hanley & Millar, *Lost revolution* (2009), pp xii, 71.   44 Joe Tiernan, *The Dublin and Monaghan bombings* (n.p., 2004), esp. pp 214–27. On Jackson (1948–98), there is an article by Patrick Maume in *D.I.B.* 45 *Ir. Indep.*, 17 June 1979.

occupation from the six occupied counties of our country'. He went on to assert, 'we share the triumph of the people of Vietnam and Cambodia, the victories of the Portuguese people and of the African colonies of Portugal, Angola and Mozambique. We share the hope of the people of Spain ...'.[46] Concern for nationalist or left-wing agitation beyond the shores of Ireland had become a norm in Official discourse. It was no doubt a reason for the presence also of a group of Chilean refugees.

THE PROVISIONALS' MILITANCY

The Bodenstown pilgrimages that attracted most attention in the 1970s were those of the Provisionals. It was they who, popularly known as the 'Provos', were the Catholic militants engaged in bloody warfare against the authorities and political opponents in Northern Ireland. The president of the Sinn Féin wing from 1970 until 1983 was Ruairí Ó Brádaigh. A university graduate, appointed a teacher of commerce in 1954, Ó Brádaigh (1932–2013) had attended his first Sinn Féin *ard-fhéis* in 1951. He took part in the I.R.A.'s Border campaign, which landed him in prison for most of 1957 and 1958 and again from November 1959 until May 1960. Between these two terms of imprisonment, he was chief-of-staff of the I.R.A. (October 1958 to May 1959) and, at the age of 26, the orator at Bodenstown (21 June 1959). After his second release he was again chief-of staff for 12 months or more.[47] The Provisionals' first pilgrimage to Bodenstown, reported by the *Irish Times* to be between 2,000 and 3,000 strong, took place on 14 June 1970 and was addressed by Dáithí Ó Conaill (an old associate of Ó Brádaigh in the 'Border campaign' and a relation by marriage). The reporter observed that 'its composition was markedly different — the contingent from the North, especially, was very much larger than normal ... The numbers they contributed to the parade made up substantially for any diminution to the southern contingents caused by the split.'[48] Similarly, the *Irish Press* reported that 'a significant feature was the size of the representation from Belfast and other Northern centres' — its estimate was 'up to 1,000' out of '3,000 people from throughout the country'. In the parade were eight bands, units of the I.R.A., contingents of Fianna Éireann and Cumann na mBan, all with their flags and banners, among them the Irish tricolour and the proletarian Plough and the Stars.[49] Like earlier pilgrimages when a need existed to outdo rivals, the first pilgrimage of the Provisionals was spectacular.

The scene was larger a year later, more 'Northern', more militarised: attendance was put at 10,000, five of the 11 bands were from the north, the flag of the Belfast brigade of the I.R.A. was drooped by a 'black-bereted colour party' whilst lines of

---

46 *Ir. Times*, 23 June 1975. **47** Robert W. White, *Ruairí Ó Brádaigh: the life and politics of an Irish revolutionary* (Bloomington, Ind., 2006?). There is an obituary in *Ir. Times*, 8 June 2013. **48** *Ir. Times*, 15 June 1970. For Ó Conaill (1938–91), see Patrick Maume's article in *D.I.B.* **49** *Ir. Press*, 15 June 1970.

'Cumann na mBan and Cumann na gCailíní from Belfast in green and white stood to attention'; the bellicose oration was delivered by a Belfast I.R.A. veteran, Joe Cahill, praised by a Republican obituarist for his 'violent background'.[50] A pattern was set for the following years. In 1972 the crowd was estimated by the chief marshal to be 23,000, by the police under 10,000; there were, a newspaper reported, 'parties from all over the country, but Belfast seemed to predominate'. The chairman, unusually, was a woman, Mrs Máire Drumm from Belfast, who dwelt upon the privations of I.R.A. men 'held behind the wire and behind prison bars'; the orator, Seán Keenan from Derry was dismissive of Protestants resentful of legal prohibitions on 'contraception and divorce'.[51]

In 1973, at a similar scene, the orator of the day, Martin McGuinness also from Derry, stated his aspiration to 'a democratic, socialist republic'; the parade from Sallins had been headed by 'a 130-strong colour party dressed in black, with black berets and dark glasses'.[52] McGuinness's speech contained the first mention of socialism at a Provisional pilgrimage, while the prominence of the men attired in black was an example of militarisation during this period. In previous decades only youths, women and girls wore uniforms. At the Provisionals' pilgrimage in 1974, the men who led the parade 'were heavily disguised. They wore dark combat jackets, wigs and dark glasses. Following them was a colour party and 14 bands'; Robert Fisk, reporting for the London *Times*, commented that 'long ranks of men in black uniforms, berets and dark glasses were allowed to parade openly'; there was, however, as the *Irish Times* reported, a police and military presence, the soldiers 'in battle-dress, half-hidden in ditches and behind bushes'.[53] Similarly in 1975 there was a conspicuous paramilitary presence — a 'colour party' of forty or so 'black-garbed men' in dark glasses leading an estimated 10,000 pilgrims, among them Sinn Féin, Cumann na mBan, Fianna Éireann, thirteen bands; police and troops with automatic weapons were in surrounding fields. The credentials of the orator, Proinsias Mac Airt, were that he was a 'veteran Belfast Republican recently released after serving a six-year term' in prison in Northern Ireland. He believed that 'Republicans owed more to Tone than they could ever repay by making pilgrimages to his grave'. Another veteran was Máire Comerford.[54] She had been one of the group of women who had made up the only pilgrimage in 1921. Mac Airt, alias Frank Card (1922–92), had been editor of Provisional Sinn Féin's Belfast newspaper, *Republican News*.[55] These scenes at Bodenstown were reminiscent of the first half of the 1930s.

50 *Ir. Times*, 14 June 1971; *Irish Republican News* (Belfast) 27 July 2004. For Cahill (1920–2004), see also *Guardian*, 26 July 2004; *Daily Telegraph*, 26 July 2004; *An Phoblacht*, 29 July 2004. Brendan Anderson's *Joe Cahill: a life in the I.R.A.* (Dublin, 2002) is hagiographical.   **51** *Ir. Press*, 12 June 1972; *Ir. Times*, 12 June 1972.   **52** *Ir. Times*, 11 June 1973.   **53** *Ir. Indep.*, 17 June 1974; *Ir. Times*, 17 June 1974; *The Times*, 17 June 1974.   **54** *Ir. Indep.*, 16 June 1975.   **55** English, *Armed struggle*, p. 98.

THE IRISH REPUBLICAN SOCIALIST PARTY

On 8 December 1974 another party in the Republican tradition was formed together with (though secretly at first) a linked paramilitary body. These were the Irish Republican Socialist Party (I.R.S.P.) and the Irish National Liberation Army (I.N.L.A.). The head of both was Seamus Costello, who had stayed with Mac Giolla and Goulding when the I.R.A. split in December 1969 and Sinn Féin a month later. Costello (1939–77), a motor-car salesman prominent in local politics at Bray, had a career in the I.R.A. which began at the age of 16; he became vice-president of Official Sinn Féin and director of operations of Official I.R.A. He opposed the 'cease-fire' declared by the latter on 29 May 1972 and consequently, eventually he left.[56] In 1975, on 8 June, the new organisation held its first pilgrimage to Bodenstown; between 250 and 300 participated and marched behind the Plough and the Stars. Already a feud with the Officials had begun. Six weeks previously the leader of the Officials in Belfast, Liam ('Billy') McMillen, the principal speaker for his party at Bodenstown in 1973, was shot dead and his murder blamed on the I.N.L.A. Costello in his oration at Bodenstown referred to this feud in accounting for the deaths of three I.R.S.P. members and, as reported in the *Independent*, 'accused the Official I.R.A. of supplying information on I.R.S.P. membership to the U.V.F. murder gangs'.[57] Despite the paucity of his audience and his hostility to his former comrades, Costello asserted that 'the most important and immediate task' of his organisation was 'the creation of a broad front in the struggle for national liberation'.[58] As will be seen, when the 'Provos' held their pilgrimage one week later they drew, it was reported, 10,000 people; Fianna Fáil drew 400 on 22 June, and 5,000 took part in Official celebrations later the same day. At Bodenstown a year later, on 6 June 1976, Costello, when the feud was vicious, urged the 'unification of all Socialist, Republican and "anti-imperialist" organisations in this country'.[59] The following month he ceased to be chief-of-staff of the I.N.L.A., though his influence in it continued. On 5 October 1977 he was himself shot dead, seemingly by a member of the Official I.R.A. The party and paramilitary body he had founded, factious as well as feuding with the Officials, never achieved the degree of fame or success of its rivals; they exceeded however their rivals' vituperation. Their pilgrimages to Bodenstown in 1978 and 1980 were reported only in the *Irish Times*; no report has been found in that paper for 1977, 1979 or for any later year in the period under consideration. About 400 marched in 1978, after which the Officials were once more denounced by the orator; in 1980 the number was down to 150 despite the news of the murder only three days before of Miriam Daly, a university lecturer, who had presided over the I.R.S.P. pilgrimage in 1978.[60] Naturally, there

---

56 For Costello and the I.R.S.P., see Micheál Ó Siochrú, 'Costello, Séamus' in *D.I.B.*; Hanley & Millar, *Lost revolution*, pp 14, 17, 25, 118, 272, 300, 402–3.   57 *Ir. Times*, 9 June 1975; *Ir. Indep.*, 9 June 1975.   58 Andrew Sanders, *Inside the I.R.A.: dissident republicans and the war for legitimacy* (Edinburgh, 2012), p. 79.   59 *Ir. Indep.*, 7 June 1976.   60 *Ir. Times*, 26 June 1978, 30 June 1980. She is the subject of an article by Patrick Maume in *D.I.B.*, xi (Cambridge, 2018).

were quite long reports of I.R.S.P. and I.N.L.A. pilgrimages in their monthly newspaper, the *Starry Plough*. One example suffices. On 27 June 1982 supporters from various parts of the island assembled at Sallins for the traditional march. The 'main speaker', Brigid Makowski, a Shannon town commissioner, employed the customary Bodenstown rhetoric. Not forgetting Tone, she held that 'the men of no property' were now 'the working-class'. But, departing from Republican tradition, she denounced 'the farmers' among the usual villains, the bankers and the multinationals; she compared 'the Irish people' with 'the people' of Central and South America, of Palestine and of Lebanon. Nor did she forget those in the party from which her own had broken away in 1974, 'those groups of lackeys, the so-called Workers' Party'.[61]

OFFICIALS AND PROVISIONALS: A COMPARISON

The narrative of the rival pilgrimages of the two Sinn Féin parties (Official and Provisional) from 1976 until 1983 was what might have been predicted from that of the pilgrimages of the six years that followed the split. Differences evident in 1970 became more marked. These rival pilgrimages will be considered here not individually but comparatively.

The pilgrimages of both the Officials and the Provisionals during the ten years following the split conformed at first, as in previous years, to the paramilitary pattern established by the Irish Volunteers in 1914. The Officials' parades, however, gradually became less militaristic, their orators less bellicose, whilst those of the Provisionals became quickly more so. The differences between the 1970s and preceding decades, and the differences between the two parties, were mostly due to the re-emergence of the Ulster question and the outbreak in 1969 and continuance throughout the 1970s and 1980s of politically motivated violence in Northern Ireland between Republicans and Loyalists and the responses of forces of law and order. Though both Officials and Provisionals had their I.R.A. wings, the Provisional I.R.A. alone was persistently proactive after 1973, while the Official I.R.A. was on the defensive and formally, but not entirely, on a 'cease-fire'. From the mid-1970s this difference was increasingly noticeable at Bodenstown, where paramilitary trappings fewer and less evident at the parades of the Officials. In its report of the Officials' parade in 1977, the *Irish Times* could state: 'only the Fianna children were in uniform this year. There was no sign of berets, dark glasses or other insignia as the parade was led into the churchyard by an advance guard from South Down and Armagh and the Cork Volunteer Band.'[62] Provisional Sinn Féin orators remained preoccupied with the political situation in the north, while the orators of Official Sinn Féin (renamed Sinn Féin the Workers' Party in January 1977) continued to concern themselves with political and economic issues on both sides of the border, and even overseas, while always appealing for a cessation of hostilities as a necessary condition for implementing the socialist policies they advocated. But in 1977 too

61 *Starry Plough*, July 1982. The file of this paper in N.L.I. is incomplete.   62 *Ir. Times*, 20 June

there was a perceptible change of policy in the speech delivered, on 12 June, by the Provisionals' orator, Jimmy Drumm. It lamented the absence of

> a positive tie-in with the mass of the Irish people who have little or no idea of the suffering in the North … We need to make a stand on economic issues and on the everyday struggles of people. The forging of the strong links between the republican movement and the workers of Ireland and radical trade-unionists will create an irrepressible mass movement and will ensure mass support for the continuing armed struggle in the North.[63]

Drumm's speech was written in fact by Gerry Adams and Danny Morrison.[64] Both were to deliver orations a few years later. To some listeners it must have brought back memories of the later 1960s. Roy Foster has remarked, in reference to this and in allusion to many earlier speeches, that 'delusionary prophecy is par for the course at Tone's grave'.[65] It was however a pointer, ignored at the time, to a significant change in the policies of Provisional Sinn Féin.

WHICH SUNDAY?

Officials and Provisionals never clashed at Bodenstown. From 1970 until 1979 the Provisionals went on their pilgrimage on the Sunday before the Officials, from 1980 until 1983 the Provisionals on the Sunday following. Until 1979 the Fianna Fáil party held its pilgrimage on the same day as the Officials, an hour or two before. So in June 1975, when again there were four pilgrimages (despite the absence of the defence forces), the fledging I.R.S.P went on the 8th, the Provisionals on the 15th, and the Officials and Fianna Fáil on the 22nd. In June 1980 there were again four. Charles Haughey laid a wreath for Fianna Fáil on the 22nd, a few hours before Pearse's 'holiest place' was occupied by Provisionals; on the previous Sunday it had been Sinn Féin the Workers' Party; on the following Sunday, the 29th, it was the I.R.S.P. In 1981 there were two June pilgrimages: Sinn Féin the Workers' Party on the 14th June, Provisional Sinn Féin on the 21st June; Fianna Fáil postponed theirs until 27 September. From then on the annual Fianna Fáil pilgrimages always took place in the autumn. Nineteen-eighty-two, the year in which Tom Dunne's book appeared, saw three June pilgrimages, but on different days, the Workers' Party (as they had become) on the 15th, Sinn Féin (no longer needing the identifier 'Provisional') on the 22nd, the Irish Republican Socialist Party on the 27th; Fianna Fáil were at Tone's grave the following October, and the Irish defence forces had not been there since 1973.

1977.　**63** *Republican News*, 18 June 1977, as cited in Henry Patterson, *The politics of illusion* (2nd ed., London, 1997), pp 180–81. Unusually, this pilgrimage was reported only very briefly in *Ir. Press* and not at all in *Ir. Indep.* The report in *Ir. Times*, 13 June 1977, gives little attention to the speech. For its importance, see also English, *Armed struggle*, p. 217.　**64** Gerry Adams, *Before the dawn: an autobiography* (London, 1996), p. 264.　**65** R. F. Foster, *Luck and the Irish: a brief history of change, c.1970–2000* (London, 2007), p. 120.

HOW MANY PILGRIMS?

It is always difficult to rely on estimates of crowd sizes. Promoters of events and sympathisers tend to overestimate, others (including the police) generally give lower figures. Gary Owens has discussed this discrepancy and the difficulties of resolving it in his treatment of the outdoor political rallies ('monster meetings') held in the 1840s to promote Repeal.[66] It is less difficult with Bodenstown pilgrims, as they walked from a fixed assembly point in an orderly manner and in a column. During the 1970s and early 1980s estimated sizes of crowds were at least a fair assessment of the comparative strengths of the two great rival factions, Officials and Provisionals. This can be seen here from a list in tabular form showing years, approximate attendances given in newspaper reports and, for good measure, names of orators or 'principal speakers'. The figures are:

Year	*Attendance* (approx.), *Orator*	*Attendance* (approx.), *Orator*
	OFFICIALS	PROVISIONALS
1970	3,000, Malachy McBurney[67]	2.000 to 3,000, or 3,000, Dáithí Ó Conaill[81]
1971	4,000 to 5,000 (or even 8,000?), Malachy McGurran[68]	8,000 or 10,000, Joe Cahill[82]
1972	'several thousand', Seán Garland[69]	10,000 or 23,000, Seán Keenan[83]
1973	5,000, Liam McMillen[70]	10,000: Martin McGuinness[84]
1974	7,000, Michael Ryan[71]	6,000, Seamus Loughran[85]
1975	5,000, Cathal Goulding[72]	10,000, Proinnsias Mac Airt[86]
1976	2,000, Des O'Hagan and Máirín de Burca[73]	6,000, Gearóid Mac Carthaigh[87]
1977	not known, Éamonn Smullen[74]	3,000, Jimmy Drumm[88]
1978	4,000, Seamus Lynch[75]	4,000, Johnny Johnson[89]
1979	1,000, Seán Ó Cionnaigh[76]	7,000, Gerry Adams[90]
1980	400, Joe Sherlock[77]	4,000, Tom Hartley and Martha McClelland[91]
1981	300 and 400, Des O'Hagan[78]	5,000, Danny Morrison[92]
1982	200, Tomás Mac Giolla[79]	5,000, Owen Carron[93]
1983	350, Proinsias de Rossa[80]	5,000, Gerry Adams[94]

66 Gary Owens, 'Nationalism without words: symbolism and ritual behaviour in the Repeal "monster meetings" of 1843–5' in James S. Donnelly, jr, and Kerby A. Miller (eds), *Irish popular culture, 1650–1850* (Dublin, 1998), pp 242–74. 67 *Ir. Times*, 22 June 1970; *Ir. Press*, 22 June 1970.

The figures for both factions, 3,000 or so, at their commemorations in 1970, the first after the split, were similar. Both enjoyed an increase until the mid-1970s. The Officials' attendances were two thirds higher before peaking at 7,000 in 1974. The Provisionals' figures doubled or trebled to 10,000 in 1971 and remained at this level (except for a drop to 6,000 in 1974) until 1975. The Officials lost numbers steadily from 1975, when Cathal Goulding addressed 5,000 faithful, half the number at their rivals' pilgrimage the previous Sunday. They did not recover and went steadily down to 200 in 1982 despite the attraction that year of the party leader, Tomás Mac Giolla. Provisional orators, too, faced smaller congregations from 1976, in which year attendance fell by 40 per cent to 6,000. In 1977 the figure was 3,000; it hovered between 4,000 and 5,000 for the remainder of the period under study except for 1979 when Gerry Adams addressed 7,000 assembled pilgrims, a figure not reached at his second coming to the rostrum in 1983.

An explanation of this phenomenon at the very end of the historical period can only be attempted. Whereas the greater fall in attendances at Official pilgrimages compared with attendances at their rivals occurring one week before (or, from 1980, one week later) can perhaps be explained by the larger public profile of the Provisionals, especially in Belfast and other parts of Northern Ireland, this explanation cannot account for the decline of both after 1974 or 1975. It does not take into account the paucity of Official pilgrims at a time when in Dublin and its environs Officials were increasingly successful at becoming public representatives. In June 1981 a Sinn Féin the Workers' Party candidate (Joe Sherlock, its orator at Bodenstown the year before) was elected to Dáil Éireann; he willingly took his seat; some days later no more than 400 of its supporters appeared at Bodenstown. The *Irish Independent*, reporting its annual pilgrimage that year, stated that 'fatigue after the election campaign and bad weather were blamed' for the S.F.W.P.'s 'smallest ever attendance'.[95] At fresh elections in February 1982 it won three seats, yet four months later (by which time it was simply the Workers' Party) attendance at its Bodenstown demonstration was down by half. Had marching along the road to Bodenstown become less important than walking streets in quest of votes? This was the opinion

68 *Ir. Times*, 21 June 1971. The *Ir. Indep.*, 21 June 1971, insisted on the highest figure; the *Ir. Press*, 21 June 1971, reported 7,000.   **69** *Ir. Times*, 19 June 1972.   **70** *Ir. Press*, 18 June 1973; *Ir. Indep.*, 18 June 1973.   **71** *Ir. Press*, 24 June 1974.   **72** *Ir. Times*, 23 June 1975.   **73** *Ir. Times*, 21 June 1976.   **74** *Ir. Times*, 20 June 1977. Smullen (1923?–90) died shortly after leaving the Workers' Party (*Ir. Press*, 26 Sept. 1990).   **75** *Ir. Indep.*, 19 June 1978; *Ir. Press*, 19 June 1978.   **76** *Ir. Times*, 25 June 1979.   **77** *Ir. Times*, 16 June 1980.   **78** *Ir. Indep.*, 15 June 1981; *Ir. Times*, 15 June 1981. **79** *Ir. Times*, 14 June 1982.   **80** *Ir. Times*, 13 June 1983.   **81** *Ir. Times*, 15 June 1970, or *Ir. Press*, 15 June 1970, respectively.   **82** *Ir. Indep.*, 14 June 1971, or *Ir. Times*, and *Ir. Press*, 14 June 1971, respectively.   **83** *Ir. Press*, 12 June 1972. The police reckoned 'less than 10,000', the chief marshal claimed 23,000.   **84** *Ir. Press*, 11 June 1973; *Ir. Indep.*, 11 June 1973.   **85** *Ir. Press*, 24 June 1974. **86** *Ir. Press*, 16 June 1975.   **87** *Ir. Press*, 14 June 1976.   **88** *Ir. Times*, 13 June 1977.   **89** *Ir. Press*, 12 June 1978.   **90** *Ir. Indep.*, 18 June 1979.   **91** *Ir. Times*, 23 June 1980; *Ir. Indep.*, 23 June 1980. **92** *Ir. Times*, 22 June 1981.   **93** *Ir. Press*, 11 June 1982.   **94** *Ir. Indep.*, 20 June 1983.   **95** *Ir. Indep.*, 15 June 1981.

of some of 'a totally new breed of recruits' in the 1970s and 1980s 'attracted to the socialist aspect of Official republicanism'.[96] The Workers' Party was to win seven seats in Dáil Éireann 1989 and one in the European Parliament, the assembly of the institution that one of the party's principals, Goulding, had denounced at Bodenstown in 1967.[97]

A FINAL COMPARISON

This survey of the Bodenstown pilgrimages ends with 1983. It is illustrative to look more closely at the two Republican pilgrimages held in that year. The Irish defence forces and Fianna Fáil no longer upheld the June tradition. One of the newly-elected Workers' Party deputies, Proinsias de Rossa, delivering his oration on 12 June, said, no doubt with the Provisionals and the I.N.L.A. in mind, that no group that killed 'man, woman or child for their religious or political beliefs' could claim Tone as their inspiration. De Rossa had been mentioned in a police report of Bodenstown in 1959 (when he was barely 19) as being a member of the I.R.A. The parade from Sallins had been 'led by a pipe band and with the Tricolour, Starry Plough and the flags of the Four Provinces' flying.[98] The custom of a colour party wearing berets and combat fatigues had been discontinued by the Officials in 1977.[99] In contrast, one week after De Rossa, Gerry Adams, who ten days previously had been elected to the British parliament but was refusing to take a seat, began his graveside address to Provisionals and sympathisers — it would appear only ironically — with the words, 'Fellow gunmen and gunwomen'.[100] He had just taken part in the parade 'led by a colour party in dark-green uniforms with black berets and pale-green handkerchief arranged to conceal their faces'; behind them were 'a party of women, some in black, others in green uniforms carrying banners, and uniformed boys and girls of the Fianna'. The Provisionals' colour party, not to be outdone by the Officials', also held aloft 'the Tricolour, the Plough and the Stars and the flags of the four provinces'.[101]

THE ULSTER DIMENSION

Ulster as a factor in the Bodenstown pilgrimages in the period to 1939 has been discussed above. Arguably the revival of the Ulster question occurred with the speech made to Republicans at Bodenstown by Seán MacBride on 18 June 1944. 'The country was partitioned', he said, 'and while this portion' — meaning independent Ireland — 'enjoyed comparative freedom, a portion of Ulster was

---

96 Kacper Rekawek, *Irish republican terrorism and politics: a comparative study of the Official and Provisional I.R.A.* (London, 2011), p. 87.   97 *Ir. Press*, 19 June 1967.   98 *Ir. Indep.*, 13 June 1983; *Ir. Times*, 13 June 1980.   99 Hanley & Millar, *Lost revolution*, p. 381.   100 *Ir. Indep.*, 20 June 1983; *An Phoblacht*, 23 June 1983. The latter, the Sinn Féin party's newspaper, after referring to 'Volunteers in the colour party' wearing 'battle fatigues', stated that Adams's words were spoken 'ironically'.   101 *Ir. Times*, 20 June 1983.

occupied by foreign troops and ruled by an autocratic government'.[102] Ten years after MacBride's speech, Bodenstown was the focus of attention again when, on 20 June 1954, a few days after the I.R.A. seized arms from the military barracks at Armagh, in Northern Ireland, the orator of the day, Gearóid Ó Broin, took the opportunity to assert that they would be 'for use against the British occupation forces in the six counties'.[103] Yet only three Bodenstown orators were from Northern Ireland during the thirty-year period from 1940 to 1969: Seán MacGloin of Belfast (1942), Joe McGurk of Belfast (1952) and Seán Dougan, County Antrim (1957). They focussed on what they perceived to be Britain's exercise of military force to keep the six disputed counties within the United Kingdom, the root cause, they asserted, of 'partition'. In the 1960s there was no principal orator from the north. During the same thirty-year period to 1969 (for which, however, information is less complete before 1960) four Northerners were on occasion prominent: one was Manus Canning (of Derry), chairman in 1960, the second was Seán Keenan (also of Derry), 'chief marshal' in 1962 and a supporting speaker in 1966; the other two were Malachy McBurney and Liam McMillen (both of Belfast) who presided in 1968 and 1969 respectively, when disturbances in Northern Ireland were beginning. Significantly, of the fifteen members of the *ard chomhairle* (national executive) of Sinn Féin in 1965, not one was from Northern Ireland.[104] Yet Ulster was a topic that was to exclude almost all others at Bodenstown a year or two later.

During the subsequent fifteen-year period, from 1970 to 1984, when the 'Troubles' were a perennial theme of Bodenstown orations, the orator at Provisional Sinn Féin pilgrimages was from Northern Ireland in every year but two: Joe Cahill (1971), Máire Drumm (1972), Martin McGuinness (1973), Seamus Loughran (1974), Proinnsias Mac Airt (1975), Jimmy Drumm (1977), Johnny Johnson (1978), Gerry Adams (1979), Tom Hartley and Martha McClelland (1980), Danny Morrison (1981), Owen Carron (1982), Gerry Adams again (1983), Jim McAllister (1984). All were from Belfast except for McGuinness, Johnson and Martha McClelland, who were from Derry, and Carron, who was from Enniskillen. In the two missing years Northerners presided: James Steele (1970) and Jimmy Drumm (1976). Only four Northerners gave an oration at pilgrimages organised by the Officials: Malachy McBurney (1970), Malachy McGurran (1971), Liam McMillen (1973) and Des O'Hagan (1976 and 1981).

The Irish government's prohibition of the Republican pilgrimage planned for 25 June 1939, three months before the outbreak of the Second World War, did not prevent a contingent of 500 Republicans travelling by train from Belfast and emerging in Dublin at Amiens Street Station in the forlorn and thwarted hope of reaching Bodenstown. But war-time transport shortages and travel restrictions seem to have reduced the number of northerners almost to zero. What must have been a very small group of 'Sinn Féiners from Belfast' managed to visit Bodenstown in June 1942, travelling the final stage of their journey by taxi from Dublin.[105] There

---

102 *Ir. Press*, 19 June 1944. No other source examined mentions Ulster.   **103** *Ir. Indep.*, 22 June 1954.   **104** Treacy, *I.R.A.*, p. 58.   **105** *Ir. Times*, 9 June 1942.

was no further mention in the sources examined of pilgrims from Ulster until 1947 when two Northern Ireland buses reached Sallins from Belfast.[106] Small or indeterminate numbers of Northerners were observed in the following three years years.[107] In 1951 the Garda Síochána reported the presence of Ulster Transport Authority buses and an Ulster contingent of I.R.A.; in 1952, when a Belfast man, Joseph McGurk, was the orator, more buses arrived from the north, some perhaps transporting the 200 I.R.A. men who marched in their parade. No less significantly, in 1953 nine Ulster Transport Authority buses were noticed by the Garda Síochána and in 1954 five.[108] The latter occasion was shortly after the successful raid for arms by the I.R.A. on the Armagh military barracks in Northern Ireland. There are references in newspapers to northern contingents in 1955 (explicit), 1956, 1957 and 1958 (all vague) and in a Garda report in 1959 to '168 members of Sinn Féin, Northern contingent'.[109] Bodenstown was almost too far from Ulster counties for an easy day trip. But an added attraction — one that partly explains why some Northerners travelled by chartered bus rather than train — was after the pilgrimage a *céilí* (a social with Irish traditional music) at a venue in Dublin organised by the National Commemoration Committee, a custom dating from the 1930s.[110] It necessitated a very late return home, whilst Dubliners could socialise and still be home early, a point illustrating the popularity of Bodenstown with Dubliners especially. During the first half of the 1960s there were only vague mentions in the Dublin morning papers of participants from Northern Ireland. Those who did attend from north of the border in the middle years of the century must have been disappointed that the orator of the day was almost always a southerner and that references to the part of Ireland from which they came were so few. In 1966, the half-centenary of the Easter rising and the prospect of a veteran of the Border campaign, a Derryman, Seán Keenan, presiding could explain why suddenly whole contingents arrived from north of the border.[111] In 1967 there was scant mention of northerners in the papers, none at all in the *United Irishman*. In 1968, a Belfast 'contingent', members of the Belfast Wolfe Tone Society and a Newry children's band appeared.[112] In 1969, buses arrived from the north and the Belfast Young Socialists were observed in the parade, which, though not reported in the press, was headed by Ulster units of the I.R.A. In the same year, Mac Giolla, a Tipperary man, referred directly to the Ulster question. Whilst characterising it as a case of 'British imperialism in Ireland' and imagining 'the Irish people of Northern Ireland' as being kept divided over the years 'by an intricate system of privileges for the

106 *Ir. Press*, 23 June 1947.   107 *Ir. Press*, 20 June 1949; Nat. Arch., Dublin, JUS/8/900 (1948, 1949).   108 Nat. Arch., Dublin, JUS/8/900 (1952, 1953, 1954).   109 *Ir. Times*, 20 June 1955, 13 June 1957; *United Irishman*, July 1956, July 1958, July 1959; Nat. Arch., Dublin, JUS/8/900 (1947).   110 *Ir. Press*, 24 June 1935, 17 June 1963; *Ir. Indep.*, 11, 20 June 1938; *Evening Herald*, 11 June 1949, 20 June 1950, 16 June 1954, 18 June 1960 (at Sallins); *United Irishman*, July 1951; Hanley, *I.R.A.*, pp 51, 226; Nat. Arch., Dublin, JUS/8/900 (1959). For buses from Belfast to Bodenstown and *céilithe* in Dublin, see also Brendan Anderson, *Joe Cahill: a life in the I.R.A.* (Dublin, 2002), p. 123.   111 *Ir. Times*, 20 June 1966; *Ir. Indep.*, 20 June 1966; *Ir. Press*, 20 June 1966.   112 *Ir. Times*, 24 June 1968; *Ir. Indep.*, 24 June 1968.

Protestants and penalties for the Catholics', he held to an optimistic vision: 'the workers will eventually see problems not in terms of Protestant and Catholic or Unionist v. Nationalist but of power and privilege v. power and persecution'.[113] These were presages of what was to be heard at Bodenstown in later years. Mac Giolla did not however mention recent outbreaks of violence or consequent political crises, a silence that was to have repercussions.

During the early 1970s occurred what can be characterised as the 'ulsterisation' of Bodenstown. Throughout the decade and into the 1980s the marchers along the pilgrims' path to Bodenstown churchyard were in much larger measure from Ulster. It can only be imagined that the main subject of their private discourse was the political situation in Northern Ireland, just as it was the recurring theme of the orations. The Ulster dimension was most conspicuous at Provisionals' pilgrimages; in contrast the Officials continued to extend their gaze to parts of the wider world where they perceived revolution to be desirable and attainable, though Ulster was always a greater concern than any of these and a greater concern than in the later 1960s. Bodenstown became a rallying ground for Provisional Sinn Féin, a parade ground for the Provisional I.R.A. and a place of brief 'rest and recreation' for war-weary Ulster Catholic militants. 'When the Provisionals come to Bodenstown', Mary Holland recalled in 1987, 'their buses stretch down the winding lanes of Kildare as far as Sallins. Northern voices fill the churchyard and children from the Falls and Ballymurphy play among the graves. The parents swagger into the cemetery as though they owned Tone's grave, which, in a sense, they do.'[114] They could trail their coats with impunity in Kildare, where, unlike their home counties, they had no opponents on the day. Ironically, the destruction done by enemy action at Bodenstown in 1969 was an opportunity, seized by the National Graves Association, to erect on the Tone family grave not a replacement tombstone but an edifice designed — expressly? — as suitable for annual political rallies. In the orations at those rallies after completion of the edifice in April 1971 deep grievances were aired but little by way of tribute to Tone was said.

---

113 *Ir. Times*, 23 June 1969; info. Brian Hanley.   114 *Ir. Times*, 14 Oct. 1987.

11

Women, religion and labour

V ARIOUS THEMES in the history of Bodenstown have the potential for further treatment. Three stand out:

WOMEN

It was a woman, Tone's widow Matilda, who, by writing to John Gray in December 1843, ensured that a memorial would be placed on Tone's grave. Indeed, Tone family concern for the state of the grave passed down into the twentieth century through female lines. Women were always among the pilgrims. Two women accompanied their menfolk to Bodenstown in 1861 on the earliest known visit that could be characterised as a 'pilgrimage'. They were named only as 'Mrs Doheny' (Ellen Doheny, wife of Michael Doheny) and 'Miss McManus' (Isabella McManus, sister of Terence Bellew McManus). They were in a group led by Doheny visiting Tone's grave the day before McManus's funeral. 'Dun Padruic', when proposing, in 1872, excursions to Bodenstown and other places of historic memory envisaged mixed company. To the imagined picnics each 'excursionist' was 'to bring his *or her* commissariat in his *or her* pocket' (italics mine). The *Leinster Express*, reporting the mass excursion to Bodenstown in 1873 for the laying of a new stone, made mention of 'the female portion of the crowd' colourfully sporting 'green veils'.[1] The *Leinster Leader* reported in 1893 that two special trains arriving from Dublin 'were closely packed' with both men and women; four years later it stated, patronisingly, that contingents of pilgrims from Dublin, Meath and Kildare consisted 'of not only brave men but fair women, these latter by the way taking a lively interest in the proceedings'; in 1899 it reported that 'a conspicuous feature' of the crowds 'was the proportion of the feminine element thronging towards Bodenstown' whilst suggesting that their participation gave the event that year 'all the air of a general holiday'.[2] The first woman to be remembered for her participation was Maud Gonne, who took part in the pilgrimage of 1901. A woman of considerable wealth, she was accompanied from Dublin by a party of children. This she did under the auspices of a group of proselytising nationalist women, Inghinidhe na hÉireann ('Daughters of Erin'). The trip was to treat the forty children who had the best attendance and application at the group's classes. These women, who were mainly

1 *Leinster Express*, 20 Sept. 1873. 2 *Leinster Leader*, 1 July 1893, 26 June 1897, 1 July 1899.

of the leisured upper middle class, had come together in 1900 as a result of opposition to a visit to Ireland by Queen Victoria.[3] After marriage to and quick separation from John MacBride and a long residence in Paris, she reappeared occasionally at Bodenstown rallies in the 1920s and 1930s.

Expectation of an increasing role for women at Bodenstown when the custom of pilgrimages was being revived in 1911 is evident in the advance notice published in *Irish Freedom* of the pilgrimage arranged for 8 July. It was addressed to 'men and women'.[4] The famous 1913 pilgrimage drew 'a large number of ladies' who 'marched' to Bodenstown churchyard, no doubt the women of Inghinidhe na hÉireann who placed a wreath on Tone's grave.[5] In the procession in June 1914 was a section referred to as 'women and girls, 200 strong'.[6] The women were most likely members of Cumann na mBan. This militantly nationalist association, formed two months before, soon incorporated the Inghinidhe na hÉireann and became, in effect, an auxiliary of the Irish Volunteers.[7] The girls may have been members of the Irish National Guards ('Sluagh Wolfe Tone'), a nationalist youth group formed in 1912, open — remarkably for the epoch — to both boys and girls (aged 14 to 16) and recalled by one member, John Kenny, as 'an off-shoot of Fianna Éireann' (nationalist Boy Scouts); Kenny was able to name thirteen of the girls, and in a later recollection (1966) remembered at least eight girls in the Irish National Guards as having joined Cumann na mBan and been active during the war of Irish independence.[8] Another member, one F. Taylor, recalled in some detail nearly sixty years later how the girls on the day of a pilgrimage (in 1912?) made the journey to Bodenstown and back by train, although the boys had the previous day 'marched to Bodenstown pulling a handcart with rations and gear to the music of the pipers and buglers', camping overnight at Kill before the ceremony, an adventure denied to the girls.[9] The Irish National Guard is mentioned in the *Irish Independent*'s account of the 1914 pilgrimage as parading 80 strong. In 1915, Cumann na mBan was identified by name in a report of the parade from Sallins and of Clarke's 'pep talk' to the gathered pilgrims.[10] Females were conspicuous in the small group — 'mostly women and young girls and boys, with perhaps a dozen men' — who paid a furtive visit to Tone's grave on 25 June 1916, shortly after the suppression of the Easter rising. In 1917, for the first time, a speech was made by a woman, Countess Markievicz. One of her female companions, Kathleen Lynn, a physician, was to take part in at least four future pilgrimages.[11] In 1918, there was a report of some Cumann na mBan women reaching the churchyard from Dublin 'on foot' and, though there was 'no

3 *Freeman's Jn.*, 22 June 1901; *Ir. Daily Indep.*, 24 June 1901; Ann Matthews, *Renegades: Irish Republican women, 1900–1922* (Cork, 2010), pp 28–30, 56–8. 4 *Irish Freedom*, July 1911. 5 *Ir. Indep.*, 23 June 1913. 6 *Freeman's Jn.*, 22 June 1914. 7 Margaret Ward, *Unmanageable revolutionaries: women and Irish nationalism* (London, 1983), pp 88–93. 8 John Kenny, 6 Nov. 1957 (B.M.H., W.S. 1693, pp 1–2; Jack K. (evidently Kenny) to editor, n.d. (*Evening Herald*, 21 Apr. 1966). 9 F. Taylor to editor, n.d. (*Sunday Press*, 22 Aug. 1971). 10 *Leinster Leader*, 26 June 1915. 11 *Kildare Observer*, 30 June 1917; *Ir. Indep.*, 23 June 1924, 22 June 1925, 21 June 1926. Her pilgrimage in 1920 is in 'The diary of Dr. Kathleen Lynn, 1919–1921', ed. Margaret Ó hÓgartaigh, in *Irish Sword*, xxvii, no. 110 (winter 2010), pp 443–522 at p. 479.

regularly organised procession', large bodies of women and men, alike, 'marched in formation to Bodenstown from centres ten miles away, carrying Sinn Féin flags, banners and other emblems'.[12] In 1919 and 1920 there was mention of 'Clann na Gaedheal Girl Scouts placing a wreath on the grave; in 1920, a larger affair, it was reported that these Girl Scouts, together with Fianna Éireann (their male counterpart) and Cumann na mBan, all three groups in uniform, made 'a remarkable display'.[13] In 1920 wreaths were placed too by Countess Markievicz and Áine Ceannt (widow of the executed Éamonn Ceannt); Margaret Pearse (mother of the executed Pearse brothers) circulated in the crowd.[14] As has been noted above, but for the brief appearance of five members of Cumann na mBan in 1921 on the orders of Michael Collins, and of another group of women (mainly?) thirteen days later, there would have been no 'Bodenstown' in that year.

In the tense atmosphere of June 1922 five women, all well known in nationalist circles, three of them close relatives of men executed in 1916, joined the irreconcilable anti-Treatyites of the Dublin brigade of the I.R.A. led by Rory O'Connor in going to Bodenstown on a Tuesday afternoon a few days before the demonstration organised by the Wolfe Tone Memorial Committee. A year later, the intervening civil war almost over, Mary MacSwiney, whose brother died on hunger strike in the war of independence, addressed with passion a largely female Republican crowd at Tone's grave. As in 1921, women were able to be proxies for men in hiding or in prison. A contingent of Cumann na mBan was present at almost every Republican pilgrimage from 1922 until 1938 and from 1942 until the late 1970s. The contingent that marched in formation with Sinn Féin and Fianna Éireann contingents in 1924 was conspicuous for its members wearing, unlike the men, military-style uniforms. But sometimes women were considered by the organisers to be no more than helpers, as in 1925 when four members of Cumann na mBan were delegated to distribute pro-Republican leaflets to Irish Free State troops on duty at the official pilgrimage earlier on the day of the Republican pilgrimage; at the latter a group of Cumann na mBan women were in charge of catering at the request of the organisers.[15] Their quasi-military role should still be taken seriously. There is a description in the *Irish Press* of the contingents of women and girls taking part in the I.R.A. parade from Sallins on the third Sunday of June 1933:

> The procession itself composed mainly of contingents of the I.R.A. and Cumann na mBan was about a mile long ... Into the cemetery marched, file after file, the men in ordinary clothes, the Cumann na mBan in their green uniforms with the new brown beret which has replaced the slouched hat. The young girls, some of them five and six years of age, of Cumann na gCailíní, came in new uniforms too — saffron and purple for Leinster, green for Munster, and Ulster with a banner bearing the Red Hand ... The girls of the

12 *Freeman's Jn.*, 24 June 1918.   13 *Ir. Indep.*, 23 June 1919, 21 June 1920.   14 *Freeman's Jn.*, 21 June 1920.   15 Matthews, *Dissidents*, pp 148–9, 211–12.

Clann na Gaedheal wore their green and gold. When the whole procession had gathered the scene was full of colour ... Eighty men and women marched at the rear of the procession behind a banner bearing the inscription: 'Communist Party of Ireland, Dublin Local.'[16]

The presence of women of Cumann na mBan would have been necessary if only for the safety of small children. It can be imagined that many of the women setting off from home to join a pilgrimage to Bodenstown were, if not travelling in a Cumann na mBan or local contingent, accompanied by their menfolk and that in some cases their children were with them too. Some of the girls in Cumann na gCailíní were perhaps soon to graduate into Clann na Gaedheal, known now also as the Republican Girl Scouts. In the reports examined, the Girl Scouts (started in 1910) were perhaps at Bodenstown in 1914 and certainly were there in 1919; they are last mentioned in 1962 and may have merged with Cumann na mBan.[17] The Cailíní were started by Cumann na mBan in 1930 (or perhaps earlier) and were to be aged (according to their formal constitution) from 8 to 16; they flourished greatly for the first few years, and are mentioned in reports from Bodenstown as late as 1971.[18] The two girls' groups provided social bonding and ideological formation for eventual membership of the women's organisation.[19] The annual outing to the Kildare countryside was an opportunity. In 1934 a police superintendent estimated that as many as 1,500 women and girls marched in uniform.[20] Cumann na mBan, which was after 1922 tied to the I.R.A., was not the only women's organisation to march at Bodenstown. Another was Mná na Poblachta, women led by Mary MacSwiney, who broke away from Cumann na mBan in 1934. Mná na Poblachta marched behind the I.R.A. in that and the following year.[21] Naturally they went on the pilgrimage organised by Sinn Féin on 9 August 1936 and addressed by Miss MacSwiney herself.[22] They marched again at the I.R.A.-organised pilgrimage the following year and for the last time in 1938 until reappearing in 1948.[23] It must be significant that in 1931 and later years women taking part in Republican parades were in uniform whilst the men were not. The Cumann na mBan uniform was described as 'grey green skirt, grey green military pattern tunic coat, brown beret, brown shoes and stockings'; officers wore a Sam Browne belt and all ranks gloves when on parade.[24] Obviously this added to the military air of Republican pilgrimages. The implication is that women in paramilitary uniform, unlike the men in the I.R.A., could be tolerated by the authorities. Women were useful auxiliaries who could, when the men

---

16 *Ir. Press*, 19 June 1933.   **17** *Ir. Indep.*, 23 June 1919; *United Irishman*, July 1962; Matthews, *Renegades*, p. 74. Clann na Gaedheal is sometimes spelt Clan na Gael. It should not be confused with Clan na Gael the American Fenian body led by Devoy.   **18** *Ir. Times*, 14 June 1971; Matthews, *Dissidents*, pp 202, 247, 254, 297–8.   **19** There are mentions of these Republican women's organisations in an elucidating memoir by a veteran in Trevor Ó Clochartaigh, 'Marion Steenson: laoch imeasc na mban' in *An Phoblacht*, 13 Mar. 2014.   **20** Hanley, *I.R.A.*, pp 98, 241. **21** *Ir. Press*, 18 June 1934, 24 June 1935.   **22** *Ir. Times*, 10 Aug. 1936.   **23** *Ir. Indep.*, 21 June 1937, 20 June 1938, 21 June 1948.   **24** Hanley, *I.R.A.*, p. 101. The quoted matter is from police files.

who organised pilgrimages were put under restriction by the authorities, still be relied upon to turn out for Bodenstown.

Women identified by name are quite common in reports of Bodenstown pilgrimages after 1916. The earliest instance of a woman addressing the crowd was Countess Markievicz in 1917. By the mid-1920s, however, they are being mentioned usually as companions or figureheads or celebrities and hardly ever as orators. Those women who appeared as guests of the Cumann na nGaedheal government at the defence forces' pilgrimages in the 1920s and at those of the Fianna Fáil party in the 1930s had roles little more than honorific. In some cases they were regarded as representatives of the dead giving approval to the proceedings, as has been illustrated above in chapter five; in other cases they accompanied their high-profile husbands or brothers and in many cases were identified conventionally only as 'Mrs' or 'Miss'. The earliest was in 1923, when W. T. Cosgrave's sister and the wives of Richard Mulcahy and Hugh Kennedy (minister for defence and attorney-general respectively) were present on the platform. A different case on the same occasion, apparently unaccompanied, was 'Senator Mrs Wyse-Power'.[25] This was Jennie Wyse-Power (née O'Toole) who had a distinguished political career dating back to the early 1880s.[26] Another illustrative case was in 1935 when at the Fianna Fáil pilgrimage Frank Aiken was accompanied by his wife while the Pearse brothers' sister Margaret presided.[27] Maud Aiken's name is not given, she had married Frank fifteen months before. Margaret Pearse, a progressive woman with informed ideas on education elected to Dáil Éireann in 1933 when aged 54, was chairman of the organising committee. Kathleen Clarke, widow of Thomas Clarke, a senator since 1928 and an independent-minded member of Fianna Fáil, laid the party's wreath at the I.R.A. pilgrimage in 1932. But De Valera's wife, Sinéad, never accompanied him on any of his thirty or so pilgrimages to Bodenstown. Even if Margaret Pearse, Kathleen Clarke and other female members of the 'republican nobility' were to be seen at Republican or Fianna Fáil pilgrimages until long after 1916, no such women were seen among Cumann na nGaedheal pilgrims in the 1920s. One woman, Mary MacSwiney, twice made a speech at Bodenstown: in 1923 before a largely female crowd and at the defiant Sinn Féin pilgrimage in 1936 after the prohibition of the I.R.A.'s. Her oratorical efforts for republicanism were made at times of tension. In 1937 a woman, Margaret Buckley, née Goulding (1879–1962), was elected president of Sinn Féin and remained so until the early 1950s. A member of Cumann na mBan, she was first reported at Bodenstown in 1932; she made a short address at a small Sinn Féin gathering at Tone's grave in 1941; annually from then until 1952 she laid the party's wreath whilst apparently remaining silent.[28]

After Margaret Buckley was succeeded as president of Sinn Féin by Patrick McLogan no woman had a prominent role in the ceremony at the grave for the next

25 *Freeman's Jn.*, 25 June 1925.   26 William Murphy and Lesa Ní Mhunghaile, 'Power, Jennie Wyse (1858–1941)' in *D.I.B.*   27 *Ir. Press*, 17 June 1935.   28 McCarthy, *Cumann na mBan*, pp 222, 225, 227; *Ir. Press*, 18 June 1934; *Ir. Indep.*, 23 June 1941. Margaret Buckley's wreath-laying is mentioned in reports from 1945. There is an article on her by Frances Clarke in *D.I.B.*

twenty years. Not until 1972 did a woman address a large crowd at Bodenstown. This was Mrs Máire Drumm, introduced as acting chairman of the *ard-chomhairle* (central committee) of Sinn Féin — more exactly (though unstated there) of the so-called 'Provisional' Sinn Féin. She was, like Mary MacSwiney in 1923 and 1936, a proxy for a man. As she explained herself, 'it was very unusual to find a woman chairman at Bodenstown. Several things had led to this. Several leaders who should have been in charge were now behind bars.'[29] She said nothing of particular concern to women in general.[30]

In 1976, probably for the first time, there was a speech at Tone's grave by a woman whose chief concern was for women. At the 'Official' Sinn Féin pilgrimage on 20 June the party's general secretary and a campaigning feminist, Máirín de Burca, presiding on the occasion, turned attention to the subject of 'women's rights'. Forthrightly she declared that, despite statements from the Catholic church about mothers working outside the family home being harmful to their children, 'women are on the move, they demand their legal, economic and social rights'.[31] Miss de Burca (b. 1937) was more dedicated than most to changing the status of women in Irish society, having been a founder in 1970, and then an active member, of the Irish Women's Liberation Movement.[32] Her speech at Bodenstown marked, more significantly than any previous appearance by a woman, a feminist presence.

Contingents of Cumann na mBan and associated junior groups were annually to be seen in parades at Bodenstown from 1914 until the mid-1970s. They were acknowledged as auxiliaries of the Irish Volunteers in the early years and of the I.R.A. after 1922. After the split in Sinn Féin and the I.R.A. in 1970 they were seen only at Provisional pilgrimages and were predominantly from Ulster. It appears that women in the Official faction had the option of joining the I.R.A. and girls of joining Fianna Éireann.[33] The belief that women should be restricted to separate, auxiliary military corps was obsolescent. In 1974 women were, for the first time, recruited into the Irish defence forces; none of these, however, were seen at Bodenstown, as the Irish government in that year discontinued the defence forces' annual Bodenstown ceremony. In 1966, Mary Maher, reporting a Bodenstown pilgrimage for the *Irish Times*, reckoned that 'about a fifth of those present were women'.[34] This suggests that not all women parading there were regimented, but that some were walking as individuals.

The first Bodenstown pilgrimages, in the 1870s, and the revived pilgrimages in the 1890s and early 1900s, were at the very least opportunities for women to socialise on outings into the countryside. They became opportunities for political formation and acquisition of the nationalist opinions that in Tone's day had been the preserve of men. Even before the pilgrimages were revived in 1911 there was evident militancy among women of nationalist opinions. The declaration in 1916 of an Irish

29 *Ir. Times*, 21 June 1976.   **30** For Máire Drumm (1919–76), see Diarmaid Ferriter's article on her in *D.I.B.*   **31** *Ir. Times*, 12 June 1972.   **32** Anne Stopper, *Mondays at Gaj's: the story of the Irish Women's Liberation Movement* (Dublin, 2006), esp. pp 21–32.   **33** Hanley & Millar, *Lost revolution*, pp 22, 67.   **34** *Ir. Times*, 20 Jan. 1966.

republic, and the uprising that brought the deaths of the signatories and other Volunteer fighting men, became points of reference in orations no less important than Tone himself. It was to be expected that their womenfolk would be at Bodenstown to commemorate them. In 1916, 1921 and on the anti-Treatyite side in 1923 women appeared at Tone's grave in the absence of men. For the remainder of the 1920s and until the 1970s women generally played minor roles and were conspicuous only as strikingly-attired marchers in the parade from Sallins.

RELIGION

In June 1966, Roy Johnston, a left-wing intellectual — a physicist of Protestant antecedents — and very active member of the Dublin Wolfe Tone Society, a group associated with Sinn Féin, wrote to the party's newspaper, the *United Irishman*, objecting to Catholic prayers — he mentioned in particular the Rosary — being recited at Republican commemorations.[35] Though he did not refer to Bodenstown, he might have done so, as Tone was not a Catholic and yet the reciting of the Rosary was on occasion part of the Bodenstown ritual. Certainly in reports over the years there are mentions of prayers at Tone's grave, the earliest in 1876 when 'those assembled uncovered and offered up a prayer for the departed patriot', and another in 1881, when 'the whole assemblage knelt down and prayed for the happy repose of the dead patriot's soul'.[36] No prayers were reported during the fifteen years of pilgrimages begun in 1891 by the National Club Literary Society. Was there a lull in religious enthusiasm? At the pilgrimage held on 8 July 1911, the year that pilgrimages were revived, the procession from Sallins, on reaching Bodenstown, reformed two abreast and 'filed slowly by the tomb of Tone' while 'prayers were recited in Irish'.[37] The organiser, Clarke, was an agnostic.[38] The few who made their way to Tone's grave in 1916, two months after the rebellion, held a short ceremony consisting of little more than kneeling and reciting prayers.[39] From then on prayers were for many years a regular part of the Bodenstown ritual. At the very large pilgrimage in 1918 'a particularly impressive feature ... was the recital of the Rosary in Irish', a certain Michael O'Sullivan of Dublin 'leading in the prayers, while the vast majority of the gathering on bended knees and with bared heads joined in the responses'.[40] Prayers in Irish are also mentioned in accounts of pilgrimages each years from 1920 to 1923. A recent chronicler of Dublin life during the troubled period of the war of Irish independence has noted 'increasingly conspicuous religiosity' among 'crowds attending public events', particularly the reciting of the Rosary.[41] After the split in 1922, there were regular reports of prayers at Republican pilgrimages. At the graveside in 1924, 'those present knelt and prayers were recited',

35 *United Irishman*, June 1966; Hanley & Millar, *Lost revolution*, p. 57.   36 *Freeman's Jn.*, 14 Aug. 1876, 15 Aug. 1881.   37 *Freeman's Jn.*, 10 July 1911.   38 MacAtasney, *Clarke*, p. 113. 39 *Kildare Observer*, 8 July 1916.   40 *Freeman's Jn.*, 24 June 1918.   41 Pádraig Yeates, *A city in turmoil: Dublin, 1919–1921* (Dublin, 2012), pp 185–6, 234–5, 237, 268–9 and esp. 293.

and in 1926 a decade of the Rosary was recited by Donal O'Donoghue.[42] In 1928 even the speech of George Gilmore (an atheist with a Protestant upbringing) in which he made an 'appeal to the young men present to join the Republican Army' was preceded by prayers.[43] It seems that the custom of saying prayers, by choice or obligation the Rosary, continued throughout the 1930s at Republicans' pilgrimages. A case reported in 1958 was when a Sinn Féin deputy, J. J. Rice, recited a decade of the Rosary.[44] These were reminders, though none was needed, that the Bodenstown pilgrimages were an element in the movement for Catholic empowerment which was the salient feature of Irish politics in the nineteenth and twentieth centuries. There may have been another, profane reason for Republicans' observance of Catholic ritual: to ward off damaging accusations by Catholic bishops of socialism and communism. Another may have been simply personal piety, as in the case of Brian O'Higgins. No instance has been found of prayers (or priests) at any of the official commemorations at Bodenstown which began in 1923, notwithstanding the ostensibly irreproachable character of those present and the official deference to the Catholic church which quickly became routine. The Fianna Fáil party did without collective worship at Tone's grave at their annual pilgrimages despite De Valera's personal piety. On laying a wreath in 1933 he merely 'paused for a few moments in prayer'.[45] He laid a wreath for Fianna Fáil many times between then and the late 1950s and in each case seems to have prayed or meditated silently. But in the fraught situation that existed in 1969 a party member, Ruairí Brugha, 'led a decade of the Rosary'. This drew a retort in a public letter, whether naive or ironical, from Malachy McKenna of Belfast, pointing out the oddness of the Rosary being recited at a Protestant's grave and suggesting a Protestant cleric be invited.[46] The custom of praying at the grave seems to have died out completely in the 1970s commensurately with decline in Catholic practice. Tone, on the evidence of his writings, had no time for prayers. Yet Johnston's letter in 1966 was ill received, especially by Seán Mac Stiofáin and Ruairí Ó Brádaigh.[47]

No Catholic priest is mentioned as being present at a Bodenstown pilgrimage until the early 1930s. An unnamed priest intervened in a fracas when police attempted to make an arrest at the I.R.A. pilgrimage in 1931.[48] Six priests from overseas were named as present at the large I.R.A. pilgrimage in 1932, and also an Irish diocesan priest, Michael Carton of Kill, County Kildare. No doubt the visitors were in Ireland mainly to take part in the Eucharistic Congress in the same month. It is credible that some Republicans were at both events too. Carton's name is almost hidden in a list of names in the report in the *Irish Press*. He was the curate in the Catholic parish in which Bodenstown was situated, known as Kill and Lyons. Could he have been the Kill priest who (according to a local I.R.A. source) in the same year advised young men in his parish to join the I.R.A.?[49] The only other possibility

42 *Leinster Leader*, 28 June 1924, 26 June 1926.   43 *Ir. Indep.*, 18 June 1928.   44 *Ir. Press*, 16 June 1958.   45 *Ir. Press*, 26 June 1933.   46 *Ir. Times*, 23 June 1969, 1 July 1969.   47 Robert W. White, *Ruairí Ó Brádaigh: the life and politics of an Irish revolutionary* (Bloomington, 2006?), pp 131–2; Hanley & Millar, *Lost revolution*, p. 57.   48 *Ir. Times*, 22 June 1931.   49 *Ir. Press*, 20 June

was the parish priest, Michael Byrne.[50] The independent-minded, sometimes recalcitrant diocesan priest, Michael O'Flanagan, took part in the pilgrimage of the very small Sinn Féin party in 1932 and recited a decade of the Rosary; in the next three years he turned up at the I.R.A. commemorations.[51] A Benedictine priest of a similar disposition, John Francis Sweetman, was also present in 1934. He was under an ecclesiastical ban on account of his extreme Republican politics. A pupil of his at the school he had conducted at Gorey, County Wexford, was Seán MacBride.[52] At the first large Fianna Fáil pilgrimage, in 1933, a priest of the diocese of Kildare and Leighlin, Thomas Burbage, was present with other dignitaries; he had joined the I.R.A.'s pilgrimage the previous Sunday; Burbage (1879–1966), a strong and intrepidly outspoken nationalist, acted as a chaplain to the I.R.A. during the war of independence and was a particular clerical friend of De Valera, in whose company he was to reappear at Bodenstown in 1947, 1948 and 1951.[53] In 1935, Byrne attended the military ceremony and a little later was on the platform at the Fianna Fáil commemoration.[54] A local man, the late Seán Meaney, recalled seeing his successor, James O'Brien, parish priest from 1936 until 1943, in the company of De Valera at Bodenstown. The next parish priest of Kill, Edmund Campion, entertained De Valera to lunch after the Fianna Fáil ceremony in 1945, and on at least six later occasions was present with him during the ceremony; he was also there in 1952, when De Valera was away in County Limerick electioneering.[55] Campion, who died in December 1953, was known for his Republican opinions; when visiting schools he was eager to hear children sing 'A nation once again' and would suppose the teacher to be unpopular if their performance was not up to expectations.[56] His successor at Kill, Thomas Hughes, attended the military ceremony in 1954 and probably stayed on for the Fianna Fáil ceremony that followed.[57] Byrne, O'Brien, Campion and Hughes must have been affected by the consideration that as Bodenstown lay within their parish of Kill and Lyons, they might, as parish priests, attend a political event there freely without breach of ecclesiastical discipline. Other priests would have been trespassers and in breach. It seems that no priest, whether from Kill or elsewhere, appeared at Bodenstown again until 1971. In April of that year, for the dedication of the new memorial at Tone's grave, both the parish priest and the curate of Kill were present, together with a Capuchin friar, a Presbyterian minister and a Church of Ireland clergyman.[58] Bodenstown became part of the new Catholic parish of Sallins in 1972. If no Sallins priest appeared at any Bodenstown rally afterwards, it was probably because the events had become too controversial.

1932; Hanley, *I.R.A.*, pp 67, 231. **50** *Irish Catholic Directory*, 1932, p. 226. Carton d. in Feb. 1934; Byrne d. in Nov. 1936 after leaving Kill (ibid., 1935, p. 519; ibid., 1937, p. 526). **51** *Ir. Press*, 28 June 1932, 19 June 1933, 18 June 1934, 24 June 1935. **52** *Ir. Press*, 18 June 1934; Mark Tierney, 'Sweetman, John Francis (1872–1953)' in *D.I.B.* **53** *Ir. Press*, 19, 26 June 1933, 16 June 1947, 28 June 1948, 25 June 1951, 10 Jan. 1966. **54** *Ir. Indep.*, 17 June 1935. **55** *Ir. Press*, 18 June 1945, 17 June 1946, 16 June 1947, 28 June 1948, 27 June 1949, 25 June 1951, 23 June 1952, 22 June 1953. **56** For information on the parish and incumbents, I am indebted to Jim Tancred, Ardclough. **57** *Ir. Indep.*, 21 June 1954. **58** *Leinster Leader*, 1 May 1971.

Why were priests, even local parish priests, so rarely at Bodenstown? One reason may be the oft-stated hostility of Catholic ecclesiastics to the I.R.A. Certainly this is consistent with conventional wisdom. One bishop, Patrick Morrisroe of Achonry, denouncing 'ultra-Nationalists' in an address in the 1930s to students at St Nathy's, his diocesan college at Ballaghadeereen, criticised even Pearse (without naming him) by stating that 'when a man enjoying the reputation of a devout Catholic openly declares to an assembly of political enthusiasts that Bodenstown is holier than the place where Patrick sleeps in Down, there is something wrong with his religious outlook'.[59] But conventional wisdom and a single example of episcopal censure ignore the evidence that even extreme Republicans were pious people and did not entirely lack friends among the Catholic clergy. For example, in 1950, a different kind of pilgrimage, the Irish national pilgrimage to Rome, received fulsome coverage in the *United Irishman*.[60] And when, in 1972, Ó Brádaigh, then chief-of-staff of the I.R.A., was on hunger-strike in Dublin after being convicted of unlawful membership of that organisation, both the Catholic archbishop and the former Catholic archbishop paid him a visit. A predecessor in the archdiocese, William Walsh, famously a nationalist, had in 1898 donated £20 towards erection of the planned memorial to Tone and the United Irishmen, by far the largest individual contribution.[61] These are examples of the 'highly sophisticated form of inter-communication and interaction' between Irish nationalism and religion on which Conor Cruise O'Brien reflected in his autobiography.[62] Another explanation is that some Catholic ecclesiastics objected to Tone himself. Laurence Kieran, recalling the moment in 1887 when he and other clerical students stood at Tone's grave and were moved to pray but were refused permission by their accompanying dean of studies, inferred that the dean's objection was that Tone was a Protestant. Another possible objection was that Tone had committed suicide, for which there was some evidence in the 1826 edition of Tone's *Life*, and which was accepted on other evidence by Madden in the volume of his *United Irishmen* treating of Tone published in 1846.[63] Another objection, more an aggravating circumstance, was Tone's antipathy to Catholic ritual, to Catholic clergy in general and to the papacy in particular, of which similarly there was evidence in the *Life*.[64] Kieran's dean of studies, more perceptive than Mac Stiofáin and Ó Brádaigh, was probably also sounder in his theology. More conclusively, there was an imperative reason for rarity of priests among the pilgrims or on the platform with other dignitaries: diocesan clergy were restricted by their bishops to their own parishes, only the parish priest of Kill and Lyons could attend and, with his permission, his curate too. Significantly, on most of those occasions when an ecclesiastic was to be seen near Tone's grave it was the local parish priest present at a pilgrimage of the Fianna Fáil party, which by the mid

59 *Evening Herald*, 3 Jan. 1935. **60** *United Irishman*, Oct. 1950. **61** 'National Memorial to Theobald Wolfe Tone and the United Irishmen' (N.L.I., Clarke papers, MS 49,355/1/27). **62** Conor Cruise O'Brien, *Memoir: my life and themes* (Dublin, 1998), pp 139–40, 155, 319. **63** *Life*, ii, 526–7, 539–40; Madden, *United Irishmen*, 3rd ser. (1846), i, 151, 156–7. **64** *Life*, i, 164, 173, 176, 197, ii, 68, 359–60, 464, 466.

1930s was less strongly nationalist even if many of its leaders had previously been active in the I.R.A.

The Sunday excursions to Bodenstown were designed for Catholics. No self-respecting Protestant would have wanted to be seen at a political meeting on the Sabbath. Arranging trains to leave Dublin until after the earlier masses allowed the many pilgrims resident in the city or its suburbs to complete their religious duties before setting out. Locals would obviously have had no difficulty in going to their usual places of worship. When in 1902 the Celtic Literary Society at Tullamore were arranging a train for groups of 'nationalists from the Midlands' to join the pilgrimage, the earliest departure time was fixed for 10.30 a.m. up-line at Athlone (no doubt after early masses), the train to stop at Tullamore and all other intermediate stations and to arrive at Sallins at about 1 p.m.[65] An indication of how the logistics of participation in Bodenstown pilgrimages from very distant parts of Ireland could allow attendance at Sunday mass is to be found in an advertisement in June 1959 of a special train to start at 7.45 a.m. from Listowel, County Kerry; it would call at Tralee and stop at Killarney to allow 'ample time' for its pilgrim-passengers to attend mass; it would eventually leave them at Sallins at 1.40 p.m. and collect them at 7.10 p.m.[66] One can imagine that pilgrims travelling long-distance on special trains and buses would have to be allowed time for mass attendance. The need to facilitate attendance at mass on Sunday mornings is a reminder that devotees of Theobald Wolfe Tone had not one but two devotional exercises to do on a Sunday close to 20 June.

LABOUR

When in 1899 an I.R.B. man, Maurice Moynihan, addressed a lively crowd at Bodenstown presided over by another I.R.B. man, P. N. Fitzgerald, the proceedings were vociferously interrupted by James Connolly, editor of the *Workers' Republic* and an energetic socialist activist, prompted by a favourable allusion by Moynihan to another I.R.B. man, Fred Allan. Once the fracas was over, Moynihan resumed his advocacy of the single-minded Fenian approach to Irish independence, which avoided association with mere reformist bodies. Obviously alluding to Connolly, as well as to the agrarian agitation that remained a political factor in rural Ireland, he declared that 'he did not wish to decry any existing organisation in connection with land or labour, but they only promoted class interest, they did not voice the nationalist sentiment, they did not assert the unalienable right of Irishmen to independence'.[67] This received no contradiction from within the crowd, much of it from Dublin. Significantly too, Connolly's objection to Allan (himself a trade-union official at that time) was not on a labour issue but that he had three weeks before drunk 'the health of the Queen'. This little episode illustrates a paradox of the

---

65 *Leinster Express*, 7, 14 June 1902.   66 *Kerryman*, 13 June 1959.   67 *Leinster Leader*, 1 July 1899.

Bodenstown pilgrimages: whereas the participants were working men the content of the orations and the responses of the audiences lacked concern for the bread-and-butter matters that elsewhere were the staple of speeches by trade-unionists and labour advocates and politicians. It is ironical that the only words known to have been spoken publicly at Bodenstown by Connolly, much celebrated as the pre-eminent Irish socialist, were about a royal toast.

Connolly was to appear again at Bodenstown in 1915 at the head of a contingent of the Irish Citizen Army, a body formed in the autumn of 1913 to give muscular or martial support to members of the Irish Transport Union 'locked out' by their employers. His allusion afterwards, in the *Workers' Republic*, to the 'drunkenness and gambling which once marked Wolfe Tone's day in Bodenstown' bears the interpretation that he had been there on earlier occasions.[68] As shown by O'Casey in his history of the Citizen Army, which he perceived as having been an essentially 'labour' organisation, its participation in the Bodenstown pilgrimage of June 1914 was what brought about its alliance with the Irish Volunteers and so with the I.R.B., an alliance that accounts for its participation in the Easter rising two years later. Its militaristic character made it acceptable to the Irish Volunteers. Contingents of both marched from Sallins in 1914, 1915, in 1917 (a year after the rising), probably in 1918 (when a trade unionist was the orator), but perhaps not again — they are not mentioned in reports — until 1922. Its sensational appearance at the Dublin anti-Treatyites' pilgrimage on 20 June in that year is evidence that it was still vigorous: 'as vehicles approached', reported the *Dublin Evening Mail*, 'there was a shout of "Hands up", and half a dozen revolvers were presented menacingly by young men wearing the large slouch hats and dark green uniform of the Irish Citizen Army'; nearly all the marching men were armed, only those of the Citizen Army were in uniform.[69]

Although Liam Mellows, the orator on that occasion in 1922, surmised correctly 'that they did not assemble that day to sing the swan-song of Irish republicanism', the event did prove to be the swan-song of the Irish Citizen Army. It was already divided over the Anglo-Irish treaty, some members were pro-Treaty, some had drifted away, it was the anti-Treaty remnant, probably still a majority, who joined Rory O'Connor and became absorbed into the I.R.A.[70] After 1922 what remained of the Citizen Army was largely out of the public eye, much more a Dublin social club than a revolutionary organisation. Significantly it is not mentioned again in any report of Bodenstown until 1934. It was there and then that it breathed its last. A contingent, was present 'under the command' of Séamus McGowan, who was attempting, ineffectually, a revival. The legendary story of its participation with the I.R.A. in that year has been recounted above and elsewhere. Its action in going to the aid of men of the Irish Republican Congress under attack at Sallins was probably its last in public. It refused to participate in 1935 on the ground, it argued, that the I.R.A. was neglecting social injustice. By 1936 one of its best-known members,

68 Matthews, *Irish Citizen Army*, pp 59–60. **69** *Dublin Evening Mail*, 21 June 1922. **70** Matthews, *Irish Citizen Army*, pp 59–60.

Roddy Connolly (son of James Connolly), was in the Labour Party persuading it to adopt as an aim a 'workers' republic'.[71] The last mention of it found in a report of a Bodenstown pilgrimage is in 1970 when Laurence McLoughlin, 'a veteran of the Citizen Army', laid the wreath at the so-called 'Official' Sinn Féin ceremony.[72] Connolly was to appear at Bodenstown in April 1971 for the dedication of a new Tone memorial, by which time he was his party's chairman and politically in the centre.[73] The Irish Citizen Army had its origins in the trade-union movement, not in the Fenian movement. After 1922 it was, arguably, an anachronism. In the history of Bodenstown it is significant for being the only large solidly labour organisation to have taken part in an annual commemoration.

The Irish Labour Party never took part in a Bodenstown pilgrimage, nor did any trade union. Both the Labour Party and the Irish Trade Union Congress (a combined organisation from 1912 until 1930), as well as the main Irish trade unions, always distanced themselves from Republican politics, whilst Republicans maintained a somewhat patronising, even disdainful, attitude towards organised labour even as late as the 1960s.[74] The Labour Party and the Irish Trade Union Congress adhered to a custom of keeping apart from advanced nationalist and paramilitary bodies, principally the I.R.B., the Irish Volunteers, the Irish Citizen Army and the I.R.A. In its early years, in the words of Tony Hepburn in his revision and rewriting of Erhard Rumpf's *Nationalismus und Sozialismus in Irland* (1959), the party, 'mindful that its only industrial base was in Protestant Ulster' — hostile to Irish nationalism, 'stood aloof from the synthesis which Connolly was forging between the I.T.G.W.U. and nationalism, and at its 1916 congress passed a neutral resolution on the subject of the recent Dublin rising'.[75] (The I.T.G.W.U., the Irish Transport and General Workers' Union, was the largest of the 'general' unions.) Perhaps another reason for the absence of Labour from the Bodenstown pilgrimages from when the party was formed in 1912 was that Labour eschewed militarism. In later decades some in Labour may have found it repulsive that some orators had been convicted of crimes of a subversive or terrorist kind, even of murder, for example Michael Conway (an orator in 1938) and Tomás Mac Curtáin (1948). There is evidence that two well-known orators, Frank Aiken (1932–6) and Seán MacBride (1935 and 1944), both in high state office later in life, had parts in atrocities or politically motivated murders.[76] Beyond doubt participants in so-called 'Republican' pilgrimages were generally perceived as associates or admirers of the I.R.A., even if not as active members. The I.R.A. was an unlawful and violent organisation. It may

71 *Ir. Times*, 18 June 1934; Brian Hanley, 'The Irish Citizen Army after 1916' in *Saothar*, xxviii (2003), pp 37–47.   72 *Ir. Press*, 22 June 1970.   73 L. W. White, 'Connolly, Roderic James (1901–80)' in *D.I.B.*   74 Henry Patterson, *The politics of illusion: a political history of the I.R.A.* (2nd ed., London, 1997), p. 114; Brian Hanley, 'The I.R.A. and trade unionism, 1911–72' in Francis Devine et al. (eds), *Essays in Irish labour history: Festschrift for Elizabeth and John W. Boyle* (Dublin, 2008), esp. pp 159–60.   75 E. Rumpf and A. C. Hepburn, *Nationalism and socialism in twentieth-century Ireland* (Liverpool, 1977), p. 13.   76 For Aiken, MacBride and politically-motivated murders, see Bew, *Politics of enmity*, pp 436, 476. Conor Cruise O'Brien, however, found Aiken in the 1950s to be 'profoundly ecumenical by disposition, bordering on pacifism' (Cruise

be for such reasons as these that the Bodenstown pilgrimages were not events in which the Labour Party could comfortably participate. Nonetheless, the essence of the matter was that the 'primary concern' of the Labour Party was 'the social and economic conditions of the ordinary people';[77] it was not the constitutional status of independent Ireland, even if the party did aspire eventually to 'a workers' republic'; Labour had nothing to gain from Bodenstown, bread-and-butter issues were hardly ever mentioned by the graveside orators.

This is the essential story, but not the full story. As early as 1874, at the pilgrimage to mark the placing of a railing around the grave, two of the four Dublin bands present were Dublin trades bands: the coopers' and the bakers'; the reporter of the *Nation* described how 'the fine brass band of the coopers proceeded in a drag drawn by four horses and displaying their trade banner'.[78] There was in 1893 mention in the *Irish Daily Independent* of the presence of the president of the Tramwaymen's Union, E. F. Quinn.[79] There were in 1895 mentions in the *Evening Herald* of 'the United Labourers' brass and reed band' and of the 'Naas Labour Union brass and drum band'.[80] At the centenary pilgrimage in 1898 it was the secretary of Dublin Trades Council, John Simmons, who moved the vote of thanks to the main orator, but he was probably acting, as in 1897, as a member of the '98 Centenary Committee.[81] There was in 1903 a brief mention in the *Freeman's Journal* of the presence at Bodenstown of 'representatives of trades bodies' and the names of two members of Dublin Trades Council acting as stewards.[82] But any other such mentions are elusive. There were ill-defined 'labour bodies' appearing in the early 1930s. They were, however, as their positions towards the rear of the parade in 1932 suggests,[83] of relatively little importance in either Republican or labour politics. Positioned nearer the front, it can be imagined, was the Workers' Union of Ireland Band when it appeared at Bodenstown in 1930, 1934 and 1935 (and perhaps on other occasions). There is evidence in the bandsmen twice siding with the Republican Congress in a fracas that some had strong political sympathies, but the band seems not to have represented the union formally.

A long-established socialist party that did participate was the Communist Party. It seems to have first appeared in 1932, under the guise of the Revolutionary Workers' Party.[84] Its most prominent leader in Ireland was Sean Murray, one of those who addressed the impromptu protest meeting of Republican Congress pilgrims at Sallins in 1935 after they were discouraged by 'physical force' from joining the I.R.A. men marching to Bodenstown. Murray (1898–1961) studied for three years at the Lenin School in Moscow; on his return to Ireland in 1931 he was full-time organiser of the Revolutionary Workers' Groups formed by the

O'Brien, *Memoir*, p. 165). **77** The words of Andrée Sheehy Skeffington in referring to the Irish Labour Party in the 1930s in her biography of her husband, *Skeff: a life of Owen Sheehy Skeffington, 1909–1970* (Dublin, 1991), p. 76. **78** *Freeman's Jn.*, 23 Mar. 1874; *Nation*, 28 Mar. 1874. **79** *Ir. Daily Indep.*, 26 June 1893. **80** *Evening Herald*, 25 June 1895. **81** *Freeman's Jn.*, 21 June 1897, 20 June 1898. **82** *Freeman's Jn.*, 22 June 1903. **83** *Ir. Indep.*, 16, 20 June 1932. **84** *Ir. Indep.*, 16, 20 June 1932.

Comintern; in 1933 they were transformed, with Murray as general secretary, into the Communist Party of Ireland; in the same year Dublin members joined the Republican procession. In the mid-1930s the party was closely associated with the Republican Congress; a month after speaking at Sallins, Murray was in Moscow again for the Comintern's seventh congress.[85] The Communist Party was dissolved south of the border in 1941 until revived there after the Emergency as the Irish Workers' League. On rare occasions it put in an appearance at Bodenstown on days of Republican pilgrimage, as in 1954 when followers sold copies of their newspaper, the *Irish Workers' Voice*, at Sallins, though apparently their daring fell short of doing so nearer to Tone's grave. In 1968, now known as the Irish Workers' Party, it sent a contingent to the Republicans' pilgrimage.[86] In June 1970, after the Republicans split into two rival camps, the well-known Belfast Communist Betty Sinclair was present at the ceremony of the 'Official' faction. She represented however not her party but, perhaps unofficially, the Belfast Trades Council.[87] Earlier that year the Communist parties north and south had united to form the Communist Party of Ireland. Under this name a contingent attended the Official faction's ceremony in 1971; the party organised its own in June 1984, drawing bus-loads of supporters from Dublin, Belfast and Cork to mark the fiftieth anniversary of the legendary Republican pilgrimage of 1934, in which it had participated (as in 1933 and 1935).[88] The Communist Party of Ireland was always small compared with nationalist parties and with the Labour party; it was important only for its close relations with Soviet Russia.

An important distinction has to be drawn between labour and trade-union bodies on one hand and individuals active, even prominent, as members of trade unions, on the other. An early case in point is that of P. T. Daly, the orator in 1902; sworn into the I.R.B. in or before 1897, he was secretary of the Wolfe Tone Memorial Committee in 1903, and was prominent as an Irish labour activist for the next forty years, exercising influence as secretary of Dublin Trades Council throughout the 1920s.[89] Another case is that of Cathal O'Shannon, the orator in 1918 and a senior official of the I.T.G.W.U. Peadar O'Donnell (orator in 1931) was for three years a full-time organiser for the same union, and many years later Christy O'Neill, having spoken for the I.R.A. at Bodenstown in 1949, also became one of its officials. Barney Conway (1880?–1965), who has been mentioned above for his part in the brawl at Bodenstown in 1935, was an official of the Workers' Union of Ireland; a Dublin docker, he was in the Citizen Army during the lock-out in 1913 and took part in the Easter rising; in the mid 1930s he was in the Communist Party and a confidant of James Larkin; he was during the 1940s and 1950s a Labour member of the city council.[90] Then there is Michael Fitzpatrick, the chairman at the Republicans'

85 *Ir. Press*, 24 June 1935; L. W. White, 'Murray, Sean' in *D.I.B.*   86 *Ir. Times*, 24 June 1968. 87 *Ir. Times*, 22 June 1970.   88 *Ir. Press*, 21 June 1971; *Ir. Times*, 11 June 1984.   89 *Ir. Daily Indep.*, 23 June 1902, 22 June 1903.   90 Quidnunc, 'Old warrior' in *Ir. Times*, 16 July 1960; 'Funeral: Mr Bernard Conway' in ibid., 6 Jan. 1965; Emmet O'Connor, *James Larkin* (Cork,

commemoration in 1937 who was assistant secretary of the Grocers' Union.[91] Another case is Margaret Buckley, who as vice-president of Sinn Féin was at Bodenstown in 1932 and as president throughout the 1940s. From 1919 until 1957 she was an official of the Irish Women Workers' Union with special responsibility for the semi-autonomous Domestic Workers' Union. Yet when a privileged prisoner in Mountjoy Jail in 1923, she took a supercilious attitude to 'charwomen' and was condescending towards 'poor derelicts' in the women's wing. Other officials of the I.W.W.U. were active in the Labour Party and a political levy was paid.[92]

There are more cases. Michael 'Mick' Price (1896–1944), the secretary of the Wolfe Tone Commemoration Committee who came to public attention when arrested a few hours before the Republicans' ceremony in 1930 and who presided over and spoke at their ceremony in 1932 and 1933, may well have got involved in union affairs after he obtained a clerkship in the Irish Hospitals Commission (created in 1933); he joined the Irish Labour Party in 1935 (not long after ceasing to be director of intelligence in the I.R.A.) and quickly rose among the active Dublin membership.[93] Another defector from the I.R.A. was Michael Mullen, a factory worker interned during the Emergency and later a Labour deputy, who was in 1969, as general secretary of the I.T.G.W.U., one of the seventeen signatories (most with previous I.R.A. associations) to the National Graves Association's appeal for funds to repair (or replace?) the damaged churchyard monument. Luke Duffy (1890–1961), a draper's assistant in his youth and later an official of the Irish Union of Distributive Workers and Clerks, is a rare case of a senior official of the Irish Labour Party being publicly involved in a Bodenstown pilgrimage. The energetic general secretary of the party from 1933 until 1949, Duffy was in May 1942 named as joint secretary (with Seán MacBride) of the committee set up by the National Graves Association to organise a Republican pilgrimage after a lapse of three years. Although he went on the pilgrimage organised for 21 June, his name does not appear in reports of earlier or later pilgrimages. As a strong nationalist, he was untypical of officials of his party.[94] A factor that may explain his role is that the committee was intended to be 'representative of various shades of opinion' and so he would have added to its respectability. Justifiable on the same ground was the appearance in the same year of James Larkin accompanied by other members of his Workers' Union of Ireland.[95] This was a union of mainly unskilled and semi-skilled workers started by Larkin's brother Peter and son James 'junior' in 1923 in a split from the I.T.G.W.U. Larkin was attempting in 1942 to position himself prominently in the Irish Labour Party. He had been at Bodenstown in 1914 as commander of the Irish Citizen Army. After returning to Ireland in 1923 after a long stay in America he was notoriously disruptive, despite which he was admitted to membership of the Labour

2002), p. 97.   **91** Hanley, 'The I.R.A. and trade unionism', pp 161–2.   **92** Margaret Buckley, *The jangle of the keys* (Dublin, 1938), p. 50; Mary Jones, *These obstreperous lassies: a history of the I.W.W.U.* (Dublin, 1988), esp. pp 173, 197, 226, 232.   **93** For Price, see Brian Hanley, 'Price, Michael' in *D.I.B.*   **94** For Duffy, see Angela Murphy, 'Duffy, Luke J.' in *D.I.B.*   **95** *Ir. Press*, 22 June 1942.

Party in December 1941. By the summer of 1942 he was at odds (again) with the dominant influence in the party — that of the I.T.G.W.U. led by his nemesis William 'Bill' O'Brien and of the Irish Trades Union Congress.[96] This conflict and a desire for publicity may have been a reason for Larkin and his followers going to Bodenstown. At the general election held on 23 June 1943 (three days after another appearance by him at Bodenstown) he was elected a Labour member of Dáil Éireann.[97] These peregrinations were unusual.

Only rarely was a speech made at Bodenstown by a 'labourite' or a socialist, whether a member of the Irish Citizen Army, an official in a trade union or an activist in the Labour Party. P. T. Daly in 1902, six months after being appointed to the Dublin Trades Council, spoke only of Tone's career. Cathal O'Shannon, a senior official of the I.T.G.W.U., instead of taking his opportunity in 1918 to raise issues of particular concern to the working class, launched into nationalist rhetoric, imitating Pearse in holding that 'they stood on the holiest ground in Ireland', beseeching the crowd to 'renew their faith in the principles given to them by Wolfe Tone', crediting Tone with 'the whole movement in its modern aspect which had shaken Irishmen within the last few years', asserting that 'there could be no friendship or alliance between England and Ireland until Ireland had her freedom and independence' and asserting further that 'persecutions' and 'internments' could not 'kill the spirit of the Irish people nor the Irish nation'. He finished by repeating the rallying words Clarke had spoken at Tone's grave in 1915: 'the time for oratory has gone'. O'Shannon's oration was preceded by a recital of the Rosary in Irish 'while the vast majority of the gathering on bended knees and with bared heads joined in the responses'.[98]

O'Shannon's deeply nationalistic oration differed in essence very little from earlier and later Bodenstown orations by men without any pretensions to solidarity with the working class. It accords remarkably with what Roy Foster has distilled from a retrospective source concerning the Irish Citizen Army:

> James Connolly's Citizen Army could have made the case that they were enslaved in terms of economic power — but very few actually articulated this. It is extremely striking how seldom a sense of economic or class grievance comes through the recollections recorded by the Bureau of Military History. Far more frequent are the traditional nostrums of Catholicism, historical victimhood, glorification of past struggles and resentment of English dominance.[99]

Remarkably too, only two orators so much as mentioned Connolly before the late 1960s. The first was De Valera in 1925, who, however, merely strung out the names 'Clarke, Pearse, Connolly, Cathal Brugha and Liam Mellows' as martyrs of 1916.[100]

96 Emmet O'Connor, *James Larkin* (Cork, 2002), pp 104–10; idem, 'Larkin, James (1874–1947)' in *D.I.B.*   97 *Ir. Press*, 21 June 1943; *Ir. Indep.*, 21 June 1943; Walker, *Ir. parlty election results, 1918–92*, pp 154, 156.   98 *Freeman's Jn.*, 24 June 1918.   99 Foster, *Vivid faces*, p. 328. 100 *Leinster Leader*, 27 June 1925.

The second was Brian O'Higgins, who in 1945 quoted Tone, Pearse and Connolly on the need for unity to achieve 'Tone's purpose'.[101] Neither referred to Connolly's trade-union career or his socialist writings.

After O'Shannon in 1918 the next instance of a socialist being given his say at Bodenstown was Peadar O'Donnell in 1931. Despite his three years of service as a full-time organiser for the I.T.G.W.U. between 1918 until 1921, the brief reports of his speech contain nothing of a specifically socialist nature other than vesting 'all power in a free republic in the Irish working class and working farmers'.[102] His characterisation of the masses as 'the slaves of the exploiting interests of our imperial masters' — rather than 'of our *capitalist* masters' — belonged to the rhetoric of the anti-Treatyite nationalists who were his audience. In a reminiscence of the period O'Donnell wrote over thirty years later it is manifest that his main sympathies in the 1920s and early 1930s were for the small farmers — the new landowning class — and not for the labourers; he recalls delivering the oration at Bodenstown in 1931 in place of Russell, but gives no detail.[103] Presented with a grand opportunity during a time of severe economic depression to argue labour questions before a large audience and attentive newspaper reporters, he gave a nationalist rant.

Other orators seem also to have been silent on labour matters despite the general militancy of the early 1930s. What is surprising is that Fianna Fáil orators were silent. Their party stole the Labour party's clothes and made, after obtaining political power in 1932, numerous social and economic changes that benefited appreciably the Dublin working class and was arguably a means of attaching that class to the party.[104] Even in 1935 and 1936, when challenged on the streets by irreconcilable Republicans, the opportunity was not taken to publicise these benefits in the Bodenstown speeches of Lemass and Derrig. The silence of the orators was total until the mid 1960s.

Beginning with Séamus Costello in 1966, four men holding high positions in the I.R.A. or Sinn Féin or both addressed the crowd. Costello urged listeners to organise militant trade-union groups and to spread a Republican policy based on compulsory acquisition of land owned by absentees and acquisition of the nation's key industries, in brief 'ownership by the people'.[105] In the following year Cathal Goulding, though less explicit, denounced as economically harmful both the recent Anglo-Irish free-trade agreement and the proposed Irish membership of the European Common Market.[106] Seán Garland declared unambiguously in 1968: 'the fight for freedom is a class struggle. It cannot be divorced from the fight for better housing or working conditions ... Our objective is, and must be, a socialist republic in which the producers of wealth can exercise complete control over the means of

101 *Ir. Indep.*, 28 June 1945. 102 *Ir. Indep.*, 22 June 1931; *An Phoblacht*, 27 June 1931. 103 Peadar O'Donnell, *There will be another day* (Dublin, 1963), esp. pp 1, 124–6. 104 Rumpf & Hepburn, *Nationalism & socialism*, pp 119–21, 125–8; Richard Dunphy, *The making of Fianna Fáil power in Ireland, 1923–1948* (Oxford, 1995), pp 159–60, 164. 105 *Ir. Times*, 20 June 1966. 106 *Ir. Times*, 19 June 1967.

production, distribution and exchange. This is our definition of Irish republicanism in 1968.'[107] This appears to have been the first time socialism was commended unambiguously in a Bodenstown oration. It was appropriate for 1968. From then on almost every orator felt obliged to allude to the interests of the working class even if not actually to embrace socialism wholeheartedly. In the following year Tomás Mac Giolla, by now a convert to socialism, insisted however, 'we do not regard socialism as a fashionable cloak to be worn or discarded'; Irish republicans should recognise that 'the Irish socialist tradition' was characteristically separatist; he dismissed socialists in the Irish Labour Party and, with no less vehemence, socialists in the Northern Ireland Labour Party, as 'the sham followers of Connolly' on the ground that they had no share in this tradition.[108] The four were untypical socialists, none was a member of a labour party, none seems to have been active in a trade union. Their aloofness from the mainstreams of the labour movement, made plain at Bodenstown by Mac Giolla, is another indication of the separateness of republicanism and socialism despite their common social base.

During the 1970s, at one time or another, orators of all three Republican factions or parties endorsed socialism or at least raised labour issues. In 1971, Malachy McGurran, speaking at the pilgrimage of the Official faction of what in the 1960s was referred to as the 'Republican movement', asserted that 'the main task today was to unite the working classes'.[109] In 1972, another Official, Seán Garland, delivered what the *Irish Times*'s reporter described as 'one of the most revolution-conscious speeches delivered at Bodenstown for many years'; Garland called for an alliance of the Left, which would embrace 'those who were now struggling within the Labour Party' and invited 'those genuine representatives of the working class' to form 'the only possible alliance of the Left with the Republican movement'.[110] Undoubtedly it was the most 'revolution-conscious' of all. Significantly too, in 1973 the orator at the Provisionals' pilgrimage, Martin McGuinness, declared that the Irish future was 'a democratic, socialist republic'. One week later, not to be outdone and wanting to appeal widely, Mac Giolla, welcomed to Bodenstown members of the Irish Labour Party and representatives of the French Communist Party, whose country, he said, 'symbolised the internationalism of Tone and the United Irishmen'.[111] At Bodenstown in 1975, Costello, now the leader of a new Republican faction, the Irish Republican Socialist Party — appropriately named as if to match the changed ethos of Bodenstown — very ambitiously looked for 'the support of the Loyalist working class' which he thought 'essential for a socialist republic'.[112] In 1977, at the Provisionals' pilgrimage, Jimmy Drumm urged 'the forging of strong links between the Republican movement and the workers of Ireland and radical trade unionists'.[113] A year later another Provisional, Johnny Johnson, called on listeners 'to make a stand on economic issues and the everyday struggles of the working people'.[114] Also in 1978, the message of an Official, Séamus Lynch, was that

107 *Ir. Times*, 24 June 1968. See also *United Irishman*, July 1968.   108 *United Irishman*, July 1969.
109 *Ir. Indep.*, 21 June 1971.   110 *Ir. Times*, 19 June 1972.   111 *Ir. Times*, 11, 18 June 1973.
112 *Ir. Times*, 9 June 1975.   113 *Ir. Times*, 13 June 1977.   114 *Ir. Press*, 12 June 1978.

'lasting peace cannot be built without hard, economic solutions to the crucial problems of unemployment, poverty and the other factors which have institutionalised violence in Northern Ireland'.[115] All this was reminiscent of Bodenstown orations of the later 1960s. But the recurring, dominant theme (except for Garland's) was the Ulster question. It was still nationalism, not socialism, that largely inspired Bodenstown orators and pilgrims.

The working-class men and women who went to Bodenstown every June, ostensibly at least to pay tribute to Theobald Wolfe Tone, did so as nationalists, not as socialists. The explanation of why so many of that class in Ireland were nationalists at all may well lie in the campaign for Irish self-government, and after 1922, for the removal of the remaining vestiges of British rule being represented and so perceived (as so often in nationalist movements) as a contest between haves and have-nots. This would explain the strikes organised by trades-unions (in the three southern provinces) during the war of independence to prevent the movement of armed troops and munitions, to force the release of Sinn Féin and I.R.A. men held in prison and generally to disrupt civil authority.[116] Although such strikes did not occur in similar situations after 1922, working-class nationalist fervour generated by the experience persisted amongst rank-and-file even if not amongst all the labour and trade-union leadership, no doubt more aware of the wider interests of their movement. Labour was *de facto* pro-Treaty. Arthur Mitchell posits that the 'great majority' of those who might 'have been attracted to socialism concluded that trade-union membership was adequate to protect their economic interests, while their political interests were bound up in Irish nationalism ... Why have just one affiliation when you can have two?'[117] A few years before his death in 1986 Peadar O'Donnell tried to explain why he and 'the masses in Dublin' were more committed to nationalism than to socialism — it was that 'Labour had deserted the Republic' at the time of Irish independence being achieved. He acknowledged that trades-union leaders had been 'afraid to identify themselves with independence in case it would affect the prospects of trade-unionism in the north'.[118] He might have probed deeper. Nationalism was part of the culture of the Catholic population, who formed a large majority of the working class of Dublin and other towns in the southern provinces, if only a minority of the working class in Belfast and other industrial towns in Ulster; it was almost exclusively Catholic, as was made evident at Tone's grave by the Rosary being recited as part of the annual ritual.

115 *Ir. Times*, 19 June 1978. **116** Arthur Mitchell, *Labour in Irish politics, 1890–1930* (Dublin, 1974), pp 104, 119–22. **117** Idem, 'The course of Irish labour history' in *Saothar*, xxii (1997), pp 101–04 at p. 103. **118** Uinseann MacEoin, *Survivors: the story of Ireland's struggle as told through some of her memorable living people recalling events* (Dublin, 1980?), pp 23–4.

Conclusion

THIS STORY OF Bodenstown is a parallel history of Ireland from 1798. It is about the grave of Theobald Wolfe Tone as a 'place of memory', discovered in Bodenstown churchyard thirty-one years after his death, marked by a stone fifteen years later, and eventually turned into a destination of organised pilgrimages by Irish nationalists. Several generations of political pilgrims took part in an annual procession to the grave and then in a ceremony that was oddly political, religious, theatrical and social. One of the remarkable features of the custom was how little it changed in its essentials during the 110 years from when it began in 1873.

That Tone really was buried at Bodenstown is proven almost to certainty despite the lack of contemporary evidence. The evidence that can be found is extensive. It is circumstantial evidence complemented by the evidence of contemporaries passed on to others. Regrettably, owing to the levelling and concreting of the Tone family grave in 1971 it would now be difficult to carry out an archaeological dig to obtain D.N.A. evidence from remains. This might have provided conclusive evidence.

The first 'discovery' of Tone's grave was made public in October 1829 only three years after the arrival in Ireland (no later than the beginning 1827) of copies of Tone's *Life*, his literary remains. The grave was poorly marked: only the name of his grandfather, William Tone, was on a tombstone. The publicity, a few lines in Dublin newspapers, was too slight to attract much attention. The lasting discovery came in 1843, when Thomas Davis, a nationalist with a poetic flair, visited the spot and then immortalised it in a poem and, with his companion at Bodenstown, the newspaper proprietor John Gray, organised the laying of a stone. Coincidentally, an initiative to mark the place of Tone's mortal remains was taken by his widow Matilda in writing to Gray at about the time that Davis and Gray were conceiving the same idea. It was on Matilda Tone's initiative that Tone's literary remains were published in 1826. A stone was laid, probably in the autumn of 1844, by Davis and others of his circle of Young Irelanders. It is from Davis's time as a promoter of Tone that the history of Bodenstown really begins. Yet that history was uneventful during the next seventeen years. Not until the early 1870s, when members of the Dublin Wolfe Tone Band visited the grave to replace the stone, does the history become rich in detail. The bandsmen's outing in 1873 proved to be the first of the series of pilgrimages that have continued, with breaks in the 1880s and 1900s, to the present day.

THE MONUMENTS

Five flat or upright stones (perhaps six) have, at different times, marked the family grave where Tone lies. The earliest was that bearing the name of Tone's grandfather William Tone. It may have been the stone seen by the anonymous visitor in 1829, or that visitor may have seen a later stone of which no other record has been found and which disappeared before Davis and Gray's visit in 1843. That Davis and his associates got a stone erected is put beyond doubt by comparing the wording given by Davis in his letter to John Pigot of 17 April 1844 with that decipherable on the gravestone fragment held since 1941 by the National Museum of Ireland. Frustratingly, the exact date of its being laid has not be ascertained, and if any picture was ever made it has not been found. What is certain is that the stone was broken in two by about 1870 and needed replacing, which in 1873 some Dublin bandsmen and local enthusiasts organised. Months later they erected a protective railing around the new stone. Dilapidation continued with the consequence that less than twenty years later another stone was needed. This replacement, provided by the Kildare Gaelic Athletic Association, lasted half a century before refurbishment was needed. The National Graves' Association, a 'republican' body, did the necessary. Alas! in 1969 both William Tone's stone and the stone erected by the Kildare Gaels were damaged in an explosion, the latter however only superficially. The consequence was a gigantic new structure in the graveyard which resembled much more an arena for party political rallies than a traditional sepulchral monument.

THE PILGRIMAGES

The original purpose of the men of the Dublin Wolfe Tone Band was simply to replace the stone laid on Tone's grave by the Young Irelanders, it was not to begin a custom of annual pilgrimages. The only previous excursion of which particulars are known had taken place in 1861 when a small party of men and women, some of whom had come from America with the body of Terence Bellew McManus for reburial in Dublin, took the opportunity to visit the grave. Not long after the replacement stone was laid in 1873 a rumour spread that it too had been damaged. The result was another descent on Bodenstown by the Dublin bandsmen to join locals who had raised money for the erection of a protective railing. The inauguration was a grand ceremony attended by a large number of people and addressed by a popular nationalist. This event in March 1874 was, as much as the event the previous September, the precedent for the organised visits to Tone's grave which soon came to be known as 'pilgrimages'. The history of the pilgrimages divides chronologically into four distinct periods: the 1870s; from 1891 until 1905; from 1911 to 1921; and from 1922 onwards. Subsequent excursions to Bodenstown until 1881 had political purposes and political statements were made by orators. The absence of pilgrimages for the next nine years has not been adequately explained. Their revival in 1891 can be seen as an emotional response to the Parnellite split by a younger generation of nationalists. Their cessation again in 1905 was due to the weakness of the Wolfe Tone Memorial Committee, no longer willing or able to organise what had become a popular event. The revival in 1911 was due largely to chance, to the coincidence of an official plan for a royal visit and a contest in the I.R.B. between older and younger generations. The split over the Anglo-Irish treaty in 1922, evident at Bodenstown that year, made threefold a few years later, was perpetuated at Bodenstown for almost fifty years until another split produced in 1970 and subsequent years the phenomenon of four rival pilgrimages, adverted to by Tom Dunne in his *Theobald Wolfe Tone, colonial outsider* (1982).

Many of the customary features of the Bodenstown pilgrimages begun in the 1870s remained little changed in the two hundred or so cases until the early 1980s identified in this study. After 1922, when rival pilgrimages began, they persisted in the pilgrimages of the anti-Treatyites, the Republicans. Not all customary features, however, were present in the official commemorations at Bodenstown in the early years of the Irish Free State, which were rather formal military ceremonies with a civilian presence and a ministerial speech. In the 1930s the Fianna Fáil party, those Republicans who took office, attempted by having separate party pilgrimages to challenge those Republicans who foreswore office; the army's ceremonies became even more formal. The pattern of three separate and rather different pilgrimages remained unchanged until the 1970s. While some old customs disappeared, new customs began. Customarily, 'pilgrims', typically from Dublin, arrived by railway or by road and assembled at Sallins; people from other villages in County Kildare made their own way; all proceeded (some, from 1914, marching), flags flying, bands playing, to the grave in the churchyard, where wreaths were laid, prayers said and speeches made, and then the pilgrims would amble back to Sallins. The speeches, 'orations', were by invited speakers of advanced nationalist opinions and usually a reputation for activism, militancy, or, after 1922, for 'physical force'. After 1922 also, government ministers would make speeches of a different nature. Ostensibly the purpose was always to commemorate and honour Tone; the real purpose of the organisers was political. A purpose of many pilgrims was no doubt as much social as respectful and political. The most significant new feature came with growing popularity of long-distance travel, in consequence of which groups arrived at Sallins on trains from places further along the line — from as far in 1903 as Cork and Limerick. In the 1930s groups travelled from towns as distant as Galway and Belfast, this last place becoming the provenance of large contingents in the 1970s.

Great significance must be attached to the factors of place and time. Bodenstown was situated at a suitable distance from Dublin for day trips by rail and road. A particular advantage was the proximity of a railway station in the village of Sallins less than two kilometres distant from Bodenstown churchyard. This allowed not merely rapid access from the metropolis but also the convenience of a meeting point and assembly place near the station for marshalled processions to the grave. The time of the year, mostly August during the 1870s, but from 1891 almost always June on a Sunday close to Tone's birthday, the 20th, allowed visitors to enjoy the most hours of daylight and usually the pleasantest of weather. These two factors made the pilgrimages social occasions, with opportunities for walking along leafy roads, hearing visiting bands, picnicking and other pastimes, which endowed them with a lasting popularity that merely formal commemoration of a national figure would not have ensured. The combination of nationalist politics and a day out in the country resulted in mutual bonding between persons of nationalist tendencies and modest means.

From the time of Davis and Gray's discovery of Tone's grave 45 years after his death Bodenstown was a place of memory and, from the 1860s, an attraction for Irish nationalists. Over the years its visitors, 'pilgrims', were generally of the more 'advanced' type, militant, and increasingly (from 1914) militaristic. The abortive 'rising' in 1916 turned nationalists into republicans; the Anglo-Irish treaty of 1921 split the republicans into two rival parties, the pro-Treaty party becoming the government party, the anti-Treaty or republican party loud and sometimes violent dissidents, some anti-Treatyites becoming reconciled to the new state in 1927 and replacing in 1932 the pro-Treaty party in office, others remaining irreconcilables even into the 1980s. This split resulted in two rival pilgrimages (even on the same day): an official pilgrimage, with Irish defence forces, government ministers, parliamentarians and officials, Cumann na Gaedheal party members and general public together; the anti-Treaty opposition, the Sinn Féin party and their followers separately. Splits among the anti-Treatyites, their military wing (the I.R.A.) becoming dominant and a new, peaceable party (Fianna Fáil) emerging, resulted in three pilgrimages in 1928 and afterwards; Fianna Fáil, once in office, separated their party organisation from the defence forces, whilst usually, conveniently, holding their own commemoration on the same day, the army soon after midday, the party an hour later. After the mid-1930s the pilgrimages became smaller; for the first three years of the Second World War the Republicans were not permitted to go; from 1944 they were resurgent, especially at times of I.R.A. activity in the 1950s; a new revival, socialist in tendency, came in the mid 1960s, a split in 1970, another in 1974, and so until 1983 (with which this study ends) as many as four rival pilgrimages. But after 1973 the defence forces no longer appeared, and in 1980 Fianna Fáil made its last June pilgrimage, in later years going in the autumn. These 'separate annual pilgrimages', commented Tom Dunne, writing in 1982, 'combine elements of Feydeau-like farce with reminders of contemporary tragedy and horror'.[1]

The continuation of the pilgrimages after 1921 was a confounding of the prediction made by D. P. Moran in 1901 that 'Bodenstown will be forgotten when Ireland comes into her own'.[2] One explanation is that the declaration of an Irish republic in 1916 as a warrant for the rebellion in which men heroically lost their lives

---

1 Dunne, *Tone*, p. 14.   2 Patrick Maume, *Long gestation: Irish nationalist life, 1891–1918* (Dublin, 1999), p. 258. The prediction was Moran's, the words quoted were Griffith's.

remained a point of reference during the war for independence that began in 1919 and during the debates on the Anglo-Irish treaty in the early months of 1922; when therefore in June 1922, on the eve of the expected civil war, uncompromising Republicans took initiatives and gathered at Bodenstown in as great a strength as supporters of the treaty, it became imperative for the government of the infant Irish Free State, as soon as the civil war was over, to continue the custom of pilgrimages and to appear in greater strength than its sadly weakened opponents. Challenges to the authorities of independent Ireland by Republican purists never ceased. Recently, Gearóid Ó Tuathaigh has cited Bodenstown as an example of 'contestation' where there are 'competing needs' for the same 'commemorative event'; he perceives this 'contested ownership of the same cultural resource or asset' as a way of the rivals 'establishing their own political pedigree or credentials, of affirming their continuity with and succession from the Wolfe Tone republican separatism of the 1790s'.[3] A simpler explanation of the persistence of the phenomenon is also possible. It was put forward, implicitly or explicitly, by generations of anti-Treatyite orators, it was a continuing, underlying theme of Bodenstown orations — Ireland had not yet come into her own.

The routines and rituals established in the early 'pilgrimages' to Bodenstown and persisting throughout the period justify use of a word ordinarily reserved for excursions with a religious purpose — even though the procession had also, in some years, a theatrical and, later, a military appearance. Dunne's use of the word 'pilgrimage' was amply justified. The commemorations manifested many of the characteristics of a religious pilgrimage. Tim Pat Coogan makes the point that the Sunday after (or before) Tone's birthday 'occupies a position in the Republican calendar analogous to that of Easter in the Christian religion'.[4] It may not be out place here to draw attention to a cultural historian, George Greenia, and a sociologist, Paul Hollander, both interested in the phenomenon of pilgrimages, who have compared religious and secular pilgrimages. Greenia writes of periodic journeys to sites, even citing as one example rallies of motor-cyclists; Hollander writes of desire to venerate symbols of belief found at distant locations, communal rituals on arrival and enhancing illusions of Utopia.[5] Though they do not mention Bodenstown, some of their comparisons implicitly show Bodenstown to resemble a religious pilgrimage more closely, in certain respects, than it resembles a secular pilgrimage. The Bodenstown pilgrimage at its most glorious would begin with an ostentatious procession along a well-trodden route, in prearranged order, the most committed devotees uniformly attired, banners and other symbols held aloft proudly, musical accompaniment, altogether a colourful, enrapturing display;

3 Gearóid Ó Tuathaigh, 'Commemoration, public history and the professional historian: an Irish perspective' in *Estudios Irlandeses*, no. 9 (2014), pp 137–45 at p. 143, published on-line only. 4 Coogan, *I.R.A.* (revd ed., London, 2002), p. 238.   5 George Greenia, 'Pilgrimage and the American myth' in Antón M. Pazos (ed.), *Redefining pilgrimage: new perspectives on historical and contemporary pilgrimages* (Farnham, Surrey, 2014), pp 47–70; Paul Hollander, 'Heaven on Earth: political pilgrimages and the pursuit of meaning and self-transcendence' in ibid., pp 71–86.

eventually there was the sanctuary of the graveyard, the shrine of the railed gravestone; then would begin the respectful walk around the grave, some devotees laying wreaths, contemplating the tragedy of the hero's fall, the mystery of the saint's end, sometimes standing silently (or kneeling?) for prayers, a general feeling of desire to emulate him, perhaps a fanfare; at the end would come a sermon or homily in which the preacher would laud the virtues of the cult figure, draw on a sacred text for dicta and injunctions (uncannily like a Gospel reading), denounce the unfaithful, the heretics and the infidels, and project the hero as a saintly figure always to be imitated. The appointed day in the calendar came to be known as 'Bodenstown Sunday'. But by the time that Dunne was writing, the word 'pilgrimage' was no longer regularly used in reports of the ceremonies; 'pilgrims' had gone out of use in the mid 1930s; 'commemoration' had become the usual word for the event. Allowedly, it was not always feasible or desirable for pilgrimage organisers to include all or even most of the aforementioned features. The commemorations of the Irish defence forces and Fianna Fáil were usually brief, sober affairs after 1937. Yet true-believing Republicans endeavoured to keep up all the old Bodenstown customs.

The Bodenstown 'pilgrimages' became ever more clearly military events. Their revival in 1891 and again in 1911 was the idea of men of the Irish Republican Brotherhood, a body with military aspirations albeit little if any military experience. From 1911 units of the National Boy Scouts, 'Fianna Éireann', a militaristic youth organisation, would march from Dublin to take part in the pilgrimage, sometimes travelling the day before and camping overnight in the vicinity. In 1914 and 1915, the main body of pilgrims consisted of different units of the similarly militaristic Irish Volunteers, the Fianna and ancillary bodies, particularly Cumann na mBan (women auxiliaries), marching in uniform, flags flying, bands playing. On the eve of the 1916 'rising' local Kildare units were to assemble at the graveyard for orders to march to Dublin which however never came. During the war for independence the Irish Republican Army and ancillary bodies endeavoured to put in appearances on the appointed day in June. On the eve of the outbreak of civil war in June 1922 rival militaristic groups congregated there. In 1923 began a great display of military pomp at Bodenstown by the defence forces of the infant Irish Free State: infantry, cavalry, artillery, ancillary units, hundreds of men on parade, aircraft overhead, a military band, volleys fired over the grave, the Last Post sounded, the minister for defence making an inspection, taking the salute and then addressing an admiring crowd of spectators that included other government ministers, members of Dáil Éireann, even civil servants and judicial figures. By the late 1920s the scale of this had been reduced. After the change of government in 1932 the scale was reduced further by the removal of civilian elements (save for the defence minister); it was reduced again after 1937, the need ostentatiously to challenge the I.R.A. having ended. The event became a purely military affair but unmilitaristic, which it remained until 1974, when it ceased. The I.R.A. too, rivalling and imitating the 'national army', the lawful defence forces of the Irish Free State, turned the

Republicans' pilgrimages into pseudo-military events in the mid 1920s. These became increasingly militaristic until banned by the government in 1936. Another, longer ban was imposed in 1939; the I.R.A. recovered control of Republican pilgrimages by 1949 and probably before, but not until the 1970s did the pseudo-military ostentation of the 1930s reappear. At all times limits to the I.R.A.'s displays of militarism were understood and respected. Men of the I.R.A., the so-called 'Volunteers', did not wear uniforms (though the ancillaries did), arms were not carried, volleys were not fired over the grave, military commands were *sotto voce*. Ironically, one innovation of the I.R.A., the sounding of Reveille after the Last Post, heard at Bodenstown in 1947, seems not to have been adopted as a custom by the Irish defence forces at Bodenstown until 1952.

Bodenstown was also an annual open-air theatre. Its playbill was almost Shakespearian in offering a mixture of history, musical and colourful entertainment, the occasional light comedy of mild disorder, hushed scenes to remind the audience of death, mourning and resurrection, and earnest soliloquy appealing to its deeply-held beliefs and ineradicable prejudices. There was the farce, tragedy and horror posited by Professor Dunne. Sometimes an interval between performances was farcical: a rival, antipathetic troupe of players would quickly occupy the stage almost before the first troupe had vacated it. The theatrical production also had the predictability of pantomime, but with villains tantalisingly off-stage, despite which many in the audience returned year after year. All this was part of what Professor Roy Foster has characterised, with regard to the period from 1890 to 1923, as the 'theatre of revolution' which was a 'potent form of national consciousness-raising'.[6] He does not however cite Bodenstown. The observation he makes could be applied to later 'Bodenstowns' too, most of all to Fianna Fáil's spectacular in 1933. The point made by Dunne in 1982 about the theatrical aspect was well made, as the area of the Tone family grave had by then been converted by the National Graves Association into an amphitheatre.

The management of the pilgrimages has its own history. If the early pilgrimages ceased for want of a permanent organising body, the revival a decade later owed much to the organisers, the National Club Literary Society and the Young Ireland League, having permanent accommodation in central Dublin. What ensured the continuity of the pilgrimages was the permanence of the Wolfe Tone Memorial Committee — its eventual name — that came into existence on the eve of the 'Ninety-eight centenary celebrations. It might have been otherwise, as the celebrations exhausted its funds, a cause of the discontinuance of the pilgrimages after 1905. But the inspirational aim of a 'memorial' to Tone kept the committee in existence, as did its function as a cover for the clandestine Irish Republican Brotherhood, and so provided a readily-available organising body for the sudden revival of pilgrimages in 1911. The Wolfe Tone Memorial Committee continued to

---

6 R. F. Foster, *Vivid faces: the revolutionary generation in Ireland, 1890–1923* (London, 2014), esp. chs 3 and 7.

organise the annual pilgrimages until 1922. The anti-Treaty or Republican pilgrimage in 1923, a women's affair, was most likely organised by Cumann na mBan. In 1924 and 1925 initiatives was taken by De Valera as president of Sinn Féin. In 1925 a new body, the Wolfe Tone Commemoration Committee, was involved; in successive years, under its auspices, certainly from 1929, the I.R.A. was in control. Sinn Féin organised its own pilgrimage in 1928, held three days after what was perceived as a pilgrimage organised for, if not by, the I.R.A. Until the eve of the Second World War the main Republican pilgrimages, which always attracted kindred bodies as well as senior members and contingents of the I.R.A., were attributed to the Wolfe Tone Commemoration Committee. During the same period there were occasional pilgrimages organised by the diminished Sinn Féin party, most noticeably in 1936 when the I.R.A.'s pilgrimage was banned. The Fianna Fáil party had separate pilgrimages in 1929 and 1930, joined the I.R.A.'s pilgrimage in 1931 for tactical reasons, always thereafter going to Bodenstown separately. Owing to a need for tight security during the Emergency years, I.R.A. pilgrimages were prohibited in 1939, 1940 and 1941. Republicans were able to go in 1942 and 1943 under the auspices of the National Graves Association, a body whose primary function was the care of graves of 'patriots'. The Wolfe Tone Commemoration Committee was behind this arrangement and ostensibly at least was the organising body of Republican pilgrimages for several years after; in 1948 and each year until 1970 credits were given in the press to the National Commemoration Committee. Despite the differences of name, both committees almost certainly were a joint-committee of the I.R.A., Sinn Féin and associated bodies. From 1923 until 1931 there were official pilgrimages primarily military in character but accommodating officialdom and the general public. Fianna Fáil once in office in 1932 established the custom of the Irish defence forces commemorating Tone with few civilians present. In 1933 and the following three years the Fianna Fáil party held rather grand commemorations of its own immediately after the military ceremony. This began another custom, continuous whenever the party was in office until military commemorations ceased in 1973, of separating by an hour or so defence forces and party. After 1937 the presence of Fianna Fáil was on a reduced scale: there was apparently no parade from Sallins, perhaps just a short walk along the boreen to the gate of the churchyard; the minister for defence would precede his party colleagues to play his role in the small military ceremony; a short while later, in a separate ceremony, De Valera, the party leader, would lay a wreath on behalf of his party; little organisation was needed beyond the military. The example of small military ceremonies was followed by future coalition governments; the coalition parties were not as such represented, whilst Fianna Fáil in opposition sometimes appeared on a different day. The continuity of the various organising bodies, and the routine established in 1911, ensured the continuance of the custom of pilgrimages to Tone's grave, whatever the travails of Ireland in the twentieth century.

Orations at Bodenstown were intended to serve political purposes. They tell us much more about the concerns of the orator and his audience, and about the preoccupations of the time, than about Tone and his times. They may now seem tedious, but a few are historically important. Pearse's oration in 1913 is the best-known example. Bellicose orations on the eve of the First World War, in the early 1930s, in the mid and late 1950s and throughout the 1970s had consequences. From the beginning, in the 1870s, 'advanced nationalists', Fenians, members of, or sympathisers with, the Irish Republican Brotherhood, the I.R.B., were involved in Bodenstown pilgrimages, as organisers, as participants and as orators. Among the last were some famous Fenian names: John Daly, Charles Doran, John O'Leary, Maurice Moynihan, P. N. Fitzgerald and John MacBride. It was chiefly 'an old Fenian', Thomas Clarke, who revived the pilgrimages in 1911 and kept them going until the rising in 1916, of which he was the principal leader. After 1922 ministers of the new, independent government, beginning with Mulcahy in 1923 and Cosgrave in 1924, stood up to make speeches at Bodenstown, as did their rivals, most notably De Valera, twice before he entered office himself, after which, until 1937, ministerial colleagues were given their chance. Nearly all of the Republican orators from the late 1920s can be identified as significant in the history of the I.R.A. Most famous is MacBride's son Seán (twice). In the 1940s and 1950s they were generally men who had been imprisoned for seditious or violent activities in pursuit of their political objectives. In the 1960s and into the 1970s Republican orators were without exception veterans of the I.R.A.'s 'Border campaign' of the late 1950s. In the 1970s and into the 1980s they were all political militants and in many cases I.R.A. operators. At least eleven Bodenstown speakers subsequently met violent deaths connected with their political activities: James Carey (murdered in 1883), John MacBride, Tom Clarke and Patrick Pearse (all three shot as rebels in 1916), Cathal Brugha (killed in fighting in 1922 in the civil war), Liam Mellows (executed in 1922), Patrick McLogan (died in 1966 of gunshot wounds in suspicious circumstances), Liam McMillen (shot dead in 1975), Máire Drumm (shot dead in 1976), Séamus Costello (shot dead in 1977) and Miriam Daly (a similar fate in 1980). But these deaths were off stage. No death was ever reported as having occurred at a pilgrimage. Only rarely were there outbreaks of violence at the scene, famously in 1934 and 1935 of brief scuffles, menacingly in 1979 when policemen were injured. If these incidents can be disregarded, the ambiance was a mixture of heated politics, relaxed enjoyment and silent reverence.

The outbreak and prolongation of politically motivated violence in Northern Ireland brought about great changes in Bodenstown churchyard and to the June pilgrimages. The explosion at the Tone family plot in 1969, the phenomena in the 1970s of rival Republican pilgrimages caused by ideological disagreements about socialism and nationalism, the ulsterisation of pilgrimages and the transformation of the plot into an architect-designed area for the unspoken purpose of political rallies and speeches, all these were consequences of the 'Troubles'. An irony was that the enemy Ulster Volunter Force, in causing the explosion, unwittingly helped Republicans make a more convenient space in Bodenstown churchyard for holding their rallies and denouncing their enemies. With ulsterisation came apathy to the

Tone legend. No orator made more than a passing mention of the man purportedly being honoured. The new memorial stood out less as a memorial to Theobald Wolfe Tone than as a purpose-designed place of assembly for political rallies by Sinn Féin and kindred bodies. On the large panel, words of Pearse about Tone took pride of place over words of Tone himself.

Were all who went to Bodenstown in June genuine pilgrims, or did some go for the spectacle or for social reasons? The music and song, the flags and banners, the colourful costumes, the pageantry, the theatre, all these were attractions. Opportunities for socialising and 'networking', meeting old friends and making new ones, were many. Tim Pat Coogan's recollections of Bodenstown in the 1960s of people enjoying a day out in the country are probably little different from those of many an observer during the hundred years or so of the Bodenstown phenomenon. As early as the 1840s there was an element of entertainment in the outdoor political rallies ('monster meetings') to promote Repeal. In his nuanced study of the ritual of these events Gary Owens argues that there was a symbiotic relationship between the theatre of rallies and the political messages of the orators. He holds, for example, that the procession before the oration was no less important than the orator's message, which was beyond the hearing of many in a large crowd; it was the sights and sounds enjoyed by participants and spectators that instilled political consciousness.[7] (Not until 1933 was there a report of a loudspeaker at Bodenstown.[8]) A point made by R. V. Comerford in his consideration of 'patriotism' as a pastime is that there was in the 1860s (the growth period of fenianism) much fraternal association in places of public entertainment of men who were in the I.R.B. or likemindedly sympathetic to Irish nationalism. Their camaraderie was typical of young men of a similar social background and with a common purpose, be it political or non-political, and it extended to common enjoyment of pastimes.[9] 'Dun Padruic' expressly recommended summer excursions to places significant for Irish nationalists 'to combine patriotism and pleasure' and envisioned picnics and popular music. Organisers of annual pilgrimages to Bodenstown were aware that a political speech would not be enough to attract pilgrims and that entertainment would be necessary. In the 1870s and the 1890s a miscellany of bands playing popular 'Irish' music was a *sine qua non*. This remained so after the revival of annual pilgrimages in 1911. In that year, after the speeches were over, an *aeraíocht* was held under the supervision of Cathal Brugha, an I.R.B. man who was to lose his life in the civil war; an *aeraíocht* remained an attraction in following years. From the mid 1930s until the late 1950s *céilithe* were held in Dublin as evening entertainment specially for Republican pilgrims from afar. Was Bodenstown any different from traditional religious pilgrimages in that some participants were not true believers, but simply conformists or sympathetic well-wishers or even 'just there for the crack'? Or were

---

7 Gary Owens, 'Nationalism without words: symbolism and ritual behaviour in the Repeal "monster meetings" of 1843–5' in James S. Donnelly, jr, and Kerby A. Miller (eds), *Irish popular culture, 1650–1850* (Dublin, 1998), pp 242–74.   8 *Ir. Press*, 19 June 1933.   9 R. V. Comerford, 'Patriotism as pastime: the appeal of fenianism in the mid-1860s' in *Irish Historical Studies*, xxii,

most Bodenstown pilgrims serious-mindedly dressing up, enjoying a country walk, listening to music and having a picnic on a pleasant early summer day thereby 'making a public statement and co-operating in building a collective message'?.[10]

THE PILGRIMS

What is rather striking about the sort of people who went regularly to Bodenstown is that until the 1920s they were generally from certain social strata fixable between the labouring poor and those who were securely in the middle class. To be able to have sufficient means to make the journey, pilgrims had to be in steady employment whether as an employee or employer. Indicators of this means are the train fare to Sallins, or the purchase price of a bicycle, relative to incomes. The labouring poor were missing, as were the *grande bourgeoisie* and country gentry. It is easier to identify the organisers, chairmen and orators than those among the crowd, as usually they had careers that ended with at least obituaries. For the first two periods of pilgrimage, from 1873 to 1905, the social composition has been discussed in some detail in chapter 5. After 1911, whilst the social composition of members of the organising body (the Wolfe Tone Memorial Committee) remained unchanged, some men of a higher social class, and women too, began showing an interest, most conspicuously, Countess Markievicz. Good evidence of this was the appreciative attendance at a weekday afternoon showing of the film of Bodenstown in 1913. The transformation of nationalist politics in 1917 widened the social basis. The appearance of motor-cars at Bodenstown in the early 1920s is also telling evidence. The beginning of Irish independence in 1923 brought to the churchyard government ministers, parliamentarians, state officials and soldiers on duty. Only the government's opponents on rival pilgrimages were still discernibly of a lower class. The change of government in 1932 resulted in three separate and socially distinct groups at Tone's grave: (1) the military; (2) socially rising members and supporters of the Fianna Fáil party that was now in power; (3) old Fenian types, still predominantly from the same social strata as pilgrims in the 1870s.

A paradox is that, although the pilgrims of the earlier years, and still most of them in later years, were of the 'class above the masses' which typically organised itself in trade unions, they were unconcerned about labour matters when they reached Bodenstown if the silence of orators of their class on the subject is evidence. What is also striking about the pilgrims is the firmness and universality of their dual loyalty to catholicism and nationalism whatever the conflicts between the two. What is observed of women at Bodenstown largely confirms that their roles in society were secondary and auxiliary to the roles of men until as late as the 1960s.

no. 87 (Mar. 1981), pp 239–50.   10 These are the words of Marta Ramón, to whom I am grateful for a discussion of this paragraph.

TONE HIMSELF?

What had pilgrimages to Tone's grave to do with Tone himself? Praise was for long lavished on him by Bodenstown orators. Some showed great extent (if not always depth) of reading of his autobiography and diaries, particularly John Murphy (1896), Patrick Pearse (1913), Art O'Connor (1927), Thomas Derrig (1936) and Ruairí Ó Brádaigh (1959). Orators such as these would recount his career, acknowledge and praise his dedication, perseverance and suffering for the Catholic and the nationalist or republican causes; they would even quote a few lines from his writings (usually from his autobiography). But they were rhetoricians, not historians. The orations were not lectures on late eighteenth-century Irish and French history. The orators' words when discoursing on Tone and his career are reminders of what the historian Edmund Curtis called 'the panegyric mind'.[11] And the example of Tone and the words of his quoted would be used to make points about present-day politics. Most would create out of narrowly selected dicta political slogans advocating national unity, national independence, and, above all, ill-defined 'republicanism' and preparedness for taking up arms. At the early pilgrimages in the 1870s speakers seem to have gone no further than to praise Tone; Daly's unmistakably 'Fenian' speech in 1880 set a precedent followed after the resumption of annual pilgrimages in 1891. Much attention was then given to the Tone story (selectively), to Tone's 'principles' (not always defined) and to the encouragement of the kind of national sentiment that Tone represented in the minds of the pilgrims, though the only speech that could be construed as seditious was MacBride's speech in 1905. During the 'revolutionary period', from 1911 or 1912 until 1922 or 1923, the emphasis was on Tone's martial spirit. When comparison is made of orations delivered at Bodenstown from 1923 to 1936 by representatives of the governments of the Irish Free State with orations of their Republican opponents two rival Tones emerge: Tone was the hero whose vision had materialised with the coming of Irish independence, conversely he was the hero whose vision had been betrayed and was still to be fulfilled. In the words of Peter Collins, 'speeches at Bodenstown, as well as alluding to '98, reflected the current political stances of various strands of republicanism and the internecine warfare within them'.[12] In the 1960s Tone became temporarily a socialist. By the 1970s, however, even paying lip-service to Tone at his grave had become a formality virtually ignored, the orator's main purpose being to announce political policy and to denounce political enemies. It could not have escaped the attention of detached observers that Theobald Wolfe Tone was receiving in the orations much less attention than the policies of the competing political parties, a change anticipated in the replacement of the two Tone gravestones and the surrounding railing by a large permanent stone platform for an audience and a

11 Edmund Curtis, 'Irish history and its popular versions' in *Irish Rosary*, xxix, no. 5 (May 1925), pp 321, 328, cited in Ian McBride, 'The shadow of the gunman: Irish historians and the I.R.A.' in *Journal of Contemporary History*, xlvi, no. 3 (July 2011), pp 686–710 at p. 691.   12 Collins, *Who fears to speak?*, p. 77.

rostrum for a speaker. What mostly orators sought and saw in Tone was historical warrant for their opinions. Only a few gave themselves time to show their knowledge and understanding of Tone and his political principles; they became fewer and fewer as the twentieth century progressed. By the penultimate decade of the century there was little reference to Tone's writings; mentions of Tone were cursory, empty, merely routine. The contributor of a piece headed 'Ritual' in an opinion column in the *Irish Times* shortly after a pilgrimage in 1980 began, 'they bury Tone deeper and deeper every year'. The columnist argued that those who go to Bodenstown have a poor understanding of Tone, just as Tone had insufficient understanding of 'the tribal drumbeats' of Ulster and believed it needed only 'reason to bring them all to amity'. More attentive than the orators to Tone's Ulster diaries, the writer pointed out that 'the Peep of Day Boys and the Defenders spoiled one of his Northern trips for him in 1792'. They were in 1980, he observed, 'still at it, under different names'.[13] A silent and yet telling answer to the question of relevance has been given by Matt Treacy in his full-length study of the various ideological influences on the most faithful of the Bodenstown pilgrims. Much attention is given by him to the Dublin Wolfe Tone Society, which flourished throughout the 1960s as a 'think-tank' and whose archives he was able to examine. Treacy makes not even the faintest allusion to the political ideas of Tone himself.[14]

Yet Tone and his grave were necessary for the Bodenstown phenomenon to begin and to continue. Tone's revolutionary politics and his adventurous career as lucidly and engagingly recounted by him in his writings published in 1826 and republished, again and again, and now abridged to contain only the parts interesting to Irish nationalists, are the most outstanding of all Irish political narratives. The Tone 'legend' was written by himself. No other Irish political figure, except O'Connell, is knowable and known so personally and intimately as Tone. His writings became a sort of Bible for his followers. O'Connell left no apologia or testament. The existence of Tone's grave and its precise location were essential conditions for the pilgrimages. O'Connell's grave at Glasnevin attracts visitors mainly for its spectacular appearance — its deep vault and *faux* Round Tower. In contrast, other Irish nationalist heroes are little known and less inspiring. Of other heroes from Tone's time, Lord Edward FitzGerald died a romantic, tragic figure, but he wrote nothing of lasting interest. Bartholomew Teeling's dying speech remained unnoticed, and his grave remains unmarked. Robert Emmet may have had an heroic demise, but his ideas are known only from a single speech and his grave remains unknown. Thomas Russell's writings, except for a pamphlet, remained unnoticed for nearly two centuries, his grave in County Down undisturbed.

Professor Dunne's contention that 'Tone did not become a central figure for later nineteenth-century nationalists, not even for the Fenians', has been considered by this study of annual organised pilgrimages to his grave. In fact the earliest known

13 *Ir. Times*, 23 June 1980.   14 Matt Treacy, *The I.R.A., 1956–69: rethinking the republic* (Manchester, 2011).

visit to the grave after those of Davis and his associates in 1843 and 1844 and local Kildare Confederates in 1848 was that made by Michael Cavanagh and other Fenians who accompanied the body of Terence Bellew McManus for reburial in Dublin in 1861. The organising of outings by the Dublin Wolfe Tone Band in 1873 and 1874 for the purpose of replacing the damaged gravestone placed by Davisites and erecting a railing was no doubt done by a group of men well aware of Tone's legacy. The outings, or pilgrimages, in 1875 and 1876 were organised by the Fenian-influenced Amnesty Association and addressed by James O'Connor, a man active in the I.R.B. since shortly after its creation. Most likely the pilgrimages of the Martyrs' Band in 1880 and 1881 were organised by the band's president, Thomas Bracken, a known Fenian. Certainly the 'orator' in 1880 was a Fenian, John Daly. The revival and organisation of the pilgrimages in the 1890s was the work of men involved in the I.R.B. and successive orators were sworn members of the same organisation. Daly, through his connexion with John Devoy and close friendship and family relationship with Thomas Clarke, played a vital, crucial role in the revival of the I.R.B. between 1909 and 1916 and so indirectly in the Easter rising that occurred in the latter year.

LIEUX DE MÉMOIRE

Patrick Pearse's designation of Tone's grave as 'the holiest place in Ireland'[15] evokes Pierre Nora's characterisation of certain places in France as *lieux de mémoire* ('places of memory'). Tone's grave, indeed Bodenstown churchyard and its environs, meet several of Nora's criteria for this characterisation: monuments, commemorations, festivals, emblems, elegies.[16] An argument is that places and memory interact and determine concepts of history. But Nora warns us that 'la mémoire est toujours suspecte à l'histoire, dont la mission vraie est de la détruire et de la refouler'.[17] This warning is one that Bodenstown audiences should heed. Surprisingly, neither Nora nor any of his contributors discusses places of pilgrimage. Other graves cared for by the National Graves Association attract regular visitors. None, however, comes close to meeting Nora's criteria. The place of death in rural Cork of Michael Collins is indeed a place of memory regularly receiving visits from his admirers. Ironically, despite Collins having been president of the Irish Republican Brotherhood when he died, his grave is not tended by the National Graves Association as he is not considered by this body to be qualified as a 'patriot'.

George Greenia and Paul Hollander emphasise place as a destination in their writings on secular pilgrimages. Neither however mentions any *regular* secular

---

15 Pearse's words as stated in the report of his speech at Bodenstown in June 1913 in *Irish Freedom*, the newspaper controlled by Clarke. Pearse's mother in a report of a pilgrimage in 1922 was stated to have attributed to him the words 'holiest spot'. The sense is the same.   16 Pierre Nora (ed.), *Les lieux de mémoire, 1: République*, ed. Pierre Nora (Paris: Gallimard, 1984), p. vii. 17 Ibid., p. xx.

pilgrimage that resembles Bodenstown. Few close comparisons in respect of place are to be found. One such case appears at first consideration to be the 'Highland gathering' at Glenfinnan on a Saturday close to 19 August, the place and date of Charles Edward Stuart raising in 1745 his standard after landing from France to oust the Hanoverian king and reclaim his kingdoms for his father — James VIII of Scotland to his Jacobite supporters there. But, though Stuart was like Tone a classically tragic figure, and though the memory evoked at Glenfinnan may for some be as deep as evoked for many at Bodenstown, the annual gathering is unlike the century-long custom of looking back to 1798 to mourn a splendid failure and to make resolutions to redress it. The gathering dates back no further than the 1960s and is no more than an enjoyable social and sporting occasion in a remote and idyllic spot with little or no contemporary political agenda. Indeed politics is considered taboo.[18] Another such case is the annual pilgrimage to Franco's grave in the Valle de los Caídos, 50 kilometres north of Madrid, on the Saturday after 20 November, the anniversary of Franco's death. Like Bodenstown and Glenfinnan the spot is sequestered and evokes memory. The appearance of a large enthusiastic crowd with flags and banners, eager to contemplate their hero's tomb, is a reminder of Bodenstown. But the ethos of the Valle de los Caídos is both political *and* religious. While at Bodenstown the clergy are conspicuously absent among Catholic pilgrims gathered for a solemn ceremony, in the Valle de los Caídos they are conspicuosly present, Benedictine priests with their abbot saying prayers, not laymen.[19] But these pilgrimages in Scotland and Spain are hardly historical. A closer comparison with Bodenstown is perhaps the annual visit of ten thousand or more Protestants to Mas Soubeyran, a sequestered hamlet in the *département* of the Gard, which for them is a *lieu de mémoire*, being the birthplace of Rolland, a leader of the Huguenot rising in the Cévennes in 1704; their *assemblée* (the word *pèlerinage* is avoided), whilst primarily religious, evokes historical memory and contains many of the customary features of gatherings at Tone's grave: a fixed day (the first Sunday of September), a procession to Rolland's house (now a sort of shrine), an oration, a history lesson, picnicking, entertainment and most remarkably the pilgrimages to Mas Soubeyran began in 1911, the year pilgrimages to Bodenstown resumed.[20]

Despite Tone's fame, despite his grave being visited and revisited, no heritage centre or building for the reception of visitors ever existed at Bodenstown, nor any official information for visitors other than a discreet sign, 'Wolfe Tone's grave', pointing the way from the main Clane-Sallins road, and a similar sign at the entrance to the churchyard, a short distance along the boreen. The contrast with other sites associated with famous men is almost too obvious to be stated. Robbie Burns, a national cult-figure in Scotland, was by 1992 being commemorated in

18 E.g. Scottish independence, for which see 'Political area a ban' in *Scotland on Sunday*, 13 Apr. 2014.   19 For an account of pilgrimages to the Valle de los Caídos, see Giles Tremlett, 'Looking for the generalíssimo' in his *Ghosts of Spain: travels through a country's hidden past* (London, 2006), pp 34–68.   20 Patrick Cabanel, 'Impansable pèlerinage protestant?: l'assemblée annuelle du Musée du Désert' in *Archives de Sciences Sociales des Religions*, lvi, no. 3 (juillet–septembre 2011),

almost a dozen 'Great Man museums' in that country.[21] Popular commemorative visits to Bodenstown of the kind discussed in this book occurred on no more than two or three days each year and were brief, for which reason there would have been no strong case for a reception centre. The idea of converting the ruined church into a museum, put forward by the National Graves Association and mentioned by Katherine Dickason in April 1971 at the inauguration of its new memorial, was surely impractical, as the building was in poor repair. A more likely place for a building for the information and refreshment of visitors would have been Sallins, the village that was already providing facilities for the pilgrims. There were other reasons too. Tone was always widely acknowledged, on the basis of his writings and of popular discourse, as a prophet of Irish independence; but the annual appearance at Bodenstown of pseudomilitary or paramilitary bodies and of orators making controversial, bellicose political speeches may have made it an unsuitable place for a heritage centre at which Tone's local connexion, his political career and the historical context could be treated of historically. There may have been another reason still: the ownership of the graveyard and the surrounding land. The National Graves Association's interest in and concern for the grave from the late 1920s did ensure that it was maintained; but its legal status was never made clear, the churchyard was a local graveyard in the ownership of the county council, whilst the land around was agricultural and privately owned. The arrangement that existed throughout the twentieth century, which was *ad hoc*, had the merit of suiting all pilgrims and all bodies irrespective of their political orientation. Any serious proposal for a Wolfe Tone heritage centre would have brought this arrangement into question. Construction of such a centre, with necessary infrastructure, would have transformed Bodenstown beyond recognition from the sequestered spot romanticised by Davis. The sheer convenience of Bodenstown for annual pilgrimages by men and women often in conflict with the authorities would always have been an argument for preserving the *status quo*.

By the penultimate decade of the twentieth century the charm of the spot described in verse by Davis in 1843 had vanished. There was no longer a recognisable sepulchral monument to a local Protestant family, but in its place, ironically, a small arena used for grandstanding, airing grievances of Ulster Catholics, forcefully stating terms for redress and black-guarding rivals and opponents. Bodenstown had become, long before the 1980s, a convenient and seductive venue for political rallies by nationalist *intégristes*. More censoriously, with regard to these rallies, another historian, Professor Diarmaid Ferriter, refers to 'the manner in which the message of Wolfe Tone and the 1798 rebellion — to promote the "common name of Irishman" in place of the existing political and religious divisions — was "cruelly mocked"'.[22]

pp 149–64. **21** George Rosie, 'Museumry and the heritage industry' in Ian Donnachie and Christopher Whatley (eds), *The manufacture of Scottish history* (Edinburgh, 1992), pp 157–70 at pp 167–8. **22** Diarmaid Ferriter, review of Paul Bew, *Ireland: the politics of enmity, 1789–2006* (Oxford, 2007), in *T.L.S.*, 7 Dec. 2007, p. 8.

Terminology and taxonomy

T HE MEN AND WOMEN who went, as if pilgrims, to Tone's grave at Bodenstown can rightly be regarded as Irish nationalists. The term 'nationalist' was, however, not used in Tone's day, nor for many years to come. Tone and many of his associates called themselves 'United Irishmen', and were so called by others. The name came from the two political clubs formed by Irish democrats in the autumn of 1791, the first, in Belfast in October, with a constitution drawn up by Tone and sent to his friend Thomas Russell, the second, in Dublin in November, with Tone himself present. The name 'United Irishmen' and its adjectival form 'United Irish' continued in use during the second half of the 1790s to refer to the revolutionary movement that derived partly from the political clubs and culminated in the Irish rebellion in 1798. After 1803, when another rebellion was attempted led by Robert Emmet and Thomas Russell, the words acquired purely historical connotations. Another word used by Tone to describe men of his own political opinions, one 'borrowed from France' — and with modern connotations though in Tone's day used with limited intent — was 'democrat'.[1] Another new word, 'liberal', appeared after 1812 as a synonym for 'democrat'. Its origin was the assembly that met at Cádiz in 1812 in an attempt to create a democratic constitution for Spain. The Irish liberals in the following decades were men who advocated broadening the basis of power in Ireland, most particularly by removing legal disabilities of Catholics, an objective not finally reached until the 1870s. Another term, 'repealer', came into use in the 1830s for those led by Daniel O'Connell, very largely Catholics, who sought to repeal the 'act of union'. This was the act of parliament that in 1801 had abolished the Irish parliament and removed Irish parliamentarians to a united British parliament sitting at Westminster.

'Nationalist' first occurs in relation to Ireland in the early 1840s. It seems first to have been used in the *Freeman's Journal*, a Dublin newspaper much read by Catholics, in 1842. This was in an article arguing for repeal of the act of union by drawing an analogy with Scotland and mentioning Tone: if certain Scotsmen — they are named — who resisted the union of Scotland with England or who would have repealed it 'were not base fools, then surely Grattan was a patriot and Wolfe Tone a holy martyr, and the Nationalists of this day are justified in striving for independence'.[2] In its report of the great demonstration at Tara in August 1843 in support of repeal, it referred to the scene as being 'so charming to the nationalist'; a month later it referred to opponents of repeal as 'anti-nationalists'; by the end of the year it was using 'nationalist' to mean Repealer.[3] The word 'nationalist' characterised those Irishmen imbued with a high regard for Ireland as a nation in addition to a belief in the desirability of repeal of the 'union' and, by long-term implication, greater empowerment of the Catholic majority. In 1847, shortly before the death of O'Connell, young Repealers, 'Young Ireland', broke away

1 Tone, *Writings*, ii, 295. 2 *Freeman's Jn.*, 3 Jan. 1842.

from the movement, now in decline, and formed Confederate clubs that had rather more radical aims and which were the instigators of short-lived and fairly harmless rebellions in 1848 and 1849.

Another new term entered Irish political vocabulary in 1858: 'Irish Republican Brotherhood'. Its founders, the first 'Fenians', were men affected by the experience of exile in France and subsequent emigration to the United States. They advocated an independent Irish republic. Now the word 'republican' in nineteenth- and twentieth-century Irish history needs elucidation.[4] Before 1916, it does not occur in newspaper reports of men now known by historians, and by well-informed contemporaries, to have been members of the Irish Republican Brotherhood — usually known by just its initials. Such men were commonly known as Fenians. This nomenclature is lucidly explained by Professor R. V. Comerford in his *Fenians in context* (1985).[5] The Irish Republican Brotherhood was formed by James Stephens in Ireland in 1858 using ideas taken from Continental secret societies, most notably a requirement of recruits to swear oaths and the adoption of a cellular system of organisation. The following year some of Stephens' allies in the United States formed a similar but hardly secret Irish nationalist society. This quickly came under the leadership of John O'Mahony, who gave it the name Fenian Brotherhood, after the *Fianna* of Gaelic legend. Although 'Fenian' came to be used in Ireland to refer to members of the I.R.B., it was not much used by I.R.B. men in referring to each other — they were 'advanced men' or members of 'the Organisation'.[6] The term 'Fenian' was to be found in the newspapers, moreover some historians, notably T. W. Moody, F.S.L. Lyons, Paul Bew and Frank Callanan as well as Comerford, have used this word definitively for members of the I.R.B. The last-named prefers the term Fenian because 'it was almost universally used' from about 1863 and uses it, sensibly, 'for convenience'.[7] Dr Matthew Kelly accepts the term whilst drawing attention to the difficulties of constructing 'a taxonomy of Irish nationalists' owing to 'the variety of political tendencies' — the many 'shades of green'; he argues that identification of a man as a member of the I.R.B. is more positive than designation of him as a Fenian to be fingered in the police files.[8] Dr Owen McGee, writing at the same time as Dr Kelly, rejects 'Fenian' as too indiscriminate; he continually uses the word 'republican'.[9] For this however there is little warrant in contemporary documents. The preferred term of the men of the I.R.B. in public discourse was 'nationalist'. An instance of this is to be found in the statement issued by the I.R.B.'s supreme council in May 1880 denouncing parliamentary involvement by members and ex-members; it refers to them as 'the Nationalists'.[10] At that time the term 'home ruler' was used to designate a follower of

---

3 *Freeman's Jn.*, 16 Aug., 27 Sept., 28 Dec. 1843. 4 The perceptions stated here are my own. The meaning of 'republican' has been discussed in Frank Callanan, '"In the name of God and of the dead generations": nationalism and republicanism in Ireland' in Richard English and Joseph Morrison Skelly (eds), *Ideas matter: essays in honour of Conor Cruise O'Brien* (Dublin, 1998), pp 109–22. 5 R. V. Comerford, *The Fenians in context: Irish politics and society, 1848–82* (Dublin, 1985; repr. 1998), pp 47–8, 51–3, 110, 131, 156, 169. 6 Ó Broin, *Revolutionary underground*, p. 9. 7 Comerford, *Fenians in context*, p. 48; idem, 'Review' in *Saothar*, xxxi (2006), pp 106–07; idem, 'Fenianism: the scope and limitations of a concept' in Fearghal McGarry and James McConnell (eds), *The black hand of republicanism: Fenianism in modern Ireland* (Dublin, 2009), pp 179–89. 8 Matthew Kelly, *The Fenian ideal and Irish nationalism* (Woodbridge, Suffolk, 2006), p. 6. See also his 'Dublin Fenianism in the 1880s' in *Historical Journal*, xliii (2000), pp 729–50. 9 McGee, *I.R.B.* (2005), p. 33. 10 This instance is given in Callanan, '"In the name of God"', p. 111.

Isaac Butt and of his successor Charles Stewart Parnell, advocates of Irish autonomy but not of separation from Great Britain. By 1890 'nationalist' was being used to refer to Parnell's supporters in parliament and in the country; at about the same time, the term 'advanced nationalist' came into use, this to indicate a tendency to republicanism. But when Maurice Moynihan referred to 'an Irish republic' at Bodenstown in 1899 there were murmurs of disapproval among his audience.[11] And when John MacBride, declaiming at Tone's grave in 1905, spoke of the possibility of armed Irishmen placing Ireland 'in a position to add a new republic to the republics of the West',[12] he was probably thinking wistfully, if seditiously, of the Boer republics in South Africa, on whose side he had made his military reputation, and of the French and American republics in which he had stayed before returning to Ireland. Thomas Clarke, writing in 1912 or 1913 and referring to the time he was in prison in the 1880s and 1890s, states proudly: 'I was then what I had been, and what I am still, an Irish Nationalist'.[13] Patrick Pearse, in his famous speech at Bodenstown in June 1913, does not use the word 'republican', he calls Tone 'the greatest of Irish nationalists'. But Michael Collins at the funeral in 1917 of Thomas Ashe, born in 1885, uninhibitedly referred to Ashe as 'a dead Fenian'.[14] The word 'republican' gradually came into common use after April 1916 when an 'Irish republic' was declared by insurgents in the 'Easter rising'; it was used to refer to adherents of Sinn Féin — inaccurately, as republicanism was not a dogma of the original Sinn Féin.

The word 'Sinn Féin' first occurs in 1911 in this account of Bodenstown. The Sinn Féin party was formally instituted in November 1905. Its leader Arthur Griffith took the initiative in forming a committee in March 1911 to oppose the forthcoming royal visit, an initiative that resulted in the revival of the pilgrimages, in abeyance since 1905. The word occurs again in June 1917 when reports appeared in the press of Sinn Féin branches from Dublin, Kildare and adjoining counties appearing at Tone's grave in large numbers and a profusion there of so-called Sinn Féin flags, colours and favours in what was said to be a 'spontaneous display'.[15] 'Sinn Féin' in its varying forms and various factions was present at almost every Bodenstown pilgrimage from then until the 1980s and beyond. In some reports its name was a disguise for the I.R.A.

A name that first occurs three years after the revival of the pilgrimages is 'volunteer'. These volunteers, given here an initial capital, appear ambiguously in the sources as both 'Irish Volunteers' and 'National Volunteers'. The term used by Clarke, Pearse and Hobson in the early months of their existence was 'Irish Volunteers'.[16] In press reports of the 1914 pilgrimage 'National Volunteers' appears. Before then splits had occurred when John (or Eoin) MacNeill invited John Redmond to nominate to the national committee. Only a daring minority of uniformed Volunteers took part in the Easter rising. After 1916 and a revival they formed contingents in parades from Sallins. In press reports of Bodenstown in June 1922 Volunteers were referred to as 'I.R.A.', these letters standing for 'Irish Republican Army'. They were the Volunteers who had thrown in their lot with the anti-Treaty party. Many of those who accepted the treaty were incorporated into the defence forces of the Irish Free State, known as the National Army. Both the

11 *Leinster Leader*, 1 July 1899.   12 *Leinster Leader*, 15 July 1905.   13 Clarke, *Glimpses of an Irish felon's prison life*, p. 102.   14 Michael Hopkinson, *The Irish war of independence* (Dublin, 2002), p. 98.   15 *Ir. Times*, 26 June 1917; *Leinster Leader*, 30 June 1917.   16 *Devoy's post bag*, ii, 439–40, 444–5, 456–7.   17 John P. Duggan, *A history of the Irish army* (Dublin, 1991), pp 138–9.

Irish Republican Army and the National Army considered themselves to be linear successors of the Volunteers formed in 1913. Both bodies on occasion called themselves Óglaigh na hÉireann (Army of Ireland), a name used by the pre-1922 Volunteers.[17] While so-called Republican pilgrimages from 1926 were organised for the I.R.A., presumably by a committee of I.R.A. activists and supporters, the I.R.A. was not referred to by this name in press reports of Bodenstown until 1931. Its proclamation as an unlawful organisation in 1936 was discreetly evaded by referring to some pilgrims as 'ex I.R.A.' or 'Old I.R.A.'. Indeed at the official pilgrimage in 1926 the old Fenian, George Lyons, a Wolfe Tone Memorial Committee man in 1899 and implicitly a '1916 man', laid a wreath on behalf of the 'old Dublin Brigade, I.R.A.'. Commonly at Fianna Fáil pilgrimages from the 1930s, and at I.R.A.-sponsored pilgrimages after 1936, the words 'old' or 'veteran' coming before 'I.R.A.' had a disarming effect and were true descriptions as more and more I.R.A. men became veterans. Suddenly in 1949 caution was cast aside by the *Irish Times* and the *Irish Press* in reporting the orator's undisguised appeal on behalf of the I.R.A. This audacity disappeared after the beginning of the I.R.A.'s 'Border campaign' in 1956 and reappeared in 1966, as Ireland was entering an age of greater permissiveness. From 1970 the qualifications 'Official I.R.A.' and 'Provisional I.R.A.' were needed, as explained below.

Associated with the Volunteers before and after 1922 were other uniformed bodies: for adolescent men the Fianna Éireann ('Irish Warriors'), for women Cumann na mBan ('Association of Women') and for girls Clann na Gaedheal (National or Republican Girl Scouts). The first of these was formed in 1909, partly in imitation of Baden Powell's Boy Scouts and were often referred to as National Boy Scouts or, after 1922, as Republican Boy Scouts. The Cumann na mBan came into existence in April 1914 and, apparently, the Girl Scouts at about the same time. In the 1930s there were mentions of Republican Girl Scouts (or Guides) and of a similar body for younger girls, Cumann na gCailíní. All were to be seen at Bodenstown into the 1970s. All these auxiliary bodies wore quasi-military-style uniforms as they walked or marched; the I.R.A. contingents, however, did not do so after 1922 even if they adopted a military demeanour.

In 1922 'republican' acquired and retained a more precise meaning — continuing respect for the authority of the second Dáil Éireann (elected in May 1921), the legitimacy of the faction of the I.R.A. that rejected the Anglo-Irish treaty and the continuing authenticity of Sinn Féin as the party formed by Arthur Griffith in 1905. Whilst Ireland became self-governing and constitutionally no longer part of the United Kingdom, it remained nominally part of the territories of the king of England, to whom formally the ministers and judges of the Irish Free State were obliged to take an oath of fidelity or allegiance. This oath was the bugbear of Irish republicans. The ambiguity of the term 'republican' in Irish politics returned in 1926 when Éamon de Valera and his closest followers broke away from Sinn Féin and formed a new party, which they named Fianna Fáil ('Soldiers of destiny'). De Valera's party remained consciously and avowedly 'republican' while distancing itself from Sinn Féin and, after 1932, from the I.R.A.[18] In my treatment of the pilgrimages to Bodenstown I retain the word 'republican', with an initial capital, to refer both to Sinn Féin and to the I.R.A. after 1921 whilst referring to De Valera's party by its formal name, 'Fianna Fáil'. This is not to confound Sinn Féin and the I.R.A., which were separate bodies even though there was probably some overlap

18 Ronan Fanning, *Independent Ireland* (Dublin, 1983), pp 99, 106, 175.

of membership, whilst their members' attitudes to Irish politics were virtually indistinguishable; nor is Fianna Fáil to be regarded as no longer 'republican', indeed its proud subtitle was always 'the Republican Party'. More splits occurred. The Republican Congress, formed in 1934, was conspicuous but short-lived and did not have a military wing. The same was true of Clann na Poblachta, formed by Republicans, whether disillusioned or inspired, in 1946. It dissolved itself in 1965. Another split occurred in the 'republican movement' in the final days of the 1960s. Both new factions called themselves Sinn Féin and I.R.A.; they were bizarrely distinguished in common parlance as Officials and Provisionals. Both split again, in 1974 and 1986 respectively. Evidently one of the things all these nationalists and republicans had in common was the custom of going on pilgrimages to Tone's grave, usually on a Sunday close to the anniversary of Tone's birth.

The great adversary of Republicans of various hues was Cumann na nGaedheal ('Association of the Gael'), formed by W. T. Cosgrave as the party of government in 1923. It absorbed minor parties in September 1934 and took the name Fine Gael. Its reluctant but reliable ally at different times was the Labour Party, the name of which needs no glossary. Cumann na nGaedheal was never royalist, nor was Fine Gael, nor was the Labour Party. When in office from 1923 to 1932 Cumann na nGaedheal did participate in the official pilgrimages to Bodenstown, as did Fine Gael ministers for defence in 1948 and later. After Ireland's formal declaration of a republic in 1949 and the severing of her tenuous remaining ties to the British crown, initiated by the coalition government in which Fine Gael, Labour and Clann na Poblachta were the main partners, all the political parties in the former Irish Free State could rightly be described as 'republican'. Just the same, the convention followed is to reserve the word 'republican' (often with an initial capital) for the anti-Treatyites and their spiritual successors, whether Sinn Féin, I.R.A., Fianna Fáil, Clann na Poblachta, Irish Republican Socialist Party or Workers' Party.

In the context of Tone's grave at Bodenstown the word 'national' has a limited meaning, as Peadar O'Donnell and George Gilmore pointed out indignantly in 1935. The National Graves Association and the National Commemoration Committee were not national bodies in the usual sense; their members were exclusively Republican activists, their names were not generally known, and the bodies did not publish annual reports. As for the word 'nationalist', commonly heard at Bodenstown until the 1920s, by the 1980s it was no more than a code word for Catholics in Northern Ireland.[19]

---

19 E.g. as used by Gerry Adams and Charles Haughey at Bodenstown, in 1983 and 1984 respectively (*Ir. Press*, 20 June 1983, 1 Oct. 1984).

Chronology of pilgrimages

FROM 1873 TO 1881, from 1891 to 1905, and from 1911, there were annual pilgrimages to Tone's grave at Bodenstown. This is a chronological list indicating exact dates, sponsoring or organising bodies, names of orators and principal speakers and page numbers in the text where information is given. In some cases after 1936 there was no oration or speech, in which cases the name of the principal wreath layer is substituted. The pilgrimages listed are generally mentioned in the text, but in some cases detail is lacking. All of the detail given here can be confirmed in newspaper sources.

Until 1921 only one pilgrimage each year was reported. In the 1870s, beginning with the Dublin Wolfe Tone Band in 1873, the sponsoring or organising body varied. Those of the Martyrs' Band in 1880 and 1881 were the last for ten years. The revival in 1891 was by the National Club Literary Society; it was continued by the Young Ireland League until 1897, when the 'Ninety-eight Centenary Committee assumed responsibility. This committee evolved into the Wolfe Tone Memorial Committee. There was a cessation in 1905 and a second revival in 1911, after which the pilgrimages organised by this committee (which was Fenian-dominated) became annual rallies for militant Irish nationalists.

In the troubled conditions of 1922 anti-Treatyites held a mid-week pilgrimage five days before that previously announced by the Wolfe Tone Memorial Committee for 25 June 1922. From then on there were two rival pilgrimages, or ceremonies, one organised by the defence forces of the Irish Free State at which Cumann na nGaedheal government ministers, parliamentarians, officials and other civilians were present, the other by anti-Treatyites, increasingly known as Republicans. The Republicans soon adopted the model of the pilgrimages of the Wolfe Tone Memorial Committee between 1911 and 1915. They themselves split in the mid 1920s between Sinn Féin (a political party), the I.R.A. (a paramilitary body with associated youth and women's auxiliaries) and Fianna Fáil (a new political party). All three organised pilgrimages at different times. After Fianna Fáil entered office in March 1932 the defence forces' ceremony was held separately from that of the Fianna Fáil party. The minister for defence was the only civilian present at the former, and only party leaders, members and supporters attended the latter.

As the I.R.A. was an illegal body — or barely legal — its pilgrimages were never advertised as such. From 1925 to 1947 the organising body was reported to be the Wolfe Tone Commemoration Committee. In 1939 they were prohibited until 1942, when, the I.R.A. having gone underground and Sinn Féin replaced it at the fore, they were revived under the auspices of the National Graves Association. From 1948 to 1971 the organising body was named as the National Commemoration Committee. It can only be supposed that the personnel of both this and the Wolfe Tone Commemoration Committee was drawn from the I.R.A. and associated bodies. These were until the late 1930s principally Cumann na mBan and Fianna Éireann. With the end of the

Emergency all four could co-operate again. As 'Republicans' was the word generally preferred by newspaper reporters and covered all associates, it is used here.

As the 1970s were beginning, both the I.R.A. and Sinn Féin split into factions distinguished oddly as 'Officials' and 'Provisionals'. A result was the new adversaries holding two rival pilgrimages, always on separate days. The Officials split in 1974 and another rival pilgrimage began, that of the Irish Republican Socialist Party with its associate, the Irish National Liberation Army. There were throughout the 1970s and into the 1980s three or four separate political pilgrimages to Bodenstown. The names 'Officials' and 'Provisionals' are used here for convenience

Two other changes of custom affect the detail in this list. After 1936 there was no longer an oration by the responsible minister at Irish defence forces' pilgrimages, he simply laid a wreath; in 1973 their ceremonies at Tone's grave ceased. After 1937 there was no oration at Fianna Fáil pilgrimages; a wreath was still laid, usually by the party's leader; the custom of orations was restored in 1968. Some of the detail (e.g. names of some ministers for defence) is not given in the main text.

For further explanation of the changing sponsoring bodies, see above, pp 180–81, 226–7, 239–40.

1873
Sept. 14, Wolfe Tone Band, Richard Keegan

1874
March 22, Wolfe Tone Band, T. D. Sullivan

1875
Sept. 26, Amnesty Association, Robert Dunne & James O'Connor

1876
Aug. 13, Amnesty Association, Robert Dunne & James O'Connor

1877
Aug. 12, Irish National Foresters, Robert Dunne & James Carey

1878
March 17, no further info.

1879
Aug. 17, Wolfe Tone Band, no further info.

1880
Aug. 22, Martyrs' Band, John Daly

1881
Aug. 14, Martyrs' Band, Thomas Bracken

1882–90 hiatus

1891
June 21, National Club Literary Society, Henry Dixson & J. L. Carew

1892
June 19, Young Ireland League, no further info.

1893
June 25, Young Ireland League, J. L. Carew

1894
June 24, Young Ireland League, George Lynch

1895
June 23, Young Ireland League, Edward R. Whelan

1896
June 21, Young Ireland League, John Murphy

1897
June 20, '98 Centenary Committee, Charles G. Doran

1898
June 19, '98 Centenary Committee, W. J. Ryan, John O'Leary presiding

1899
June 25, Wolfe Tone Memorial Cttee, Maurice Moynihan

1900
June 24, Wolfe Tone Memorial Cttee, William O'Leary Curtis

1901
June 23, Wolfe Tone Memorial Cttee, P. N. Fitzgerald

1902
June 22, Wolfe Tone Memorial Cttee, P. T. Daly

1903
June 21, Wolfe Tone Memorial Cttee, John T. Keating

1904
June 26, Wolfe Tone Memorial Cttee, small gathering, no orator

1905
July 9, Wolfe Tone Memorial Cttee?, Patrick Devlin, John MacBride presiding

1906–10 hiatus

1911
July 8, Wolfe Tone Memorial Cttee, John Mark Sullivan, John MacBride presiding

1912
June 23, Wolfe Tone Memorial Cttee, Cathal Brugha & Bulmer Hobson, Tom Clarke presiding

1913
June 22, Wolfe Tone Memorial Cttee, Patrick Pearse, Tom Clarke presiding

1914
June 21, Wolfe Tone Memorial Cttee, W. J. Ryan, Tom Clarke presiding

1915
June 20, Wolfe Tone Memorial Cttee, Tom Clarke

1916
June 25, apparently spontaneous, no speeches

1917
June 24, apparently spontaneous, Countess Markievicz

1918
June 23, prob. Wolfe Tone Memorial Cttee, Cathal O'Shannon

1919
June 22, Wolfe Tone Memorial Cttee, P. S. O'Hegarty

1920
June 20, Wolfe Tone Memorial Cttee, Seán Ó Murthuile

1921
June 19, Wolfe Tone Memorial Cttee but prohibited
July 3, Wolfe Tone Memorial Cttee, Mrs Margaret Pearse

1922
June 20, anti-Treatyites, Liam Mellows

June 25, Wolfe Tone Memorial Cttee, Barney Mellows, Áine Ceannt, Mrs Margaret Pearse, Countess Markievicz & P. S. O'Hegarty

1923
June 23, Cumann na mBan?, Mary MacSwiney
June 24, Irish defence forces, Richard Mulcahy

1924
June 22, Irish defence forces, W.T. Cosgrave
June 22, Sinn Féin, Brian O'Higgins

1925
June 21, Irish defence forces, Peter Hughes
June 21, Sinn Féin, Éamon de Valera

1926
June 20, Irish defence forces, Peter Hughes
June 20, Republicans, John Madden

1927
June 19, Irish defence forces, Peter Hughes
June 19, Republicans, Art O'Connor

1928
June 17, Irish defence forces, Desmond FitzGerald
June 17, Republicans, George Gilmore.
June 20, Sinn Féin, John Madden

1929
June 16, Republicans, Seán Buckley
June 17, Irish defence forces, Desmond FitzGerald
June 30, Fianna Fáil, Éamon de Valera

1930
June 22, Irish defence forces, Desmond FitzGerald
June 22, Fianna Fáil, Éamon de Valera
June 29, Republicans, Tom Maguire

1931
June 21, Irish defence forces, Desmond FitzGerald
June 21, Republicans, Peadar O'Donnell

1932
June 19, Republicans, Seán Russell
June 27, Sinn Féin, Peadar McAndrews
June 28, Irish defence forces, Frank Aiken

1933
June 18, Republicans, Maurice Twomey
June 25, Irish defence forces, Frank Aiken
June 25, Fianna Fáil, Seán T. O'Kelly

1934
June 17, Republicans, Patrick McLogan
June 24, Irish defence forces, Frank Aiken
June 24, Fianna Fáil, Patrick Ruttledge

1935
June 16, Irish defence forces, Frank Aiken
June 16, Fianna Fáil, Seán Lemass
June 23, Republicans, Seán MacBride

1936
June 14, Irish defence forces, Frank Aiken
June 14, Fianna Fáil, Thomas Derrig
June 21, Republicans, Mary MacSwiney, but
   prohibited
Aug. 9, Sinn Féin, Mary MacSwiney

1937
June 13, Irish defence forces, Frank Aiken
   (wreath only)
June 13, Fianna Fáil, Seán MacEntee
June 20, Republicans, Tom Barry

1938
June 19, Republicans, Maurice Twomey &
   Michael Conway
June 26, Irish defence forces, Frank Aiken
   (wreath)
June 26, Fianna Fáil, Éamon de Valera
   (wreath only)

1939
June 18, Irish defence forces, Frank Aiken
   (wreath)
June 18, Fianna Fáil, Éamon de Valera (wreath)
June 25, Republicans, but prohibited

1940
June 16, Irish defence forces, Oscar Traynor
   (wreath)
June 16, Fianna Fáil, Éamon de Valera
   (wreath)
June 23, Sinn Féin, J. J. O'Kelly, but
   prohibited

1941
June 22, Irish defence forces, Oscar Traynor
   (wreath)
June 22, Sinn Féin, Margaret Buckley
June 27, Fianna Fáil, Seán T. O'Kelly
   (wreath)

1942
June 7, Sinn Féin, Seán MacGloin
June 17, Sinn Féin, Margaret Buckley
June 21, Irish defence forces, Oscar Traynor
   (wreath)

June 21, Fianna Fáil, Éamon de Valera (wreath)
June 21, National Graves Association, James
   Killean

1943
June 18, Sinn Féin, no more info.
June 20, Irish defence forces, Oscar Traynor
   (wreath)
June 20, National Graves Association, Donal
   O'Donoghue

1944
June 18, National Graves Association, Seán
   MacBride
June 25, Irish defence forces, Oscar Traynor
   (wreath)
June 25, Fianna Fáil, Éamon de Valera
   (wreath)

1945
June 17, Irish defence forces, Oscar Traynor
   (wreath)
June 17, Fianna Fáil, Éamon de Valera
   (wreath)
June 24, Republicans, Brian O'Higgins

1946
June 16, Irish defence forces, Oscar Traynor
   (wreath)
June 16, Fianna Fáil, Éamon de Valera
   (wreath)
June 23, Republicans, Frank Driver

1947
June 15, Irish defence forces, Oscar Traynor
   (wreath)
June 15, Fianna Fáil, Éamon de Valera (wreath)
June 22, Republicans, Seán McCool

1948
June 20, Irish defence forces, Thomas
   O'Higgins (wreath)
June 20, Republicans, Tomás Mac Curtain
June 27, Fianna Fáil, Éamon de Valera (wreath)

1949
June 19, Irish defence forces, Thomas
   O'Higgins (wreath)
June 19, Republicans, Christy O'Neill
June 26, Fianna Fáil, Éamon de Valera (wreath)

1950
June 18, Irish defence forces, Thomas
   O'Higgins (wreath)
June 18, Republicans, Gearóid Ó Broin
June 25, Fianna Fáil, Éamon de Valera
   (wreath)

1951
June 17, Irish defence forces, Oscar Traynor (wreath)
June 24, Fianna Fáil, Éamon de Valera (wreath)
June 24, Republicans, Anthony Magan

1952
June 22, Irish defence forces, Oscar Traynor (wreath)
June 22, Fianna Fáil, Oscar Traynor (wreath)
June 22, Republicans, Joe McGurk

1953
June 21, Irish defence forces, Oscar Traynor (wreath)
June 21, Fianna Fáil, Éamon de Valera (wreath)
June 21, Republicans, Tomás Mac Curtáin

1954
June 20, Irish defence forces, Seán Mac Eoin (wreath)
June 20, Éamon de Valera (wreath) & Eoin Ryan (reading)
June 20, Republicans, Gearóid Ó Broin

1955
June 19, Irish defence forces, Seán Mac Eoin (wreath)
June 19, Republicans, Éamonn Mac Thomáis
June 26, Fianna Fáil, Éamon de Valera (wreath)

1956
June 17, Irish defence forces, Liam Cosgrave (wreath)
June 17, Fianna Fáil, Éamon de Valera (wreath)
June 17, Republicans, George Dearle

1957
June 23, Irish defence forces, Kevin Boland (wreath)
June 23, Fianna Fáil, James Ryan (wreath)
June 23, Republicans, Seán Dougan

1958
June 15, Republicans, J. J. McGirl
June 22, Irish defence forces, Kevin Boland (wreath)
June 22, Fianna Fáil, Éamon de Valera (wreath)

1959
June 21, Fianna Fáil, Seán Lemass (wreath)
June 21, Irish defence forces, Kevin Boland (wreath)

June 21, Republicans, Ruairí Ó Brádaigh

1960
June 19, Irish defence forces, Kevin Boland (wreath)
June 19, Fianna Fáil, Seán Lemass (wreath)
June 19, Republicans, Seán Mac Stiofáin

1961
June 18, Irish defence forces, Kevin Boland (wreath)
June 18, Fianna Fáil, Seán Lemass (wreath)
June 18, Republicans, John Joe Rice

1962
June 17, Irish defence forces, Gerald Bartley (wreath)
June 17, Fianna Fáil, Seán Lemass (wreath)
June 17, Republicans, Tomás Mac Giolla

1963
June 23, Irish defence forces, Gerald Bartley (wreath)
June 23, Fianna Fáil, Seán MacEntee (wreath)
June 23, Republicans, Thomas Mitchell

1964
June 24, Irish defence forces, Gerald Bartley (wreath)
June 24, Fianna Fáil, Seán MacEntee (wreath)
June 24, Republicans, Martin Shannon

1965
June 20, Irish defence forces, Michael Hilliard (wreath)
June 20, Fianna Fáil, Frank Aiken (wreath)
June 20, Republicans, Tony Meade

1966
June 19, Irish defence forces, Michael Hilliard (wreath)
June 19, Fianna Fáil, Frank Aiken (wreath)
June 19, Republicans, Seamus Costello

1967
June 18, Irish defence forces, Michael Hilliard (wreath)
June 18, Fianna Fáil, Jack Lynch (wreath)
June 18, Republicans, Cathal Goulding

1968
June 23, Irish defence forces, Michael Hilliard (wreath)
June 23, Fianna Fáil, Jack Lynch (wreath) and Ruairí Brugha (oration)
June 23, Republicans, Seán Garland

1969
June 22, Irish defence forces, Michael Hilliard (wreath)
June 22, Fianna Fáil, Michael Hilliard (wreath) and Frank McDonnell (oration)
June 22, Republicans, Tomás Mac Giolla

1970
June 14, Provisionals, Dáithí Ó Conaill
June 21, Irish defence forces, Jerry Cronin (wreath)
June 21, Fianna Fáil, Neville Keery (oration)
June 21, Officials, Malachy McBurney

1971
June 13, Provisionals, Joe Cahill
June 20, Irish defence forces, Jerry Cronin (wreath).
June 20, Fianna Fáil, Cathal Brugha (oration)
June 20, Officials, Malachy McGurran

1972
June 11, Provisionals, Seán Keenan & Máire Drumm
June 18, Irish defence forces, Jerry Cronin (wreath)
June 18, Fianna Fáil, Neville Keery (oration)
June 18, Officials, Seán Garland

1973
June 10, Provisionals, Martin McGuinness
June 17, Irish defence forces, Paddy Donegan (wreath)
June 17, Fianna Fáil, George Colley (wreath)
June 17, Officials, Liam McMillen

1974
June 16, Provisionals, Seamus Loughran
June 23, Fianna Fáil, Joe Groome (oration)
June 23, Officials, Michael Ryan

1975
June 8, I.R.S.P., Seamus Costello
June 15, Provisionals, Proinnsias Mac Airt
June 22, Fianna Fáil, Jack Lynch (wreath)
June 22, Officials, Cathal Goulding

1976
June 6, I.R.S.P., Seamus Costello

June 13, Provisionals, Gearóid Mac Carthaigh
June 20, Fianna Fáil, Paddy Power (wreath).
June 20, Officials, Des O'Hagan and Máirín de Burca

1977
June 12, Provisionals, Jimmy Drumm
June 19, Officials, Éamonn Smullen
June, Fianna Fáil, apparently absent

1978
June 11, Provisionals, Johnny Johnson
June 18, Fianna Fáil, George Colley
June 18, Mac Giolla & Seamus Lynch
June 25, I.R.S.P., Miriam Daly

1979
June 17, Provisionals, Gerry Adams
June 24, Fianna Fáil, Brian Lenihan (wreath)
June 24, Officials, Seán Ó Cionnaigh

1980
June 15, Officials, Joe Sherlock
June 22, Charles Haughey (wreath)
June 22, Tom Hartley & Martha McClelland
June 29, I.R.S.P., Liam Ó Comáin

1981
June 14, Officials, Des O'Hagan
June, 21, Fianna Fáil, cancelled
June 21, Provisionals, Danny Morrison
Sept. 27, Fianna Fáil, Charles Haughey (wreath)

1982
June 13, Workers' Party (Officials), Tomás Mac Giolla
June 20, Sinn Féin (Provisionals), Owen Carron
June 27, I.R.S.P., Brigid Makowski (née Sheils)
Sept. 26, Fianna Fáil, Charles Haughey (speech)

1983
June 12, Workers' Party (Officials), Proinsias de Rossa
June 19, Sinn Féin (Provisionals), Gerry Adams
Oct. 16, Fianna Fáil, Charles Haughey (speech)

Note on sources

A CONVENTIONAL BIBLIOGRAPHY would make little sense. Newspapers are the main primary source. Over three hundred reports of Bodenstown pilgrimages have been examined. After 1798 and for many years, however, the newspapers seldom mentioned Tone. From 1873, when regular organised visits began with the Dublin Wolfe Tone Band going down to Bodenstown to place a new stone on Tone's grave, reports from Bodenstown were regular in the *Freeman's Journal* until it ceased publication in 1925. The *Irish Daily Independent* after it began in 1891, and under its shorter title, *Irish Independent*, from 1905, gave similar coverage. Both were Dublin morning newspapers. Another, the *Irish Times*, reported Bodenstown pilgrimages unfailingly only from 1922. Another, the *Irish Press*, started in September 1931, was in its early years almost obsessive about Theobald Wolfe Tone. Two Dublin evening papers, the *Evening Herald* and the *Dublin Evening Mail*, sometimes give new information. The local Kildare weeklies, both published at Naas, the *Kildare Observer* (which began in 1879 and ceased in 1935) and the *Leinster Leader* (which began in 1880), regularly reported Bodenstown pilgrimages, often supplying detail not given by the dailies, though on other occasions simply drawing reports from the *Irish Independent*. Another local paper, the longer-established *Leinster Express*, published at Maryborough in Queen's County (renamed Portlaoise and County Leix respectively in the 1920s) sometimes reported from Kildare. The information all these papers gave, on proceedings, attendances, speeches, could be very detailed and is all the more reliable for being recorded within hours of the events. Generally the reports were sympathetic; liberal tedencies were common among newspaper men; a day in the country was seductive. They do at least enable us to see the main public features and changes over time even if entirely deficient in telling what was happening behind the scenes. Partisan papers like *An Phoblacht* are no better in this respect and can be very disappointing. For the 'secret history' of Bodenstown some resort has been made to printed primary sources. Of these, editions of letters or diaries are the most reliable; memoirs and reminiscences must be treated with caution. For the identification of Bodenstown churchyard as the site of Tone's grave and laying of the first stone in 1844 most invaluable are five letters in the collection held by the late Mrs Katherine Dickason of Short Hills, New Jersey, a great-great-granddaughter. Many in this collection have been used by Marianne Elliott in her *Wolfe Tone* (1982) and by T. W. Moody, R. B. McDowell and myself in our *Writings of Theobald Wolfe Tone* (3 vols, 1998–2008). Some use has been made by me of police reports for the periods from 1892 to 1901, from 1911 to 1915 and from 1942 to 1959. For the years covering the rise of the Irish Volunteers and advent of Irish independence in 1922 the depositions ('witness statements') made by surviving activists some thirty years later and made accessible on-line by the (Irish) Bureau of Military History contain many gems of information. But passions of the period and lapse of time must have distorted memories of experiences.

There are significant mentions of Bodenstown in secondary sources (biographies, histories, studies). Two have been found invaluable for Republican pilgrimages in the twentieth century: Owen McGee, *The I.R.B.: the Irish Republican Brotherhood from the Land League to Sinn Féin* (Dublin, 2005), and Brian Hanley, *The I.R.A., 1926–1936* (Dublin, 2002). For Fianna Fáil none surpasses in thoroughness Donnacha Ó Beacháin, *Destiny of the soldiers: Fianna Fáil, Irish republicanism and the I.R.A., 1926–1973* (Dublin, 2010). Worthy of mention here, because the author, a former editor of the *Irish Press*, was probably kept well informed by his republican readers, is Tim Pat Coogan, *The I.R.A.*, (revd ed., London, 2000). On Cumann na mBan, the most faithful of pilgrims, there is Cal McCarthy, *Cumann na mBan and the Irish revolution* (revd ed., Cork, 2014). No comparable history exists of the Irish defence forces. Other sources are eclectic and mostly give little more than a few lines about Bodenstown. A work of reference much used, invaluable for being comprehensive, detailed and, in many cases, definitive, is the *Dictionary of Irish biography*, edited by James McGuire and James Quinn (9 vols, Cambridge, 2009). Some 'missing persons' are in a supplement edited by James Quinn (2 vols, 2018). The *D.I.B.* is cited with acknowledgement to the respective contributors. Other sources much cited can be found in the list of abbreviations.

A survey covering so long a period of a subject not previously studied inevitably leaves some sources untapped. Old age allows insufficient time for examination of more than a very small proportion of the extensive archival sources for the period of 185 years covered by the treatment. These sources are now very rich for the twentieth century, beyond the period with which I am most familiar — the 'long nineteenth century'. Questions about, for example, the sentiments and motivations of protagonists will no doubt in future be answered by later generations of researchers. Meantime they may find that the sources examined by me do at least make possible a convenient narrative of events and the identification of participants with which to engage in deeper research.

Index